Lecture Notes in Computer Science   5836

Commenced Publication in 1973
Founding and Former Series Editors:
Gerhard Goos, Juris Hartmanis, and Jan van Leeuwen

Editorial Board

David Hutchison
Lancaster University, UK

Takeo Kanade
Carnegie Mellon University, Pittsburgh, PA, USA

Josef Kittler
University of Surrey, Guildford, UK

Jon M. Kleinberg
Cornell University, Ithaca, NY, USA

Alfred Kobsa
University of California, Irvine, CA, USA

Friedemann Mattern
ETH Zurich, Switzerland

John C. Mitchell
Stanford University, CA, USA

Moni Naor
Weizmann Institute of Science, Rehovot, Israel

Oscar Nierstrasz
University of Bern, Switzerland

C. Pandu Rangan
Indian Institute of Technology, Madras, India

Bernhard Steffen
TU Dortmund University, Germany

Madhu Sudan
Microsoft Research, Cambridge, MA, USA

Demetri Terzopoulos
University of California, Los Angeles, CA, USA

Doug Tygar
University of California, Berkeley, CA, USA

Gerhard Weikum
Max Planck Institute for Informatics, Saarbruecken, Germany

Sven-Bodo Scholz   Olaf Chitil (Eds.)

Implementation and Application of Functional Languages

20th International Symposium, IFL 2008
Hatfield, UK, September 10-12, 2008
Revised Selected Papers

 Springer

Volume Editors

Sven-Bodo Scholz
University of Hertfordshire
Department of Computer Science
Hatfield, AL10 9AB, UK
E-mail: s.scholz@herts.ac.uk

Olaf Chitil
University of Kent
School of Computing
Kent, CT2 7NF, UK
E-mail: o.chitil@kent.ac.uk

ISSN 0302-9743   e-ISSN 1611-3349
ISBN 978-3-642-24451-3   e-ISBN 978-3-642-24452-0
DOI 10.1007/978-3-642-24452-0
Springer Heidelberg Dordrecht London New York

Library of Congress Control Number: 2011937065

CR Subject Classification (1998): F.3, D.3, D.2, F.4.1, D.1, D.2.4

LNCS Sublibrary: SL 1 – Theoretical Computer Science and General Issues

Typesetting: Camera-ready by author, data conversion by Scientific Publishing Services, Chennai, India

Printed on acid-free paper

Springer is part of Springer Science+Business Media (www.springer.com)

Preface

This volume presents revised and selected papers from the 20th International Symposium on Implementation and Application of Functional Languages (IFL 2008). Following the tradition of the IFL symposia, the papers presented here have been selected from revised versions of the 31 papers that were presented at the event which was organized by the Compiler Technology Group of the University of Hertfordshire in Hatfield, UK.

In its 20-year-old tradition, IFL has been held at various places throughout Europe including The Netherlands, UK, Germany, Sweden, Spain, Ireland and Hungary. The symposium brings together researchers actively engaged in the implementation and application of functional and function-based programming languages. It provides an open forum for researchers who wish to present and discuss new ideas and concepts, work in progress, preliminary results, etc. related primarily but not exclusively to the implementation and application of functional languages. Topics of interest cover a wide range, from novel language designs, theoretical underpinnings, compilation and optimization techniques for diverse hardware architectures, to applications, programming techniques and novel tools.

IFL 2008 had 58 participants including researchers from outside Europe such as from the USA and Canada. The presentations covered a wide range of aspects and we believe that the present volume gives a good impression of that range. Although mainly intended for the participants, preprint versions of all presentations are available as a technical report from the University of Hertfordshire (TR 474).

This volume starts with Ralf Hinze's paper on Moessner's Theorem. Its compelling use of a theory of scans and convolutions enables a nice and concise proof of that theorem, showing how a programming language perspective can help mathematical reasoning. The paper's beauty has gained the author the Peter Landin Prize, which is awarded to the best paper of each year's IFL symposium.

The subsequent three papers focus on novel ways for implementing declarative languages: Bernd Braßel and Sebastian Fischer propose a novel way for mapping functional logic programs to purely functional programs which preserves laziness. Ian Mackie suggests interaction nets as an implementation vehicle for closed reductions that promises substantial performance improvements. Clemens Grelck and Frank Penczek introduce a streaming-based coordination language named S-Net and describe an avenue for its effective implementation. These more holistic papers are followed by papers that aim at improving individual aspects of the implementation of functional languages. Nils Anders Danielsson and Ulf Norell present a surprisingly simple approach to parsing mixfix operator expressions which they have implemented for Agda. Kai Trojahner and Clemens Grelck present an optimization for the compilation of programs that operate generically on n-dimensional arrays. They found an elegant way to use dependent types to

get rid of array descriptors at runtime. Olha Shkaravska, Marco van Eekelen and
Alejandro Tamalet stretch the boundaries of type-based analyses to determine
the possible relations between the sizes of input and output lists of functions.

In the remaining papers, the focus shifts from language implementation aspects toward the application of functional languages. At the boundary between
implementations and application, we have papers on embedded languages. George
Giorgidze and Henrik Nilsson expose nicely how Template Haskell can be used
to embed functional hybrid modelling. Joel Svensson, Mary Sheeran and Koen
Claessen introduce Obsedian, an embedded DSL for unleashing the power of
graphics cards in a high-level way. Yan Wang and Verónica Gaspes show how
the data description calculus can be embedded into Haskell in order to better
support short-lived data formats.

The next two papers are concerned with iTasks, a combinator library in Clean
that enables rapid development of Web-based multi-user work-flow systems. The
first paper, authored by Jan Martin Jansen, Rinus Plasmeijer and Pieter Koopman, proposes a seamless extension of iTasks that enables advanced forms of
user-interaction through plug-in technology. The second paper is authored by
Jan Martin Jansen, Rinus Plasmeijer and Pieter Koopman. It tries to capture
the behavior of iTasks in a high-level semantics facilitating formal reasoning and
testing of such systems.

Mauro Jaskelioff's paper on monad transformer libraries identifies shortcomings of the existing monad transformer libraries and proposes an improved approach that substantially simplifies the way several effects can be combined.
David Teller, Arnaud Spiwack and Till Varoquaux suggest a neat way of improving exception handling in OCaml without requiring additional new language
features. This paper demonstrates nicely how advanced language features such
as polymorphic variants can be harnessed to create intriguing new functionality.

The final paper, in a way constitutes the most applied contribution. The authors, Bas Lijnse and Rinus Plasmeijer, try to investigate novel ways of bridging
between databases and functional programming languages. Their key idea is to
start from an abstraction layer on top of databases and then to map the operations on that level down to generically defined boiler-plate code that implements
the required functionalities on the database as well as on the corresponding data
structures.

We hope that the current volume will not only provide the reader with some
fascinating new ideas on how to implement or use declarative programming
languages, but will also encourage readers to participate in future IFL symposia.

August 2009

Sven-Bodo Scholz
Olaf Chitil

Organization

Program Committee

Umut Acar	Toyota Technological Institute	USA
Kenichi Asai	Ochanomizu University	Japan
Lennart Augustsson	Credit Suisse	UK
Olaf Chitil	University of kent	UK
Koen Claessen	Chalmers University of Technology	Sweden
Marko van Eekelen	Radboud University Nijmegen	The Netherlands
Martin Erwig	Oregon State University	USA
Andy Gill	University of Kansas	USA
Neal Glew	Intel Research	USA
Clemens Grelck	University of Lübeck	Germany
Jurriaan Hage	Utrecht University	The Netherlands
Frédéric Loulergue	University of Orléans	France
Greg Michaelson	Heriot-Watt University	UK
Zoltán Horváth	Eötvös Loránd University	Hungary
Frank Huch	University of Kiel	Germany
Rinus Plasmeijer	Radboud University Nijmegen	The Netherlands
Sven-Bodo Scholz	University of Hertfordshire	UK (Chair)
Martin Sulzmann	IT University of Copenhagen	Denmark

Additional Reviewers

Tim Bauer	Pieter Koopman	Joel Svensson
Bernd Braßel	Leonard Lensink	Wouter Swierstra
Wonsoek Chae	Mónica Mászáros	Mt Tejfel
Chris Chambers	Michal Palka	Kai Trojahner
Jan Christiansen	Frank Penczek	Bernard van Gastel
Gergely Devai	Leaf Petersen	John van Groningen
Peter Divianszky	Daniel Rolls	Eric Walkingshaw
Sebastian Fischer	Olha Shkaravska	Viktoria Zsok

Local Organization

Jing Guo	Frank Penczek	Jeyan Thiyagalingam
Carl Joslin	Daniel Rolls	
Stephan Herhut	Sven-Bodo Scholz	

Table of Contents

Scans and Convolutions—
A Calculational Proof of Moessner's Theorem

Ralf Hinze

Computing Laboratory, University of Oxford
Wolfson Building, Parks Road, Oxford, OX1 3QD, England
ralf.hinze@comlab.ox.ac.uk
http://www.comlab.ox.ac.uk/ralf.hinze/

Abstract. The paper introduces two corecursion schemes for stream-generating functions, scans and convolutions, and discusses their properties. As an application of the framework, a calculational proof of Paasche's generalisation of Moessner's intriguing theorem is presented.

1 Introduction

In the 1950s Alfred Moessner discovered the following intriguing scheme for generating the natural kth powers [1]: From the sequence of natural numbers, delete every kth number and form the sequence of partial sums. From the resulting sequence, delete every $(k-1)$-st number and form again the partial sums. Repeat this step $k-1$ times.

The second simplest instance of the process yields the squares by summing up the odd numbers. (Of course if we repeat the transformation 0 times, we obtain the 1st powers of the naturals.)

$$1 \; \not 2 \; 3 \; \not 4 \; 5 \; \not 6 \; \; 7 \; \not 8 \; \dots$$
$$1 \quad\;\; 4 \quad\;\; 9 \quad\;\; 16 \quad \dots$$

For generating the cubes we perform two deletion-and-summation steps.

$$1 \; 2 \; \not 3 \; 4 \; \;\; 5 \; \not 6 \; \; 7 \; \;\; 8 \; \not 9 \; 10 \; 11 \; \not{12} \; \dots$$
$$1 \; \not 3 \quad\; 7 \; \not{12} \quad\; 19 \; \not{27} \quad\; 37 \; \not{48} \quad\quad \dots$$
$$1 \quad\quad\; 8 \quad\quad\;\; 27 \quad\quad\;\; 64 \quad\quad\quad\; \dots$$

The second sequence is probably unfamiliar—the numbers are the "three-quarter squares" ($A077043$[1])—but the final sequence is the desired sequence of cubes.

Actually, it is not surprising that we get *near* the kth powers by repeated summations. If we omit the deletions, we obtain the columns of Pascal's triangle, the *binomial coefficients*, which are related to the *falling factorial powers* [3].

$$1 \; 2 \;\; 3 \;\; 4 \;\; 5 \dots$$
$$1 \; 3 \;\; 6 \; 10 \; 15 \dots$$
$$1 \; 4 \; 10 \; 20 \; 35 \dots$$
$$1 \; 5 \; 15 \; 35 \; 70 \dots$$

---

[1] Most sequences defined in this paper are recorded in Sloane's On-Line Encyclopedia of Integer Sequences [2]. Keys of the form $Annnnnn$ refer to entries in that database.

S.-B. Scholz and O. Chitil (Eds.): IFL 2008, LNCS 5836, pp. 1–24, 2011.

It *is* surprising that the additional deletion step is exactly what is needed to generate the kth powers. However, the magic does not stop here. In the original scheme we deleted numbers at regular intervals. What happens if we steadily increase the size of the intervals?

$$
\begin{array}{rrrrrrrrrrrrrr}
\not{1} & 2 & \not{3} & 4 & 5 & \not{6} & 7 & 8 & 9 & \not{10} & 11 & 12 & 13 & 14 & \not{15} & \ldots \\
 & \not{2} & & 6 & \not{11} & & 18 & 26 & \not{35} & & 46 & 58 & 71 & \not{85} & & \ldots \\
 & & \not{6} & & & & 24 & \not{50} & & & 96 & 154 & \not{225} & & & \ldots \\
 & & & & & & \not{24} & & & & 120 & \not{274} & & & & \ldots \\
 & & & & & & & & & & \not{120} & & & & & \ldots
\end{array}
$$

We obtain the factorials! The crossed-out numbers form the right sides of $\vee$-shaped triangles of increasing size. The numbers in the lower left corner make up the resulting sequence. What sequence do we obtain if we start off by deleting the squares or the cubes? The general scheme becomes visible if we rewrite the preceding example slightly. We began by deleting the numbers

$$
\begin{aligned}
1 &= 1*1 \\
3 &= 2*1 + 1*1 \\
6 &= 3*1 + 2*1 + 1*1 \\
10 &= 4*1 + 3*1 + 2*1 + 1*1
\end{aligned}
$$

and obtained at the end of Moessner's process the sequence

$$
\begin{aligned}
1 &= 1^{\wedge}1 \\
2 &= 2^{\wedge}1 * 1^{\wedge}1 \\
6 &= 3^{\wedge}1 * 2^{\wedge}1 * 1^{\wedge}1 \\
24 &= 4^{\wedge}1 * 3^{\wedge}1 * 2^{\wedge}1 * 1^{\wedge}1 .
\end{aligned}
$$

Now if we delete, say, the numbers

$$
\begin{aligned}
2 &= 1*2 \\
11 &= 2*2 + 1*7 \\
26 &= 3*2 + 2*7 + 1*6 \\
46 &= 4*2 + 3*7 + 2*6 + 1*5 ,
\end{aligned}
$$

where $2, 7, 6, 5$ is the prefix of some arbitrary sequence, we obtain the numbers

$$
\begin{aligned}
1 &= 1^{\wedge}2 \\
4 &= 2^{\wedge}2 * 1^{\wedge}7 \\
1152 &= 3^{\wedge}2 * 2^{\wedge}7 * 1^{\wedge}6 \\
2239488 &= 4^{\wedge}2 * 3^{\wedge}7 * 2^{\wedge}6 * 1^{\wedge}5 .
\end{aligned}
$$

Quite magically, factors have become exponents and sums have become products.

A purpose of this paper is to formalise Moessner's process, in fact, Paasche's generalisation of it [4], and to establish the relationship between the sequence of deleted positions and the resulting sequence of numbers. Of course, this is not the first published proof of Moessner's theorem: several number-theoretic arguments have appeared in the literature [5,4,6]. We approach the problem from a different angle: Moessner's process can be captured by a *corecursive* program that operates on *streams*, which are infinite sequences. In this setting Moessner's theorem amounts to an equivalence of two corecursive functions.

A central message of the paper is that a programming-language perspective on concrete mathematics is not only feasible, but also beneficial: the resulting proofs have more structure and require little mathematical background. Last but not least, since the artifacts are executable programs, we can play with the construction, check conjectures, explore variations etc.

The overall development is based on a single proof method: the *principle of unique fixed points* [7]. Under some mild restrictions, recursion equations over a coinductive datatype possess unique solutions. Uniqueness can be exploited to prove that two elements of a codatatype are equal: if they satisfy the same recursion equation, then they are!

Along the way we introduce two corecursion schemes for stream-generating functions, *scans* and *convolutions*, which are interesting in their own right. Scans generalise the anti-difference or summation operator, which is one of the building blocks of *finite calculus*, and convolutions generalise the convolution product, which is heavily used in the theory of *generating functions*. Using the unique-fixed-point principle, we show that the two combinators satisfy various fusion and distributive laws, which generalise properties of summation and convolution product. These laws are then used to establish Moessner's theorem.

The rest of the paper is structured as follows. To keep the development self-contained, Section 2 provides an overview of streams and explains the main proof principle; the material is taken partly from "Streams and Unique Fixed Points" [7]. Sections 3 and 4 introduce scans and convolutions, respectively. Using this vocabulary, Section 5 then formalises Moessner's process and Section 6 proves it correct. Finally, Section 7 reviews related work and Section 8 concludes.

2   Streams

The type of streams, *Stream* α, is like Haskell's list datatype $[\alpha]$, except that there is no base constructor so we cannot construct a finite stream. The *Stream* type is not an inductive type, but rather a *coinductive type*, whose semantics is given by a *final coalgebra* [8][2].

$$
\begin{aligned}
\textbf{data } Stream\,\alpha \;=\; & Cons\,\{\,head \;\;::\;\; \alpha, \\
& \qquad\quad\; tail \;\;::\;\; Stream\,\alpha\,\}
\end{aligned}
$$

$$
\begin{aligned}
&\textbf{infixr } 5 \prec \\
&(\prec) \qquad :: \;\; \alpha \to Stream\,\alpha \to Stream\,\alpha \\
&a \prec s \;=\; Cons\,a\,s
\end{aligned}
$$

---

[2] The definitions are given in the purely functional programming language Haskell [9]. Since Haskell has a CPO semantics, initial algebras and final coalgebras actually coincide [10].

Streams are constructed using $\prec$, which prepends an element to a stream. They are destructed using *head* and *tail*, which yield the first element and the rest of the stream, respectively.

We say a stream s is *constant* iff $tail\ s = s$. We let the variables s, t and u range over streams and c over constant streams.

2.1   Operations

Most definitions we encounter later on make use of the following functions, which lift n-ary operations ($n = 0, 1, 2$) to streams.

$$
\begin{aligned}
&repeat &&::\ \ \alpha \to Stream\ \alpha \\
&repeat\ a &&=\ \ s\ \ \textbf{where}\ \ \ s\ =\ a \prec s \\
&map &&::\ \ (\alpha \to \beta) \to (Stream\ \alpha \to Stream\ \beta) \\
&map\ f\ s &&=\ \ f\ (head\ s) \prec map\ f\ (tail\ s) \\
&zip &&::\ \ (\alpha \to \beta \to \gamma) \to (Stream\ \alpha \to Stream\ \beta \to Stream\ \gamma) \\
&zip\ f\ s\ t &&=\ \ f\ (head\ s)\ (head\ t) \prec zip\ f\ (tail\ s)\ (tail\ t)
\end{aligned}
$$

The call *repeat* 0 constructs a sequence of zeros (*A000004*). Clearly a constant stream is of the form *repeat k* for some k. We refer to *repeat* as a *parametrised stream* and to *map* and *zip* as *stream operators*.

The definitions above show that *Stream* is a so-called *applicative functor* or *idiom* [11]: *pure* is *repeat* and idiomatic apply can be defined in terms of *zip*.

$$
\begin{aligned}
&pure &&::\ \ \alpha \to Stream\ \alpha \\
&pure &&=\ \ repeat \\
&\textbf{infixl}\ 9\ \diamond \\
&(\diamond) &&::\ \ Stream\ (\alpha \to \beta) \to (Stream\ \alpha \to Stream\ \beta) \\
&s \diamond t &&=\ \ zip\ (\$)\ s\ t
\end{aligned}
$$

Here, \$ denotes function application. Conversely, we can define the 'lifting operators' in terms of the idiomatic primitives: $repeat = pure$, $map\ f\ s = pure\ f \diamond s$ and $zip\ g\ s\ t = pure\ g \diamond s \diamond t$. We will freely switch between these two views.

Of course, we have to show that *pure* and $\diamond$ satisfy the *idiom laws*.

$$
\begin{aligned}
pure\ id \diamond s &= s &&\text{(identity)} \\
pure\ (\cdot) \diamond s \diamond t \diamond u &= s \diamond (t \diamond u) &&\text{(composition)} \\
pure\ f \diamond pure\ a &= pure\ (f\ a) &&\text{(homomorphism)} \\
s \diamond pure\ a &= pure\ (\$\ a) \diamond s &&\text{(interchange)}
\end{aligned}
$$

We postpone the proofs until we have the prerequisites at hand.

Furthermore, we lift the arithmetic operations to streams, for convenience and conciseness of notation. In Haskell, this is easily accomplished using type classes. Here is an excerpt of the necessary code.

instance $(Num\ a) \Rightarrow Num\ (Stream\ a)$ **where**

$$
\begin{aligned}
(+) &= zip\ (+) \\
(-) &= zip\ (-) \\
(*) &= zip\ (*) \\
negate &= map\ negate \quad \text{-- unary minus} \\
fromInteger\ i &= repeat\ (fromInteger\ i)
\end{aligned}
$$

This instance declaration allows us, in particular, to use integer constants as streams—in Haskell, unqualified 3 abbreviates $fromInteger\ (3 :: Integer)$. Also note that since the arithmetic operations are defined point-wise, the familiar arithmetic laws also hold for streams.

Using this vocabulary we can define the usual suspects: the natural numbers ($A001477$) and the factorial numbers ($A000142$).

$$
\begin{aligned}
nat &= 0 \prec nat + 1 \\
fac &= 1 \prec nat' * fac
\end{aligned}
$$

Note that we use the convention that the identifier x' denotes the tail of x. Furthermore, note that $\prec$ binds less tightly than $+$. For instance, $0 \prec nat + 1$ is grouped $0 \prec (nat + 1)$.

Another useful function is $iterate$, which builds a stream by repeatedly applying a given function to a given value.

$$
\begin{aligned}
iterate &:: (\alpha \rightarrow \alpha) \rightarrow (\alpha \rightarrow Stream\ \alpha) \\
iterate\ f\ a &= a \prec iterate\ f\ (f\ a)
\end{aligned}
$$

Thus, $iterate\ (+1)\ 0$ is an alternative definition of the stream of naturals.

2.2 Definitions

Not every legal Haskell definition of type $Stream\ \tau$ actually defines a stream. Two simple counterexamples are $s = tail\ s$ and $s = head\ s \prec tail\ s$. Both of them loop in Haskell; when viewed as stream equations they are ambiguous.[3] In fact, they admit infinitely many solutions: every constant stream is a solution of the first equation and every stream is a solution of the second. This situation is undesirable from both a practical and a theoretical standpoint. Fortunately, it is not hard to restrict the *syntactic form* of equations so that they possess *unique solutions*. We insist that equations adhere to the following form:

$$
x = h \prec t \ ,
$$

---

[3] There is a slight mismatch between the theoretical framework of streams and the Haskell implementation of streams. Since products are lifted in Haskell, $Stream\ \tau$ additionally contains partial streams such as $\bot$, $a_0 \prec \bot$, $a_0 \prec a_1 \prec \bot$ and so forth. We simply ignore this extra complication here.

where x is an identifier of type $Stream\,\tau$; h is an expression of type τ; and t is an expression of type $Stream\,\tau$ possibly referring to x, or some other stream identifier in the case of mutual recursion. However, neither h nor t may use $head\;x$ or $tail\;x$.

If x is a parametrised stream or a stream operator

$$x\;x_1\;\ldots\;x_n\;=\;h\prec t\;,$$

then h or t may use $head\;x_i$ or $tail\;x_i$ provided x_i is of the right type. Furthermore, t may contain recursive calls to x, but we are not allowed to take the head or tail of a recursive call. There are no further restrictions regarding the arguments of a recursive call. For a formal account of these requirements, we refer the interested reader to "Streams and Unique Fixed Points" [7], which also contains a constructive proof that equations of this form indeed have unique solutions.

2.3 Proofs

Uniqueness can be exploited to prove that two streams are equal: if they satisfy the same recursion equation, then they are! If $s = \varphi\,s$ is an admissible equation in the sense of Section 2.2, we denote its unique solution by $fix\;\varphi$. (The equation implicitly defines a function in s. A solution of the equation is a fixed point of this function and vice versa.) The fact that the solution is unique is captured by the following universal property of fix.

$$fix\;\varphi\;=\;s\;\Longleftrightarrow\;\varphi\,s\;=\;s$$

Read from left to right it states that $fix\;\varphi$ is indeed a solution of $x = \varphi\,x$. Read from right to left it asserts that any solution is equal to $fix\;\varphi$. So, if we want to prove $s = t$ where $s = fix\;\varphi$, then it suffices to show that $\varphi\,t = t$.

As an example, let us prove the *idiom homomorphism law*.

$$\begin{aligned}
&\quad pure\;f \diamond pure\;a\\
=\;&\quad\{\text{ definition of }\diamond\,\}\\
&\quad (head\;(pure\;f))\,(head\;(pure\;a))\;\prec\;tail\;(pure\;f) \diamond tail\;(pure\;a)\\
=\;&\quad\{\text{ definition of }pure\,\}\\
&\quad f\;a\;\prec\;pure\;f \diamond pure\;a
\end{aligned}$$

Consequently, $pure\;f \diamond pure\;a$ equals the unique solution of $x = f\;a \prec x$, which by definition is $pure\;(f\;a)$.

So far we have been concerned with proofs about streams, however, the proof technique applies equally well to parametrised streams or stream operators! As an example, let us show the so-called *iterate* fusion law, which amounts to the free theorem of $(\alpha \to \alpha) \to (\alpha \to Stream\,\alpha)$.

$$map\;h \cdot iterate\;f_1\;=\;iterate\;f_2 \cdot h\;\Longleftarrow\;h \cdot f_1\;=\;f_2 \cdot h$$

We show that both $map\;h \cdot iterate\;f_1$ and $iterate\;f_2 \cdot h$ satisfy the equation $x\;a = h\;a \prec x\;(f_1\;a)$. Since the equation has a unique solution, the law follows.

$$(map\ h \cdot iterate\ f_1)\ a$$
$$=\quad \{\ \text{definition of } iterate\ \}$$
$$map\ h\ (a\ \prec\ iterate\ f_1\ (f_1\ a))$$
$$=\quad \{\ \text{definition of } map\ \}$$
$$h\ a\ \prec\ (map\ h \cdot iterate\ f_1)\ (f_1\ a)$$

$$(iterate\ f_2 \cdot h)\ a$$
$$=\quad \{\ \text{definition of } iterate\ \}$$
$$h\ a\ \prec\ iterate\ f_2\ (f_2\ (h\ a))$$
$$=\quad \{\ \text{assumption: } h \cdot f_1 = f_2 \cdot h\ \}$$
$$h\ a\ \prec\ (iterate\ f_2 \cdot h)\ (f_1\ a)$$

The fusion law implies $map\ f \cdot iterate\ f = iterate\ f \cdot f$, which in turn is the key for proving that $iterate\ f\ a$ is the unique solution of $x = a \prec map\ f\ x$.

$$iterate\ f\ a$$
$$=\quad \{\ \text{definition of } iterate\ \}$$
$$a\ \prec\ iterate\ f\ (f\ a)$$
$$=\quad \{\ \text{iterate fusion law: } h = f_1 = f_2 = f\ \}$$
$$a\ \prec\ map\ f\ (iterate\ f\ a)$$

Consequently, $nat = iterate\ (+1)\ 0$.

3 Scans

Let's meet some old friends. Many list-processing functions can be ported to streams, in fact, most of the functions that *generate* lists, such as *repeat* or *iterate*. Functions that *consume* lists, such as *foldr* or *foldl*, can be adapted with varying success, depending on their strictness. The tail-strict *foldl*, for instance, cannot be made to work with streams. We can however turn *scanr* and *scanl*, the list-producing variants of *foldr* and *foldl*, into stream operators.

$$scanr\ ::\ (\alpha \to \beta \to \beta) \to \beta \to (Stream\ \alpha \to Stream\ \beta)$$
$$scanr\ (\circledast)\ e\ s\ =\ t\ \textbf{where}\ \ t\ =\ e\ \prec\ zip\ (\circledast)\ s\ t$$
$$scanl\ ::\ (\beta \to \alpha \to \beta) \to \beta \to (Stream\ \alpha \to Stream\ \beta)$$
$$scanl\ (\circledast)\ e\ s\ =\ t\ \textbf{where}\ \ t\ =\ e\ \prec\ zip\ (\circledast)\ t\ s$$

If we follow our convention of abbreviating $zip\ (\circledast)\ s\ t$ by $s \circledast t$, the definitions of the ts become $t = e \prec s \circledast t$ and $t = e \prec t \circledast s$, emphasising the symmetry of the two scans. The schema below illustrates the working of $scanr\ (\circledast)\ e\ s$.

	s_0	s_1	s_2	s_3	s_4	s_5	s_6	s_7	s_8	s_9	$\cdots$
	$\circledast$	$\circledast$	$\circledast$	$\circledast$	$\circledast$	$\circledast$	$\circledast$	$\circledast$	$\circledast$	$\circledast$	$\cdots$
e	t_0	t_1	t_2	t_3	t_4	t_5	t_6	t_7	t_8	t_9	$\cdots$
$\parallel$	$\parallel$	$\parallel$	$\parallel$	$\parallel$	$\parallel$	$\parallel$	$\parallel$	$\parallel$	$\parallel$	$\parallel$	$\cdots$
t_0	t_1	t_2	t_3	t_4	t_5	t_6	t_7	t_8	t_9	t_{10}	$\cdots$

The diagram makes explicit that $scanr\ (\cdot)\ e\ (s_0 \prec s_1 \prec s_2 \prec s_3 \prec \cdots)$ generates

$$e\ \prec\ s_0 \cdot e\ \prec\ s_1 \cdot (s_0 \cdot e)\ \prec\ s_2 \cdot (s_1 \cdot (s_0 \cdot e))\ \prec\ \cdots\ ,$$

that is, the expressions are nested to the right, but the elements appear in *reverse* order.[4] For instance, *scanr* $(:) []$ generates partial reversals of the argument stream and *scanr* $(\cdot)$ *id* partially 'forward composes' a stream of functions.

We shall also need unary versions of the scans.

$$
\begin{array}{rcl}
scanr1 & :: & (\alpha \to \alpha \to \alpha) \to (Stream\ \alpha \to Stream\ \alpha) \\
scanr1\ (\circledast)\ s & = & scanr\ (\circledast)\ (head\ s)\ (tail\ s) \\
scanl1 & :: & (\alpha \to \alpha \to \alpha) \to (Stream\ \alpha \to Stream\ \alpha) \\
scanl1\ (\circledast)\ s & = & scanl\ (\circledast)\ (head\ s)\ (tail\ s)
\end{array}
$$

Note that the types of *scanr1* and *scanl1* are more restricted than the types of *scanr* and *scanl*.

Two important instances of *scanr* are summation, which we will need time and again, and product.

$$
\begin{array}{rclcrcl}
\Sigma & = & scanr\ (+)\ 0 & \qquad & \Sigma' & = & scanr1\ (+) \\
\Pi & = & scanr\ (*)\ 1 & \qquad & \Pi' & = & scanr1\ (*)
\end{array}
$$

Both stream operators satisfy a multitude of laws [7]. For instance,

$$
\begin{array}{rclcrcl}
\Sigma(c * s) & = & c * \Sigma\ s & \qquad & \Pi(s \mathbin{\widehat{}} c) & = & \Pi\ s \mathbin{\widehat{}} c \\
\Sigma(s + t) & = & \Sigma\ s + \Sigma\ t & \qquad & \Pi(s * t) & = & \Pi\ s * \Pi\ t \ .
\end{array}
$$

The laws are in fact instances of general properties of scans. First of all, scans enjoy two fusion properties.

$$
\begin{array}{rcll}
map\ h\ (scanr\ (\circledast)\ e\ s) & = & scanr\ (\oplus)\ n\ s & \text{(fusion)} \\
\multicolumn{3}{c}{\Longleftarrow \quad h\ e\ =\ n\ \ \wedge\ \ h\ (a \circledast b)\ =\ a \oplus h\ b} \\
scanr\ (\circledast)\ e\ (map\ h\ s) & = & scanr\ (\oplus)\ e\ s & \text{(functor fusion)} \\
\multicolumn{3}{c}{\Longleftarrow \quad h\ a \circledast b\ =\ a \oplus b} \\
scanr\ (\circledast)\ e & = & scanl\ (flip\ (\circledast))\ e & \text{(flip)}
\end{array}
$$

The flip law relates *scanr* to *scanl*; the function *flip* is given by *flip* $f\ a\ b = f\ b\ a$.

The fusion laws can be shown using parametricity [12]. The type of *scanr* contains two type variables, α and β, the *fusion law* amounts to the free theorem in β and the *functor fusion law* to the free theorem in α. However, we need not rely on parametricity as we can also employ the unique-fixed-point principle. For fusion we show that $map\ h\ (scanr\ (\circledast)\ e\ s) = pure\ h \diamond scanr\ (\circledast)\ e\ s$ satisfies $x = n \prec s \oplus x$, the recursion equation of *scanr* $(\oplus)\ n\ s$.

$$
\begin{array}{cl}
& pure\ h \diamond scanr\ (\circledast)\ e\ s \\
= & \{\ \text{definition of } scanr \text{ and } \diamond\ \} \\
& h\ e\ \prec\ pure\ h \diamond (s \circledast scanr\ (\circledast)\ e\ s) \\
= & \{\ \text{assumption: } h\ e = n \text{ and } h\ (a \circledast b) = a \oplus h\ b \text{ lifted to streams}\ \} \\
& n\ \prec\ s\ \oplus\ (pure\ h \diamond scanr\ (\circledast)\ e\ s)
\end{array}
$$

---

[4] While *scanl* is the true counterpart of its list namesake, *scanr* isn't. The reason is that the list version of *scanr* is *not incremental*: in order to produce the first element of the output list it consumes the entire input list.

The proof of functor fusion can be found in Appendix A, along with most of the remaining *purely structural* proofs.

Scans also satisfy two distributive laws: if $\circledast$ distributes over $\oplus$, then $\circledast$ also distributes over $scanr\,(\oplus)$; furthermore, $scanr\,(\oplus)$ distributes over $\oplus$.

$$
\begin{aligned}
scanr\,(\oplus)\,(c \circledast e)\,(c \circledast s) \;&=\; c \circledast scanr\,(\oplus)\,e\,s \\
\Longleftarrow \quad c \circledast (a \oplus b) \;&=\; (c \circledast a) \oplus (c \circledast b) && \text{(distributivity 1)} \\
scanr\,(\oplus)\,(a \oplus b)\,(s \oplus t) \;&=\; scanr\,(\oplus)\,a\,s \oplus scanr\,(\oplus)\,b\,t \\
\Longleftarrow \quad \oplus\ \text{AC} && && \text{(distributivity 2)}
\end{aligned}
$$

Note that we use $\oplus$ and $\circledast$ both lifted and unlifted; likewise, c stands both for a constant stream and the constant itself. Finally, AC is shorthand for associative and commutative.

The first law is in fact a direct consequence of the fusion laws.

$$
\begin{aligned}
&\quad scanr\,(\oplus)\,(c \circledast e)\,(c \circledast s) \\
=\;&\quad \{\ \text{functor fusion: } h\,a = c \circledast a\ \} \\
&\quad scanr\,(\lambda a\,b \to (c \circledast a) \oplus b)\,(c \circledast e)\,s \\
=\;&\quad \{\ \text{fusion: } h\,a = c \circledast a \text{ and } c \circledast (a \oplus b) = c \circledast a \oplus c \circledast b \text{ by assumption}\ \} \\
&\quad c \circledast scanr\,(\oplus)\,e\,s
\end{aligned}
$$

For the second law, we show that $scanr\,(\oplus)\,a\,s \oplus scanr\,(\oplus)\,b\,t$ satisfies $x = (a \oplus b) \prec (s \oplus t) \oplus x$, the recursion equation of $scanr\,(\oplus)\,(a \oplus b)\,(s \oplus t)$.

$$
\begin{aligned}
&\quad scanr\,(\oplus)\,a\,s \oplus scanr\,(\oplus)\,b\,t \\
=\;&\quad \{\ \text{definition of } scanr\ \} \\
&\quad (a \prec s \oplus scanr\,(\oplus)\,a\,s) \oplus (b \prec t \oplus scanr\,(\oplus)\,b\,t) \\
=\;&\quad \{\ \text{definition of } zip\,(\oplus)\ \} \\
&\quad (a \oplus b) \prec (s \oplus scanr\,(\oplus)\,a\,s) \oplus (t \oplus scanr\,(\oplus)\,b\,t) \\
=\;&\quad \{\ \text{assumption: } \oplus\ \text{AC}\ \} \\
&\quad (a \oplus b) \prec (s \oplus t) \oplus (scanr\,(\oplus)\,a\,s \oplus scanr\,(\oplus)\,b\,t)
\end{aligned}
$$

4 Convolutions

Now, let's make some new friends. Moessner's theorem is about repeated summations. We noted in the introduction that repeated summation of *repeat* 1 yields the columns of Pascal's triangle: $repeat\,1 = \binom{nat}{0}$ and $\Sigma\binom{nat}{k} = \binom{nat}{k+1}$ where $\binom{s}{t}$ is the binomial coefficient lifted to streams. What happens if we repeatedly sum an arbitrary stream? For instance, $\Sigma' \cdot \Sigma'$ takes $t_1 \prec t_2 \prec t_3 \prec \cdots$ to

$$
1 * t_1 \prec 2 * t_1 + 1 * t_2 \prec 3 * t_1 + 2 * t_2 + 1 * t_3 \prec \cdots .
$$

Note that the factors are going down whereas the indices are going up: double summation is an example of a so-called *convolution*. To understand the workings of a convolution, imagine two rows of people shaking hands while passing in opposite directions.

$$\ldots s_4\, s_3\, s_2\, s_1 \longrightarrow \qquad \ldots s_4\, s_3\, s_2\, s_1 \longrightarrow \qquad \ldots s_4\, s_3\, s_2\, s_1 \longrightarrow$$
$$\longleftarrow t_1\, t_2\, t_3\, t_4 \ldots \qquad \longleftarrow t_1\, t_2\, t_3\, t_4 \ldots \qquad \longleftarrow t_1\, t_2\, t_3\, t_4 \ldots$$

Firstly, the two leaders shake hands; then the first shakes hand with the second of the other row and vice versa; then the first shakes hand with the third of the other row and so forth. Two operations are involved in a convolution: one operation that corresponds to the handshake and a second operation, typically associative, that combines the results of the handshake.

$$\ldots s_4\, s_3\, s_2\, s_1 \longrightarrow \qquad \ldots s_4\, s_3\, s_2 \quad s_1 \longrightarrow \qquad \ldots s_4\, s_3 \quad s_2 \quad s_1 \longrightarrow$$
$$\circledast \qquad\qquad \circledast \;\oplus\; \circledast \qquad\qquad \circledast \;\oplus\; \circledast \;\oplus\; \circledast$$
$$\longleftarrow t_1\, t_2\, t_3\, t_4 \ldots \qquad \longleftarrow t_1 \quad t_2\, t_3\, t_4 \ldots \qquad \longleftarrow t_1 \quad t_2 \quad t_3\, t_4 \ldots$$

Unfortunately, when it comes to the implementation, the symmetry of the description is lost. There are at least three ways to set up the corecursion (we abbreviate *head s* by s_0 and *tail s* by s').

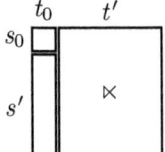 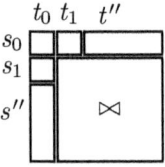 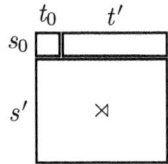

Assume that $\circledast$ implements the handshake. The first element of the convolution is $s_0 \circledast t_0$. Then we can either combine $s' \circledast pure\, t_0$ with the convolution of s and t' (diagram on the left) or we can combine the convolution of s' and t with *pure* $s_0 \circledast t'$ (diagram on the right).

$$convolutel \;::\; (\alpha \to \beta \to \gamma) \to (\gamma \to \gamma \to \gamma)$$
$$\to (Stream\,\alpha \to Stream\,\beta \to Stream\,\gamma)$$
$$convolutel\,(\circledast)\,(\oplus) \;=\; (\ltimes)\,\textbf{where}$$
$$s \ltimes t \;=\; head\,s \circledast head\,t \;\prec\; zip\,(\oplus)\,(map\,(\circledast head\,t)\,(tail\,s))\,(s \ltimes tail\,t)$$

$$convoluter \;::\; (\alpha \to \beta \to \gamma) \to (\gamma \to \gamma \to \gamma)$$
$$\to (Stream\,\alpha \to Stream\,\beta \to Stream\,\gamma)$$
$$convoluter\,(\circledast)\,(\oplus) \;=\; (\rtimes)\,\textbf{where}$$
$$s \rtimes t \;=\; head\,s \circledast head\,t \;\prec\; zip\,(\oplus)\,(tail\,s \rtimes t)\,(map\,(head\,s\,\circledast)\,(tail\,t))$$

It is not too hard to show that the two variants are equal if $\oplus$ is associative, see Appendix A. The proof makes essential use of the symmetric definition in the middle. We shall now assume associativity and abbreviate *convolutel* and *convoluter*, by *convolute*.

Two instances of this corecursion scheme are convolution product and convolution exponentiation.

$$\textbf{infixl}\,7\,\ast\!\ast$$
$$s \ast\!\ast t \;=\; convolute\,(\ast)\,(+)\,s\,t$$
$$\textbf{infixr}\,8\,\frown$$
$$s \frown t \;=\; convolute\,(\,\widehat{}\,)\,(\ast)\,s\,t$$

If you are familiar with generating functions [3], you will recognise $\ast\!\ast$ as the product of generating functions. Exponentiation $\frown$ is comparatively unknown; we shall need it for formalising Moessner's process, but more on that later.

Both operators satisfy a multitude of laws which merit careful study.

$$
\begin{array}{rclcrcl}
(c \ast s) \ast\!\ast t &=& c \ast (s \ast\!\ast t) & \qquad & (s \,\widehat{}\, c) \frown t &=& (s \frown t) \,\widehat{}\, c\\
(s + t) \ast\!\ast u &=& s \ast\!\ast u + t \ast\!\ast u & & (s \ast t) \frown u &=& s \frown u \ast t \frown u\\
\Sigma\, s \ast\!\ast t &=& \Sigma(s \ast\!\ast t) & & \Pi\, s \frown t &=& \Pi(s \frown t)\\[1.5ex]
s \ast\!\ast (t \ast c) &=& (s \ast\!\ast t) \ast c & & s \frown (t \ast c) &=& (s \frown t) \,\widehat{}\, c\\
s \ast\!\ast (t + u) &=& s \ast\!\ast t + s \ast\!\ast u & & s \frown (t + u) &=& s \frown t \ast s \frown u\\
s \ast\!\ast \Sigma\, t &=& \Sigma(s \ast\!\ast t) & & s \frown \Sigma\, t &=& \Pi(s \frown t)
\end{array}
$$

Note that we can shift Σ in and out of a convolution product. This allows us to express repeated summations as convolutions:

$$
\begin{aligned}
&\Sigma\, s\\
=\;& \{\,(1 \prec repeat\,0) \ast\!\ast t = t\,\}\\
&\Sigma((1 \prec repeat\,0) \ast\!\ast s)\\
=\;& \{\,\Sigma\, t \ast\!\ast u = \Sigma(t \ast\!\ast u)\,\}\\
&\Sigma(1 \prec repeat\,0) \ast\!\ast s\\
=\;& \{\,\Sigma(1 \prec repeat\,0) = 0 \prec repeat\,1\,\}\\
&(0 \prec repeat\,1) \ast\!\ast s\\
=\;& \{\,(0 \prec t) \ast\!\ast u = 0 \prec t \ast\!\ast u\,\}\\
&0 \prec repeat\,1 \ast\!\ast s\ .
\end{aligned}
$$

Hence, $\Sigma'\, s = repeat\,1 \ast\!\ast s$ and (see motivating example),

$$
\begin{aligned}
&\Sigma'(\Sigma'\, s)\\
=\;& \{\,\text{see above}\,\}\\
&\Sigma'(repeat\,1 \ast\!\ast s)\\
=\;& \{\,\Sigma'\, t \ast\!\ast u = \Sigma'(t \ast\!\ast u)\,\}\\
&\Sigma'(repeat\,1) \ast\!\ast s\\
=\;& \{\,\Sigma'(repeat\,1) = nat'\,\}\\
&nat' \ast\!\ast s\ .
\end{aligned}
$$

Perhaps unsurprisingly, the laws above are instances of general properties of convolutions. Like scans, convolutions satisfy two fusion properties and a flip law.

$$map\ h\ (convolute\ (\circledast)\ (\oplus)\ s\ t)\ =\ convolute\ (\boxtimes)\ (\boxplus)\ s\ t \qquad \text{(fusion)}$$
$$\Longleftarrow\quad h\,(c_1 \oplus c_2)\ =\ h\,c_1 \boxplus h\,c_2\ \wedge\ h\,(a \circledast b)\ =\ a \boxtimes b$$
$$convolute\ (\circledast)\ (\oplus)\ (map\ h\ s)\ (map\ k\ t)\ =\ convolute\ (\boxtimes)\ (\oplus)\ s\ t$$
$$\Longleftarrow\quad h\,a \circledast k\,b\ =\ a \boxtimes b \qquad \text{(functor fusion)}$$
$$flip\ (convolute\ (\circledast)\ (\oplus))\ =\ convolute\ (flip\ (\circledast))\ (\oplus) \qquad \text{(flip)}$$

The laws for ⁂ and ⌣ suggest that convolutions enjoy three different types of distributive laws. Let $s \bowtie t = convolute\ (\circledast)\ (\oplus)\ s\ t$, then

$$(c \boxtimes s) \bowtie t\ =\ c \circledast (s \bowtie t) \qquad \text{(distributivity 1)}$$
$$\Longleftarrow\quad c \circledast (c_1 \oplus c_2)\ =\ (c \circledast c_1) \oplus (c \circledast c_2)$$
$$\wedge\quad c \circledast (a \circledast b)\ =\ (c \boxtimes a) \circledast b$$
$$(s \boxplus t) \bowtie u\ =\ (s \bowtie u) \oplus (t \bowtie u) \qquad \text{(distributivity 2)}$$
$$\Longleftarrow\quad \oplus\ AC\ \wedge\ (a_1 \boxplus a_2) \circledast b\ =\ (a_1 \circledast b) \oplus (a_2 \circledast b)$$
$$(scanr\ (\boxplus)\ n\ s) \bowtie t\ =\ scanr\ (\oplus)\ e\ (s \bowtie t) \qquad \text{(distributivity 3)}$$
$$\Longleftarrow\quad \oplus\ AC\ \wedge\ (a_1 \boxplus a_2) \circledast b\ =\ (a_1 \circledast b) \oplus (a_2 \circledast b)$$
$$\wedge\quad n \circledast b\ =\ e\ \wedge\ a \oplus e\ =\ a\ .$$

Again, the proofs of the laws can be found in Appendix A. Furthermore, there are analogous laws for right distributivity.

5 Moessner's Process Formalised

We are finally in a position to formalise Moessner's process. Consider the examples in the introductory section and note that the process generates a sequence of equilateral triangles. In the case of natural powers, the triangles were of the same size

1	2	3	4	5	6	7	8	9	10	11	12
1	3		7	12		19	27		37	48	
1			8			27			64		

for the factorials, we steadily increased their size

1	2	3	4	5	6	7	8	9	10	11	12	13	14	15
	2		6	11		18	26	35		46	58	71	85	
			6			24	50			96	154	225		
						24				120	274			
										120				

Our goal is to relate the elements in the upper right corners, the sequence of deleted positions, to the elements in the lower left corners, the sequence generated by Moessner's process. It turns out that this is most easily accomplished through a third sequence, the sequence of *size differences*. Assuming that we start off with an invisible triangle of size 0, the size differences for the above examples are $3 \prec repeat\,0$ and $repeat\,1$, respectively.

Paasche's generalisation of Moessner's theorem then reads: If d is a sequence of size differences, then

$$nat' \ast\!\ast\, d$$

is the sequence of deleted positions and

$$nat' \frown d$$

is the sequence obtained by Moessner's process.

The first part of this beautiful correspondence is easy to explain: if d is the sequence of size differences, then $\Sigma'\,d$ is the sequence of sizes and $\Sigma'(\Sigma'\,d) = nat' \ast\!\ast\, d$ is the sequence of deleted positions. Before we tackle the second part, let's have a look at some examples first.[5]

> $nat' \ast\!\ast\, (2 \prec repeat\,0)$
$\langle 2, 4, 6, 8, 10, 12, 14, 16, 18, 20, 22, 24, 26, 28, 30, 32, \ldots \rangle$
> $nat' \frown (2 \prec repeat\,0)$
$\langle 1, 4, 9, 16, 25, 36, 49, 64, 81, 100, 121, 144, 169, 196, 225, 256, \ldots \rangle$
> $nat' \ast\!\ast\, (3 \prec repeat\,0)$
$\langle 3, 6, 9, 12, 15, 18, 21, 24, 27, 30, 33, 36, 39, 42, 45, 48, \ldots \rangle$
> $nat' \frown (3 \prec repeat\,0)$
$\langle 1, 8, 27, 64, 125, 216, 343, 512, 729, 1000, 1331, 1728, 2197, 2744, 3375, \ldots \rangle$
> $nat' \ast\!\ast\, repeat\,1$
$\langle 1, 3, 6, 10, 15, 21, 28, 36, 45, 55, 66, 78, 91, 105, 120, 136, \ldots \rangle$
> $nat' \frown repeat\,1$
$\langle 1, 2, 6, 24, 120, 720, 5040, 40320, 362880, 3628800, 39916800, 479001600, \ldots \rangle$
> $nat' \ast\!\ast\, (2 \prec 7 \prec 6 \prec 5 \prec repeat\,0)$
$\langle 2, 11, 26, 46, 66, 86, 106, 126, 146, 166, 186, 206, 226, 246, 266, 286, \ldots \rangle$
> $nat' \frown (2 \prec 7 \prec 6 \prec 5 \prec repeat\,0)$
$\langle 1, 4, 1152, 2239488, 9555148800, 2799360000000, 219469824000000, \ldots \rangle$

It is not too hard to calculate the results: We have $s \ast\!\ast (k \prec repeat\,0) = s \ast repeat\,k$ and $s \frown (k \prec repeat\,0) = s \,\widehat{}\, repeat\,k$, which implies Moessner's original theorem. Furthermore, $s \ast\!\ast 1 = \Sigma'\,s$ and $s \frown 1 = \Pi'\,s$ which explains why we obtain the factorials when we increase the size of the triangles by 1.

Let's get more adventurous. If we increase the *size difference*, we obtain the so-called *superfactorials* (*A000178*), the products of the first n factorials: $nat' \frown nat = nat' \frown \Sigma\,1 = \Pi(nat' \frown 1) = \Pi(\Pi'\,nat') = \Pi\,fac'$. Taking this one step further, recall that $\Sigma\binom{nat}{k} = \binom{nat}{k+1}$. Consequently, $nat' \frown \binom{nat}{2}$ yields the *superduperfactorials* (*A055462*), the products of the first n superfactorials: $nat' \frown \binom{nat}{2} = nat' \frown \Sigma(\Sigma\,1) = \Pi(\Pi\,fac')$.

---

[5] This is an interactive session. The part after the prompt ">" is the user's input. The result of each submission is shown in the subsequent line. The actual output of the Haskell interpreter is displayed; the session has been generated automatically using lhs2TeX's active features [13].

In the introduction we asked for the sequences we obtain if we start off by deleting the squares or the cubes. This is easily answered using the left-inverse of Σ', the difference operator $\nabla\, s = head\, s \prec \Delta\, s$ where $\Delta\, s = tail\, s - s$ is the left-inverse of Σ. We have $\nabla\,(\nabla\,(nat' \wedge 2)) = 1 \prec repeat\, 2$ (A040000). Consequently, Moessner's process generates $nat' \frown (1 \prec repeat\, 2) = 1 \prec (nat + 2) * (nat' \frown 2) = 1 \prec (nat + 2) * fac' \wedge 2 = fac * fac'$ (A010790). We leave the cubes as an instructive exercise to the reader.

6 Moessner's Process Verified

> ⟨...⟩ *obtaining a correct solution demands particular attention*
> *to the avoidance of unnecessary detail.*
>
> The Capacity-C Torch Problem—Roland Backhouse

We have noted that Moessner's process generates a sequence of triangles. Let's look at them more closely. Below is the process that generates the cubes, now with an additional row of ones on top.

	0	0	0	0		0	0	0	0		0	0	0	0
1	1	1	1	1		1	1	1	1		1	1	1	1
0	1	2	3			4	5	6			7	8	9	
0	1	3				7	12				19	27		
0	1					8					27			

Every element within a triangle is the sum of the element to its left and the element above. The values in the two margins are zero, except for the topmost element in the left margin, which is 1 and acts as the initial seed.

The verbal description suggests that the sequences are formed from top to bottom. An alternative view, which turns out to be more fruitful, is that they are formed from left to right. We start with the vector $(0\,0\,0\,1)$ (left margin read from bottom to top). The vector goes through a *binomial process*, which yields the diagonal vector $(1\,3\,3\,1)$. This vector goes through the same process yielding $(8\,12\,6\,1)$, and so forth. The first elements of these vectors are the cubes.

	0	0	0	0			0	0	0	0			0	0	0	0		
1	1	1	1	1	1		1	1	1	1	1		1	1	1	1	1	1
0	1	2	3		3		4	5	6		6		7	8	9			9
0	1	3			3		7	12			12		19	27				27
0	1				1		8				8		27					27

In general, the input and output vectors are related by

		0		0		0	0	
a_3			a_3		a_3		a_3	a_3	b_3
a_2		$a_2 + a_3$		$a_2 + 2a_3$		$a_2 + 3a_3$		b_2
a_1		$a_1 + a_2 + a_3$	$a_1 + 2a_2 + 3a_3$					b_1
a_0	$a_0 + a_1 + a_2 + a_3$							b_0 ,

or somewhat snappier,

$$b_n = \sum_k \binom{k}{n} a_k \ ,$$

where k and n range over natural numbers. (This is really a finite sum, since only a finite number of coefficients are nonzero.) As to be expected, the formula involves a binomial coefficient. At this point, we could rely on our mathematical skills and try to prove Moessner's theorem by manipulating binomial coefficients and this is indeed what some authors have done [5,14].

But there is a more attractive line of attack: Let us view the vectors as coefficients of a polynomial so that $(a_0\,a_1\,a_2\,a_3\ldots)$ represents $f(x) = \sum_n a_n x^n$. A triangle transformation is then a higher-order function, a function that maps polynomials to polynomials. We can calculate this higher-order mapping as follows.

$$\sum_n b_n x^n$$
$$=\quad \{\text{ definition of } b_n \}$$
$$\sum_n \left(\sum_k \binom{k}{n} a_k \right) x^n$$
$$=\quad \{\text{ distributive law }\}$$
$$\sum_n \sum_k \binom{k}{n} a_k x^n$$
$$=\quad \{\text{ interchanging the order of summation }\}$$
$$\sum_k \sum_n \binom{k}{n} a_k x^n$$
$$=\quad \{\text{ distributive law }\}$$
$$\sum_k a_k \left(\sum_n \binom{k}{n} x^n \right)$$
$$=\quad \{\text{ binomial theorem }\}$$
$$\sum_k a_k (x+1)^k$$

Here is the punch line: Under the functional view, each triangle maps f to $f \ll 1$ where $\ll$, the *shift operator*, is given by

$$(\ll) \quad :: \quad (\mathbb{Z} \to \mathbb{Z}) \to \mathbb{Z} \to (\mathbb{Z} \to \mathbb{Z})$$
$$f \ll n \ = \ \lambda x \to f(x+n) \ .$$

This change of representation simplifies matters dramatically. By going higher-order we avoid unnecessary detail in the sense of Roland Backhouse [15].

6.1 Moessner's Original Theorem

Moessner's original sequence, where the size of the triangles is constant, is then given by the sequence of polynomials idiomatically applied to 0—the application extracts the lowest coefficients.

$$moessner \quad :: \quad \mathbb{Z} \rightarrow Stream\,\mathbb{Z}$$
$$moessner\,k \quad = \quad iterate\,(\,\ll 1)\,id^k \diamond 0$$

$$f^k \quad = \quad \lambda x \rightarrow (f\,x)^k$$

The seed polynomial is id^k, which is then repeatedly shifted by 1. The auxiliary definition lifts exponentiation to functions, so id^k is $\lambda x \rightarrow x^k$. (Below, we also use s^k to denote exponentiation lifted to streams.)

We are now in a position to prove Moessner's theorem: $moessner\,k = nat^k$. (Of course, this equation is a special case of the relation given in Section 5, but we prove it nonetheless as it serves as a good warm-up exercise.) The central observation is that two shifts can be contracted to one: $(q \ll i) \ll j = q \ll (i + j)$. This allows us to eliminate the iteration:

$$iterate\,(\,\ll 1)\,p = pure\,(\ll) \diamond pure\,p \diamond nat \;. \tag{1}$$

The proof of this equation relies on the fact that $iterate\,f\,a$ is the unique solution of $x = a \prec map\,f\,x$, see Section 2.3.

$$pure\,(\ll) \diamond pure\,p \diamond nat$$
$$= \quad \{\text{ definition of } pure \text{ and } nat \,\}$$
$$p \ll 0 \;\prec\; pure\,(\ll) \diamond pure\,p \diamond (nat + 1)$$
$$= \quad \{\; q \ll 0 = q \text{ and } (q \ll i) \ll j = q \ll (i + j) \text{ lifted to streams }\}$$
$$p \;\prec\; pure\,(\ll) \diamond (pure\,(\ll) \diamond pure\,p \diamond nat) \diamond 1$$
$$= \quad \{\text{ idioms }\}$$
$$p \;\prec\; map\,(\,\ll 1) \diamond (pure\,(\ll) \diamond pure\,p \diamond nat)$$

The proof of Moessner's theorem then boils down to a three-liner.

$$iterate\,(\,\ll 1)\,id^k \diamond 0$$
$$= \quad \{\text{ equation (1) }\}$$
$$(pure\,(\ll) \diamond pure\,id^k \diamond nat) \diamond 0$$
$$= \quad \{\; (id^k \ll n)\,0 = n^k \text{ lifted to streams }\}$$
$$nat^k$$

6.2 Paasche's Generalisation of Moessner's Theorem

I know also that formal calculation is not a spectator sport: ⟨...⟩
Making Formality Work For Us—Roland Backhouse

Now, what changes when the size of the triangles increases by $i > 0$? In this case, the input vector must additionally be padded with i zeros to fit the size of the next triangle, for instance, $(1\,3\,3\,1)$ becomes $(0\,\cdots 0\,1\,3\,3\,1)$. In other words, the polynomial must be multiplied by id^i. Lifting multiplication to functions,

$$f * g \quad = \quad \lambda x \rightarrow f\,x * g\,x \;,$$

a 'generalised triangle transformation' is captured by $step\,i$ where i is the increase in size.

$$step \quad :: \quad \mathbb{Z} \to (\mathbb{Z} \to \mathbb{Z}) \to (\mathbb{Z} \to \mathbb{Z})$$
$$step\ i\ f \quad = \quad (id^i * f) \ll 1$$

Finally, Paasche's process is the partial 'forward composition' of the $step\ i$ functions idiomatically applied to the initial polynomial id^0 idiomatically applied to the constant 0.

$$paasche \quad :: \quad Stream\ \mathbb{Z} \to Stream\ \mathbb{Z}$$
$$paasche\ d \quad = \quad tail\ (scanr\ (\cdot)\ id\ (map\ step\ d) \diamond pure\ id^0 \diamond pure\ 0)$$

The $tail$ discards the value of the initial polynomial, which is not part of the resulting sequence. A truly functional approach: a stream of 2nd-order functions is transformed into a stream of 1st-order functions, which in turn is transformed to a stream of numbers.

It remains to show that $paasche\ d = nat' \mathbin{\widetilde{}} d$. We start off with some routine calculations manipulating the scan.

$$scanr\ (\cdot)\ id\ (map\ step\ d) \diamond pure\ id^0$$
$$= \quad \{\ \text{idiom interchange}\ \}$$
$$pure\ (\$\ id^0) \diamond scanr\ (\cdot)\ id\ (map\ step\ d)$$
$$= \quad \{\ \text{scan fusion: } h\ g = g\ id^0\ \}$$
$$scanr\ (\$)\ id^0\ (map\ step\ d)$$
$$= \quad \{\ \text{scan functor fusion: } h = step \text{ and } (f\$) = f\ \}$$
$$scanr\ step\ id^0\ d$$
$$= \quad \{\ \text{definition of } step\ \}$$
$$scanr\ (\lambda i\ g \to (id^i * g) \ll 1)\ id^0\ d$$
$$= \quad \{\ (f * g) \ll k = (f \ll k) * (g \ll k)\ \}$$
$$scanr\ (\lambda i\ g \to (id^i \ll 1) * (g \ll 1))\ id^0\ d$$
$$= \quad \{\ id^0 = id^0 \ll 1 \text{ and scan functor fusion: } h\ i = id^i \ll 1\ \}$$
$$scanr\ (\lambda f\ g \to f * (g \ll 1))\ (id^0 \ll 1)\ (map\ (\lambda i \to id^i \ll 1)\ d)$$
$$= \quad \{\ \text{definition of } scanr1\ \}$$
$$scanr1\ (\lambda f\ g \to f * (g \ll 1))\ (map\ (\lambda i \to id^i \ll 1)\ (0 \prec d))$$

How can we make further progress? Let's introduce a new operator for $scanr1$'s first argument,

$$f \triangleleft g \quad = \quad f * (g \ll 1)\ ,$$

and let's investigate what happens when we nest invocations of $\triangleleft$ (recall that $scanr1$ arranges the elements in reverse order).

$$f_2 \triangleleft (f_1 \triangleleft f_0)$$
$$= \quad \{\ \text{definition of } \triangleleft\ \}$$
$$f_2 * (f_1 * f_0 \ll 1) \ll 1$$
$$= \quad \{\ (f * g) \ll k = (f \ll k) * (g \ll k)\ \}$$

$$f_2 * f_1 \ll 1 * (f_0 \ll 1) \ll 1$$
$$= \quad \{ f = f \ll 0 \text{ and } (f \ll i) \ll j = f \ll (i+j) \}$$
$$f_2 \ll 0 * f_1 \ll 1 * f_0 \ll 2$$

The scan corresponds to a convolution! Let $s \bowtie t = convolute \,(\ll)\,(*)\, s\, t$, then

$$scanr1 \,(\lhd)\, s \;=\; s \bowtie t \quad \textbf{where} \quad t \;=\; 0 \prec t + pure\,1 \;. \tag{2}$$

In our case, t equals nat. The relation, however, holds for arbitrary operators that satisfy the three laws: $(a_1 * a_2) \ll b = (a_1 \ll b) * (a_2 \ll b)$, $(a \ll b_1) \ll b_2 = a \ll (b_1 + b_2)$ and $a \ll 0 = a$ (see also convolution distributivity 1). In general, if $(A, +, 0)$ is a monoid and 1 an element of A, then t is the so-called sequence of 'powers' of 1.

Turning to the proof of equation (2), we show that $s \bowtie t$ satisfies $x = head\, s \prec tail\, s \lhd x$, the recursion equation of $scanr1\,(\lhd)\, s$.

$$s \bowtie t$$
$$= \quad \{ \text{ definition of } \bowtie \text{ and definition of } t \}$$
$$head\, s \ll 0 \prec tail\, s \ll 0 * s \bowtie (t + pure\,1)$$
$$= \quad \{ a \ll 0 = a \}$$
$$head\, s \prec tail\, s * s \bowtie (t + pure\,1)$$
$$= \quad \{ \text{ convolution distributivity 1: } s \bowtie (t + pure\,1) = (s \bowtie t) \ll pure\,1 \}$$
$$head\, s \prec tail\, s * (s \bowtie t) \ll pure\,1$$
$$= \quad \{ \text{ definition of } \lhd \}$$
$$head\, s \prec tail\, s \lhd (s \bowtie t)$$

By rewriting the scan as a convolution we can complete the proof of Moessner's theorem—the remaining steps are again mostly routine calculations. Let $e = 0 \prec d$, then

$$scanr1 \,(\lambda f\, g \to f * (g \ll 1)) \,(map \,(\lambda i \to id^i \ll 1)\, e) \diamond pure\,0$$
$$= \quad \{ \text{ equation (2) } \}$$
$$convolute \,(\ll)\,(*)\,(map \,(\lambda i \to id^i \ll 1)\, e)\, nat \diamond pure\,0$$
$$= \quad \{ \text{ convolution functor fusion: } h\, i = id^i \ll 1 \text{ and } k = id \}$$
$$convolute \,(\lambda i\, n \to (id^i \ll 1) \ll n)\,(*)\, e\, nat \diamond pure\,0$$
$$= \quad \{ (f \ll i) \ll j = f \ll (i+j) \}$$
$$convolute \,(\lambda i\, n \to id^i \ll (1 + n))\,(*)\, e\, nat \diamond pure\,0$$
$$= \quad \{ \text{ convolution functor fusion: } h = id \text{ and } k\, n = 1 + n \}$$
$$convolute \,(\lambda i\, n \to id^i \ll n)\,(*)\, e\, nat' \diamond pure\,0$$
$$= \quad \{ \text{ idiom interchange } \}$$
$$pure \,(\$\,0) \diamond convolute \,(\lambda i\, n \to id^i \ll n)\,(*)\, e\, nat'$$
$$= \quad \{ \text{ convolution fusion: } h\, g = g\, 0 \text{ and } h\,(id^i \ll n) = n \,\hat{}\, i \}$$
$$convolute \,(\lambda i\, n \to n \,\hat{}\, i)\,(*)\, e\, nat'$$

$$= \quad \{ \text{ convolution flip } \}$$
$$\quad convolute \; (\hat{\ }) \; (*) \; nat' \; e$$
$$= \quad \{ \text{ definition of } convolute \text{ and } \smile \}$$
$$1 \prec nat' \smile d \; .$$

This completes the proof.

7 Related Work

The tale of Moessner's theorem In a one-page note, Moessner conjectured what is now known as Moessner's theorem [1]. The conjecture was proven in the subsequent note by Perron [5]. The proof mainly manipulates binomial coefficients. A year later, Paasche generalised Moessner's process to non-decreasing intervals [4,16], while Salié considered an arbitrary start sequence [6]. Paasche's proof of the general theorem builds on the theory of generating functions and is quite intricate—the generating functions are in fact the 'reversals' of the polynomials considered in this paper. A snappier, but less revealing proof of the original theorem can be found in the textbook "Concrete mathematics" [3, Ex. 7.54]. Van Yzeren observed that Moessner's theorem can be looked upon as a consequence of Horner's algorithm for evaluating polynomials [17]. His idea of viewing the diagonals as coefficients of polynomials is at the heart of the development in Section 6. Inspired by Moessner's process, Long generalised Pascal's triangle, which he then used to prove Salié's theorem [14]. The same author also wrote a more leisurely exposition of the subject [18]. The paper hints at the relationship between the sequence of deleted positions and the sequence obtained by Moessner's generalised process formalised in Section 5.

Scans and convolutions To the best of the author's knowledge the material on scans and convolutions is original. Of course, there are several papers, most notably [19,20,21,22,23], that deal with special instances of the combinators, with sums and the convolution product, in particular.

8 Conclusion

Moessner's theorem and its generalisation nicely illustrate scans and convolutions. Though the theorems are number-theoretic, programming language theory provides a fresh view leading to snappier statements and more structured proofs. While scans are well-known, convolutions are under-appreciated; I think they deserve to be better known. Liberating scans and convolutions from their number-theoretic origins seems to be worthwhile: by turning them into *polymorphic* combinators, we literally obtain theorems for free [12]. Even though we don't rely on parametricity for the proofs, we use parametricity as a guiding principle for formulating fusion laws. Of equal importance are distributive laws: convolution distributivity, for instance, allowed us to rewrite a scan as a convolution, a central step in the proof of Moessner's theorem.

All in all a nice little theory for an intriguing theorem. I hope to see further applications of scans and convolutions in the future.

Acknowledgements

Special thanks are due to Roland Backhouse for posing the challenge to prove Moessner's theorem within stream calculus. Furthermore, a big thank you to Daniel James for improving my English. Thanks are finally due to the anonymous referees for pointing out several presentational problems.

References

1. Moessner, A.: Eine Bemerkung über die Potenzen der natürlichen Zahlen. In: Aus den Sitzungsberichten der Bayerischen Akademie der Wissenschaften, Mathematisch-Naturwissenschaftliche Klasse 1951, vol. (3), p. 29 (March 1951)
2. Sloane, N.J.A.: The on-line encyclopedia of integer sequences, http://www.research.att.com/~njas/sequences/
3. Graham, R.L., Knuth, D.E., Patashnik, O.: Concrete mathematics, 2nd edn. Addison-Wesley Publishing Company, Reading (1994)
4. Paasche, I.: Ein neuer Beweis des Moessnerschen Satzes. In: Aus den Sitzungsberichten der Bayerischen Akademie der Wissenschaften, Mathematisch-naturwissenschaftliche Klasse 1952, vol. (1), pp. 1–5 (February 1952)
5. Perron, O.: Beweis des Moessnerschen Satzes. In: Aus den Sitzungsberichten der Bayerischen Akademie der Wissenschaften, Mathematisch-naturwissenschaftliche Klasse 1951, vol. (4), pp. 31–34 (May 1951)
6. Salié, H.: Bemerkung zu einem Satz von Moessner. In: Aus den Sitzungsberichten der Bayerischen Akademie der Wissenschaften, Mathematisch-naturwissenschaftliche Klasse 1952, vol. (2), pp. 7–11 (February 1952)
7. Hinze, R.: Functional pearl: Streams and unique fixed points. In: Thiemann, P. (ed.) Proceedings of the 2008 International Conference on Functional Programming, pp. 189–200. ACM Press, New York (2008)
8. Aczel, P., Mendler, N.: A final coalgebra theorem. In: Pitt, D., Rydeheard, D., Dybjer, P., Poigné, A. (eds.) Category Theory and Computer Science. LNCS, vol. 389, pp. 357–365. Springer, Heidelberg (1989)
9. Peyton Jones, S.: Haskell 98 Language and Libraries. Cambridge University Press, Cambridge (2003)
10. Fokkinga, M.M., Meijer, E.: Program calculation properties of continuous algebras. Technical Report CS-R9104, Centre of Mathematics and Computer Science, CWI, Amsterdam (January 1991)
11. McBride, C., Paterson, R.: Functional pearl: Applicative programming with effects. Journal of Functional Programming 18(1), 1–13 (2008)
12. Wadler, P.: Theorems for free! In: The Fourth International Conference on Functional Programming Languages and Computer Architecture (FPCA 1989), London, UK, pp. 347–359. Addison-Wesley Publishing Company, Reading (1989)
13. Hinze, R., Löh, A.: Guide2lhs2tex (for version 1.14) (October 2008), http://people.cs.uu.nl/andres/lhs2tex/
14. Long, C.: On the Moessner theorem on integral powers. The American Mathematical Monthly 73(8), 846–851 (1966)
15. Backhouse, R.: The capacity-C torch problem. In: Audebaud, P., Paulin-Mohring, C. (eds.) MPC 2008. LNCS, vol. 5133, pp. 57–78. Springer, Heidelberg (2008)

16. Paasche, I.: Eine Verallgemeinerung des Moessnerschen Satzes. Compositio Mathematica 12, 263–270 (1954)
17. van Yzeren, J.: A note on an additive property of natural numbers. The American Mathematical Monthly 66(1), 53–54 (1959)
18. Long, C.T.: Strike it out: Add it up. The Mathematical Gazette 66(438), 273–277 (1982)
19. Karczmarczuk, J.: Generating power of lazy semantics. Theoretical Computer Science (187), 203–219 (1997)
20. McIlroy, M.D.: Power series, power serious. J. Functional Programming 3(9), 325–337 (1999)
21. McIlroy, M.D.: The music of streams. Information Processing Letters (77), 189–195 (2001)
22. Rutten, J.: Fundamental study — Behavioural differential equations: a coinductive calculus of streams, automata, and power series. Theoretical Computer Science (308), 1–53 (2003)
23. Rutten, J.: A coinductive calculus of streams. Math. Struct. in Comp. Science (15), 93–147 (2005)

A   Proofs

Most of the proofs have been relegated to this appendix as not to disturb the flow. For conciseness, we abbreviate *head s* by s_0 and *tail s* by s'. Furthermore, s_1 is shorthand for *head (tail s)* and s'' for *tail (tail s)* and so forth.

Several proofs establish the equality of two streams by showing that they satisfy the same recursion equation. These proofs are laid out as follows.

$$
\begin{aligned}
&s \\
=\ &\{\ \text{why?}\ \} \\
&\varphi\, s \\
\subset\ &\{\ x = \varphi\, x \text{ has a unique solution}\ \} \\
&\varphi\, t \\
=\ &\{\ \text{why?}\ \} \\
&t
\end{aligned}
$$

The symbol $\subset$ is meant to suggest a link connecting the upper and the lower part; the recursion equation is given within the curly braces (below we omit the "has a unique solution" blurb for reasons of space). When reading $\subset$-proofs, it is easiest to start at both ends working towards the link. Each part follows a typical pattern: starting with e we unfold the definitions obtaining $e_1 \prec e_2$; then we try to express e_2 in terms of e.

Scan functor fusion. We show that $scanr\,(\circledast)\,e\,(pure\ h \diamond s)$ satisfies $x = e \prec s \oplus x$, the recursion equation of $scanr\,(\oplus)\,e\,s$.

$$scanr\,(\circledast)\,e\,(pure\,h\diamond s)$$
$$=\quad\{\text{ definition of } scanr \}$$
$$e\prec(pure\,h\diamond s)\circledast scanr\,(\circledast)\,e\,(pure\,h\diamond s)$$
$$=\quad\{\text{ assumption: } h\,a\circledast b=a\oplus b\}$$
$$e\prec s\oplus scanr\,(\circledast)\,e\,(pure\,h\diamond s)$$

Scan flip The straightforward proof is left as an exercise to the reader.

Equality of left and right convolution We have noted in Section 4 that there are at least three different ways to define a convolution (here we fix the two operators · and +).

$$s\ltimes t\;=\;s_0\cdot t_0\prec map\,(\cdot t_0)\,s'+s\ltimes t'$$
$$s\bowtie t\;=\;s_0\cdot t_0\prec s_1\cdot t_0+s_0\cdot t_1\prec map\,(\cdot t_0)\,s''+s'\bowtie t'+map\,(s_0\cdot)\,t''$$
$$s\rtimes t\;=\;s_0\cdot t_0\prec s'\rtimes t+map\,(s_0\cdot)\,t'$$

In general they yield different results. However, if + is associative, then $\ltimes\;=\;\bowtie\;=\;\rtimes$. To establish this equality, we first show the *shifting lemma*:

$$map\,(\cdot t_0)\,s'+s\bowtie t'\;=\;s'\bowtie t+map\,(s_0\cdot)\,t'\;.$$

Let $f\,s\,t=map\,(\cdot t_0)\,s'+s\bowtie t'$ and $g\,s\,t=s'\bowtie t+map\,(s_0\cdot)\,t'$, then

$$f\,s\,t$$
$$=\quad\{\text{ definition of } f \}$$
$$map\,(\cdot t_0)\,s'+s\bowtie t'$$
$$=\quad\{\text{ definition of } \bowtie \text{ and } + \}$$
$$s_1\cdot t_0+s_0\cdot t_1\prec s_2\cdot t_0+(s_1\cdot t_1+s_0\cdot t_2)$$
$$\prec map\,(\cdot t_0)\,s'''+(map\,(\cdot t_1)\,s''+s'\bowtie t''+map\,(s_0\cdot)\,t''')$$
$$=\quad\{\;+\text{ is associative and definition of } f \}$$
$$s_1\cdot t_0+s_0\cdot t_1\prec s_2\cdot t_0+s_1\cdot t_1+s_0\cdot t_2$$
$$\prec map\,(\cdot t_0)\,s'''+f\,s'\,t'+map\,(s_0\cdot)\,t'''$$
$$\subset\quad\{\,x\,s\,t=\cdots\prec map\,(\cdot t_0)\,s'''+x\,s'\,t'+map\,(s_0\cdot)\,t'''\,\}$$
$$s_1\cdot t_0+s_0\cdot t_1\prec s_2\cdot t_0+s_1\cdot t_1+s_0\cdot t_2$$
$$\prec map\,(\cdot t_0)\,s'''+g\,s'\,t'+map\,(s_0\cdot)\,t'''$$
$$=\quad\{\;+\text{ is associative and definition of } g \}$$
$$s_1\cdot t_0+s_0\cdot t_1\prec(s_2\cdot t_0+s_1\cdot t_1)+s_0\cdot t_2$$
$$\prec(map\,(\cdot t_0)\,s'''+s''\bowtie t'+map\,(s_1\cdot)\,t'')+map\,(s_0\cdot)\,t'''$$
$$=\quad\{\text{ definition of } \bowtie \text{ and } + \}$$
$$s'\bowtie t+map\,(s_0\cdot)\,t'$$
$$=\quad\{\text{ definition of } g \}$$
$$g\,s\,t\;.$$

Next we show that $\bowtie$ satisfies the recursion equation of $\rtimes$.

$$s \bowtie t$$
$=$ { definition of $\bowtie$ }
$$s_0 \cdot t_0 \; \prec \; s_1 \cdot t_0 + s_0 \cdot t_1 \; \prec \; map\,(\cdot\,t_0)\,s'' + s' \bowtie t' + map\,(s_0\,\cdot)\,t''$$
$=$ { shifting lemma }
$$s_0 \cdot t_0 \; \prec \; s_1 \cdot t_0 + s_0 \cdot t_1 \; \prec \; s'' \bowtie t + map\,(s_1\,\cdot)\,t' + map\,(s_0\,\cdot)\,t''$$
$\subseteq$ { $x\,s\,t = \cdots \prec \cdots \prec x\,s''\,t + map\,(s_1\cdot)\,t' + map\,(s_0\cdot)\,t''$ }
$$s_0 \cdot t_0 \; \prec \; s_1 \cdot t_0 + s_0 \cdot t_1 \; \prec \; s'' \rtimes t + map\,(s_1\,\cdot)\,t' + map\,(s_0\,\cdot)\,t''$$
$=$ { definition of $\rtimes$ and $+$ }
$$s_0 \cdot t_0 \; \prec \; s' \rtimes t + map\,(s_0\,\cdot)\,t'$$
$=$ { definition of $\rtimes$ }
$$s \rtimes t$$

An analogous argument shows that $\bowtie$ satisfies the recursion equation of $\ltimes$, which completes the proof.

Convolution fusion. We show that $s \ltimes t = pure\,h \diamond convolute\,(\circledast)\,(\oplus)\,s\,t$ satisfies $x\,s\,t = s_0 \boxtimes t_0 \prec (s' \boxtimes pure\,t_0) \boxplus x\,s\,t'$, the defining equation of $convolute\,(\boxtimes)\,(\boxplus)\,s\,t$.

$$pure\,h \diamond (s \ltimes t)$$
$=$ { definition of $\ltimes$ and $\diamond$ }
$$h\,(s_0 \circledast t_0) \; \prec \; pure\,h \diamond (s' \circledast pure\,t_0 \oplus s \ltimes t')$$
$=$ { assumption: $h\,(c_1 \oplus c_2) = h\,c_1 \boxplus h\,c_2$ and $h\,(a \circledast b) = a \boxtimes b$ }
$$(s_0 \boxtimes t_0) \; \prec \; s' \boxtimes pure\,t_0 \boxplus pure\,h \diamond (s \ltimes t')$$

Convolution functor fusion. We demonstrate that the left convolution $s \ltimes t = convolute\,(\circledast)\,(\oplus)\,(pure\,h \diamond s)\,(pure\,k \diamond t)$ satisfies $x\,s\,t = s_0 \boxtimes t_0 \prec (s' \boxtimes pure\,t_0) \oplus x\,s\,t'$, the recursion equation of $convolute\,(\boxtimes)\,(\oplus)\,s\,t$.

$$(pure\,h \diamond s) \ltimes (pure\,k \diamond t)$$
$=$ { definition of $\ltimes$ and $\diamond$ }
$$(h\,s_0 \circledast k\,t_0) \; \prec \; (pure\,h \diamond s' \circledast pure\,(k\,t_0)) \oplus ((pure\,h \diamond s) \ltimes (pure\,k \diamond t'))$$
$=$ { idiom laws and assumption: $h\,a \circledast k\,b = a \boxtimes b$ }
$$(s_0 \boxtimes t_0) \; \prec \; (s' \boxtimes pure\,t_0) \oplus ((pure\,h \diamond s) \ltimes (pure\,k \diamond t'))$$

Convolution flip. Again, we leave the straightforward proof as an exercise.

Convolution distributivity 1. This law is, in fact, a simple application of the two fusion laws.

$$(c \boxtimes s) \bowtie t$$

$= \quad \{ \text{ definition of } \bowtie \}$

$\quad convolute \ (\circledast) \ (\oplus) \ (c \boxtimes s) \ t$

$= \quad \{ \text{ functor fusion: } h \ a = c \boxtimes a \text{ and } k = id \}$

$\quad convolute \ (\lambda a \ b \rightarrow (c \boxtimes a) \circledast b) \ (\oplus) \ s \ t$

$= \quad \{ \text{ fusion: } h \ x = c \circledast x, \ c \circledast (c_1 \oplus c_2) = (c \circledast c_1) \oplus (c \circledast c_2) \text{ and }$

$\qquad c \circledast (a \circledast b) = (c \boxtimes a) \circledast b \text{ by assumption } \}$

$\quad c \circledast convolute \ (\circledast) \ (\oplus) \ s \ t$

$= \quad \{ \text{ definition of } \bowtie \}$

$\quad c \circledast (s \bowtie t)$

Convolution distributivity 2. This law can be shown using the unique-fixed-point principle.

$$(s \boxplus t) \bowtie u$$

$= \quad \{ \text{ definition of } \bowtie \text{ and } \boxplus \}$

$\quad (s_0 \boxplus t_0) \circledast u_0 \ \prec \ ((s' \boxplus t') \circledast pure \ u_0) \oplus (s \boxplus t) \bowtie u'$

$= \quad \{ \text{ assumption: } (a_1 \boxplus a_2) \circledast b = (a_1 \circledast b) \oplus (a_2 \circledast b) \}$

$\quad (s_0 \circledast u_0 \oplus t_0 \circledast u_0) \ \prec \ (s' \circledast pure \ u_0 \oplus t' \circledast pure \ u_0) \oplus (s \boxplus t) \bowtie u'$

$\subset \quad \{ \ x \ s \ t \ u = \cdots \prec (s' \circledast pure \ u_0 \oplus t' \circledast pure \ u_0) \oplus x \ s \ t \ u' \}$

$\quad (s_0 \circledast u_0 \oplus t_0 \circledast u_0) \ \prec \ (s' \circledast pure \ u_0 \oplus t' \circledast pure \ u_0) \oplus (s \bowtie u') \oplus (t \bowtie u')$

$= \quad \{ \text{ assumption: } \oplus \text{ is associative and commutative } \}$

$\quad (s_0 \circledast u_0 \oplus t_0 \circledast u_0) \ \prec \ (s' \circledast pure \ u_0 \oplus s \bowtie u') \oplus (t' \circledast pure \ u_0 \oplus t \bowtie u')$

$= \quad \{ \text{ definition of } \oplus \}$

$\quad (s_0 \circledast u_0 \ \prec \ s' \circledast pure \ u_0 \oplus s \bowtie u') \oplus (t_0 \circledast u_0 \ \prec \ t' \circledast pure \ u_0 \oplus t \bowtie u')$

$= \quad \{ \text{ definition of } \bowtie \}$

$\quad (s \bowtie u) \oplus (t \bowtie u)$

Convolution distributivity 3. Let $t = scanr \ (\boxplus) \ n \ s$, we show that $t \bowtie u$ satisfies $x = e \prec (s \bowtie u) \oplus x$, the recursion equation of $scanr \ (\oplus) \ e \ (s \bowtie u)$.

$$t \bowtie u$$

$= \quad \{ \text{ definition of } scanr \text{ and } \bowtie \}$

$\quad n \circledast u_0 \ \prec \ (s \boxplus t) \bowtie u \oplus pure \ n \circledast u'$

$= \quad \{ \text{ assumption: } n \circledast b = e \text{ and } a \oplus e = a \}$

$\quad e \ \prec \ (s \boxplus t) \bowtie u$

$= \quad \{ \text{ convolution distributivity 2 } \}$

$\quad e \ \prec \ (s \bowtie u) \oplus (t \bowtie u)$

From Functional Logic Programs to Purely Functional Programs Preserving Laziness*

Bernd Braßel and Sebastian Fischer

Christian-Albrechts-University of Kiel
{bbr,sebf}@informatik.uni-kiel.de

Abstract. Functional logic languages extend the setting of functional programming by non-deterministic choices, free variables and narrowing.

Most existing approaches to simulate logic features in functional languages do not preserve laziness, i.e., they can only model strict logic programming like in Prolog. Lazy functional logic programming however, has interesting properties supporting a more declarative style of programming search without sacrificing efficiency.

We will present a recently developed technique to reduce all logic extensions to the single problem of generating unique identifiers. The impact of this reduction is a general scheme for compiling functional logic programs to lazy functional programs without side effects.

One of the design goals is that the purely functional parts of a program should not suffer from significant run-time overhead. Preliminary experiments confirm our hope for significant improvements of run-time performance even for non-deterministic programs but suggest further work to improve the memory requirements of those.

1 Introduction

The two main paradigms of declarative programming are functional and logic programming. Logic languages support non-deterministic choice, computing with partial information and search for solutions. Conceptually, the simplest way to provide logic features in functional languages is to express non-determinism using lists [28] but in principal any instance of the class `MonadPlus` can be used for this purpose, for examples see [19,20,24]. All these approaches model non-deterministic computations like in Prolog in the sense that all computations involving non-deterministic choices are *strict*. However, the *functional logic* paradigm is mainly motivated by the insight that laziness and non-deterministic search can be combined profitably. Especially, this combination allows to program in the expressive and intuitive *generate-and-test* style while effectively computing in the more efficient style of *test-of-generate* [16]. Recent applications of this technique show that it is, for example, well suited for the demand-driven

---

* This work has been partially supported by the German Research Council (DFG) under grant Ha 2457/5-1.

S.-B. Scholz and O. Chitil (Eds.): IFL 2008, LNCS 5836, pp. 25–42, 2011.

generation of test data [27,12]. Functional logic design patterns [3] illustrate
further benefits of combining lazy functional and logic programming.

In order to realize the lazy functional logic paradigm several programming
languages have been developed [14]. Curry [13,18] extends lazy functional programming by non-deterministic choice and free variables; the syntax closely corresponds to that of Haskell 98 [25]. Further lazy functional logic programming
languages are Escher [21] and Toy [22]. Compiling lazy functional logic programs
to various target languages, including C [23], C++ [21], Java [17,5], Prolog [2]
and Haskell [7] has a long tradition.

This paper is mainly concerned with translating Curry to Haskell. Note, however, that the technique could easily be adapted to any of the functional logic languages mentioned above. Likewise, other lazy functional languages like Clean [26]
would suit equally well as target language.

As shown previously [7,8], choosing a *lazy functional* target language has
several advantages. Firstly, deterministic functions can be translated without
imposing much overhead. Additionally, Haskell allows to implement sharing of
computed values even across non-deterministic branches where existing implementations reevaluate shared expressions. Finally, in contrast to a logic target
language, the explicit encoding of non-determinism allows more fine grained
control of logic search.

The challenge of targeting Haskell, however, is to preserve the laziness of the
source language which allows the efficient execution of programs written in the
generate-and-test style. Therefore, previous approaches to non-determinism in
Haskell [28,19,20,24] do not suffice.

The translation scheme developed in this paper features all advantages mentioned above. Additionally, it comprises the following advantages.

- It is the first scheme translating lazy functional logic programs to *purely*
  functional programs. Consequently, the resulting code can be *fully optimized*,
  in contrast to our previous approach [7] which relied on unsafe side effects
  for generating labels.
- The transformation is *simple* — one could even say "off-the-shelf" as the
  technique of uniquely identifying certain expressions is employed fairly often.

In Section 2.1 we describe the general idea of the transformation scheme in comparison to naive implementations of non-determinism using lists. The general
transformation scheme is defined in Section 3, mainly Subsection 3.3. We relate the presented approach to other compilation schemes in Section 4, provide
experimental comparisons in Section 5, and conclude in Section 6.

2   Informal Presentation of the Transformation

In this section we describe the problems of translating lazy functional logic programs and informally present the idea behind our solution. We first motivate
call-time choice (Section 2.1) which describes the meaning of the interaction
between laziness and non-determinism by means of two examples — one very

simple, the other more elaborated. We then show that a naive encoding of non-determinism violates call-time choice (Section 2.2), present our approach to correctly implement it (Section 2.3), and finally draw special attention to finite failure (Section 2.4).

2.1 Non-determinism and Laziness

The interaction of laziness and logic programming features — especially non-determinism — is non-trivial both semantically, as well as operationally, i.e., from the point of view of an implementation. Current lazy functional logic programming languages have agreed on a model coined *Call-Time Choice* that supports the intuition that variables are placeholders for *values* rather than possibly non-deterministic computations. An important consequence of this computational model is that a lazy (call-by-need) computation has the same results as an eager (call-by-value) computation of the same program (if the latter terminates).

The semantic consequences of call-time choice are usually illustrated with a variation of the following tiny program:

```
coin :: Bool
coin = True
coin = False

not, selfEq :: Bool → Bool

not True  = False
not False = True

selfEq b = iff b b

iff :: Bool → Bool → Bool
iff True  b = b
iff False b = not b
```

In functional logic programs, all matching rules of an operation[1] are applied non-deterministically. Whenever there are multiple matching rules we say that these rules *overlap*. This behaviour differs from functional languages where only the topmost matching rule of a function is applied. Hence, a call to `coin` has two non-deterministic results: `True` and `False`. The function `selfEq` checks whether its argument is equivalent to itself using the Boolean equivalence test `iff`. There are two call-by-value derivations for the goal (`selfEq coin`):

```
selfEq coin
  | → selfEq True  → iff True  True  → True
  | → selfEq False → iff False False → not False → True
```

If we evaluate the same goal with call-by-name, we get two more derivations, both with a result that cannot be obtained with call-by-value:

---

[1] When non-determinism is involved, we use the term *operation* rather than *function*.

```
selfEq coin → iff coin coin
    | → iff True coin → coin
            | → True
            | → False
    | → iff False coin → not coin
            | → not True  → False
            | → not False → True
```

In a call-by-need derivation of the goal, i.e., in a lazy programming language, coin is evaluated only once and the result of (selfEq coin) is True. Shared non-deterministic sub computations evaluate to the same value.

Current lazy functional logic programming languages conform to call-time choice semantics following the *principle of least astonishment* because — like well known from functional programming — lazy computations have the same results as eager ones. Therefore, call-time choice relates to call-by-need—not to call-by-name which would give too many results. This choice simplifies formal reasoning, e.g., the result of a call to selfEq will always be True. It seems the most reasonable choice in order to not confuse programmers. Imagine, e.g., a function sort :: [Int] → [Int] and the following definition that generates tests for this function:

```
sortTests :: ([Int],[Int])
sortTests = (l, sort l) where l free
```

Programmers will expect the second component of the pair to be a sorted reordering of the first. And they will still expect this behaviour if they use a non-deterministic *generator* for non-negative numbers instead of a free variable[2]:

```
sortTests :: ([Int],[Int])
sortTests = (l, sort l) where l = natList

natList :: [Int]
natList = []
natList = nat : natList

nat :: Int
nat = 0
nat = nat + 1
```

The sort function can be defined using the *test-of-generate* pattern [16]:

```
sort :: [Int] → [Int]
sort l | sorted p = p where p = permute l

sorted :: [Int] → Bool
sorted []       = True
sorted [_]      = True
sorted (m:n:ns) = m ≤ n && sorted (n:ns)
```

---

[2] It has been shown in [4] that logic variables can be simulated using such non-deterministic generators and this result relies on call-time choice semantics.

```
permute :: [a] → [a]
permute []     = []
permute (x:xs) = insert x (permute xs)

insert :: a → [a] → [a]
insert x xs     = x : xs
insert x (y:ys) = y : insert x ys
```

The definition of sort is only reasonable with call-time choice, i.e., if both occurrences of p (in the guard and in the right-hand side of sort) denote the same value. Otherwise, an arbitrary permutation of the input would be returned if some other permutation is sorted. Thanks to lazy evaluation, permutations need to be computed only as much as is necessary in order to decide whether they are sorted. For example, if the first two elements of a permutation are already out-of-order, then a presumably large number of possible completions can be discarded. Permutations of a list are computed recursively by inserting the head of a list at an arbitrary position in the permutation of the tail. The definition of insert uses overlapping rules to insert x either as new head or somewhere in the tail of a non-empty list.

Permutation sort demonstrates nicely the semantic effect of call-time choice and the operational effect of laziness which prunes away large parts of the search space by not evaluating unsorted permutations completely. Thus, it is a characteristic example for a search problem expressed in the more intuitive *generate-and-test* style but solved in the more efficient *test-of-generate* style. This pattern generalizes to other problems and is not restricted to sorting which is usually not expressed as a search problem.

2.2 Naive Functional Encoding of Non-determinism

In a first attempt, we might consider to represent non-deterministic values using lists [28] and lift all operations to the list type. The program that computes (selfEq coin) would then be translated as follows:

```
goal :: [Bool]
goal = selfEq coin

coin :: [Bool]
coin = [True,False]

not, selfEq :: [Bool] → [Bool]
not bs = [ False | True ← bs ] ++ [ True | False ← bs ]

selfEq bs = iff bs bs

iff :: [Bool] → [Bool] → [Bool]
iff xs ys = [ y | True  ← xs, y ← ys ]
         ++ [ y | False ← xs, y ← not ys ]
```

However, this translation does not adhere to call-time choice semantics because argument variables of functions denote possibly non-deterministic computations rather than values. For example, the argument `bs` of `selfEq` represents all non-deterministic results of this argument and the function `iff` might choose different values for each of its arguments. Consequently, the result of evaluating `goal` is `[True,False,False,True]` which resembles a call-by-name derivation of the corresponding functional logic program rather than call-by-need.

In order to model call-time choice, we could translate all functions such that they take deterministic arguments and use the list monad to handle non-determinism. The same example would then be translated as follows (the definition of `coin` is unchanged):

```
goal :: [Bool]
goal = do { b ← coin; selfEq b }

not, selfEq :: Bool → [Bool]
not True  = return False
not False = return True


selfEq b = iff b b

iff :: Bool → Bool → [Bool]
iff True  b = return b
iff False b = not b
```

Here, the value of `goal` is `[True,True]` as in a call-by-value derivation of a functional logic program, i.e., it corresponds to call-time choice. Unfortunately, the resulting program is strict, e.g., the call to `coin` is evaluated before passing its result to the function `selfEq`. Strictness can lead to unexpected non-termination and performance problems due to unnecessary evaluations. In lazy functional logic programming, unnecessary evaluation often means *unnecessary search*. The consequence often is exponential overhead which is clearly unacceptable. We will see in Section 5 that for programs in generate-and-test style such overhead can be significantly reduced by laziness.

With a naive approach, and also with sophisticated optimizations [19,20,24], we have the choice between laziness and call-time choice, we cannot obtain both.

2.3   Combining Laziness and Call-Time Choice

In our approach to translating lazy functional logic programs we do not use lists to represent non-determinism. Instead, we introduce a new constructor `Choice :: ID → a → a → a` and use it to build trees of non-deterministic values. Of course, a constructor of this type cannot be defined in Haskell, but in order to keep the description of our transformation as simple as possible, we do not consider types in this paper. In an implementation we can introduce different choice constructors for every data type.

The type `ID` in the first argument of `Choice` is an abstract type with the following signature:

```
type ID
instance Eq ID
initID :: ID
leftID, rightID :: ID → ID
```

The functions `leftID` and `rightID` compute unique identifiers from a given identifier and are used to pass unique identifiers to every part of the computation that needs them. In order to ensure that the generated identifiers are indeed unique, the shown functions need to satisfy specific properties:

- `leftID` and `rightID` must not yield the same identifier for any arguments,
- they never yield an identifier equal to `initID`, and
- both functions yield different results when given different arguments.

More formally, we can state that `leftID` and `rightID` have disjoint images that do not contain `initID`, and are both injective. In the syntax of QuickCheck [10], these properties read as follows:

λi j → leftID i /= rightID j

λi → initID /= leftID i && initID /= rightID i

λi j → i /= j ⟹ leftID i /= leftID j && rightID i /= rightID j

A possible implementation of `ID` uses positive integers of unbounded size:

```
type ID = Integer   -- positive

initID :: ID
initID = 1

leftID, rightID :: ID → ID
leftID  i = 2*i
rightID i = 2*i + 1
```

This implementation satisfies the given properties for all positive integers. In fact, the choice of 1 in the definition of `initID` is arbitrary—any positive integer would suffice. This implementation is not perfect because the generated identifiers grow rapidly and many integers might not be used as identifiers depending on how the functions `leftID` and `rightID` are used. However, it is purely functional and serves well as a prototype implementation. There are more efficient implementations [6] that make selected use of side effects without sacrificing compiler optimizations.

Unique identifiers are crucial in our approach to translate lazy functional logic programs because they allow to detect sharing of non-deterministic choices. If the result of a computation contains occurrences of `Choice` with the same identifier, the same alternative of both choices needs to be taken when computing the (functional logic) *values*[3] of this expression. In order to label non-deterministic choices with unique identifiers, we need to pass them to every position in the program that eventually performs a non-deterministic choice. As a first example, we consider the translation of (`selfEq coin`) in our approach:

---

[3] We define the computation of functional logic values in Section 3.4.

```
goal :: ID → Bool
goal i = selfEq (coin i)

coin :: ID → Bool
coin i = Choice i True False

not, selfEq :: Bool → Bool
not True            = False
not False           = True
not (Choice i x y) = Choice i (not x) (not y)

selfEq b = iff b b

iff :: Bool → Bool → Bool
iff True            z = z
iff False           z = not z
iff (Choice i x y) z = Choice i (iff x z) (iff y z)
```

We pass an identifier to the operations `goal` and `coin` because they either directly create a `Choice` or call an operation which does. The functions `selfEq`, `iff`, and `not` do not need an additional parameter. We only have to extend their pattern matching to handle choices. If a value constructed by `Choice` is demanded, we return a choice with the same identifier and reapply the function to the different alternatives to compute the alternatives of the result. With these definitions (`goal initID`) evaluates to the following result (assuming `initID` yields 1).

```
Choice 1 (Choice 1 True False) (Choice 1 False True)
```

This result can be interpreted as `Choice 1 True True` because for all occurrences of `False` we would need to take once a left branch and once a right branch of a `Choice` labeled with 1. In our approach, however, choices with the same label are constrained to take the same branch when computing non-deterministic results. The invalid branches of the inner choices are, hence, pruned away. As a result, we obtain call-time choice semantics without sacrificing laziness: `coin` is evaluated by `iff` — not before passing it to `selfEq`. Moreover, the computations leading to the invalid results `False` are never evaluated (see Section 3.4).

A more complex example is the translation of `permute` (see Section 2.1):

```
permute :: ID → [a] → [a]
permute _ []    = []
permute i (x:xs) = insert (leftID i) x (permute (rightID i) xs)
permute i (Choice il xs ys) = Choice il (permute i xs) (permute i ys)

insert :: ID → a → [a] → [a]
insert i x []    = [x]
insert i x (y:ys) =
  Choice (leftID i) (x:y:ys) (y : insert (rightID i) x ys)
insert i x (Choice il xs ys) =
  Choice il (insert i x xs) (insert i x ys)
```

Both functions take an identifier as additional argument because they either directly create a `Choice` or call an operation which does and both functions make use of `leftID` and `rightID` to generate new identifiers that are passed down to sub computations.

2.4 Failing Computations

Non-determinism is only one means to model search in (functional-)logic programs. The other one is (finite) failure. Unlike in functional programs, where failing computations are considered programming errors, a functional logic programmer uses incomplete patterns or guards to restrict search. For example, the `sort` function introduced in Section 2.1 uses a guard that fails for unsorted lists in order to constrain the set of results to sorted permutations of the input.

In order to model failing computations, we introduce an additional special constructor `Failure` — again ignoring types in the scope of this description. Similar to the special rules for `Choice`, every pattern matching needs to be extended with a rule for `Failure`. For example, consider the transformed version of sort[4]:

```
sort :: ID → [Int] → [Int]
sort i l = guard (sorted p) p where p = permute i l

guard :: Bool → a → a
guard True          z = z
guard (Choice i x y) z = Choice i (guard x z) (guard y z)
guard _              _ = Failure

sorted :: [Int] → Bool
sorted []                = True
sorted [_]               = True
sorted (m:n:ns)          = m ≤ n && sorted (n:ns)
sorted (Choice i xs ys)  = Choice i (sorted xs) (sorted ys)
sorted (m:Choice i xs ys) = Choice i (sorted (m:xs)) (sorted (m:ys))
sorted _                 = Failure
```

We introduce a function `guard` to express guards in functional logic programs. This function returns its second argument if the first argument is `True`. Additionally, we have to add a rule to handle `Choice` in the first argument. We add a default case for all patterns that have not been matched to every function to return `Failure` in case of a pattern match error and to propagate such errors. Note that in the definition of the predicate `sorted` we need to handle `Choice` at every position in the nested pattern for lists with at least two elements.

3 Formal Definition of Transformation

In this section we define our program transformation formally. We introduce necessary notation (Sections 3.1 and 3.2), formalize the transformation (Section 3.3), and define the computation of non-deterministic *values* (Section 3.4).

---

[4] We omit the definitions of (≤) and (&&).

3.1 Preliminaries

We consider functional logic programs to be constructor-based term rewriting systems. For this we consider a *constructor-based signature* Σ as a disjoint union of two sets of symbols $C \cup F$ along with a mapping from each symbol to a natural number, called the symbol's *arity*. We will write $s^n \in \Sigma$ to denote that Σ contains the symbol s and that the arity of s is n. Elements of the sets C and F are called *constructor* and *function symbols*, respectively. We will use the symbols $c, c_1, \ldots, c_n$ for constructor symbols, $f, g, h, f_1, \ldots, f_n$ for function symbols and $s, s_1, \ldots, s_n$ for arbitrary symbols in $C \cup F$.

In general we use the notation $\overline{o_n}$ to denote a *sequence of objects* $o_1, \ldots, o_n$. If the exact length and elements of the sequence are arbitrary we may write $\overline{o}$.

Terms are constructed from constructor-based signatures in the usual inductive way. There are several important sets of terms. Elements of the set of *variables* X are denoted by $x, y, z, x_1, \ldots, x_n$ and the set of *values* V is defined by $V \ni v ::= x \mid c(\overline{v_n})$ where $x \in X$ and $c^n \in C$. We consider X to be fixed in the following. Finally the set of *expressions* E is defined by $E \ni e ::= x \mid s(\overline{e_n})$ where $x \in X$ and $s^n \in \Sigma$.

A special class of terms is called *linear*. In a linear term every variable appears at most once. The *sub terms* of a term t are denoted by $sub(t)$ and can be defined inductively by $sub(x) = \{x\}$; $sub(s(\overline{e_n})) = \{s(\overline{e_n})\} \cup \bigcup_{1 \leq i \leq n} sub(e_i)$. Likewise, the set of *variables* occurring in a term t, denoted by $var(t)$, is defined by $var(x) = \{x\}$; $var(s(\overline{e_n})) = \bigcup_{1 \leq i \leq n} var(e_i)$.

3.2 Programs and Operations

A *program* over a given signature Σ is a sequence of *rules*. Each rule is of the form $f(\overline{v}) \rightarrow e$ where $f(\overline{v})$ is linear. The set of all programs over a signature Σ is denoted by P_Σ but we can often simply write P when Σ is clear from the context or arbitrary. Elements of P will be denoted as p, p'. For a program p and a rule $r \in p$ where $r = f(\overline{v}) \rightarrow e$ we say that r is *a rule defining* (the operation) f (in p). The sequence of all rules defining f in p is denoted by $p(f)$.

An important subclass of programs are *uniform programs*. In a uniform program p for all rules $l \rightarrow r \in p$ holds $var(r) \subseteq var(l)$. Furthermore, the only non-deterministic operation is the binary $?^2$ defined by:

```
x ? y → x
x ? y → y
```

All other operations are defined either by a single rule without pattern matching or by a flat pattern matching on the last argument without any overlap. Formally, this means for any $f^n \neq ?^2$:

$$p(f) = f(\overline{x_n}) \rightarrow e$$
$$\vee\ p(f) = f(\overline{x_{n-1}}, c_1(\overline{y})) \rightarrow e_1, \ldots, f(\overline{x_{n-1}}, c_i(\overline{z})) \rightarrow e_i$$

where the constructors $\overline{c_i}$ are pairwise different.

It is well known that any functional logic program can be transformed into an equivalent uniform program [1]. For this it is necessary to redefine overlapping rules using ?^{2} and eventually adding auxiliary functions if the overlap is not trivial. For example the operation insert from Section 2.1 is redefined as:

```
insert  x xs      = (x:xs) ? insert2 x xs
insert2 x (y:ys) = y : insert x ys
```

Complex pattern matching also requires the introduction of fresh operations. For example sorted from Section 2.1 is redefined as:

```
sorted []      = True
sorted (m:xs) = sorted2 m xs

sorted2 _ []      = True
sorted2 m (n:ns) = m ≤ n && sorted (n:ns)
```

Some arguments are swapped like those of iff (Section 2.1). Free variables are simulated by generators as discussed in Section 2.1 and justified in [4].

The simple structure of uniform programs allows us to concisely define our transformation in the following subsection.

3.3   The Transformation of Programs

For the following, assume a given uniform program p over a signature Σ. We assume that Σ does not contain any of those symbols which we want to add as discussed in Section 2.3. We denote the set of these symbols by

$$S := \{\texttt{hnf}^1, \texttt{leftID}^1, \texttt{rightID}^1, \texttt{initID}^0, \texttt{Choice}^3, \texttt{Failure}^0\}$$

In this section we define how to produce a (purely functional) program p' over a signature Σ'.

One of the design goals of the transformation is that purely functional computations should be as efficient as possible. To achieve this we have to distinguish between purely functional and (potentially) non-deterministic operations. A necessary requirement for an operation to be non-deterministic is that it depends on the operation ?^{2}. In other words, it either calls ?^{2} directly or calls a function depending on ?^{2}. Formally, the set of non-deterministic operations $N \subseteq \Sigma$ is the smallest set such that

$$N := \{?^2\} \cup \{f \mid \exists l \to r \in p(f) : \exists g(\overline{e_n}) \in sub(r) : g^n \in N\}$$

All elements of N are extended with an extra argument to form the new signature $\Sigma' := S \cup \Sigma \setminus N \cup \{f^{n+1} \mid f^n \in N\}$.

One of the main concepts discussed in Section 2.3 is that each non-deterministic sub expression is extended by a *unique identifier* generated by leftID, rightID and initID. For this let i be an expression of type ID, i.e., an expression yielding an identifier at run time. Then the function $fresh_n(i)$ generates an expression yielding a different identifier from i for each natural number n. This is achieved by adding n times the function rightID and finally leftID.[5]

$$fresh_n(i) = \texttt{leftID}(\texttt{rightID}^n(i))$$

The next definition covers the transformation of expressions. It adds a given expression i of type ID for each call to an operation in N.

$$tr(i, x) = x$$

$$tr(i, s(\overline{e_n})) = \begin{cases} s(\overline{tr(i_n, e_n)}) & \text{, if } s^n \notin N \\ s(i_{n+1}, \overline{tr(i_n, e_n)}) & \text{, if } s^n \in N \end{cases}$$

where

$$\overline{i_{n+1}} = \overline{fresh_{n+1}(i)}$$

We are now ready to transform the rules defining an operation $f \neq ?^2$. Each rule is transformed by an application of $tr(\mathtt{i}, \cdot)$ to both the left and the right hand side of the rule where $\mathtt{i}$ is a fresh variable not occurring anywhere in p. For operations with matching rules the additional rules to lift the Choice constructor (see Section 2.3) and to produce Failure (Section 2.4) are added.

$$p'(f) := \begin{cases} tr(\mathtt{i}, l) \rightarrow tr(\mathtt{i}, r) & , p(f) = l \rightarrow r, l = f(\overline{x_n}) \\[2ex] \begin{array}{l} \overline{tr(\mathtt{i}, l_n) \rightarrow tr(\mathtt{i}, r_n)}, \\ f(\overline{x_m}, \texttt{Choice}(x, y, z)) \\ \quad \rightarrow \texttt{Choice}(x, f(\overline{x_m}, y), f(\overline{x_m}, z)), \\ f(\overline{x_m}, x) \rightarrow \texttt{Failure} \end{array} & , \begin{array}{l} p(f) = \overline{l_n \rightarrow r_n}, \\ l_1 = f(\overline{x_m}, c(\overline{y})) \end{array} \end{cases}$$

The operation $?^2$ is replaced by $?^3$ which introduces the constructor Choice.

$$?(i, x, y) = \texttt{Choice}(i, x, y)$$

Finally, the transformed program is extended by the definitions of the external operations initID, leftID, rightID and hnf. Possible implementations of initID, leftID and rightID were discussed in Section 2.3. The definition and application of hnf is the topic of the following subsection.

3.4   Evaluation to Head Normal Form and Transformation of Goals

In Section 2.3 we have seen that the transformed program yields terms of the form Choice 1 (Choice 1 True False) (Choice 1 False True) where the only valid solution is True (computed in two different ways). We will now define a function to abstract the admissible values from a given tree of choices.

---

[5] Note that we are quite wasteful in the generation of identifiers. We do so for simplicity; a transformation generating a minimal amount of calls to leftID and rightID is straightforward by counting non-deterministic sub terms.

```
hnf :: a → [a]
hnf ct = hnf' [] ct
  where hnf' choices (Choice i x y) = case lookup i choices of
              Just b  → hnf' choices (if b then x else y)
              Nothing → hnf' ((i,True) :choices) x
                     ++ hnf' ((i,False):choices) y
        hnf' _ Failure = []
        hnf' _ v       = [v]
```

The reader may check that indeed hnf applied on the tree of choices given above evaluates to [True,True].

It is unfortunate, however, that this version of hnf fixes the search strategy. In this case, hnf models depth first search. A nice opportunity provided by our approach is to let the user define the search strategy by different traversals of a representation of the search space. For this we first define the type representing *search trees*.

```
data SearchTree a = Value a
                  | Branch (SearchTree a) (SearchTree a)
                  | Stub
```

Now we can define an hnf function with the type a → SearchTree a.

```
hnf :: a → SearchTree a
hnf ct = hnf' [] ct
  where hnf' choices (Choice i x y) = case lookup i choices of
              Just b  → hnf' choices (if b then x else y)
              Nothing → Branch (hnf' ((i,True) :choices) x)
                               (hnf' ((i,False):choices) y)
        hnf' _ Failure = Stub
        hnf' _ v       = Value v
```

This function basically replaces Choice constructors with Branch constructors and prunes away invalid branches when matching a Choice constructor with a label that has already been processed.

Different search strategies can now be defined as tree traversals. We only give the definition of depth first search. See [8] for a definition of breadth first search.

```
df :: SearchTree a → [a]
df (Value v)     = [v]
df (Branch t1 t2) = df t1 ++ df t2
df Stub          = []
```

Having defined hnf, the final step of our transformation is to translate the goals given by the user, e.g., as the body of a function goal or on an interactive command line environment. For any search strategy st a given goal e is then translated to $(st\ (\mathtt{hnf}\ (tr(\mathtt{initID}, e))))$.[6]

---

[6] Curry implementations yield complete normal forms instead of head normal forms. Normal-form computation is orthogonal to our new approach to labeling and discussed elsewhere [8].

4 Related Work

The extension of lazy functional programming by logic features has by now a long tradition both in theory and application. A recent survey of the state of the art is given in [14].

There are several compilers for Curry which all follow one of three basic approaches. Compiling to *logic* languages like the PAKCS system [15], to *functional* languages like our former approach [8], or devising a *new abstract machine from scratch* [23,5]. Orthogonal to the development of a compiler for a complete language, several projects endeavor to extend functional programming by implementing *libraries* to support logic programming [19,20,24]. Each of these approaches has its own advantages and drawbacks.

Naturally, compiling to logic programming languages benefits from the efficient implementation of non-deterministic search. In addition, the target language will often feature further opportunities, e.g., to integrate constraint solvers [11]. Three main disadvantages, however, lead to handicaps with respect to both the performance of the average program and the class of applications that can be realized.

1. The *lazy evaluation of functions* has a substantial portion of *interpretation* in a logic programming language. Since in practice most functional logic programs feature more functional than logic code[7] and because laziness is very important for efficient search this results in cut backs for average performance.
2. As languages for logic programming are conceptually strict, there is no sensible notion of *sharing across non-determinism*. Sharing purely functional evaluations for each branch of a search space is, however, an important advantage for performance [7]. Especially, tabling techniques are not easily adapted to lazy semantics.
3. Since the resulting programs reuse the search facilities of Prolog it is impossible to support *control of the search*. However, the recent examples of implementing test tools [9] show that the opportunity to define sophisticated search strategies can be vital for the successful development of applications.

Obviously, when devising an abstract machine from scratch and compiling to a low level language like C or Java the implementation can support a detailed control of the search. Currently, there exists one mature implementation compiling to C, the MCC [23], and an experimental one to Java [5]. The main drawback of such an enterprise is that most of the knowledge amassed about declarative languages has to be reimplemented. Although an admirable effort in this regard has been realized for the MCC, we think that in the long run it is more promising

---

[7] This is more than just an observation about the current style of functional logic programming. It is in the essence of non-determinism that it is more expressive while being more computationally demanding in general. Therefore, sensible optimization techniques would often transform logic code to functional code when possible. Consequently, a good implementation of pure functions is crucial.

to benefit from the development of mature Haskell compilers like GHC. This includes the integration of concurrent programming, e.g. by STMs, and experiment with parallel search strategies. In contrast to the MCC the approach compiling to Java [5] also includes — like ours — sharing across non-determinism. There, however, no effort has been taken to implement any of the well known techniques to optimize declarative programs.

Libraries for logic programming in Haskell all share the same drawback in comparison to our approach: they do *not preserve laziness* for logic operations. Therefore, lazy functional logic programs cannot directly be translated to Haskell employing such a library. In contrast, it is one of the main insights of the research in functional logic programming languages that laziness and non-deterministic search can be combined profitably [16]. The next subsection shows by example that integrating laziness can significantly improve the performance of search.

5   Experimental Comparison

We have tested our approach to transform lazy functional logic programs in order to show a) the benefit of preserving laziness compared to monadic approaches in Haskell, and of b) using optimizations of an up-to-date Haskell compiler compared to other implementations of Curry.

We have applied the `sort` function defined in Section 2.1 to lists of different length and measured the run time for each investigated system. We have investigated two monadic approaches to model non-determinism: the list monad and a fair monad of streams [20] which we will call "stream monad" in the following. Additionally, we have compared our approach to existing Curry systems — especially, to the Kiel Curry System KiCS, our former approach, that uses a translation scheme similar to the one presented in this paper but uses side effects that prohibit optimizations on the generated Haskell code. We have used optimizations whenever available (optimizations have not been available in PAKCS and KiCS). The reported CPU times are user time in seconds, measured by the `time` command on a 2.2 GHz Intel Core 2 Duo Mac Book. The results of our experiments are depicted in Figure 1. The run times of the `sort` function are plotted at a logarithmic scale — they range from fractions of a second to several minutes. We clearly see that permutation sort is an exponential time algorithm even if laziness prevents the computation of unnecessary sub permutations.

However, the lazy implementations clearly outperform the strict monadic versions of `sort`. The list monad is even faster than the more sophisticated stream monad — probably because fairness is not an issue here and any sophistication to achieve it is worthless effort for this example. The missing laziness is a problem for the monadic implementations. They need minutes for lists of length 12 while the run time of the lazy implementations is insignificant for such lists.

We experienced the impure version of KiCS to be about two times slower than PAKCS, which is itself two times slower than MCC, which is three times slower than an optimized Haskell program that is transformed according to the transformation presented in this paper. A speedup of 12 compared to our

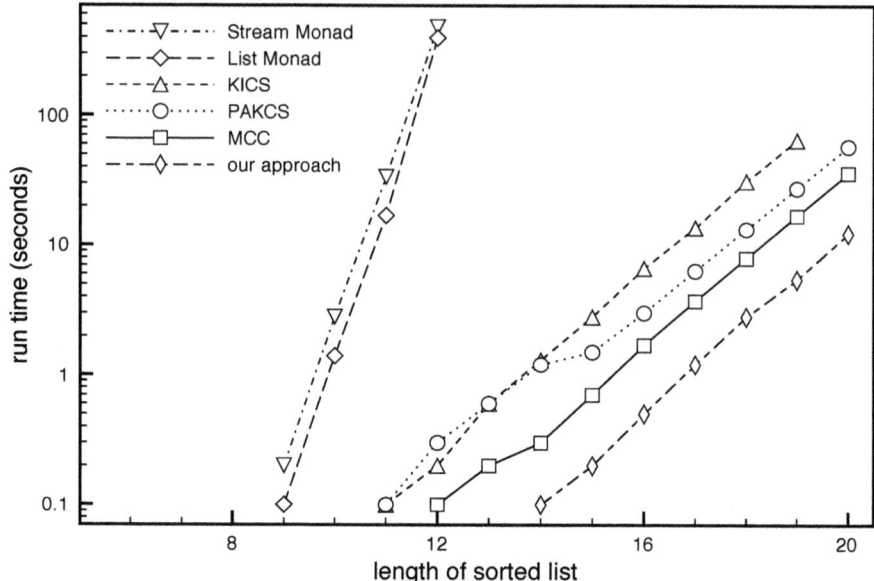

Fig. 1. Run time of Permutation Sort

old implementation of KiCS is quite encouraging, although the memory requirements of our approach should dampen our optimism. Applying permutation sort
to a list of 20 elements resulted in a memory allocation failure in the old version
of KiCS and also in our new approach the memory requirements increase with
the length of the sorted list. The MCC runs permutation sort in constant space,
which hints at a problem with garbage collection that is yet to be solved.

6   Conclusions and Future Work

We have presented a new scheme to translate lazy functional logic programs into
purely functional programs. To the best of our knowledge, we are the first to
provide such a translation that preserves laziness without using side effects. As
a consequence, the resulting programs can be fully optimized and preliminary
experiments show that the resulting code performs favorably compared to other
compilation techniques. Moreover, our transformation scheme adds almost no
overhead to purely functional parts of a program: only patterns have to be
extended with rules for choices and failure; unique identifiers only need to be
passed to operations that may cause non-determinism.

We do not prove the correctness of our approach in this paper. Conceptually, however, the approach is similar to a previously presented transformation
scheme implemented in the Curry compiler KiCS, which employs side effects.
The correctness of that scheme has been shown previously [8] also taking into
account the side effects.

We also do not discuss how to translate higher-order functions due to lack of space. Higher-order functions can be integrated in a way similar to the approach presented in [12]. This integration does not involve defunctionalization but reuses the higher-order features of the target language.

For future work we have to *implement the compilation scheme* described in Section 2.3. As the scheme is an extension of the one used in our earlier system [7] (and even simpler) we should be able to reuse much of our former work. This time, however, we plan to write the compiler in Curry rather than in Haskell.

While the run times for our compilation scheme look promising there is still work to do with regard to *memory usage*. Up to now the MCC system stands alone when regarding the combination of time and space efficiency.

A further topic of improvement concerns *constraint programming*. Our approach so far is not up to par with that of the PAKCS or the MCC system. PAKCS provides an interface to constraint solvers of the target language Prolog, MCC implements its own constraint solvers. Constraint programming could be integrated in our approach by interfacing external solvers or implementing solvers in Haskell. The details of a general framework for constraint programming in purely functional languages are still investigated in ongoing research.

References

1. Antoy, S.: Evaluation strategies for functional logic programming. Journal of Symbolic Computation 40(1), 875–903 (2005)
2. Antoy, S., Hanus, M.: Compiling multi-paradigm declarative programs into Prolog. In: Kirchner, H. (ed.) FroCos 2000. LNCS, vol. 1794, pp. 171–185. Springer, Heidelberg (2000)
3. Antoy, S., Hanus, M.: Functional logic design patterns. In: Hu, Z., Rodríguez-Artalejo, M. (eds.) FLOPS 2002. LNCS, vol. 2441, pp. 67–87. Springer, Heidelberg (2002)
4. Antoy, S., Hanus, M.: Overlapping rules and logic variables in functional logic programs. In: Etalle, S., Truszczyński, M. (eds.) ICLP 2006. LNCS, vol. 4079, pp. 87–101. Springer, Heidelberg (2006)
5. Antoy, S., Hanus, M., Liu, J., Tolmach, A.: A virtual machine for functional logic computations. In: Grelck, C., Huch, F., Michaelson, G.J., Trinder, P. (eds.) IFL 2004. LNCS, vol. 3474, pp. 108–125. Springer, Heidelberg (2005)
6. Augustsson, L., Rittri, M., Synek, D.: On generating unique names. Journal of Functional Programming 4(1), 117–123 (1994)
7. Braßel, B., Huch, F.: The Kiel Curry system KiCS. In: Seipel, D., Hanus, M., Wolf, A. (eds.) INAP 2007. LNCS, vol. 5437, pp. 215–223. Springer, Heidelberg (2009)
8. Braßel, B., Huch, F.: On a Tighter Integration of Functional and Logic Programming. In: Shao, Z. (ed.) APLAS 2007. LNCS, vol. 4807, pp. 122–138. Springer, Heidelberg (2007)
9. Christiansen, J., Fischer, S.: EasyCheck — test data for free. In: Garrigue, J., Hermenegildo, M.V. (eds.) FLOPS 2008. LNCS, vol. 4989, pp. 322–336. Springer, Heidelberg (2008)
10. Claessen, K., Hughes, J.: QuickCheck: A lightweight tool for random testing of Haskell programs. In: ICFP 2000: Proceedings of the ACM Internatioal Conference on Functional Programming, pp. 268–279. ACM, New York (2000)

11. Fernández, A.J., Hortalá-González, M.T., Sáenz-Pérez, F., del Vado-Vírseda, R.: Constraint functional logic programming over finite domains. Theory and Practice of Logic Programming (2007) (to appear)
12. Fischer, S., Kuchen, H.: Data-flow testing of declarative programs. In: Proc. of the 13th ACM SIGPLAN International Conference on Functional Programming (ICFP 2008), pp. 201–212. ACM Press, New York (2008)
13. Hanus, M.: A unified computation model for functional and logic programming. In: Proc. of the 24th ACM Symposium on Principles of Programming Languages, Paris, pp. 80–93 (1997)
14. Hanus, M.: Multi-paradigm declarative languages. In: Dahl, V., Niemelä, I. (eds.) ICLP 2007. LNCS, vol. 4670, pp. 45–75. Springer, Heidelberg (2007)
15. Hanus, M., Antoy, S., Braßel, B., Engelke, M., Höppner, K., Koj, J., Niederau, P., Sadre, R., Steiner, F.: PAKCS: The Portland Aachen Kiel Curry System (2007), http://www.informatik.uni-kiel.de/~pakcs/
16. Hanus, M., Réty, P.: Demand-driven search in functional logic programs. Research report rr-lifo-98-08, Univ. Orléans (1998)
17. Hanus, M., Sadre, R.: An abstract machine for curry and its concurrent implementation in java. Journal of Functional and Logic Programming 1999(6) (1999)
18. Hanus, M. (ed.): Curry: An integrated functional logic language (vers. 0.8.2) (2006), http://www.curry-language.org
19. Hinze, R.: Deriving backtracking monad transformers. In: Wadler, P. (ed.) Proceedings of the 2000 International Conference on Functional Programming, Montreal, Canada, September 18-20, pp. 186–197 (2000)
20. Kiselyov, O.: Simple fair and terminating backtracking monad transformer (October 2005), http://okmij.org/ftp/Computation/monads.html#fair-bt-stream
21. Lloyd, J.W.: Declarative programming in escher. Technical report cstr-95-013, University of Bristol (1995)
22. López-Fraguas, F., Sánchez-Hernández, J.: TOY: A multiparadigm declarative system. In: Narendran, P., Rusinowitch, M. (eds.) RTA 1999. LNCS, vol. 1631, pp. 244–247. Springer, Heidelberg (1999)
23. Lux, W., Kuchen, H.: An efficient abstract machine for curry. In: Beiersdörfer, K., Engels, G., Schäfer, W. (eds.) Informatik 1999 — Annual Meeting of the German Computer Science Society (GI), pp. 390–399. Springer, Heidelberg (1999)
24. Naylor, M., Axelsson, E., Runciman, C.: A functional-logic library for wired. In: Haskell 2007: Proceedings of the ACM SIGPLAN Workshop on Haskell Workshop, pp. 37–48. ACM, New York (2007)
25. Peyton Jones, S. (ed.): Haskell 98 Language and Libraries—The Revised Report. Cambridge University Press, Cambridge (2003)
26. Plasmeijer, R., van Eekelen, M.: Clean language report version 2.0 (2002), http://clean.cs.ru.nl/CleanExtra/report20/
27. Runciman, C., Naylor, M., Lindblad, F.: SmallCheck and Lazy SmallCheck: Automatic exhaustive testing for small values. In: Haskell 2008: Proceedings of the First ACM SIGPLAN Symposium on Haskell, pp. 37–48. ACM, New York (2008)
28. Wadler, P.: How to replace failure by a list of successes. In: Jouannaud, J.-P. (ed.) FPCA 1985. LNCS, vol. 201, pp. 113–128. Springer, Heidelberg (1985)

An Interaction Net Implementation of Closed Reduction

Ian Mackie

LIX, CNRS UMR 7161, École Polytechnique, 91128 Palaiseau Cedex, France

Abstract. Closed reduction is a very efficient reduction strategy for the lambda calculus, which is explained using a simple form of explicit substitutions. This paper introduces this strategy, and gives an implementation as a system of interaction nets. We obtain one of the most efficient implementations of this kind to date.

1 Introduction

At the heart of all functional programming languages lies the λ-calculus. A good, efficient, implementation of the λ-calculus is based around:

- finding an efficient *strategy* for reduction, and
- finding an efficient *implementation* of that strategy.

The reduction strategies used in functional programming languages usually stop at weak-head normal form—they do not reduce under abstractions. If we were to remove this constraint by allowing some reductions under an abstraction then sharing, and consequently efficiency, will be improved. In this paper we propose an efficient strategy for reduction in the λ-calculus, which is given as a conditional rewrite relation on lambda terms. We then implement the calculus as a system of interaction nets in such a way as to capture the conditions without additional cost.

Interaction nets [9] are a model of computation, and as an alternative to general graph rewriting, they have a number of striking features. In particular, in graph rewriting, locating (by graph matching) a reduction step is an expensive operation, as is finding the next redex. Interaction nets avoid these problems: there is a very simple mechanism to locate a redex (called an active pair in interaction net terminology), and there is no need to use expensive matching algorithms.

Just like term rewriting systems, interaction nets are user defined. Because we can write systems which correspond to term rewriting systems we can see them as specification languages. But, because we must also explain all the low-level details (such as copying and erasing) then we can see them as a low-level operational semantics or implementation language. There are interesting aspects of interaction nets for parallel evaluation, but we will not explore those here, although a parallel implementation of interaction nets does give a parallel implementation of the λ-calculus using the results of this paper.

S.-B. Scholz and O. Chitil (Eds.): IFL 2008, LNCS 5836, pp. 43–59, 2011.

Over the last years there have been several implementations of the λ-calculus using interaction nets. These include optimal reduction [7], encodings of existing strategies [12,19], and new strategies [14,16]. One of the first algorithms to implement Lévy's [11] notion of optimal reduction for the λ-calculus was presented by Lamping [10]. Empirical and theoretical studies of this algorithm have revealed several causes of inefficiency (accumulation of certain nodes in the graph rewriting formalism). Asperti et al. [1] devised BOHM (Bologna Optimal Higher-Order Machine) to overcome some of these issues.

Although many of the works cited above are known to be better than current implementations of the λ-calculus, to the best of our knowledge, none of the ideas have been used in the implementation of a functional programming language. One reason for this is that these algorithms are rarely well understood, and secondly the efficiency of these are not known. In this paper we present a simple interaction net system which is the most efficient to date. Our hope is that this implementation of the λ-calculus can find its way into the compilation of functional programming languages. Indeed, this work is part of a much larger research programme to do exactly that.

To summarise, the main contributions in this paper are:

- We give an efficient reduction strategy, which is a variant of closed reduction that has been well studied previously. This particular variant is well-adapted to implementation with interaction nets. The strategy is not β-optimal in the sense of Lévy [11], so there will be cases where optimal reduction could do better. However it does less work than many extant strategies since it allows reduction under abstractions.
- We give an interaction net encoding of precisely the above strategy, which means that we can prove correctness in a very simple and direct way. We simply need to show that we can follow the sequence of term reductions in the graphical formalism.

Relation to Previous Work. The present paper is a continuation of a programme of research by the author to use interaction nets as a mechanism for the efficient implementation of the λ-calculus. Specifically, it builds upon: [13], [14] and [16]. It is also related to the work on interaction nets for linear logic [8,15].

Overview. The rest of this paper is structured as follows. In the next section we recall interaction nets, and motivate why we use them. In Section 3 we introduce the reduction strategy for the λ-calculus that we will implement. In Section 4 we give the translation of the λ-calculus into interaction nets. Section 5 studies the reduction system. In Section 6 gives experimental evidence of our results, where we compare with other systems.

2   Interaction Nets

An interaction net system [9] is specified by giving a set Σ of symbols, and a set $\mathcal{R}$ of interaction rules. Each symbol $\alpha \in \Sigma$ has an associated (fixed) *arity*. An occurrence of a symbol $\alpha \in \Sigma$ will be called an *agent*. If the arity of α is n, then the agent has $n+1$ *ports*: a distinguished one called the *principal port* depicted by an arrow, and n *auxiliary ports* labelled $x_1, \ldots, x_n$ corresponding to the arity of the symbol. Such an agent will be drawn in the following way:

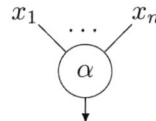

A net N built on Σ is a graph (not necessarily connected) with agents at the vertices. The edges of the graph connect agents together at the ports such that there is only one edge at every port. The ports of an agent that are not connected to another agent are called the free ports of the net. There are two special instances of a net: a wiring (no agents) and the empty net.

A pair of agents $(\alpha, \beta) \in \Sigma \times \Sigma$ connected together on their principal ports is called an *active pair*; the interaction net analog of a redex. An interaction rule $((\alpha, \beta) \implies N) \in \mathcal{R}$ replaces an occurrence of the active pair (α, β) by a net N. The rule must satisfy two conditions: all free ports are preserved during reduction (reduction is local, *i.e.*, only the part of the net involved in the rewrite is modified), and there is at most one rule for each pair of agents. The following diagram illustrates the idea, where N is any net built from Σ.

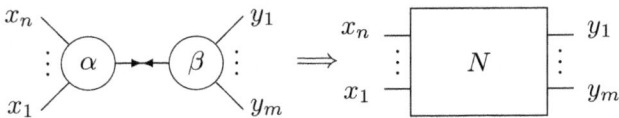

We use the notation $\implies$ for the one step reduction relation and $\implies^*$ for its transitive and reflexive closure. If a net does not contain any active pairs then we say that it is in normal form. One-step reduction ($\implies$) satisfies the diamond property, and thus we obtain a very strong notion of confluence. Indeed, all reduction sequences to normal form are permutation equivalent and standard results from rewriting theory tell us that all notions of termination coincide (if one reduction sequence terminates, then all reduction sequences terminate).

We choose to base this work on interaction nets because it expresses the algorithm as well as the memory management: there is no external copying or erasing machinery for instance. For this reason it is an ideal formalism for studying implementations and estimating the cost of evaluation.

3   λ-calculus: Closed Reduction Strategy

The origin of what we call *closed reduction* comes from a strategy for cut-elimination in linear logic [6]. We refer the reader to [4,5] for the interpretation of this strategy in the λ-calculus. In this paper we use a variant of this strategy which has a natural encoding in interaction nets.

$$\frac{\Gamma, x : A, y : B, \Delta \vdash t : C}{\Gamma, y : B, x : A, \Delta \vdash t : C} \text{ (Exchange)} \qquad \frac{}{x : A \vdash x : A} \text{ (Var)}$$

$$\frac{\Gamma, x : A \vdash t : B}{\Gamma \vdash \lambda x.t : A \to B} \text{ (Abs)} \qquad \frac{\Gamma \vdash t : A \to B \qquad \Delta \vdash u : A}{\Gamma, \Delta \vdash tu : B} \text{ (App)}$$

$$\frac{\Gamma \vdash t : B}{\Gamma, x : A \vdash E_x(t) : B} \text{ (Erase)} \qquad \frac{\Gamma, x : A, y : A \vdash t : B}{\Gamma, z : A \vdash C_z^{x,y}(t) : B} \text{ (Copy)}$$

$$\frac{\Gamma, x : A \vdash t : B \qquad \Delta \vdash v : A}{\Gamma, \Delta \vdash t[v/x] : B} \text{ (Sub)}$$

Fig. 1. Type Assignment for terms

We assume that terms are typed, which makes the proofs of various properties, specifically the duplication and erasing lemmas, simpler because we can rely on termination. However, the interaction net encoding of the next section also works also for the untyped calculus with the very same compilation and reduction rules, but we would need to rely on a weak evaluator that would not reduce disconnected nets for instance (see [18] for a weak evaluator).

To reason about the encoding, we need to be able to talk about substitutions and the propagation of substitutions through a term. The following calculus will serve this purpose, where we use a variant of the λ-calculus where erasing, copying and substitutions are explicit. In the following we assume Barendregt's variable convention [3] when talking about bound variables.

Definition 1 (Terms). *The table below summarises the terms, variable constraints and the free variables of the terms. We also add a single constant at base type, $\star : I$, which can be encoded as $\star = \lambda x.x$.*

Name	Term	Variable Constraint	Free Variables
Variable	x	—	$\{x\}$
Abstraction	$\lambda x.t$	$x \in \mathsf{fv}(t)$	$\mathsf{fv}(t) - \{x\}$
Application	tu	$\mathsf{fv}(t) \cap \mathsf{fv}(u) = \varnothing$	$\mathsf{fv}(t) \cup \mathsf{fv}(u)$
Erase	$E_x(t)$	$x \notin \mathsf{fv}(t)$	$\mathsf{fv}(t) \cup \{x\}$
Copy	$C_x^{y,z}(t)$	$x \notin \mathsf{fv}(t), y \neq z, \{y, z\} \subseteq \mathsf{fv}(t)$	$\mathsf{fv}(t) - \{y, z\} \cup \{x\}$
Substitution	$t[u/x]$	$x \in \mathsf{fv}(t), \mathsf{fv}(t) - \{x\} \cap \mathsf{fv}(u) = \varnothing$	$\mathsf{fv}(t) - \{x\} \cup \mathsf{fv}(u)$

In Figure 1 we give the typing rules, where $\Gamma \vdash t : A$ indicates that the term t has type A in the context Γ. The context is treated as an ordered sequence: $x_1 : A_1, \ldots, x_n : A_n$, and we give an explicit structural rule which allows elements of the sequence to be permuted. Note that this is the only structural rule, since copying and erasing elements of the sequence are done explicitly by the typing rules for Copy and Erase respectively.

We can compile the usual λ-calculus to this calculus by inserting the erase and copy constructs. The following definition will do this for us:

Definition 2 (Compilation). *Let t be a λ-term with $\mathsf{fv}(t) = \{x_1, \ldots, x_n\}$. Then the compilation is defined as: $[x_1] \ldots [x_n] t^\circ$ with $(\cdot)^\circ$ given by: $x^\circ = x$, $(tu)^\circ = t^\circ u^\circ$, and $(\lambda x.t)^\circ = \lambda x.[x]t^\circ$ if $x \in \mathsf{fv}(t)$, otherwise $(\lambda x.t)^\circ = \lambda x.E_x(t^\circ)$. We define $[\cdot]\cdot$ below, where $t[x := u]$ is the usual (implicit) notion of substitution, and the variables x' and x'' below are assumed to be fresh.*

$$
\begin{array}{lll}
[x]x & = x & \\
[x](\lambda y.t) & = \lambda y.[x]t & \\
[x](tu) & = C_x^{x',x''}([x'](t[x := x'])[x''](u[x := x''])) & x \in \mathsf{fv}(t), x \in \mathsf{fv}(u) \\
& = ([x]t)u & x \in \mathsf{fv}(t), x \notin \mathsf{fv}(u) \\
& = t([x]u) & x \in \mathsf{fv}(u), x \notin \mathsf{fv}(t) \\
[x]E_y(t) & = E_y([x]t) & \\
[x]C_y^{y',y''}(t) & = C_y^{y',y''}([x]t) &
\end{array}
$$

Example 1. Here are two familiar λ-terms compiled:

- $(\lambda xy.x)^\circ = \lambda xy.E_y(x)$
- $(\lambda fx.f(fx))^\circ = \lambda fx.C_f^{g,h}(g(hx))$

Definition 3 (Closed values). *A term t is a closed value if it is an abstraction, and $\mathsf{fv}(t) = \varnothing$. The predicate $\mathsf{cv}(t)$ is true if and only if t is a closed value.*

Our implementation of this calculus in interaction nets will follow a very specific strategy. We give this first for terms, and the correctness of the interaction net encoding will be given by showing that we follow this strategy.

Definition 4 (Closed value reduction). *We define a reduction relation $\rightarrow$ on terms below, where we write $\mathsf{cvnf}(t)$ if $\mathsf{cv}(t)$ and t is a normal form under $\rightarrow$.*

Name	Reduction		Condition
Beta	$(\lambda x.t)u$	$\rightarrow t[u/x]$	$\mathsf{cv}(\lambda x.t)$
Var	$x[v/x]$	$\rightarrow v$	—
App1	$(tu)[v/x]$	$\rightarrow (t[v/x])u$	$x \in \mathsf{fv}(t)$
App2	$(tu)[v/x]$	$\rightarrow t(u[v/x])$	$x \in \mathsf{fv}(u)$
Lam	$(\lambda y.t)[v/x]$	$\rightarrow \lambda y.t[v/x]$	$\mathsf{cv}(v)$
Copy1	$(C_x^{y,z}(t))[v/x]$	$\rightarrow (t[v/y])[v/z]$	$\mathsf{cvnf}(v)$
Copy2	$(C_{x'}^{y,z}(t))[v/x]$	$\rightarrow C_{x'}^{y,z}(t[v/x])$	—
Erase1	$(E_x(t))[v/x]$	$\rightarrow t$	$\mathsf{cv}(v)$
Erase2	$(E_y(t))[v/x]$	$\rightarrow E_y(t[v/x])$	—
Sub	$(t[w/y])[v/x]$	$\rightarrow t[w[v/x]/y]$	$x \in \mathsf{fv}(w)$

Below are a number of basic properties of reduction for this calculus. The first set of results show that certain properties are preserved under reduction.

Lemma 1 (Preservation Lemma)

1. *Preservation of free variables: if $t \to u$ then $\mathsf{fv}(t) = \mathsf{fv}(u)$.*
2. *Preservation of variable constraints: if t is a term satisfying the variable constraints above and $t \to u$, then u satisfies the variable constraints. In other words, if t is a well-defined term, then so is u.*
3. *Preservation of types (Subject Reduction): if $\Gamma \vdash t : A$ and $t \to u$ then $\Gamma \vdash u : A$.*

Proof. Part 1 is proved by a straightforward observation on the reduction rules: free variables are neither introduced nor erased. Part 2 by simple set theoretical arguments. Part 3 by the standard method of induction on the derivation of $t \to u$.

The reduction relation of the calculus presented contains many constraints, but it is good enough to get weak normal forms.

Lemma 2 (Adequacy). *If $t : A \to B$ is a closed term, then there is a sequence of reductions such that $t \to^* \lambda x.t'$, for some term t'. Moreover, if $t : I$ is a closed term, then there is a sequence of reductions such that $t \to^* \star$.*

Consequently, this calculus is adequate to compute the usual values that are associated to programs in the λ-calculus.

4   Interaction Net Encoding

We need to find a good way of implementing this calculus, in particular, to find an efficient way of computing all the conditions of the rewrite system. It turns out that a system of interaction nets can do this naturally.

We give a translation $\mathcal{T}(\cdot)$ of terms into interaction nets—composing this with the translation of the previous section will give a translation from λ-terms to nets. The agents required for the translation will be introduced when needed, and the interaction rules for these agents will be given in the following section. We remark that the translation given here is very similar to that used by some previous encodings [14,16], with an essential difference that we pick out closed abstractions in the translation, and that the rewrite rules of the next section are quite different. A term t with $\mathsf{fv}(t) = \{x_1, \ldots, x_n\}$ will be translated as a net $\mathcal{T}(t)$ with the root edge at the top, and n free edges corresponding to the free variables:

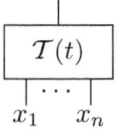

Variable. The first case of the translation function is when t is a variable, say x, then $\mathcal{T}(t)$ is translated into a wire:

$$\big|$$
$$x$$

Abstraction. If t is an abstraction, say $\lambda x.t'$, then there are two alternative translations, which are given as follows:

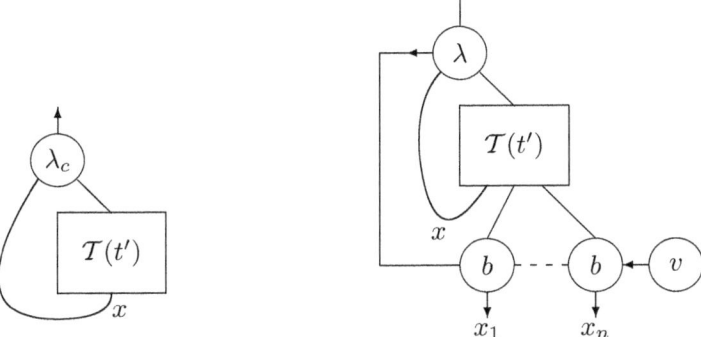

The first case, shown on the left, is when $\mathsf{fv}(\lambda x.t') = \varnothing$. Here we use one agent λ_c to represent a *closed abstraction*. This net corresponds closely to standard graph representations of the λ-calculus, except that we explicitly connect the occurrence of the variable x to the binding λ.

The second case, shown on the right, is when $\mathsf{fv}(\lambda x.t') = \{x_1, \ldots, x_n\}$. Here we introduce three different kinds of agents: λ of arity 3, for abstraction, and two kinds of agent representing a list of free variables. An agent b is used for each free variable, and we end the list with an agent v. The idea is that there is a pointer to the free variables of an abstraction. We assume, without loss of generality, that the (unique) occurrences of the variable x is in the leftmost position of $\mathcal{T}(t')$.

We remark that a closed term will never become open during reduction (although of course terms may become closed, and indeed there are interaction rules which will create a λ_c agent from a λ agent when needed). The use of the λ_c agent identifies the case where there are no free variables, and plays a crucial role in the efficient dynamics of this system.

Application. If t is uv, then $\mathcal{T}(uv)$ is given by the following net, where we have introduced an agent @ of arity 2 corresponding to an application.

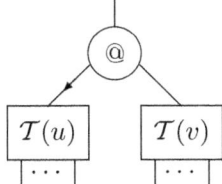

Erasing. If t is $E_x(u)$, then $\mathcal{T}(E_x(u))$ is given by the following net using a new agent ϵ, of arity 0.

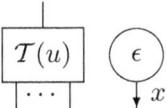

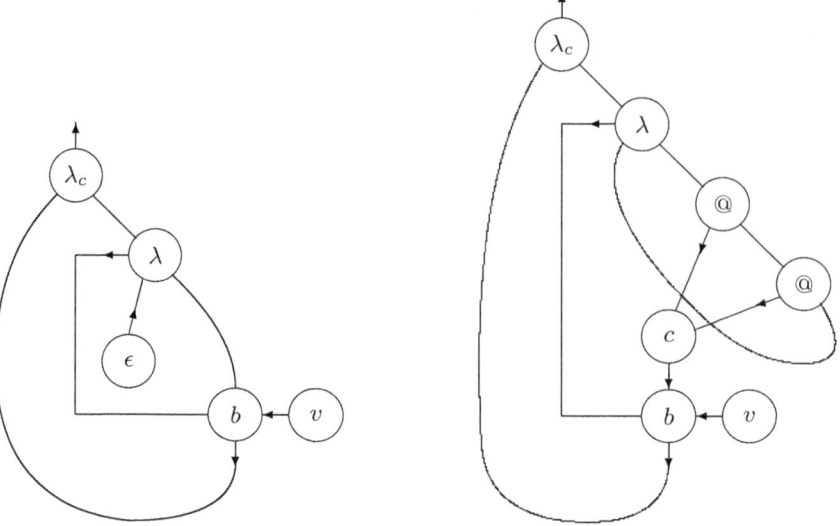

Fig. 2. Example nets: $\mathcal{T}(\lambda xy.E_y(x))$ and $\mathcal{T}(\lambda fx.C_f^{g,h}(g(hx)))$

Duplication. If t is $C_x^{y,z}(u)$, then $\mathcal{T}(C_x^{y,z}(u))$ is given by the following net using a new agent c, of arity 2. We have assumed in the diagram, without loss of generality, that the (unique) occurrences of the variables y, z are in the right-most positions of $\mathcal{T}(u)$.

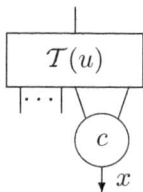

Substitution. If t is $u[v/x]$, then $\mathcal{T}(u[v/x])$ is given by the following net, where we simply connect the free edge x of $\mathcal{T}(u)$ to the root of $\mathcal{T}(v)$.

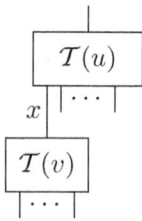

That completes the cases for the translation, which is the same whether we talk about typed or untyped terms. We state one important static result about this translation, which is a direct consequence of the fact that no active pairs are created for the translation of normal forms.

Lemma 3. *If t is a term, then* cvnf(t) *implies* $\mathcal{T}(t)$ *is a net in normal form.*

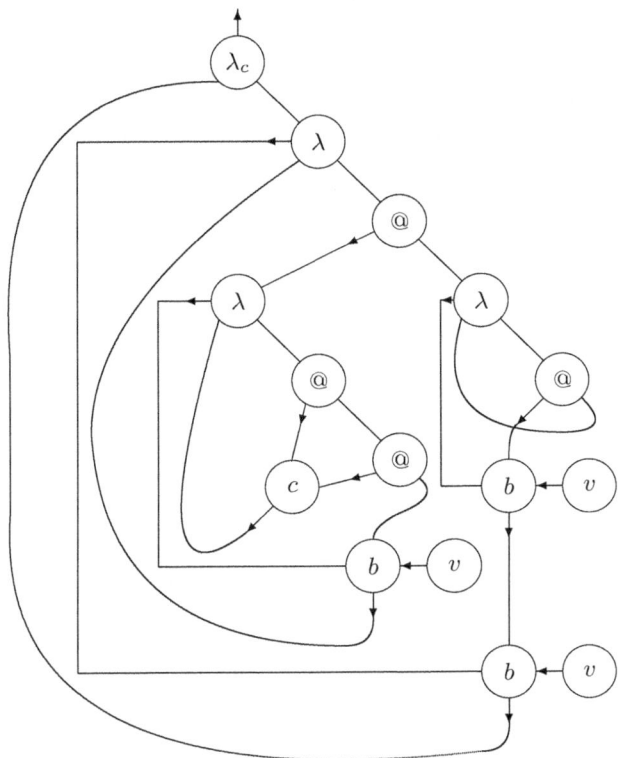

Fig. 3. Example of a net in normal form: $\mathcal{T}((\lambda xy.(\lambda z.(z(zy)))(\lambda w.xw))^\circ)$

Example 2. In Figure 2 we give two example nets corresponding to the λ-terms $\mathbf{K} = \lambda xy.x$ and $\mathbf{2} = \lambda fx.f(fx)$, which give a flavour of the kinds of structures that we are dealing with. In Figure 3 we give an additional example which is a term in closed value normal form: $\mathbf{2}' = \lambda xy.(\lambda z.(z(zy)))(\lambda w.xw)$. This is an example of a term that will not be β-optimal, as it is a net in normal form, yet there is a redex in the usual λ-calculus.

5   Reduction

The reduction system given for the calculus consists of ten rewrite rules, but the following result shows that six of these are equalities in the interaction system:

Proposition 1. *If $t \rightarrow u$ by one of the following, then $\mathcal{T}(t) = \mathcal{T}(u)$:*

$$
\begin{aligned}
&\textit{Var:} && x[v/x] \rightarrow v \\
&\textit{App1:} && (tu)[v/x] \rightarrow (t[v/x])u \\
&\textit{App2:} && (tu)[v/x] \rightarrow t(u[v/x]) \\
&\textit{Copy2:} && (C_{x'}^{y,z}(t))[v/x] \rightarrow C_{x'}^{y,z}(t[v/x]) \\
&\textit{Erase2:} && (E_y(t))[v/x] \rightarrow E_y(t[v/x]) \\
&\textit{Sub:} && (t[w/y])[v/x] \rightarrow t[w[v/x]/y]
\end{aligned}
$$

Proof. $\mathcal{T}(t)$ and $\mathcal{T}(u)$ are identical nets in each case.

Additionally, the graphical representation factors out several other syntactical differences. For instance the nets $\mathcal{T}(t[u/x][v/y])$ and $\mathcal{T}(t[v/y][u/x])$ are identical, but there is no way to make the corresponding terms reduce to each other in the calculus. The elimination of these syntactical differences is one of the main features of the graphical representation.

We now proceed to give the interaction rules which encode the remaining four rewrite rules.

Beta Rule. If $(\lambda x.t)u \rightarrow t[u/x]$, then we require a sequence of interactions which transforms $\mathcal{T}((\lambda x.t)u)$ into $\mathcal{T}(t[u/x])$, as shown in the following diagram:

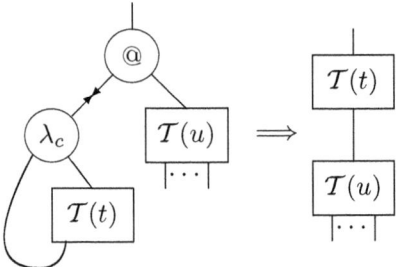

An active pair has been created on the left-hand side, and this net transformation can be simulated by one rule which captures the notion of connecting the body of the abstraction to the root, and the argument to the (unique) occurrence of the variable x in the body of the abstraction:

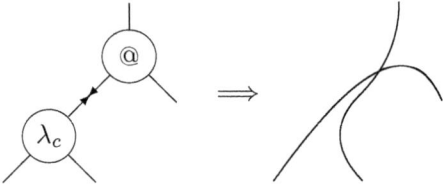

We can now state the following intermediate result:

Lemma 4 (Beta Simulation). *If $(\lambda x.t)u \rightarrow t[u/x]$, then there is a single interaction such that:* $\mathcal{T}((\lambda x.t)u) \Longrightarrow \mathcal{T}(t[u/x])$.

Lam Rule. If $(\lambda y.t)[v/x] \rightarrow \lambda y.t[v/x]$, then $\mathsf{cvnf}(v)$. We thus need a sequence of interactions which transforms $\mathcal{T}((\lambda y.t)[v/x])$ into $\mathcal{T}(\lambda y.t[v/x])$. This is given in Figure 4, where we assume $v = \lambda z.w$ (to keep the diagram simple, we show the case where there are just two free variables in the term $\lambda y.t$). An active pair has been created on the left-hand side. We need just one rule:

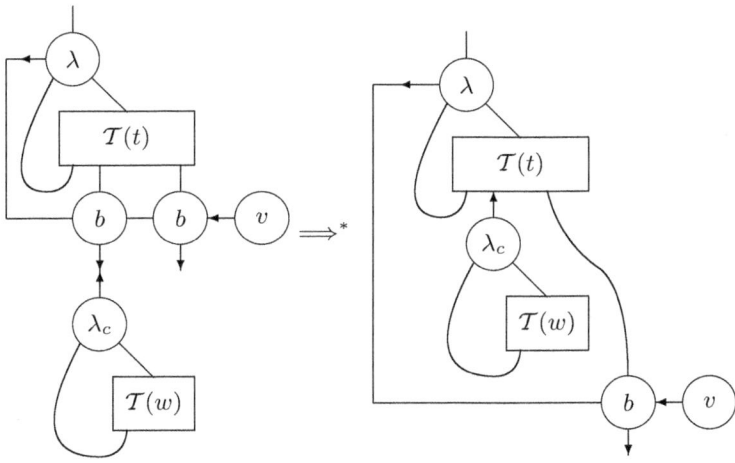

Fig. 4. Lam rule

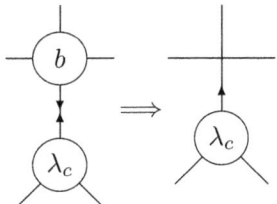

Formalizing this gives us our second intermediate result.

Lemma 5 (Lam Simulation). *If $(\lambda y.t)[v/x] \to \lambda y.t[v/x]$, then there is a single interaction such that: $\mathcal{T}((\lambda y.t)[v/x]) \Longrightarrow \mathcal{T}(\lambda y.t[v/x])$.*

In the previous case, when there are no more free variables in an abstraction, then the v and λ agents create an active pair. The following interaction rule shows that a closed abstraction is created:

$$\bigcirc\!\!\!v \longrightarrow \bigcirc\!\!\!\lambda \quad \Longrightarrow \quad \bigcirc\!\!\!\lambda_c$$

Thus far we have only been concerned with linear reductions. We now address copying and discarding.

Copy rule. If $(C_x^{y,z}(t))[v/x] \to t[v/y][v/z]$, where $\mathsf{cvnf}(v)$, then we require a transformation from $\mathcal{T}((C_x^{y,z}(t))[v/x])$ to $\mathcal{T}(t[v/y][v/z])$, as shown below:

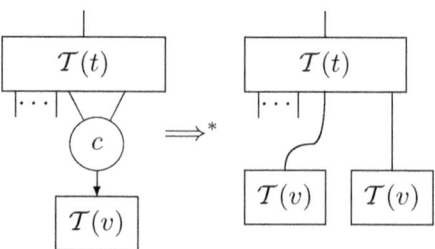

The duplication process begins when a c agent meets a closed abstraction. The λ_c agent is copied, and δ agents are propagated to duplicate the body of the abstraction, say u.

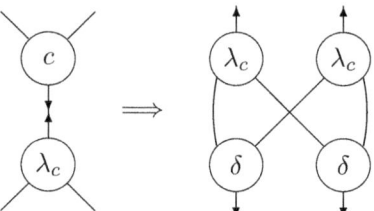

After this interaction, we are left with the following configuration, where the body of the abstraction is not yet duplicated.

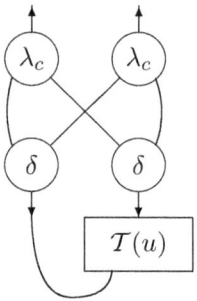

The δ agents have been introduced precisely to complete the duplication of this net. It is important to remark that we cannot use the c agent for this purpose, since there may be c agents occurring in the net that need to be duplicated. The interaction rules for δ are the following, which indicate that δ copies any other agent α, where $\alpha \neq \delta$. The interaction of a δ agent with another δ agent indicates that part of the duplication has completed.

The δ agents are used in such a way that we can assume that there are no δ agents occurring in a net to be duplicated. We remark that duplication of a net is quite delicate since δ interactions can only duplicate nets in normal form— specifically no active pairs can be duplicated. This of course is an advantage as sharing is a desirable property that we want! A net that is representing a term in normal form is in normal form (Lemma 3). Using the fact that there are δ agents connected to all the free edges of the net will allow us to fully duplicate a net.

Lemma 6 (Duplication). *Let $N = \mathcal{T}(t)$ for any term* cvnf(t). *N can be fully duplicated using δ agents giving two occurrences of the net N.*

Using this lemma, we can now state the main result about copy.

Lemma 7 (Copy Simulation). *If $C_x^{y,z}(t)[v/x] \to t[v/y][v/z]$, where* cvnf(v), *then $\mathcal{T}(C_x^{y,z}(t)[v/x]) \Longrightarrow^* \mathcal{T}(t[v/y][v/z])$.*

Erase rule. If $(E_x(t))[v/x] \to t$, then we require a sequence of interactions which transforms $\mathcal{T}((E_x(t))[v/x])$ into $\mathcal{T}(t)$. The interaction rules for ϵ follow a general pattern. For each agent α of arity n, the interaction erases the agent α and propagates n occurrences of the ϵ agent along all the auxiliary ports:

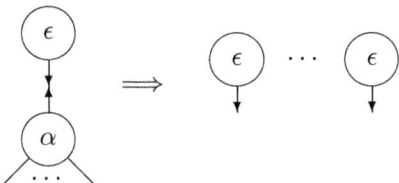

Lemma 8 (Erasing). *Let $N = \mathcal{T}(t)$, for any term* cvnf(t). *Then N can be completely erased using ϵ agents.*

Lemma 9 (Erase Simulation). *If $E_x(t)[v/x] \to t$, where* cvnf(v), *then there is a sequence of interaction rules such that: $\mathcal{T}(E_x(t)[v/x]) \Longrightarrow^* \mathcal{T}(t)$.*

This completes the dynamics of the system of interaction. In Figure 5 we summarise all the interaction rules for this system. We can now group together all the previous lemmas concerning the simulation of closed value reduction as a system of interaction nets. Each of the simulation lemmas given show the existence of a sequence of interactions simulating each reduction step in the calculus. By confluence of interaction nets, we can state a much stronger result.

Theorem 1. *Let $t : A$ be a closed term of base type, then $t \to^* c$, for some constant c, if and only if there is a finite sequence of interactions such that $\mathcal{T}(t) \Longrightarrow^* \mathcal{T}(c)$.*

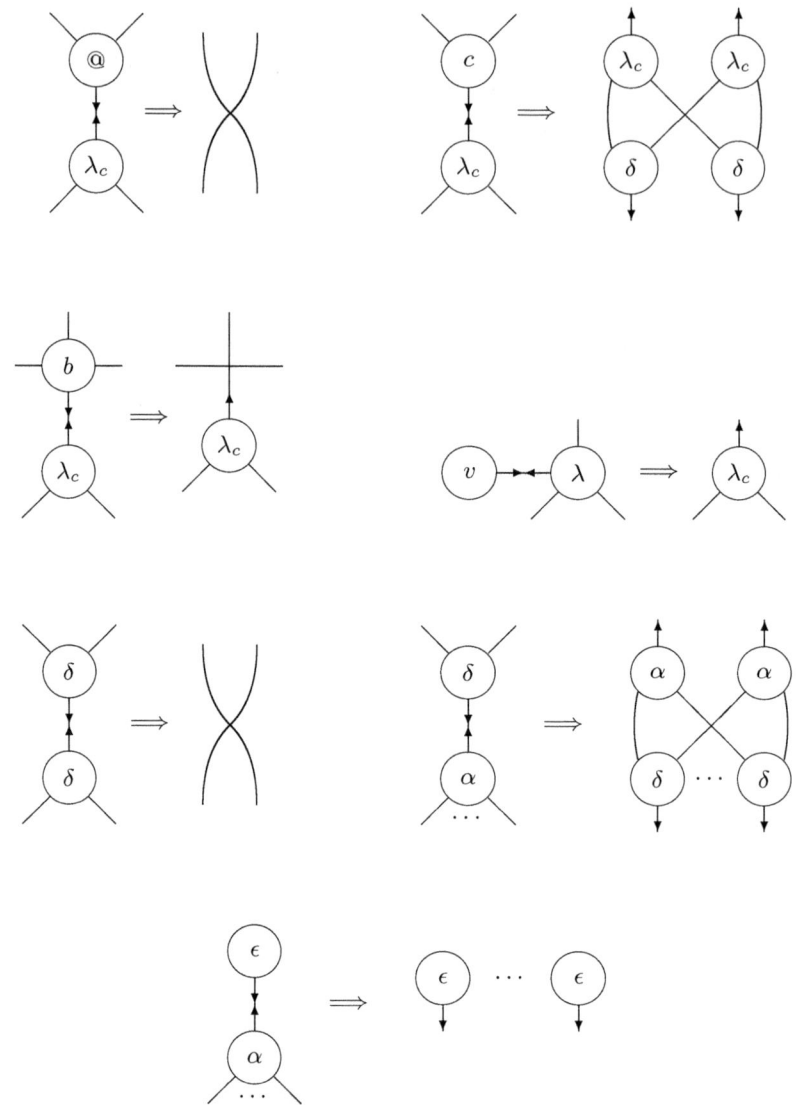

Fig. 5. Interaction Rules

6   Testing

There are a number of benchmark results that have become standard to demonstrate the performance of these kinds of evaluators. We base ours on those used to demonstrate BOHM [2], which is the system that we use as the basis of the comparison. These terms generate vast computations, and in particular include terms where sharing plays a significant role for the evaluation. Table 1 shows

Table 1. Benchmark: Church numerals

Term	CVR	β-optimal
2 *II*	8(4)	12(4)
2 2 *II*	30(9)	40(9)
2 2 2 *II*	82(18)	93(16)
2 2 2 2 *II*	314(51)	356(27)
2 2 2 2 2 *II*	983346(131122)	1074037060(61)
3 2 *II*	48(12)	47(12)
4 2 *II*	66(15)	63(15)
5 2 *II*	84(18)	79(18)
10 2 *II*	174(33)	159(33)
3 2 2 *II*	160(29)	157(21)
4 2 2 *II*	298(48)	330(26)
5 2 *2II*	556(83)	847(31)
10 2 2 *II*	15526(2082)	531672(56)
3 2 2 2 *II*	3992(542)	34740(40)
4 2 2 2 *II*	983330(131121)	1074037034(60)
2 2 2 10 *II*	1058(179)	10307(67)
2 2 2 2 10 *II*	4129050(655410)	1073933204(162)

some evaluations of Church numerals. Results of the form 8(4) should be read as 8 interactions, of which 4 were $\lambda_c - @$ (thus giving a count of the number of β-reductions performed). The number of β-reduction steps performed is only given for curiosity: it is the number of interactions which gives a measure of actual work. To give some indication as to what some of these numbers mean, current implementations of interaction nets can perform over 1 million interactions per second. Implementations of functional languages, such as Haskell, OCaml, SML, etc. are well known to not be able to cope with such terms, and indeed fail on the larger examples in the table.

A brief analysis of this table (and other data accumulated) show a general pattern from which a key observation can be made. As the terms become larger, BOHM improves with respect to the number of β-interactions, but closed value reduction becomes better with respect to the total number of interactions (*i.e.*, total cost of evaluation).

The comparison given here only touches on the testing done, and in particular we do not include results for other systems of interaction nets, or related systems of rewriting (see for instance [14,17]). We hope to provide a more complete comparison at some future occasion.

7   Conclusions

When implementing the λ-calculus efficiently, we need to take into account both the strategy and the implementation of this strategy. In this paper we have presented the closed reduction strategy and given an implementation. This has given us the most efficient interaction net implementation of the λ-calculus to date.

This work is currently being used as part of an implementation of a simple functional programming language. In this way we can build for the first time a complete programming language around interaction nets. This will allow us to identify what we do better, or worse, than existing implementation technologies.

References

1. Asperti, A., Giovannetti, C., Naletto, A.: The bologna optimal higher-order machine. Journal of Functional Programming 6(6), 763–810 (1996)
2. Asperti, A., Guerrini, S.: The Optimal Implementation of Functional Programming Languages. Cambridge Tracts in Theoretical Computer Science, vol. 45. Cambridge University Press, Cambridge (1998)
3. Barendregt, H.P.: The Lambda Calculus: Its Syntax and Semantics, 2nd edn. Studies in Logic and the Foundations of Mathematics, vol. 103. North-Holland Publishing Company, Amsterdam (1984) (revised edition)
4. Fernández, M., Mackie, I.: Closed reductions in the λ-calculus. In: Flum, J., Rodríguez-Artalejo, M. (eds.) CSL 1999. LNCS, vol. 1683, pp. 220–234. Springer, Heidelberg (1999)
5. Fernández, M., Mackie, I., Sinot, F.-R.: Closed reduction: explicit substitutions without alpha conversion. Mathematical Structures in Computer Science 15(2), 343–381 (2005)
6. Girard, J.-Y.: Geometry of interaction 1: Interpretation of System F. In: Ferro, R., Bonotto, C., Valentini, S., Zanardo, A. (eds.) Logic Colloquium 1988. Studies in Logic and the Foundations of Mathematics, vol. 127, pp. 221–260. North Holland Publishing Company, Amsterdam (1989)
7. Gonthier, G., Abadi, M., Lévy, J.-J.: The geometry of optimal lambda reduction. In: Proceedings of the 19th ACM Symposium on Principles of Programming Languages (POPL 1992), pp. 15–26. ACM Press, New York (1992)
8. Gonthier, G., Abadi, M., Lévy, J.-J.: Linear logic without boxes. In: Proceedings of the 7th IEEE Symposium on Logic in Computer Science (LICS 1992), pp. 223–234. IEEE Press, Los Alamitos (1992)
9. Lafont, Y.: Interaction nets. In: Proceedings of the 17th ACM Symposium on Principles of Programming Languages (POPL 1990), pp. 95–108. ACM Press, New York (1990)
10. Lamping, J.: An algorithm for optimal lambda calculus reduction. In: Proceedings of the 17th ACM Symposium on Principles of Programming Languages (POPL 1990), pp. 16–30. ACM Press, New York (1990)
11. Lévy, J.-J.: Optimal reductions in the lambda calculus. In: Hindley, J.P., Seldin, J.R. (eds.) To H.B. Curry: Essays on Combinatory Logic, Lambda Calculus and Formalism, pp. 159–191. Academic Press, London (1980)
12. Lippi, S.: λ-calculus left reduction with interaction nets. Mathematical Structures in Computer Science 12(6) (2002)
13. Mackie, I.: The Geometry of Implementation. PhD thesis, Department of Computing, Imperial College of Science, Technology and Medicine (September 1994)
14. Mackie, I.: YALE: Yet another lambda evaluator based on interaction nets. In: Proceedings of the 3rd International Conference on Functional Programming (ICFP 1998), pp. 117–128. ACM Press, New York (1998)
15. Mackie, I.: Interaction nets for linear logic. Theoretical Computer Science 247(1), 83–140 (2000)

16. Mackie, I.: Efficient λ-evaluation with interaction nets. In: van Oostrom, V. (ed.) RTA 2004. LNCS, vol. 3091, pp. 155–169. Springer, Heidelberg (2004)
17. Mackie, I., Pinto, J.S.: Encoding linear logic with interaction combinators. Information and Computation 176(2), 153–186 (2002)
18. Pinto, J.S.: Weak reduction and garbage collection in interaction nets. Electronic Notes in Theoretical Computer Science 84(4), 625–640 (2003)
19. Sinot, F.-R.: Call-by-name and call-by-value as token-passing interaction nets. In: Urzyczyn, P. (ed.) TLCA 2005. LNCS, vol. 3461, pp. 386–400. Springer, Heidelberg (2005)

Implementation Architecture and Multithreaded Runtime System of S-Net

Clemens Grelck[1,2] and Frank Penczek[2]

[1] University of Amsterdam, Institute of Informatics
Science Park 107, 1098 XG Amsterdam, Netherlands
c.grelck@uva.nl
[2] University of Hertfordshire, School of Computer Science
Hatfield, Herts, AL10 9AB, United Kingdom
{f.penczek,c.grelck}@herts.ac.uk

Abstract. S-Net is a declarative coordination language and component technology aimed at modern multi-core/many-core architectures and systems-on-chip. It builds on the concept of stream processing to structure networks of communicating asynchronous components, which can be implemented using a conventional (sequential) language. In this paper we present the architecture of our S-Net implementation. After sketching out the interplay between compiler and runtime system, we characterise the deployment and operational behaviour of our multi-threaded runtime system for contemporary multi-core processors. Preliminary runtime figures demonstrate the effectiveness of our approach.

1 Introduction

The free lunch is over! Excessive power consumption and heat dissipation have eventually set an end to clock frequency scaling, and the current trend in processor architecture is to go multi-core [1]. Small-scale dual-core and quad-core processors already dominate the consumer market while the roadmaps of all major hardware manufacturers promise a steep rise in the number of cores [2]. At the same time, massively parallel processors (e.g. GPGPUs, accelerator boards) already offer a degree of parallelism in computing resources that very recently could only be found in dedicated supercomputing installations [3].

This hardware trend towards multi-core/many-core designs puts immense pressure on software manufacturers: For the first time in history software does not automatically benefit from a new generation of hardware as was characteristic for the era of clock frequency scaling. Software must become parallel in order to benefit from future processor generations! However, to the present day software is predominantly sequential adhering to the von Neumann model of computing. While parallel computing is an established discipline, it has always been confined to supercomputing application areas and installations. Now, parallel computing must go mainstream, but the existing tools and technologies were developed for experts in the niche, not for the mainstream.

S.-B. Scholz and O. Chitil (Eds.): IFL 2008, LNCS 5836, pp. 60–79, 2011.

S-Net [4] is a novel approach to ease parallelisation of existing and new applications. It builds on separation of concerns as the key design principle: an *application engineer* uses domain-specific knowledge to provide application building blocks of suitable granularity in the form of (rather conventional) functions that map inputs into outputs. In a complementary way, a *concurrency engineer* uses his expert knowledge on target architectures and concurrency in general to orchestrate the (sequential) building blocks into a parallel application. In fact, S-Net turns regular functions/procedures implemented in a conventional language into asynchronous, state-less components communicating via uni-directional streams. The choice of a component language solely depend on the application domain of the components itself. In principle, any conventional programming language can be used, and a single S-Net network can manage components implemented using different languages.[1] Fig. 1 shows an example of an S-Net streaming network.

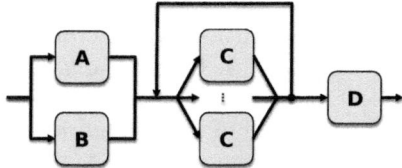

Fig. 1. Illustration of an S-Net streaming network of asynchronous components

Note that any base component is characterised by a single input and a single output stream. This restriction is motivated, again, by the principle of separation of concerns: The concern of a box is mapping input values into output values, whereas its purpose within a streaming network is entirely opaque to the box itself. Concurrency concerns like synchronisation and routing that immediately become evident if a box had multiple input streams or multiple output streams, respectively, are kept away from boxes. Our solution achieves a near-complete separation of computing and coordination aspects. We have identified four fundamental construction principles for streaming networks:

- *serial composition* of two (potentially) different components where the output stream of one component becomes the input stream of another component;
- *parallel composition* of two (potentially) different networks where some routing oracle decides on which branch data takes;
- *serial replication* of a single network where data is streamed through the same network a dynamically determined number of times; and
- *indexed parallel replication* of a single network where an index attached to the data determines which branch (or which replica of the network) is taken.

---

[1] There are, however, technical limitations on the interoperability of languages and on the technical interplay between coordination and computation layer.

These four construction principles allow concurrency engineers to define complex streaming networks of asynchronous components and to turn sequential code blocks into a parallel application ready to effectively exploit the capabilities of modern multi-core and many-core processors with very little effort.

This paper is the first to report on our implementation of S-Net. The architecture of our implementation features a target independent compiler that generates (C) code dominated by calling functions from the *S-Net common runtime interface*. Multiple implementations of the common runtime interface allow us to support varying concrete hardware platforms in a plug-in manner. In this paper, we provide an in-depth description of our multithreading based runtime system for contemporary multi-core processors with shared memory. We will describe this runtime system at a level of abstraction such that it may equally well serve as an operational semantics of S-Net.

It is a characteristic feature of our common runtime interface that it does not prejudice any concrete representation of the streaming network. This proves essential when it comes to supporting a wide range of target architectures with highly varying demands and capabilities, e.g. microthreading on the MicroGrid architecture [5,6]. As a consequence, it is up to any concrete runtime system to define the dynamic representation of the streaming network, and runtime system functionality naturally falls into one of two categories: *network deployment* and *network operation*. The former is concerned with instantiating the streaming network on the target platform while the latter defines the operational behaviour of the network constituents. As we will see later, these two aspects are not necessarily consecutive, but interleave in practice.

The specific contributions of the paper are the

- presentation of the overall architecture of our S-Net implementation;
- formal description of network deployment;
- formal specification of the operational behaviour of components;
- implementation of guarantees for package ordering; and
- preliminary performance figures.

The remainder of the paper is organised as follows: In Section 2 we provide a more detailed introduction to S-Net. Section 3 sketches out the architecture of our S-Net implementation including compiler, runtime system and their interplay. Section 4 discusses network instantiation while the operational behaviour of network components is described in Section 5. In Section 6 we elaborate on package ordering. Eventually, we provide some preliminary runtime figures in Section 7, discuss related work in Section 8 and conclude in Section 9.

2   S-Net in a Nutshell

As a pure coordination language S-Net relies on a separate component language to describe computations. Such components are named *boxes* in S-Net terminology, their implementation language *box language*. Any box is connected to the rest of the network by two typed streams: an input stream and an output stream. Messages on these typed streams are organised as non-recursive records, i.e. label-value pairs. Labels are subdivided into *fields* and *tags*. Fields are associated with values from the box language domain. They are entirely opaque to S-Net. Tags are associated with integer numbers that are accessible both on the S-Net and the box language level. Tag labels are distinguished from field labels by angular brackets.

On the S-Net level, the behaviour of a box is declared by a *type signature*: a mapping from an *input type* to a disjunction of *output types*. For example,

```
box foo ({a,<b>} -> {c} | {c,d,<e>})
```

declares a box that expects records with a field labelled a and a tag labelled b. The box responds with a number of records that either have just a field c or fields c and d as well as tag e. Both the number of output records and the choice of variants are at the discretion of the box implementation alone.

As soon as a record is available on the input stream, a box consumes that record, applies its box function to the record and emits the resulting records on its output stream. In the simple but common case of a one-to-one mapping between input and output records the box function's result value may determine the output record. In the general case, our *box language interface* provides a box language specific abstraction named snet_out to dynamically produce output records during the execution of the box function. As soon as the evaluation of the box function is complete, the S-Net box is ready to receive and process the next input record.

S-Net boxes are stateless by definition, i.e., the mapping of an input record to a stream of output records is free of side-effects or, in other words, purely functional. We exploit this property for cheap relocation and re-instantiation of boxes; it distinguishes S-Net from conventional component technologies. In particular if boxes are implemented using imperative languages, S-Net, however, can only guarantee that box functions actually adhere to the *box language contract* as far as the box language supports such guarantees. This is in the end the same in any functional language that supports calling non-functional code.

In fact, the above type signature makes box foo accept *any* input record that has *at least* field a and tag <b>, but may well contain further fields and tags. The formal foundation of this behaviour is *structural subtyping* on records: Any record type t_1 is a subtype of t_2 iff $t_2 \subseteq t_1$. This subtyping relationship extends nicely to multivariant types, e.g. the output type of box foo: A multivariant type x is a subtype of y if every variant $v \in x$ is a subtype of some variant $w \in y$.

Subtyping on the input type of a box means that a box may receive input records that contain more fields and tags than the box is supposed to process. Such fields and tags are retrieved from the record before the box starts processing and are added to each record emitted by the box in response to this input record, unless the output record already contains a field or tag of the same name. We call this behaviour *flow inheritance*. In conjunction, record subtyping and flow inheritance prove to be indispensable when it comes to making boxes that were developed in isolation to cooperate with each other in a streaming network.

It is a distinguishing feature of S-NET that we do not explicitly introduce streams as objects. Instead, we use algebraic formulae to define the connectivity of boxes. The restriction of boxes to a single input and a single output stream (SISO) is essential for this. As pointed out earlier, S-NET supports four network construction principles: static serial/parallel composition and dynamic serial/-parallel replication. We build S-NET on these construction principles because they are pairwise orthogonal, each represents a fundamental principle of composition beyond the concrete application to streaming networks (i.e. serialisation, branching, recursion, indexing), they naturally express the prevailing models of parallelism (i.e. task parallelism, pipeline parallelism, data parallelism) and, last not least, we believe that these four principles are sufficient to construct all useful streaming networks. The four network construction principles are embodied by *network combinators.* They all preserve the SISO property: any network, regardless of its complexity, again is a SISO component.

Let A and B denote two S-NET networks or boxes. Serial composition (denoted A..B) constructs a new network where the output stream of A becomes the input stream of B while the input stream of A and the output stream of B become the input and output streams of the compound network, respectively. As a consequence, instances of A and B operate asynchronously is a pipelined fashion. In the intuitive example of Fig. 1 serial composition can be identified between the left, the middle and the right subnetworks.

Parallel composition (denoted (A|B)) constructs a network where all incoming records are either sent to A or to B and the resulting record streams are merged to form the overall output stream of the compound network. By means of type inference [7] we associate each operand network with a type signature similar to the annotated type signatures of boxes. Any incoming record is directed towards the operand network whose input type better matches the type of the record itself. If both branches in the streaming network match equally well, one is selected non-deterministically. The example network in Fig. 1 features parallel composition in combining A and B.

Serial replication (denoted A*type) constructs a conceptually infinite chain of instances of A. The chain is tapped before every instance to extract records that match the type pattern given as right operand (i.e. the record's type is a subtype of specified type). Such records are merged into the output stream. In a simplifying view Fig. 1 illustrates serial replication as a feedback loop. While in a completely stateless setting feedback and replication are equivalent, the presence of synchronisation facilities (see below) requires us to make this subtle difference. From a conceptual point of view, their relationship resembles that of recursion and iteration; from a pragmatic point of view, the separation of data in different instances of the operand network contributes to an orderly system behaviour.

Indexed parallel replication (denoted A!<tag>) replicates instances of A in parallel. Unlike in static parallel composition we do base routing on types and the best-match rule, but on a tag specified as right operand. All incoming records must feature this tag; its value determines the instance of the left operand the record is sent to. Output records are non-deterministically merged into a single output stream similar to parallel composition. In Fig. 1 we can identify parallel replication of network C. To summarise we can express the S-NET sketched out in Fig. 1 by the following expression:

$$(A|B) \; .. \; (C!\texttt{<t>})*\{p\} \; .. \; D$$

assuming previous definitions of A, B, C and D. While this example remains in the abstract, concrete S-NET applications can be found in [8,9].

Last not least, S-NET features a synchronisation component that we call *synchrocell*; it takes the syntactic form [| *type*, *type* |]. Similar to serial replication the types act as patterns for incoming records. A record that matches one of the patterns is kept in the synchrocell. As soon as a record arrives that matches the other pattern, the two records are merged into one, which is forwarded to the output stream. Incoming records that only match previously matched patterns are immediately forwarded to the output stream. Hence, a synchrocell becomes an identity after successful synchronisation and may be removed by a runtime system. The extremely simplified behaviour of synchrocells captures the essential notion of synchronisation in the context of streaming networks. More complex synchronisation behaviours, e.g. continuous synchronisation of matching pairs in the input stream, can easily be achieved using synchrocells and network combinators. See [8] for more details on this and on the S-NET language in general.

3   Implementation Architecture

The implementation architecture of S-NET is designed in a modular fashion: We can identify two self-contained modules, the *compiler* and the *runtime system*. We will focus on the runtime system in the remainder of this paper, but nevertheless briefly present the entire system design in Fig. 2 to give a complete picture of our overall approach. In this two-layered architecture, a network is transformed into three conceptually different network representations while it is being processed by the system.

To illustrate this process of transformation from user-written code to an actually executed program, we apply the presented transformations to our running example. The S-NET compiler represents the example network from previous sections as the tree shown in Fig. 3. On this abstract syntax tree (AST) representation, the compiler carries out various optimisation and annotation tasks in addition to the most important task of type inference [7]. From user-defined types and patterns and from the inferred information, the compiler generates decision functions. The runtime system applies these functions to incoming records to determine routing of records and match records against patterns. We illustrate the compilation process in Fig. 3.The final stage of the compiler is code generation. Here, the compiler generates a textual representation of the AST. This representation of the network is a portable format we refer to as *common runtime interface* (CRI) representation.

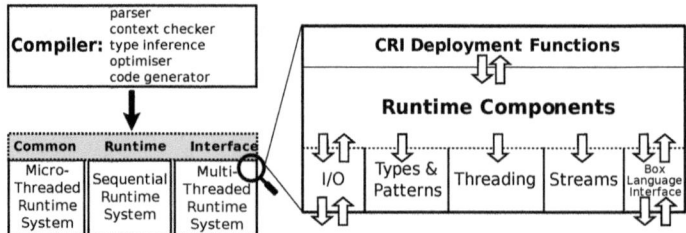

Fig. 2. The system consists of a compiler and various runtime system implementations

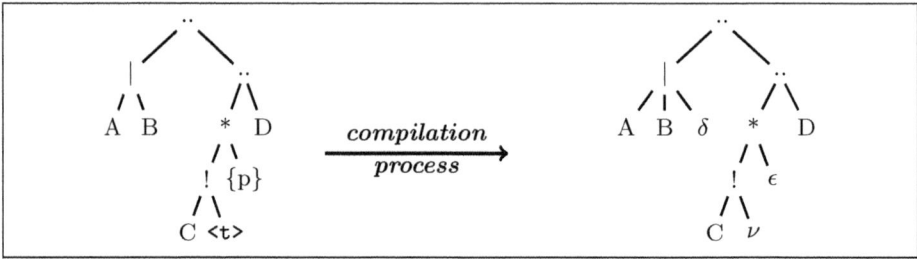

Fig. 3. The S-NET compiler reads in a network description and annotates the parse tree with runtime-specific information, as for example decision functions (ϵ, ν, δ), without dissolving the tree structure as such.

The CRI decouples the compilation process from the runtime system. The compiler does not dissolve the hierarchical structure of the network, which leaves this traditional compiler task to the runtime system. This achieves high flexibility for runtime system implementors: as the compiled structure still features a high level of abstraction, the actual decomposition, i.e. the interpretation of the CRI format, takes places in the runtime system according to the target architecture. This approach turns the compiler into a universal component which we can re-use for any concrete implementation of a runtime system.

The transformation from CRI format to the final and actually executed representation of the network is carried out by a component that any runtime-system implementation has to provide: the *deployer*. The deployer is specific to a runtime-system as it implements the final transformation of the network representation. As this is an integral part of the runtime system, it is presented in great detail in the following section. As mentioned above, the concrete implementation of the runtime representation is entirely decoupled from any stages above the deployer. For the time being, we are targeting three destination architectures:

- sequential execution,
- multithreading based on PTHREADS and
- microthreading based on μTC [5].

In this paper, however, we solely focus on the multi-threaded implementation based on PTHREADS. The main idea of this implementation is to break down the network into smaller runtime components which are connected to each other by buffered streams. The compiled program which is being executed in this implementation resembles the intuitive view of a network in which data elements are flowing from component to component for processing.

The general implementation design of the runtime system is illustrated in Fig. 2(right): Apart from the deployer, the runtime system consists of several smaller modules for type and pattern representation, thread management, communication, box language interfacing, and general I/O. These modules provide functionality for the runtime components, which form the core of the runtime system. These components implement the runtime behaviour of all S-NET combinators.

4 Network Deployment

The deployment process transforms the compiler-generated CRI representation of a network into a network of runtime components. In this section we will take a closer look at this process for each S-NET entity. In the presented source code, we shall use a teletype font for identifiers if these refer to streams.

The deployment of box and synchrocell (Fig. 4) connects an inbound stream to the appropriate runtime component. From the stream, the box resp. synchrocell reads inbound records for processing. Result records produced by the component are sent out via an outbound stream, which is created by the deployer by calling new Stream(). In addition to these streams, both components require auxiliary parameters: For the deployment of the synchrocell, the compiler generates two decision functions, μ_a and μ_b, from the user-defined patterns of the synchrocell. For box deployment, the user-defined, internal behaviour f of the box (the box implementation) is required. Additionally, the box component also requires a compiler-generated type encoding τ of the box's input type. The purpose of these parameters are explained in greater detail in Section 5. The runtime components are started by a call to spawn.

The new and spawn functions are high-level abstractions of the rather low-level code of the PTHREADS implementation. We do this for the sake of presentation, as the concrete code is less concise (but trivial).

The simplest case of combinator deployment is the deployment of a *serial* combinator (Fig. 5). Both operands are deployed recursively. The inbound stream is connected to the first operand. The outbound stream of the deployed first operand is connected to the second operand, whose outbound stream constitutes the outbound stream of the compound runtime component network, representing this serial combination.

The deployment of the *choice* combinator (Fig. 5) requires two runtime components in addition to the components of its operands. These additional components implement the implicit splitting and merging points of streams in an S-NET *choice* combination. The dispatcher, a multi-outbound stream component, forwards inbound records to one of the operands. The output streams of

```
𝒟(box_τ f, in) =
    let out = new Stream()
        box = spawn Box( in, f, τ, out)
    in out

𝒟([|μ_a, μ_b|], in) =
    let out = new Stream()
        sync = spawn Sync( in, μ_a, μ_b, out)
    in out
```

Fig. 4. Deployment of box and synchrocell

the operands are connected to a complementary multi-inbound stream component, the collector. The collector aggregates the output streams of the operands and bundles these to a single output stream. The CRI representation of the *choice* combinator requires a decision function δ, which the compiler generates. The dispatcher evaluates this function for each inbound record to determine routing destinations. The deployment of the choice combinator also deploys the operands of the combinator. This recursive process only ends once an operand does not have any more operands, i.e., if it is a box or synchrocell.

```
𝒟(A .. B, in) = let out = 𝒟(A, in) in 𝒟(B, out)

𝒟(A |_δ B, in) =
    let opin_1 = new Stream()
        opin_2 = new Stream()
        disp = spawn ChoiceDispatch( in, δ, opin_1, opin_2)
        opout_1 = 𝒟(A, opin_1)
        opout_2 = 𝒟(B, opin_2)
        out = new Stream()
        coll = spawn Collector( nil, {opout_1, opout_2}, out)
    in out

𝒟(A *_ε, in) =
    let ctrl = new Stream()
        bypass = new Stream()
        disp = spawn StarDispatch( in, A, ε, ctrl, nil, bypass)
        out = new Stream()
        coll = spawn Collector( ctrl, {bypass}, out)
    in out

𝒟(A !_ν, in) =
    let ctrl = new Stream()
        disp = spawn SplitDispatch( in, A, ν, ctrl, ∅)
        out = new Stream()
        coll = spawn Collector( ctrl, ∅, out)
    in out
```

Fig. 5. Deployment of combinators

Similar to the *choice* deployment, the deployment of a *star* combinator (Fig. 5) also sets up a dispatcher and a collector. The operand of the *star*, however, is not deployed yet — its deployment is fully demand-driven and postponed until runtime. For this reason, the operand is passed directly to the dispatcher, in conjunction with a compiler-generated decision function ϵ. The dispatcher

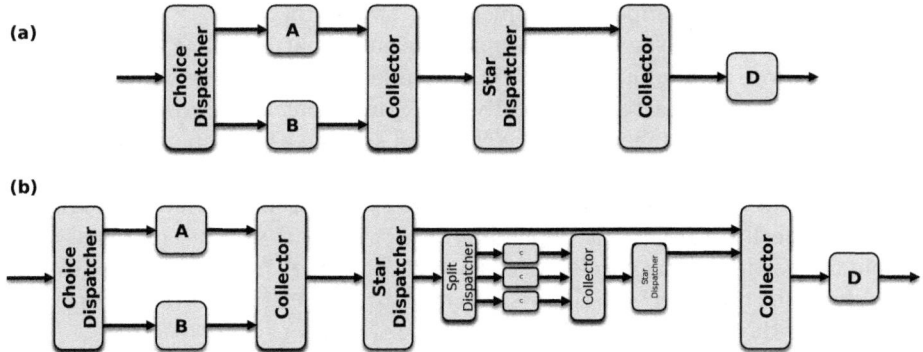

Fig. 6. Deployed component network of example network which initially only contains
A, B, D (a) Remaining operands are deployed demand-driven (b)

calls the deployment function for the operand only when needed, driven by the
outcome of the decision function. As the operand network of the *star* combinator
may evolve (unfold) over time, the associated collector has to be able to manage a
potentially growing set of inbound streams. A control stream between dispatcher
and collector is set up to serve the purpose of communicating the appearance of
new streams to the collector.

From the deployment perspective, the *split* combinator (Fig. 5) is very similar
to the *star* combinator. The operand instantiation is demand driven and triggered by a decision function ν. After the initial deployment, no operand instance
is present, and thus, the stream set of the collector is empty. A control stream
is established between dispatcher and collector to register the outbound streams
of dynamically created, new instances of the operand.

To illustrate the deployment process, the resulting component network for
the running example is shown in Fig. 6(a). Instances of C and the surrounding
splitter are not built by the deployment process until required. Instead, only
an initial connection between the star dispatcher and its collector ensures that
the network is fully connected. While processing records, instances of the star
operand and the split operand are spawned demand-driven. The component
network as it has developed after one instance of the star operand and three
instances of the split operand have been built is shown in Fig. 6(b).

5   Operational Behaviour of Components

We continue denoting streams by identifiers set in teletype. Concatenation of
records and streams are denoted by $\triangleleft$ (append as prefix) and $\triangleright$ (append as
suffix). Each definition of a component starts with the keyword **Thread** to
emphasise the fact, that the component is executed as a thread. Case differen-
tiations are introduced by a | in the source code, guard expressions of cases by
the keyword **when**.

The synchrocell component implements two main tasks. Firstly, it stores records if they match the specified synchronisation pattern. The procedure here again relies on match functions: The compiler generates one match function for each synchrocell pattern. Secondly, the component merges records, once all pattern have been matched. We model record storage as parameters to the component function, which serves a dual purpose. It stores the records if they match a pattern and also encodes the state of the synchrocell. The state determines the synchrocell's operations, depending on which pattern was matched by an inbound record. A synchrocell of two patterns (see Fig. 7; if a storage parameter does not hold a record yet, this is indicated by -) and two match functions μ_a and μ_b, has the following possible states and transitions:

State	μ_a	μ_b	Description (current)	Action	Next state
- -	•		initial state	store record	q -
- -		•	initial state	store record	- q
- -	•	•	initial state	output	id
q -	•		first pattern was matched	output	q -
q -		•	first pattern was matched	merge and output	id
q -	•	•	first pattern was matched	merge and output	id
- q	•		second pattern was matched	merge and output	id
- q		•	second pattern was matched	output	- q
- q	•	•	second pattern was matched	merge andoutput	id
id	n/a	n/a	sync replaced by identity	output	id

When a record is stored in the synchrocell, all constituents of the record which are not part of the pattern, are stripped out. This is implemented by the strip function which uses the decision functions to determine which record constituents are to be removed. Only the remainder is stored for the merging process. If a record matches a pattern for which a record has already been stored, the *output* action forwards the record to the outbound stream out. A record that matches the last remaining previously unmatched pattern, is merged if a record is available in storage, and simply output otherwise. Record merging is defined by the flow inheritance operator, which is presented in Fig. 7. For clarity, we presented an implementation where the sync component is replaced by an Id component after the last pattern has been matched. The Id component forwards all inbound records directly to the outbound stream. In practice, however, dead synchrocells are completely removed in a garbage collection step, where the cell's inbound stream is directly connected to its successor component.

The box component is a connector from the S-NET domain to the box language domain. The box component calls the box function and provides it with an inbound record and the inbound type τ of the S-NET box. The box function may produce an arbitrary amount of records during its execution, each of which needs to flow inherit fields from the original inbound record. To make this process convenient for a box programmer, an SNetOut function is provided. This function expects one result record at a time, carries out flow inheritance and

```
Thread Box( r◁in, ƒ, τ, out) =
       let t' = ƒ( r, τ, out)
       in Box( in, ƒ, τ, t')

fun SNetOut( r, τ, res, out) =
    let f  = r \ τ
        rf = f ⋈ res
    in out▷rf

Thread Sync( r◁in, μₐ, μᵦ, -, -, out) when μₐ(r) ∧ μᵦ(r) =
       Id( in, out▷r)
|      Sync( r◁in, μₐ, μᵦ, -, -, out) when μₐ(r) =
       let q = strip( r, μₐ)
       in Sync( in, μₐ, μᵦ, q, -, out)
|      Sync( r◁in, μₐ, μᵦ, -, -, out) =
       let q = strip( r, μᵦ)
       in Sync( in, μₐ, μᵦ, -, q, out)
|      Sync( r◁in, μₐ, μᵦ, q, -, out) when ¬μᵦ(r) =
       Sync( in, μₐ, μᵦ, q, -, out▷r)
|      Sync( r◁in, μₐ, μᵦ, q, -, out) =
       let m = r ⋈ q
       in Id( in, out▷m)

Thread Id(r◁in, out) = Id(in, out▷r)

fun infix ⋈ f r = r ∪ (f \ r)
```

Fig. 7. Implementation of sync, box and flow-inheritance operator

writes the record to the outbound stream. For each output the box produces, it calls SNetOut. After the execution of the box functions finishes, control is returned to the box component.

The collector (Fig. 8) is a multi-inbound stream component. This component is used where multiple operand streams are merged into one single outbound stream. The collector keeps all streams that it monitors in a stream set S. When records become available on any of the streams in the set, the record is read from the stream and forwarded to the outbound stream **out**. The collector is always deployed as part of a dispatcher-collector pair, with a control stream connecting these two. The registration of new channels is implemented using this control stream: Dispatchers send streams of dynamically created operand instances via **ctrl** to the collector, where the streams are added to the stream set.

The choice dispatcher is a multi-outbound stream component. It reads records from its single inbound stream, and forwards the records over one of the outbound streams to the operand networks. The compiler-generated δ function is an integral part of this process. The compiler generates this function from the input types of the *choice* operands. Applied to a record r, δ returns an integer value n, depending on which operand input type the record matched. The dispatcher shown in Fig. 8 reads a record r from the inbound channel **in**. If δ applied to r evaluates to 1, the record is forwarded to the inbound channel $opin_1$ of the first operand, and to the second operand via $opin_2$ otherwise. We chose to design δ as a function to integers and not to a binary set, which would be sufficient for this purpose. The integer domain enables us to implement an optimisation to reduce the overhead that multiple dispatcher would cause. The optimisation maps an n-fold choice combination to a single, n-channel choice dispatcher, as opposed to $n - 1$ binary dispatchers.

The main purpose of the star dispatcher (Fig. 8) is to decide, whether an inbound record matches the exit pattern of the *star* combinator or not. If the record matches, the dispatcher sends the record to the outbound stream. If the record does not match the pattern, the dispatcher sends the record to the operand network. To make this decision, the dispatcher employs a decision function m. This function is generated by the compiler from the exit pattern of the *star* combinator. When applied to a record, the decision function evaluates to true, if the record matches the exit pattern, and to false otherwise. The instantiation of operands is demand-driven, and hence the star dispatcher is initially not connected to any operand. After deployment, the only connections the dispatcher maintains are an outbound channel (bypass, **bps**) and a control channel (**ctrl**) to the collector. The operand has not been deployed, and the continuation stream **cont** not yet been built. This setup does not change, as long as all inbound records match the exit pattern. The dispatcher immediately sends matching records via **b** to the collector. In case a record does not match the pattern, the operand is deployed. To do this, the **cont** stream is created and connected as inbound stream to the operand. The dispatcher now sends all records that do not match the exit pattern to this continuation stream for processing by the operand. As *star* is a feed-forward combinator, all output of the operand is sent to a new instance of the combinator. This is achieved by instantiating

```
Thread  Collect ( in◁ctrl, S, out) =
            Collect ( ctrl, {in}∪S, out)
|       Collect ( ctrl, {r◁in} ∪ S, out) =
            Collect ( ctrl, {in} ∪ S, out▷r)

Thread  ChoiceDispatch ( r◁in, δ, out₁, out₂) when δ(r) = 1 =
            ChoiceDispatch ( in, δ, out₁ ▷r, out₂)
|       ChoiceDispatch ( r◁in, δ, out₁, out₂) =
            ChoiceDispatch ( in, δ, out₁, out₂▷r)

Thread
   StarDispatch ( r◁in, N, m, ctrl, cont, bps) when m(r) =
      StarDispatch ( in, N, m, ctrl, cont, bps▷r)
| StarDispatch ( r◁in, N, m, ctrl, nil, bps) =
   let cont = new Stream ()
       out = 𝒟(N, cont▷r)
       bps' = new Stream ()
       disp = spawn StarDispatch ( out, N, m, ctrl, nil , bps')
   in StarDispatch ( in, N, m, ctrl▷bps', cont, bps)
| StarDispatch ( r◁in, N, m, ctrl, cont, bps) =
      StarDispatch ( in, N, m, ctrl, cont▷r, bps)

Thread  SplitDispatch ( r◁in, A, ν, ctrl, {opin_{ν(r)}}∪S) =
            SplitDispatch (in, A, ν, ctrl, {opin_{ν(r)}▷r}∪S)
|       SplitDispatch ( r◁in, A, ν, ctrl, S) =
            let opin_{ν(r)} = new Stream ()
            opout = 𝒟(A, opin_{ν(r)}▷r)
            in SplitDispatch (in, A, ν, ctrl▷opout, {opin_{ν(r)}▷r}∪S)
```

Fig. 8. Implementation of combinator components

a new dispatcher, in the same way the current dispatcher was set up by the deployment function. No new collector needs to be instantiated: The already existing collector is notified via the control stream. The new dispatcher instance sends all records that match the exit pattern via stream bps' to the collector. If the pattern is not matched, the described process repeats itself.

The split dispatcher (Fig. 8) sends records to the proper instance of its operand. This instance is determined by the value of the given tag at runtime. To read the tag value from a record, the compiler generates a function ν. This function returns the integer value of the appropriate tag from a record. The split dispatcher deploys instances demand-driven, an thus, no instance is present initially. When a new instance is deployed, the inbound stream instance is added to the set of served channels. The dispatcher associates the tag value with the instance (more specifically, with the inbound stream) and sends the new outbound stream to the collector. All future records, which carry the same tag value, will be forwarded to this instance.

6   Guaranteeing Causal Record Order

As explained in Section 2, parallel composition as well as serial and parallel replication involve merging output streams in a non-deterministic way, i.e., any record produced by some subnetwork proceeds as soon as possible. As a consequence, records travelling on different branches through the network may overtake each other, as Fig. 9 illustrates on the simple example of parallel composition. While merging streams in a non-deterministic way enables S-NET programs to adapt to load distribution in concurrent systems and leads to efficient runtime behaviour in general, there are situations where non-deterministic system behaviour is undesirable. Therefore, S-NET provides deterministic variants of the aforementioned combinators: | |,**,!!.[2] Unlike their non-deterministic counterparts described so far, they are guaranteed to maintain the causal order along branches of the streaming network: any record created in one branch of the network as a (potentially indirect) response to a record on the compound network's input stream precedes any other such record on the compound network's output stream that stems from a subsequent record on the input stream.

Both compilation and deployment are largely unaffected by the introduction of deterministic combinators. They merely produce deterministic variants of the dispatcher and collector components with identical argument sets as the non-deterministic counterparts. However, the operational behaviour of deterministic components deserves our attention. Fig. 10 shows our solution. We leave out deterministic star and split dispatchers; their definition follows the same pattern as illustrated by means of the choice dispatcher.

Conceptually, each record that enters a deterministic subnetwork is mapped to a separate substream. Within the network, all records that are produced from

---

[2]   The choice of doubling the character of the non-deterministic combinator is motivated by the observation that the serial combinator (. .) is the only original network combinator that does maintain causal order on streams.

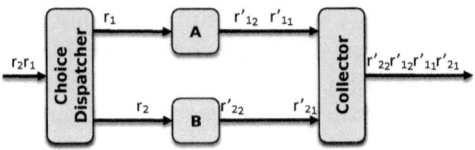

Fig. 9. Causal record order $(r'_{2_2} r'_{2_1} r'_{1_2} r'_{1_1})$ is lost if records overtake each other

```
𝒟(A ∥δ B, in) =
let opin₁ = new Stream()
    opin₂ = new Stream()
    disp = spawn DetChoiceDispatch( in, δ, 1, opin₁, opin₂)
    opout₁ = 𝒟(A, opin₁)
    opout₂ = 𝒟(B, opin₂)
    out = new Stream()
    coll =
      spawn DetCollect(nil, {opout₁,opout₂}, ∅, 1, -, out)
in out

Thread
  DetChoiceDispatch( [l,c]◁in, δ, cnt, opin₁, opin₂) when l > 0 =
    DetChoiceDispatch( in, δ, cnt, opin₁▷[l+1,c], opin₂▷[l+1,c])
| DetChoiceDispatch( r◁in, δ, cnt, opin₁, opin₂) =
  if δ(r) = 1
  then DetChoiceDispatch( in, δ, cnt+1, opin₁▷[0,cnt]▷r, opin₂)
  else DetChoiceDispatch( in, δ, cnt+1, opin₁, opin₂▷[0,cnt]▷r)

Thread
  DetCollect( ctrl, {[0,c]◁in} ∪ R, W, cnt, tosend, out) =
    if c = cnt
    then DetCollect( ctrl, {in} ∪ R, W, cnt, tosend, out)
    else DetCollect( ctrl, R, {[0,c]◁in} ∪ W, cnt, tosend, out)
| DetCollect( ctrl, {[l,c]◁in} ∪ R, W, cnt, tosend, out) =
    DetCollect( ctrl, R, {in} ∪ W, cnt, [l,c], out)
| DetCollect( ctrl, {r◁in} ∪ R, W, cnt, tosend, out) =
      DetCollect( ctrl, {in} ∪ R, W, cnt, tosend, out▷r)
| DetCollect( ctrl, ∅, W, cnt, -, out) =
    DetCollect( ctrl, W, W, cnt+1, out)
| DetCollect( ctrl, ∅, W, cnt, [l,c], out) =
    DetCollect( ctrl, W, W, cnt, -, out◁[l-1,c])
| DetCollect( in◁ctrl, R, W, cnt, tosend, out) =
    DetCollect( ctrl, {in} ∪ R, W, cnt, tosend, out)
```

Fig. 10. Deployment and implementation of deterministic choice combinator

the inbound record, remain in the same substream. The dispatcher-collector pair ensures, that any substream is completely output before any elements of another substream are forwarded to the merged output stream. We implement substreams by help of control records that act as stream delimiters. A control record $[l,c]$ has two attributes: a *level* l and a *counter* c. Only deterministic dispatch components create control records. The counter value is increased for each new control record to distinguish consecutive substreams. The purpose of the level value is to identify correct dispatcher-collector pairs in the presence of recursively nested deterministic and non-deterministic network combinators. When a new record arrives at a deterministic dispatcher, a fresh control record is sent ahead of the record itself to the appropriate output stream following consultation of the oracle function δ. Inbound control records are broadcast to all branches with the level value incremented by one.

The deterministic collector, as shown in Fig. 10, complements the deterministic (choice) dispatch, but in fact this collector is used to implement deterministic replication combinators as well. This collector ensures that different substreams appearing on its inout streams are forwarded to its output stream without interleaving and in the right order. To achieve this, the collector maintains two stream sets: The *ready* set R contains all streams on which the collector actively snoops for input while the *waiting* set W contains those input streams that are currently blocked.

When a control record appears on one of the ready input streams that was emitted by the dispatch component corresponding to this collector (level 0), we check its counter: if the counter coincides with the internal counter of the collector (*cnt*), it marks the beginning of the next substream to be sent to the collector's output. If so, the corresponding input stream remains in the ready set and the control record is discarded. Otherwise, the input stream is moved from the ready set to the waiting set without consuming the control record.

Any control record that belongs to an outer dispatcher-collector pair (level > 0) appearing on a ready input stream causes that stream to be moved to the waiting set while the control record is stored in the collector. Keep in mind that the corresponding dispatcher had broadcast this control record to all its output streams. So, the collector must retrieve them sooner or later from all of its input streams. Only after the last such instance of the control record has been received by the collector, it may issue a single instance on the output stream.

Any regular record appearing on a ready input stream is immediately forwarded to the output stream. Note that any normal record is preceded by the control record identifying the substream the subsequent regular records belong to. If an input stream is still in the ready set when a regular record arrives, this means that this is the active substream to be issued on the output stream. Only one such active input stream exists at a time. If there are still further input streams in the ready set, then only because the corresponding control record has not yet arrived.

If the ready set becomes empty, i.e. a followup control record appeared on the previously active input stream indicating the end of that substream, we restore a fresh ready set from the waiting set and increment the internal counter of the collector. This step will make the collector identify the next active substream. In case we have a pending control record belonging to an outer dispatcher-collector pair, we forward it to the output stream with a decremented level counter.

Last not least, we may at any time receive a new input stream via the control stream. In this case we add the new input stream to the ready set. This feature of the collector is only used for implementing the deterministic replication combinators, that lead to dynamically evolving networks.

To make this scheme work, some minor extensions are required for non-deterministic dispatchers and collectors: Dispatchers must broadcast control records to all output streams without touching them. Collectors must gather control records on the various input streams and discard all by one, which is issued on the output stream.

7 Performance Evaluation

For a very preliminary performance evaluation we present runtimes obtained for an application from the radar signal processing domain. In essence, the application is a serial composition of signal processing functions, which are applied to an incoming radar echo. The purpose of the application is to identify slowly moving objects on the ground from the signal of an aircraft mounted radar antenna. As classical Doppler radar approaches fail to produce good results in this area, this application employs an adaptive technique, where signal filters are computed at runtime, depending on incoming data. More detail about the concrete implementation of the application is available in [8].

For the presented runtime measurements we have used three different platforms: a conventional unicore processor (Machine A, Intel Celeron M with 1GB of memory running Linux), a modern dual-core processor (Machine B, Intel Core Duo with 2GB of memory running Linux) and a twofold dual-core multiprocessor (Machine C, 2x AMD Opteron 275 with 8GB of memory running Linux). Fig. 11 shows the outcome of our experiments.

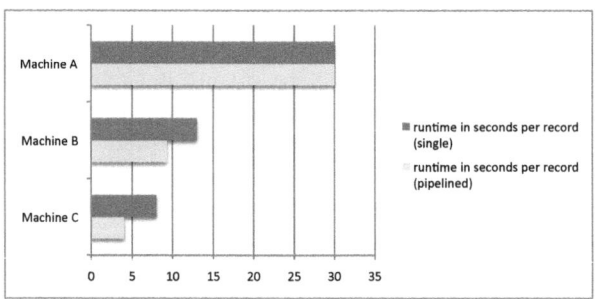

Fig. 11. Preliminary performance measurements

At first, we measure the processing time for one single record by feeding one record at a time into the network. Any subsequent record is only sent once the result of the previous record has been received. This results in sequential processing and serves as a baseline for performance. In a second experiment, we continuously feed records into the network and, thus, take advantage from multiple processing resources. As Fig. 11 shows, we indeed achieve considerable speedups on multi-core hardware by simply organising sequential legacy components into an S-Net streaming network.

8   Related Work

The concept of stream processing has a long history (see [10] for a survey). The view of a program as a set of processing blocks connected by a static network of channels goes back at least as far as Kahn's seminal work [11] and the language Lucid [12]. Kahn introduced the model of infinite-capacity, deterministic process networks and proved that it had properties useful for parallel processing. Lucid was apparently the first language to introduce the basic idea of a block that transforms input sequences into output sequences. For a more theoretical treatment of stream processing we refer to [13] and [14].

Multi-threaded execution of streaming networks with PTHREADS is offered by StreamIt [15]. In StreamIt, streaming networks are implemented in a high-level, Java like language. A network is defined by implementing boxes (called *filters* in StreamIt) and connecting these by extending the stream structure classes *SplitJoin*, *Pipeline* and *FeedbackLoop*. Filters are directly encoded in StreamIt itself. Neither coordination of legacy code nor a clear separation between computing and coordination layers can be achieved. Access to box implementations and consumer and producer rates enables the StreamIt compiler to optimise scheduling. Hence, StreamIt falls into the category of synchronous dataflow approaches like Lustre [16] and Esterel [17], whereas S-NET advocates asynchronous dataflow.

The separation between coordination and computation in S-NET is closely related to data-driven coordination approaches, of which [18] gives an overview. The earliest related proposal, to our knowledge, for a complete separation as advocated by S-NET, is the coordination language HOPLa [19].

Relating to our modular design of the runtime system, we cite the work on Borealis [20]. The Borealis stream processing engine is based on typed streams of attribute-value pairs (based on [21]), not unlike S-NET records. The values, however, are accessible by Borealis operators and are consequently limited to a pre-defined set of data types. The architecture of the system is composed of several modules which provide a wealth of features as for example load balancing, runtime optimisations and failure recovery. Networks are described in an XML based query language. Compared to S-NET, the description language is rather low-level, but it does not require a compiler as such, as networks can be directly deployed to a Borealis node. Another recent advancement in stream-based coordination technology is the language Reo [22]. It concerns itself primarily with issues of channel and component mobility and does not exploit static connectivity or type-theoretical tools for network analysis.

In the specific area of functional programming we mention Eden [23], that extends Haskell with process abstraction and process instantiation facilities. Processes communicate via FIFO channels, just as in S-NET, but process topologies are completely dynamic including mobile channels. On the other end of the spectrum we see Hume [24], which combines Haskell-like boxes with synchronous data flow processing. The emphasis with Hume lies in the inference of exact bounds on resource consumption for applications in embedded systems.

9   Conclusion and Future Work

We have presented the architecture of our implementation of the coordination language S-NET that allows legacy code to be assembled into a streaming network of asynchronous components in a minimally intrusive way. The concept of a common runtime interface proves essential in separating our target-independent compiler from target platform specific runtime system implementations. In the sequel we have put the emphasis on describing a single implementation in-depth: a runtime systems that targets contemporary multi-core processors. We have recognised the distinction between deployment of networks and the operational behaviour of components within the network and explicated their mutual dependence and interplay.

We have developed both a high-level coordination language and a complete, portable tool chain that enables users to harness the computational power of modern multi-core architectures while at the same time they can stick to their familiar (sequential) programming environment for the bulk of an application. Some runtime figures based on an application from the radar signal processing domain demonstrate the effectiveness of our approach.

While the design of S-NET as a language is an area of active research, we can identify three main directions of current and future work with respect to the implementation of S-NET: implementations of the common runtime interface for on-chip microgrids on the one hand and distributed memory workstation clusters on the other hand as well as a refinement of the multithreaded runtime system described here that exercises tighter control on the usage of threads by managing thread scheduling, etc, in the S-NET runtime system ourselves rather than delegating this vital task to the operating system.

Acknowledgements

The development of S-NET is funded by the European Union through the FP-VI Integrated Project ÆTHER, *Self-adaptive Embedded Technologies for Pervasive Computing Architectures,* (www.aether-ist.org).

References

1. Sutter, H.: The free lunch is over: A fundamental turn towards concurrency in software. Dr. Dobb's Journal 30 (2005)
2. Held, J., Bautista, J., Koehl, S.: From a few cores to many: a Tera-scale computing research overview. Technical report, Intel Corporation (2006)
3. Owens, J.D., Houston, M., Luebke, D., Green, S., Stone, J.E., Phillips, J.C.: GPU Computing. Proceedings of the IEEE 96, 879–899 (2008)
4. Grelck, C., Scholz, S.-B., Shafarenko, A.: A Gentle Introduction to S-Net. Parallel Processing Letters 18(2), 221–237 (2008)
5. Jesshope, C.: μTC – an intermediate language for programming chip multiprocessors. In: Jesshope, C., Egan, C. (eds.) ACSAC 2006. LNCS, vol. 4186, pp. 147–160. Springer, Heidelberg (2006)

6. Bousias, K., Jesshope, C., Thiyagalingam, J., et al.: Graph walker: implementing S-Net on the self-adaptive virtual processor. In: Æther-Morpheus Workshop: From Reconfigurable to Self-Adaptive Computing, Lugano, Switzerland (2008)
7. Cai, H., Eisenbach, S., Grelck, C., Penczek, F., Scholz, S.B., Shafarenko, A.: S-Net Type System and Operational Semantics. In: Æther-Morpheus Workshop: From Reconfigurable to Self-Adaptive Computing, Lugano, Switzerland (2008)
8. Grelck, C., Shafarenko, A.: S-Net Language Report. University of Hertfordshire, School of Computer Science, Hatfield, United Kingdom (2006)
9. Grelck, C., Scholz, S.B., Shafarenko, A.: Coordinating Data Parallel SAC Programs with S-Net. In: 21st IEEE International Parallel and Distributed Processing Symposium (IPDPS 2007), Long Beach, USA. IEEE Press, Los Alamitos (2007)
10. Stephens, R.: A survey of stream processing. Acta Informatica 34, 491–541 (1997)
11. Kahn, G.: The semantics of a simple language for parallel programming. In: Information Processing 1974, Stockholm, Sweden, pp. 471–475. North-Holland, Amsterdam (1974)
12. Ashcroft, E.A., Wadge, W.W.: Lucid. CACM 20, 519–526 (1977)
13. Broy, M., Stefanescu, G.: The algebra of stream processing functions. Theoretical Computer Science, 99–129 (2001)
14. Stefanescu, G.: Network Algebra. Springer, Heidelberg (2000)
15. Thies, W., Karczmarek, M., Amarasinghe, S.P.: StreamIt: A language for streaming applications. In: Computational Complexity, 179–196 (2002)
16. Halbwachs, N., Caspi, P., Raymond, P., Pilaud, D.: The synchronous data-flow programming language LUSTRE. Proceedings of the IEEE 79, 1305–1320 (1991)
17. Berry, G., Gonthier., G.: The Esterel synchronous programming language: Design, semantics, implementation. Science of Computer Programming 19, 87–152 (1992)
18. Papadopoulos, G.A., Arbab, F.: Coordination models and languages. In: Advances in Computers, vol. 46. Academic Press, London (1998)
19. Florijn, G., Bessamusca, T., et al.: Ariadne and HOPLa: flexible coordination of collaborative processes. In: Hankin, C., Ciancarini, P. (eds.) COORDINATION 1996. LNCS, vol. 1061. Springer, Heidelberg (1996)
20. Abadi, D., Ahmad, Y., Balazinska, M., et al.: The design of the Borealis stream processing engine. In: CIDR, pp. 277–289 (2005)
21. Abadi, D.J., Carney, D., Çetintemel, U., et al.: Aurora: a new model and architecture for data stream management. VLDB Journal 12, 120–139 (2003)
22. Arbab, F.: Reo: a channel-based coordination model for component composition. Mathematical. Structures in Comp. Sci. 14, 329–366 (2004)
23. Loogen, R., Ortega-Mallén, Y., Peña-Marí, R.: Parallel functional programming in Eden. Journal of Functional Programming 15, 431–475 (2005)
24. Hammond, K., Michaelson, G.: The design of hume: A high-level language for the real-time embedded systems domain. In: Lengauer, C., Batory, D., Blum, A., Vetta, A. (eds.) Domain-Specific Program Generation. LNCS, vol. 3016, pp. 127–142. Springer, Heidelberg (2004)

Parsing Mixfix Operators

Nils Anders Danielsson[1],[*] and Ulf Norell[2]

[1] University of Nottingham
[2] Chalmers University of Technology

Abstract. A simple grammar scheme for expressions containing mixfix operators is presented. The scheme is parameterised by a precedence relation which is only restricted to be a directed acyclic graph; this makes it possible to build up precedence relations in a modular way. Efficient and simple implementations of parsers for languages with user-defined mixfix operators, based on the grammar scheme, are also discussed. In the future we plan to replace the support for mixfix operators in the language Agda with a grammar scheme and an implementation based on this work.

1 Introduction

Programming language support for user-defined infix operators is often nice to have. It enables the use of compact and/or domain-specific notations, especially if a character set with many symbols is used. The feature can certainly be abused to create code which the intended audience finds hard to read, but the inclusion of user-defined infix operators in a number of programming languages, including Haskell (Peyton Jones 2003), ML (Milner et al. 1997), Prolog (Sterling and Shapiro 1994), and Scala (Odersky 2009), suggests that this is a risk which many programmers are willing to take.

Some languages, such as Coq (Coq Development Team 2009), Isabelle (Paulson et al. 2008), and Obj (Goguen et al. 1999), take things a step further by supporting the more general concept of *mixfix* (also known as *distfix*) operators. A mixfix operator can have several name parts and be infix (like the typing relation _⊢_:_), prefix (if_then_else_), postfix (array subscripting: _[_]), or closed (Oxford brackets: ⟦_⟧). With mixfix operators the advantages of binary infix operators can be taken one step further, but perhaps also the disadvantages.

An important criterion when designing a programming language feature is that the feature should be easy to understand. In the case of mixfix operators the principle explaining how to parse an arbitrary expression should be simple (even though abuse of the feature may lead to a laborious parsing process). Mixfix operators are sometimes perceived as being difficult in this respect. Our aim with this work is to present a method for handling mixfix operators which is elegant, easy to understand, and easy to implement with sufficient efficiency.

We show how to construct a simple expression grammar, given a set of operators with specified precedence and associativity (see Sect. 3). We want to avoid

---

[*] The author would like to thank EPSRC for financial support.

S.-B. Scholz and O. Chitil (Eds.): IFL 2008, LNCS 5836, pp. 80–99, 2011.

monolithic precedence relations in which every operator is related to every other, so we only require the precedences to form a directed acyclic graph (Sect. 2). To abstract from source language details the language mechanisms used to specify the operators, precedence graphs etc. are left unspecified.

In Sect. 5 the grammars are defined formally, using the total, dependently typed language Agda (Norell 2007; Agda Team 2009). The grammars are defined using parser combinators with a well-defined semantics, so as a side effect a provably correct implementation of a mixfix expression parser is obtained. The formalisation also shows that the expressions generated by the grammars correspond exactly to a notion of precedence correct expressions. Furthermore the Agda code provides a number of examples of the use of mixfix operators.

The restriction of precedence relations to *acyclic* graphs ensures that the constructed grammars are unambiguous, assuming that all operator name parts are unique (Sect. 4). Acyclicity also ensures that parsers corresponding to the generated grammars can be implemented using (backtracking) recursive descent. However, naive use of recursive descent leads to poor performance. In a prototype which uses *memoising* parser combinators (Frost and Szydlowski 1996) we have achieved sufficient efficiency along with a simple implementation (Sect. 6). In the future we plan to use this approach to handle mixfix operators in Agda.

The paper ends with a discussion of related work and some conclusions in Sects. 7–8.

2   Precedence and Associativity

In some languages it is very easy to introduce mixfix operators. For instance, in Agda a name is an operator if it includes an underscore character. Every underscore stands for an operator *hole*, i.e. a position in which an argument expression is expected. The examples from Sect. 1 are valid operator names in Agda:[1] _⊢_:_, _[_], if_then_else_, and ⟦_⟧. However, typically one wants to combine operators into larger expressions, and then it is important to specify if and how they can be combined. How should an expression like

$$\text{if } b \wedge n + n == n \text{ ! then } n \text{ else } (n + n - n) \qquad (1)$$

be parsed, for instance?

The traditional way to disambiguate such expressions is to use *precedence* and *associativity* (Aho et al. 1986; Aasa 1995), and we follow this approach. Precedence specifies if an operator "binds tighter" than another. Associativity specifies how sequences of infix operators of the same precedence should be interpreted; an operator can be left associative, right associative, or non-associative. The expression x + y * z parses as x + (y * z) if _*_ binds tighter than _+_, and x + y - z parses as (x + y) - z if the two operators have the same precedence and are both left associative. See Table 1 for a summary of how precedence and associativity affect parsing of infix operators.

---

[1] Unless the wrong colon character is used.

Table 1. Possible outcomes of parsing x + y * z, where _+_ and _*_ are infix operators. Here + < * means that _*_ binds tighter than _+_, and + = * means that the operators have equal precedence.

Precedence	Associativity	Result of parsing x + y * z
+ < *		x + (y * z)
* < +		(x + y) * z
+ = *	Both left	(x + y) * z
+ = *	Both right	x + (y * z)
None of the above		Parse error

Unlike languages like Coq and Isabelle, but following Aasa (1995), we do not assign any form of precedence to the internal holes of mixfix operators (i.e. the holes which are surrounded by name parts). Instead, to keep things simple, expressions of arbitrary precedence are allowed in the holes. This means that one can effectively define parentheses as a closed mixfix operator (_), binding tighter than everything else, with the semantics of the polymorphic identity function (as long as the name parts (and) are unambiguous).

Many languages require the precedence relation to be a total order. However, this can make reading source code more difficult, because it means that every operator is related to every other, which is likely to make it harder for programmers to remember the precedence relation. It also means that one needs to make unnecessary, possibly arbitrary choices. Why should one have to specify a relation between _+_ and _∧_, two semantically unrelated operators, for instance? This goes against modularity.

One might think that partial orders are a good alternative. However, under the (reasonable) assumption that _+_ binds tighter than _==_, which binds tighter than _∧_, transitivity would imply that _+_ binds tighter than _∧_, which we want to avoid.

Instead we just require that the precedence relation forms a directed acyclic graph (DAG), where an edge from one node to another means that the operators in the second node bind tighter than those in the first one, and operators in the same node have equal precedence. This makes it possible to define a small domain-specific library (language) with a couple of operators and a natural, possibly domain-specific precedence relation, without relating these operators to those from other libraries. However, we note that partial and total orders are DAGs, so the results below apply also to those cases.

We require the graphs to be acyclic because cyclic precedence relations very easily lead to ambiguous grammars. Furthermore acyclicity ensures that the grammars are not left recursive, thus enabling backtracking recursive descent as an implementation technique.

Figure 1 contains a small precedence graph. To keep things simple the grammar scheme introduced below is concerned solely with operators, so the precedence graph includes some variables (b and n) and parentheses ((_)). These are treated as closed mixfix operators which bind more tightly than all other

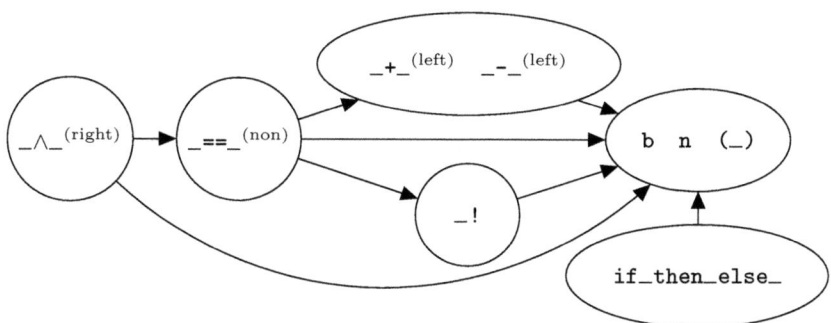

Fig. 1. A precedence graph. An arrow from node p to node q means that operators in node q bind tighter than operators in node p. Infix operators are annotated with their associativity.

operators. Let us interpret the example (1) given above using this precedence graph.

We can start by noticing that all the operators' name parts are unique, so it is easy to identify which name parts belong to which operator. We can then isolate the internal arguments of if_then_else_ and (_):

$$\text{if } [\text{b} \wedge \text{n + n == n !}] \text{ then } [\text{n}] \text{ else } (\ [\text{n + n - n}]\ ). \qquad (2)$$

Furthermore parentheses bind more tightly than if_then_else_, so the parenthesised expression has to be the last argument to the conditional:

$$\text{if } [\text{b} \wedge \text{n + n == n !}] \text{ then } [\text{n}] \text{ else } \big[(\ [\text{n + n - n}]\ )\big]. \qquad (3)$$

In b ∧ n + n == n ! the operator _∧_ is only related to _==_ (plus the variables), and it binds weaker, so the only possible parse is

$$[\text{b}] \wedge \Big[\big[[\text{n}] + [\text{n}]\big] == \big[[\text{n}]\ !\big]\Big]. \qquad (4)$$

Note that when reading source code which is known to be syntactically correct (which is the case here) "the only possible parse" translates into "the one and only correct parse". Note also that the interpretation of this subexpression would have been slightly less straightforward if the precedence relation had been a partial order.

Finally the operators _+_ and _-_ have the same precedence and are both left associative, so we end up with

$$\text{if } \Big[[\text{b}] \wedge \Big[\big[[\text{n}] + [\text{n}]\big] == \big[[\text{n}]\ !\big]\Big]\Big]$$
$$\text{then } [\text{n}] \text{ else } \Big[(\ \Big[\big[[\text{n}] + [\text{n}]\big] - [\text{n}]\Big]\ )\Big]. \qquad (5)$$

3   A Grammar Scheme for Mixfix Operators

Section 2 may have given some intuition about precedence and associativity, but there are still some design choices left. This section makes things precise by giving a grammar scheme which, when instantiated with a precedence graph, yields a context-free grammar specifying the syntax of expressions.

First some definitions:

- A mixfix operator consists of a finite sequence of holes (denoted by _ above) and name parts (if, then and else in if_then_else_), plus in the case of an infix operator an associativity (left, right or "non"; note that we do not restrict the term "infix operator" to binary operators). To reduce the risk of ambiguity we require that operators contain at least one name part, and that two holes may not occur next to each other in an operator. Furthermore, for simplicity, we require that two name parts may not occur next to each other either.
- A precedence graph is a finite directed acyclic simple graph with unlabelled edges, whose nodes are annotated with finite sets of operators.

Given such a precedence graph a grammar is constructed. The terminals of the grammar are the name parts used by the operators in the graph.

We make no assumptions about uniqueness of name parts or operators (except that a given operator may only occur once in a given node). The resulting grammar can hence be ambiguous. We feel that it is overly restrictive to require the grammar to be unambiguous. For instance, it seems unnecessary to reject a program just because two imported libraries both define a particular operator, even though this operator is never used, or only used in such a way that it can be disambiguated based on context. As another example, the designer of some library may want to include both if_then_ and if_then_else_, and in order to keep the library simple it seems reasonable to give both operators the same precedence. Given the rules below this makes the grammar ambiguous, because if e then if e then e else e can be parsed in two ways.[2] Instead of rejecting ambiguous grammars we suggest that ambiguous *parses* should be rejected, preferably together with error messages showing all possible parses, thus aiding debugging. Language designers are of course free to impose further restrictions to ensure unambiguity. (Ambiguity is discussed further in Sect. 4.)

As mentioned above the language of the constructed grammar *only* contains operator applications (possibly nullary). Expressions in a real language usually contain other constructions as well, like parentheses, let or lambda expressions and non-operator symbols. To keep things simple such constructs are not treated here, but we note that it is easy to incorporate several of them by modifying the grammar scheme (see Sect. 5.4 for one example).

Let us now build up the grammar scheme step by step, starting with a precedence graph where every node is labelled with exactly one infix, non-associative

---

[2] Assuming that e binds tighter than the conditionals.

operator with no internal holes. In this case an expression headed by the operator op from graph node p consists of an expression headed by an operator which
binds tighter, then op's only name part, and finally another expression headed
by an operator which binds tighter. We can encode this using the non-terminals

$$\widehat{p} ::= p{\uparrow}\ op_p^{\mathrm{non}}\ p{\uparrow} \quad \text{and} \tag{6}$$

$$p{\uparrow} ::= \bigvee \{ \widehat{q} \mid p < q \}. \tag{7}$$

Here $\bigvee S$ stands for a choice between all the elements in the finite set S, op_p^{non}
is the single name part of the (non-associative) operator in node p, and $p < q$
means that there is an edge from node p to node q. An arbitrary expression is an
expression headed by an arbitrary operator, so the non-terminal for expressions is

$$expr ::= \bigvee \{ \widehat{p} \mid p \text{ is a graph node} \}. \tag{8}$$

It is straightforward to extend this grammar scheme to infix, non-associative
operators with multiple name parts. All the internal holes can contain arbitrary
expressions, so we can just let op_p^{non} stand for the non-terminal

$$op_p^{\mathrm{non}} ::= n_1\ expr\ n_2\ expr\ \cdots\ n_k, \tag{9}$$

where n_i is the i-th name part of the non-associative infix operator with k name
parts annotating node p. For graphs whose nodes are annotated with sets of
operators we change the definition of op_p^{non} to include one production for every
operator in node p.

Finally let us include other kinds of operators. This amounts to adding more
productions to $\widehat{p}$. When is an expression headed by a right associative infix
operator precedence correct? Both arguments should be allowed to be expressions
headed by operators which bind tighter, and the right argument should also be
allowed to be an application of another right associative operator of the same
precedence. There is scope for allowing other combinations to be precedence
correct as well, though. We choose to view prefix operators as right associative
by including the productions

$$\widehat{p} ::= \overrightarrow{p}^{+}\ p{\uparrow} \quad \text{and} \tag{10}$$

$$\overrightarrow{p} ::= op_p^{\mathrm{prefix}} \mid p{\uparrow}\ op_p^{\mathrm{right}}. \tag{11}$$

Here e^{+} stands for a positive number of repetitions of e, and op_p^{prefix} and op_p^{right}
are the analogues of op_p^{non} for prefix and right associative operators, respectively.
(In Sect. 7 a grammar scheme due to Aasa (1995) which handles prefix operators
differently is discussed.)

Note that the parse trees generated for prefix and right associative operators
are not the correct ones; for prefix operators they have the shape $(op \cdots op)\,rest$
rather than $op(\cdots(op\ rest)\cdots)$. However, this is easily corrected by a post-
processing pass. In our implementation based on parser combinators one simply

$$expr ::= \bigvee \{\, \widehat{p} \mid p \text{ is a graph node} \,\}$$

$$\widehat{p} ::= op_p^{closed}$$

$$\mid p{\uparrow}\; op_p^{non}\; p{\uparrow}$$

$$\mid \overrightarrow{p}^{\,+}\; p{\uparrow}$$

$$\mid p{\uparrow}\; \overleftarrow{p}^{\,+}$$

$$\overrightarrow{p} ::= op_p^{prefix} \mid p{\uparrow}\; op_p^{right}$$

$$\overleftarrow{p} ::= op_p^{postfix} \mid op_p^{left}\; p{\uparrow}$$

$$p{\uparrow} ::= \bigvee \{\, \widehat{q} \mid p < q \,\}$$

$$op_p^{fix} ::= \bigvee \left\{\; n_1\; expr\; n_2\; expr\; \cdots\; n_k \;\middle|\; \begin{array}{l} n_1, \ldots, n_k \text{ are the name parts of} \\ \text{an operator in node } p \text{ with fix-} \\ \text{ity/associativity } \textit{fix} \end{array} \right\}$$

Fig. 2. A grammar scheme for mixfix expressions, parameterised by a precedence graph

$$\widehat{p} ::= \widehat{p}^{\,closed} \mid \widehat{p}^{\,non} \mid \widehat{p}^{\,right} \mid \widehat{p}^{\,left}$$

$$\widehat{p}^{\,closed} ::= op_p^{closed}$$

$$\widehat{p}^{\,non} ::= p{\uparrow}\; op_p^{non}\; p{\uparrow}$$

$$\widehat{p}^{\,right} ::= \left(op_p^{prefix} \mid p{\uparrow}\; op_p^{right} \right) \left(\widehat{p}^{\,right} \mid p{\uparrow} \right)$$

$$\widehat{p}^{\,left} ::= \left(\widehat{p}^{\,left} \mid p{\uparrow} \right) \left(op_p^{postfix} \mid op_p^{left}\; p{\uparrow} \right)$$

Fig. 3. An alternative formulation of $\widehat{p}$ which leads to grammars which are left and right recursive, but whose parse trees do not require post-processing

needs to include a right fold in the semantic action attached to the $\widehat{p}$ production (see Sect. 5). Furthermore this formulation has the advantage of not being right recursive.

Note also that it would be reasonable to allow prefix operators to be non-associative. For instance, if the operators if_then_ and if_then_else_ from the example above were both non-associative then if e then if e then e else e could only be parsed in one way:[3] if e then (if e then e) else e. To keep things simple we treat all prefix operators as right associative in this presentation, though.

Postfix operators, left associative infix operators and closed operators can be handled analogously. The full grammar scheme is shown in Fig. 2. Note that, because precedence graphs are acyclic, the instantiated grammars are neither left nor right recursive (see Sects. 5.4–5.5). An alternative definition of $\widehat{p}$ which avoids the need to post-process the parse trees and accepts the same strings is

---

[3] Unless the grammar contains some other ambiguity.

given in Fig. 3. The grammars resulting from this definition can be left and right recursive, though.

To make things more concrete, let us instantiate the grammar scheme for the precedence graph in Fig. 1. After some simplification—removal of productions which are unused or always fail, together with inlining—we get the following grammar (with terminals underlined):

$$
\begin{aligned}
expr &::= and \mid eq \mid term \mid fac \mid if \mid closed \\
and &::= (and\uparrow \ \underline{\wedge})^+ \ and\uparrow \\
and\uparrow &::= eq \mid closed \\
eq &::= eq\uparrow \ \underline{==} \ eq\uparrow \\
eq\uparrow &::= term \mid fac \mid closed \\
term &::= closed \ ((\underline{+} \mid \underline{-}) \ closed)^+ \\
fac &::= closed \ \underline{!}^+ \\
if &::= (\underline{if} \ expr \ \underline{then} \ expr \ \underline{else})^+ \ closed \\
closed &::= \underline{b} \mid \underline{n} \mid \underline{(} \ expr \ \underline{)}
\end{aligned}
\tag{12}
$$

4   Unambiguity

An important property of the grammar scheme introduced in Sect. 3 is that, while the instantiated grammars can in general be ambiguous, this ambiguity is necessarily introduced by reusing the same name part in several operators: if all operator name parts in a precedence graph are unique, then the resulting grammar is unambiguous.

If no operators have internal holes then this result can be proved by adapting a theorem due to Lotfallah (2009). The general case can be reduced to the simpler one by using the following observation (following Aasa (1995)): Operators with internal name parts act like generalised brackets, so given a precedence graph with unique name parts and a syntactically correct string one can uniquely identify the substrings corresponding to the non-terminals op_p^{fix}. One can then treat every instance of one of the op_p^{fix} non-terminals as a terminal of a new grammar. For instance, the string if b ∧ b else n then n would be treated as a string containing two terminals: if b ∧ b else n then and n. This new grammar only contains atoms, unary prefix and postfix operators and binary infix operators, so unambiguity follows from Lotfallah's theorem. It remains to show that the internal expressions of the op_p^{fix} "terminals" are unambiguous, but this follows by applying the same argument inductively to the proper substrings corresponding to the $expr$ non-terminal.

Note that Lotfallah's theorem requires a form of acyclicity. Cyclic precedence graphs easily lead to ambiguous grammars, even if all name parts are unique. Consider the graph in Fig. 4, for instance. The grammar corresponding to this graph can generate the string 0 * 0 + 0 in two ways: with * as the outermost operator (0 * (0 + 0)) or with + as the outermost operator ((0 * 0) + 0).

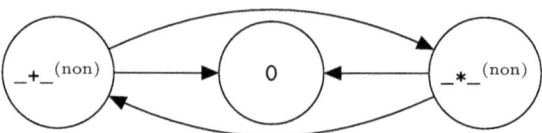

Fig. 4. A cyclic precedence graph

5   Formalisation

The unambiguity result from Sect. 4 indicates that the grammars are, in some sense, useful: reasonable expressions will not be rejected because of ambiguities, as long as all name parts are unique. In this section a notion of precedence correct expression is defined, and it is proved that the grammars generate exactly the precedence correct expressions. This amounts to a different aspect of usability: no precedence correct expression will be rejected because the grammar is too limited.

We perform this exercise formally, in the total, dependently typed functional programming language Agda (Agda Team 2009). As part of this development the grammar scheme introduced above is defined formally using parser combinators. First operators, precedence graphs and precedence correct expressions are defined (Sects. 5.1–5.3), then a parser combinator library is introduced (Sect. 5.4), the grammar scheme is defined (Sect. 5.5), and finally the proof mentioned above is outlined (Sect. 5.6). Note that some minor details of Agda have been changed in order to aid the presentation.

5.1   Operators

Before defining what an operator is we encode associativities and fixities using two simple data types. Fixities are combined with associativities, but only for infix operators; prefix, postfix and closed operators are viewed as being right, left and non-associative, respectively:

 data *Associativity* : *Set* **where**
  left : *Associativity*
  right : *Associativity*
  non : *Associativity*
 data *Fixity* : *Set* **where**
  prefx : *Fixity*
  infx : *Associativity* → *Fixity*
  postfx : *Fixity*
  closed : *Fixity*

(The constructors of a data type are introduced by giving their type signatures. Note that **infix** is a reserved word in Agda, hence the strange names.)

An operator is then represented by its fixity plus a vector containing its name parts. Note that the fixity is exposed in the type, along with the internal arity, i.e. the number of internal arguments:

> **record** *Operator* (*fix* : *Fixity*) (*arity* : $\mathbb{N}$) : *Set* **where**
>   **field** *nameParts* : *Vec NamePart* (*1* + *arity*)

(*Vec A n* is a list of *A*s of length *n*. *NamePart* is the type of name parts.) The operator `if_then_else_` is represented as follows:

> *if-then-else* : *Operator* prefx *2*
> *if-then-else* = **record** {*nameParts* = `"if"` :: `"then"` :: `"else"` :: []}

5.2   Precedence Graphs

For simplicity precedence graphs are represented by their unfoldings as forests, with one tree (*Precedence*) for every node in the graph:

> **data** *Precedence* : *Set* **where**
>   precedence : ((*fix* : *Fixity*) → *List* ($\exists$ (*Operator fix*))) →
>   *List Precedence* → *Precedence*
>
> *PrecedenceGraph* : *Set*
> *PrecedenceGraph* = *List Precedence*

Two projection functions are defined for the *Precedence* nodes, one returning the operators of the given precedence, and one returning the successor nodes:

> *ops* : *Precedence* → (*fix* : *Fixity*) → *List* ($\exists$ (*Operator fix*))
> *ops* (precedence *o s*) = *o*
>
> ↑ : *Precedence* → *List Precedence*
> ↑ (precedence *o s*) = *s*

(Dependent function spaces are written as $(x : A) \to B$.) Note that the *set* of operators annotating a graph node is represented by a function mapping a fixity to a *list* of operators of that fixity; the stronger invariants of a set are not needed for this development.

The type $\exists$ is used to hide the arity argument of *Operator fix*, so that operators of different arity can be members of the same list. It is a variant of the pair type:

> **data** $\exists$ {*A* : *Set*} (*B* : *A* → *Set*) : *Set* **where**
>   _,_ : (*x* : *A*) → *B x* → $\exists$ *B*

(Note that arguments in braces, like {*A*}, are *implicit*; they do not need to be given explicitly if Agda can infer them.)

5.3   Expressions

The type of expressions which are precedence correct with respect to a given precedence graph is defined in a module parameterised by the graph:

> **module** *PrecedenceCorrect* (*g* : *PrecedenceGraph*) **where**

The definition consists of four mutually inductive types:

- *Expr ps* stands for expressions where the head operator has one of the precedences in *ps*:

> **data** *Expr* (*ps* : *List Precedence*) : *Set* **where**
> _•_ : ∀ {*p assoc*} → *p* ∈ *ps* → *Ex p assoc* → *Expr ps*

Ex p assoc, introduced below, stands for expressions where the head operator has precedence *p* and associativity *assoc*. The type _∈_ encodes list membership:

> **data** _∈_ {*A* : *Set*} : *A* → *List A* → *Set* **where**
> here : ∀ {*x   xs*}   → *x* ∈ *x* :: *xs*
> there : ∀ {*x y xs*} → *x* ∈ *xs* → *x* ∈ *y* :: *xs*

- *In ops* stands for the application of one of the operators in *ops* to all its internal arguments:

> **data** *In* {*fix*} (*ops* : *List* (∃ (*Operator fix*))) : *Set* **where**
> _•_ : ∀ {*arity op*} →
>   (*arity, op*) ∈ *ops* → *Vec* (*Expr g*) *arity* → *In ops*

Note that the internal arguments are unrestricted expressions (*Expr g*). Note also that constructors are overloaded in Agda.

- *Out p assoc* contains expressions where the head operator either has precedence *p* and associativity *assoc*, or binds strictly tighter than *p*:

> **data** *Out* (*p* : *Precedence*) (*assoc* : *Associativity*) : *Set* **where**
> similar : *Ex p assoc* → *Out p assoc*
> tighter : *Expr* (↑ *p*) → *Out p assoc*

Out p left stands for the left arguments of left associative operators of precedence *p*, and similarly for *Out p* right.

- Finally *Ex p assoc* is defined. Note the use of mixfix operators:

> **data** *Ex* (*p* : *Precedence*) : *Associativity* → *Set* **where**
> ⟪_⟫   :   *In* (*ops p* closed   )   → *Ex p* non
> ⌟_⟫   : *Out p* left → *In* (*ops p* postfx)   → *Ex p* left
> ⟪_⌞   :   *In* (*ops p* prefx   ) → *Out p* right → *Ex p* right
> ⌟_⌞   : *Expr* (↑ *p*) → *In* (*ops p* (infx non)) → *Expr* (↑ *p*) → *Ex p* non
> ⌟_⌞ℓ : *Out p* left → *In* (*ops p* (infx left)) → *Expr* (↑ *p*) → *Ex p* left
> ⌟_⌞ʳ : *Expr* (↑ *p*) → *In* (*ops p* (infx right)) → *Out p* right → *Ex p* right

Two "weakening" functions will also be used. The function *weakenE* takes an expression headed by an operator which has one of the precedences in *ps* and converts it to an expression headed by an operator with one of the precedences in $p :: ps$, and *weakenI* is similar:

$$weakenE \ : \ \forall \ \{p \ ps\} \rightarrow Expr \ ps \rightarrow Expr \ (p :: ps)$$
$$weakenE \ (p{\in}ps \bullet e) \ = \ \mathsf{there} \ p{\in}ps \bullet e$$
$$weakenI \ : \ \forall \ \{\mathit{fix} \ ops\} \ \{op \ : \ \exists \ (Operator \ \mathit{fix})\} \rightarrow In \ ops \rightarrow In \ (op :: ops)$$
$$weakenI \ (op{\in}ops \bullet args) \ = \ \mathsf{there} \ op{\in}ops \bullet args$$

5.4 Parser Combinators

In order to define the grammar scheme we will use a parser combinator library based on that described by Danielsson and Altenkirch (2009), but tailored specifically for this task. The type *Parser* defines the parser combinators:

data *Parser* : $Set \rightarrow Set$ **where**
- fail   : $\forall \ \{A\} \rightarrow Parser \ A$
- _|_   : $\forall \ \{A\} \rightarrow Parser \ A \rightarrow Parser \ A \rightarrow Parser \ A$
- _‖_   : $\forall \ \{I \ i\} \ \{A : I \rightarrow Set\} \rightarrow$
              $Parser \ (A \ i) \rightarrow Parser \ (\exists \ A) \rightarrow Parser \ (\exists \ A)$
- _⊛_   : $\forall \ \{A \ B\} \rightarrow Parser \ (A \rightarrow B) \rightarrow Parser \ A \rightarrow Parser \ B$
- _<$>_   : $\forall \ \{A \ B\} \rightarrow (A \rightarrow B) \rightarrow Parser \ A \rightarrow Parser \ B$
- _+   : $\forall \ \{A\} \rightarrow Parser \ A \rightarrow Parser \ (List^{+} \ A)$
- _between_   : $\forall \ \{A \ n\} \rightarrow \infty \ (Parser \ A) \rightarrow Vec \ NamePart \ (1 + n) \rightarrow$
              $Parser \ (Vec \ A \ n)$

The semantics of the parser combinators is given by the following inductively defined type:

data $\_{\in}\_{\cdot}\_$: $\forall \ \{A\} \rightarrow A \rightarrow Parser \ A \rightarrow List \ NamePart \rightarrow Set$ **where**
  . . .

The type $x \in p \cdot s$ is inhabited if and only if one of the possible results of applying the parser p to the string s is x. The parser combinators come with a parser backend which takes a parser and a string and computes all parses matching the string. Because Agda is total (modulo any bugs in the implementation) this backend is guaranteed to terminate, and it has been proved to be sound and complete with respect to the semantics.

Let us now explain all the combinators. The parser fail always fails, so there is no constructor for it in $\_{\in}\_{\cdot}\_$. The combinator _|_ encodes symmetric choice:

$$|^{\ell} \ : \ x \in p_1 \ \cdot \ s \rightarrow x \in p_1 \mid p_2 \ \cdot \ s$$
$$|^{r} \ : \ x \in p_2 \ \cdot \ s \rightarrow x \in p_1 \mid p_2 \ \cdot \ s$$

(The introduction of the bound variables x, s, p_1 and p_2 has been omitted here to avoid clutter.) The combinator _‖_ is a variant of _|_:

$$\|^{\ell} \; : \; x \in p_1 \cdot s \to (\_ \, , \, x) \in p_1 \| p_2 \cdot s$$
$$\|^{r} \; : \; x \in p_2 \cdot s \to x \quad\;\; \in p_1 \| p_2 \cdot s$$

(The underscore tells Agda to try to infer what the corresponding expression should be.) The $\_\circledast\_$ operator is *applicative functor application* (McBride and Paterson 2008): the result of $p_1 \circledast p_2$ is the result of p_1 (a function) applied to the result of p_2. The combinator $\_{<\$>}\_$ maps a function over the results of a parser:

$$\_\circledast\_ \; : \; f \in p_1 \cdot s_1 \to x \in p_2 \cdot s_2 \to f\,x \in p_1 \circledast p_2 \cdot s_1 +\!\!\!+ s_2$$
$$<\$>\_ \; : \qquad\qquad\qquad x \in p \;\cdot\; s \to f\,x \in f <\$> p \cdot s$$

(The function $\_+\!\!\!+\_$ concatenates two lists.) The parser $p+$ parses one or more occurrences of p:

$$+_{[]} \; : \; x \in p \cdot s \qquad\qquad\qquad\quad \to [x] \quad \in p+ \cdot s$$
$$+_{::} \; : \; x \in p \cdot s_1 \to xs \in p+ \cdot s_2 \to x :: xs \in p+ \cdot s_1 +\!\!\!+ s_2$$

Here $List^+ \; A$ is the type of non-empty lists containing elements of type A. Finally p between ns parses strings matching p between the name parts in the non-empty vector ns, returning a vector containing the results from p:

$$\text{between}_{[]} \; : \; [\,] \in p \text{ between } (t :: [\,]) \cdot t :: [\,]$$
$$\text{between}_{::} \; : \; x \in \flat\, p \cdot s_1 \to xs \in p \text{ between } ts \cdot s_2 \to$$
$$x :: xs \in p \text{ between } (t :: ts) \cdot t :: s_1 +\!\!\!+ s_2$$

The definition of $\_$between$\_$ uses ∞, which marks its argument as being coinductive. It can be read as a suspension, and comes with "force" and "delay" operators:

$$\infty \; : \; Set \to Set$$
$$\flat \; : \; \forall \, \{A\} \to \infty\, A \to A$$
$$\sharp \; : \; \forall \, \{A\} \to A \to \infty\, A$$

The rest of the *Parser* data type is inductive, so the only way to define cyclic or infinite parsers/grammars is to use $\_$between$\_$. Note that because the first and last name parts accepted by p between ns are the first and last name parts in ns the cycles introduced by $\_$between$\_$ are neither left nor right recursive.

Figure 5 contains a precedence graph for the parser combinators. Note that in Agda ordinary function application (juxtaposition), non-operator identifiers, parenthesised expressions and closed operators all bind strictly tighter than every other operator. This amounts to modifying the grammar in Fig. 2 by removing op_p^{closed} from $\widehat{p}$ and adding the following productions:

$$expr ::= closed^+, \tag{13}$$

$$p{\uparrow} ::= closed^+, \quad \text{ and} \tag{14}$$

$$closed ::= identifier \mid \text{(} \; expr \; \text{)} \mid \bigvee \{ \, op_p^{\text{closed}} \mid p \text{ is a graph node} \, \}. \tag{15}$$

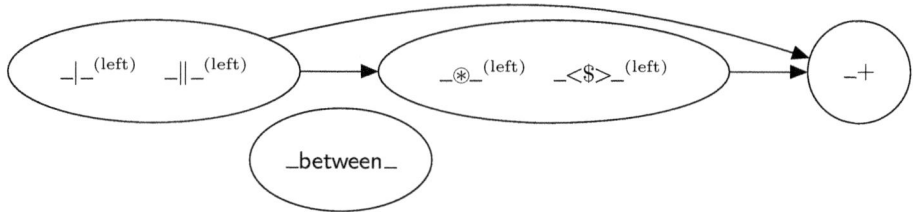

Fig. 5. A precedence graph for the parser combinators

The non-terminal *identifier* stands for ordinary identifiers; this includes the *names* of operators, like `if_then_else_`, but not operator name parts, unless they are also ordinary identifiers. (Note that this grammar does not correspond exactly to Agda's current expression syntax, partly because it omits constructs like lambda abstractions and dependent function spaces. It should give enough intuition to enable following the examples in the paper, though.)

5.5   The Grammar Scheme

Now the implementation of the grammar scheme can be presented. The definition is yet again given in a module parameterised by a precedence graph:

> **module** *Mixfix* (*g* : *Precedence Graph*) **where**

A grammar will be defined for *g*. The grammar is defined by mutual structural recursion/guarded corecursion.

   The only delayed parser is *expr*, which corresponds to the non-terminal *expr*:

$$expr \ : \ \infty \ (Parser \ (Expr \ g))$$
$$expr \ = \ \sharp \ (precs \ g)$$

   The parser *precs ps* corresponds to $\bigvee \{\, \widehat{p} \mid p \in ps \,\}$, and *inner* (*ops p fix*) corresponds to op_p^{fix}:

$$precs \ : \ (ps \ : \ List \ Precedence) \rightarrow Parser \ (Expr \ ps)$$
$$precs \ [] \qquad\quad = \ \mathsf{fail}$$
$$precs \ (p :: ps) \ = \ (\lambda \ (\_ \ , \ e) \rightarrow \mathsf{here} \bullet e) \ \mathtt{<\$>} \ prec \ p$$
$$\qquad\qquad\quad | \quad weakenE \qquad\qquad\quad \mathtt{<\$>} \ precs \ ps$$
$$inner \ : \ \forall \ \{fix\} \ (ops \ : \ List \ (\exists \ (Operator \ fix))) \rightarrow Parser \ (In \ ops)$$
$$inner \ [] \qquad\qquad\quad = \ \mathsf{fail}$$
$$inner \ ((\_ \ , \ op) :: ops) \ =$$
$$\qquad (\lambda \ args \rightarrow \mathsf{here} \bullet args) \ \mathtt{<\$>} \ (expr \ \mathsf{between} \ nameParts \ op)$$
$$\qquad | \quad weakenI \qquad\qquad\quad \mathtt{<\$>} \ inner \ ops$$

   Finally we get to *prec p*, which corresponds to the non-terminal $\widehat{p}$. The definition of *prec* follows the grammar scheme given in Sect. 3 closely:

$prec\ :\ (p\ :\ Precedence) \rightarrow Parser\ (\exists\ (Ex\ p))$
$prec\ p@(\mathsf{precedence}\ ops\ sucs)\ =$

    $\langle\!\langle\_\rangle\!\rangle$ `<$>` $[\mathsf{closed}\quad]$
  $\|\ \underset{\ }{_\langle_\rangle_}\ $ `<$>` $\ p\!\uparrow\ \circledast\ [\mathsf{infx\ non}]\quad\circledast\ p\!\uparrow$
  $\|\ app^{r}\ $ `<$>`$\qquad\quad preRight\ +\ \circledast\ p\!\uparrow$
  $\|\ app^{\ell}\ $ `<$>`$\ p\!\uparrow\ \circledast\ postLeft\ +$
  $\|\ \mathsf{fail}$

where

$[\_]\ =\ \lambda\ (fix\ :\ Fixity) \rightarrow inner\ (ops\ fix)$
$p\!\uparrow\ =\ precs\ sucs$
$preRight\ :\ Parser\ (Out\ p\ \mathsf{right} \rightarrow Ex\ p\ \mathsf{right})$
$preRight\ =\ \langle\!\langle_\rangle\!\rangle_\ $ `<$>`$\qquad\quad [\mathsf{prefx}\quad]$
$\qquad\qquad\quad|\ \underset{\ }{_\langle_\rangle^{r}_}\ $ `<$>`$\ p\!\uparrow\ \circledast\ [\mathsf{infx\ right}]$
$postLeft\ :\ Parser\ (Out\ p\ \mathsf{left} \rightarrow Ex\ p\ \mathsf{left})$
$postLeft\ =\ (\lambda\ op\quad e_1 \rightarrow e_1\ \langle\ op\ \rangle\!\rangle\quad)\ $ `<$>`$\ [\mathsf{postfx}\quad]$
$\qquad\qquad\quad|\ (\lambda\ op\ e_2\ e_1 \rightarrow e_1\ \langle\ op\ \rangle^{\ell}\ e_2)\ $ `<$>`$\ [\mathsf{infx\ left}]\ \circledast\ p\!\uparrow$
$app^{r}\ =\ \lambda\ fs\ e \rightarrow foldr\ (\lambda\ f\ e \rightarrow f\ (similar\ e))\ (\lambda\ f \rightarrow f\ (tighter\ e))\ fs$
$app^{\ell}\ =\ \lambda\ e\ fs \rightarrow foldl\ (\lambda\ e\ f \rightarrow f\ (similar\ e))\ (\lambda\ f \rightarrow f\ (tighter\ e))\ fs$

Here $[fix]$ corresponds to op_p^{fix}, $p\!\uparrow$ to $p\!\uparrow$, $preRight$ to $\overrightarrow{p}$ and $postLeft$ to $\overleftarrow{p}$. Note the use of *foldl* and *foldr* to handle the post-processing of the parse trees. These functions are folds for non-empty lists:

$$foldr\ :\ \{A\ B\ :\ Set\} \rightarrow (A \rightarrow B \rightarrow B) \rightarrow (A \rightarrow B) \rightarrow List^{+}\ A \rightarrow B$$
$$foldl\ :\ \{A\ B\ :\ Set\} \rightarrow (B \rightarrow A \rightarrow B) \rightarrow (A \rightarrow B) \rightarrow List^{+}\ A \rightarrow B$$

The right fold *foldr* applies the argument of type $A \rightarrow B$ to the last element of the list, and the left fold *foldl* applies it to the first element.

The code above is accepted as total by Agda because it uses a lexicographic combination of guarded corecursion and structural recursion: every call path from one definition to itself consists solely of constructors and recursive calls, and either at least one of the constructors is the coinductive constructor ♯, or one argument becomes structurally smaller.

5.6   Correctness

Finally let us show that the grammar scheme is sound and complete with respect to the type of precedence correct expressions, i.e. that the generated expressions are exactly the precedence correct ones.

Due to the precise types used in the definition of the grammar scheme we have already established soundness: all expressions generated by the *expr* non-terminal have to be precedence correct with respect to the relevant precedence graph.

In order to show completeness we first define a function *show* which flattens expressions (the code is omitted here):

$$show \ : \ \forall \ \{ps\} \rightarrow Expr \ ps \rightarrow List \ NamePart$$

We then show, for every expression e, that e is one of the possible results of parsing $show \ e$:

$$complete \ : \ (e \ : \ Expr \ g) \rightarrow e \in \flat \ expr \ \cdot \ show \ e$$

The proof, which is not included here, is by induction over the structure of e.

6 Implementation

Section 5 describes a (not necessarily efficient) method which, given a precedence graph, parses expressions containing mixfix operators. However, for a programming language with support for user-defined mixfix operators the precedence graph is not predetermined, and different precedence graphs can be in effect at different source locations. If the programming language is defined in a suitable way, then the following procedure can be used to parse a program:

1. Parse the program, treating expressions as flat lists of tokens.
2. Compute the precedence graph in effect for every expression.
3. Parse the flat token lists into real expressions, using the relevant precedence graphs.

This requires that one can identify the extent of an expression without parsing it completely, and also that the relevant precedence graph does not change halfway through an expression. If expressions can bind new operators—consider lambda abstractions, for instance—then the procedure does not quite work, but a reasonable workaround is to include all binding constructs in the "outer" grammar used by the first step above. Note that similar methods are used to parse several existing languages with user-defined infix operators, for instance Haskell.

Using parser combinators to implement the grammar scheme, like in Sect. 5, can be nice: the implementation is almost a direct transliteration of the intended grammar, so it should be easy to understand and modify the code. However, to ensure sufficient efficiency of parsing one has to choose the implementation of the parser combinators (the backend) carefully. There are at least two problems to watch out for:

- The generated grammars are often far from being left factorised.
- The sharing of the precedence DAG might be lost when the DAG is converted into a parser.

If Wadler's "list of successes" implementation of parser combinators (1985) is used, then one can expect worst-case parse times which are (at least) exponential in the size of the graph, even if the grammar is completely unambiguous. However, as observed by Norvig (1991), inefficient backtracking parsers can be made efficient by using memoisation. We have a prototype implementation which uses memoising parser combinators based on those of Frost and Szydlowski (1996)

and memoises the $\widehat{p}$ non-terminals. This means that when the parser backend
has found all substrings, starting at a given input position, which match $\widehat{p}$, then
the corresponding results and the substrings' endpoints are stored for later reuse.
Our experiments indicate that this gives sufficient performance for typical programming language applications, involving limited ambiguity and moderately
sized graphs and input strings. If precedence graphs are very large (due to large
libraries of operators) it is perhaps a good idea to prune them before parsing,
keeping only those parts of the graphs which are relevant based on the name
parts present in the current expression.

7   Related Work

Peyton Jones (1986) shows how user-defined mixfix operators can be described
using a *fixed* grammar (as opposed to the grammar scheme defined in this work)
by distinguishing initial, middle and final tokens of mixfix operators lexically.
Support for user-defined precedences is not discussed, and seems hard to incorporate. Peyton Jones argues that operators *should* be lexically distinguishable
from other syntactic constructs, to make them easier to parse for humans. We
partly agree, but think that this task can be performed by syntax highlighting
instead of lexical conventions; in any way, lexical restrictions fit well with the
approach developed in this paper. Peyton Jones also discusses how mixfix operator sections can be handled. A section is a partial application of an operator; for
instance, the sections _[i] and if_then_else y stand for λ x → x [i]
and λ b x → if b then x else y, respectively. Sections can be straightforwardly integrated into our grammar scheme. To avoid a combinatorial explosion
of the number of productions one can let the lexer distinguish between hole mark-
ers (_) placed before, between and after name parts (similarly to Peyton Jones'
PRE_TOKEN, IN_TOKEN and POST_TOKEN), and take advantage of this
distinction in the grammar scheme.

The work of Aasa (1995, 1992) is probably closest to ours. She shows how a
class of possibly ambiguous context-free grammars, whose productions are annotated with disambiguating precedences and associativities, can be translated
into unambiguous context-free grammars. She also shows how a parser for user-
defined mixfix operators can be implemented using parser combinators. In contrast to our work Aasa only considers total precedence orders. Furthermore her
notion of what it means to be precedence correct is more liberal than ours (the
strings accepted are claimed to be exactly those which an operator-precedence
parser (Floyd 1963; Aho et al. 1986) accepts). This might seem like an advantage, but in order to achieve this result Aasa ends up with an arguably rather
complicated grammar scheme, while we have striven to keep the grammars simple and hence easy to understand. The difference lies in how prefix and postfix
operators are handled. As an example of how Aasa's system differs from ours,
consider the precedence graph in Fig. 6. In our system the string 0 + $ 0 is
syntactically incorrect since $_ binds weaker than _+_, whereas Aasa's system
accepts arbitrary prefix operators immediately to the right of an infix operator, so in her system the string can be unambiguously parsed as 0 + ($ 0). It

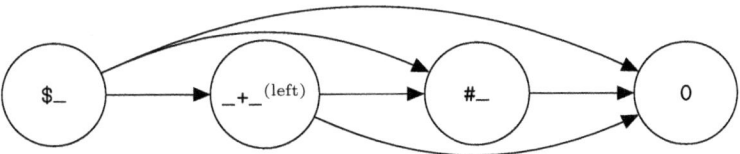

Fig. 6. A precedence graph corresponding to a total precedence order (based on a precedence relation due to Aasa (1995))

does not stop there, though. The string # $ 0 + 0, which is also syntactically incorrect in our system, is parsed as # ($ (0 + 0)) in Aasa's. It is accepted because, even though #_ binds tighter than _+_, the occurrence of _+_ is *covered* by $_. Our system has the advantage that one can tell whether a syntax tree is precedence correct by inspecting every node in isolation and considering the relation between the node's operator and the operators of the child nodes. In Aasa's system this is not enough: even though the syntax tree # ($ 0) (where the parentheses indicate the structure of the syntax tree) is precedence correct and #_ binds strictly tighter than _+_ the syntax tree (# ($ 0)) + 0 is not precedence correct.

Several languages and formalisms which support user-defined mixfix operators rely on *type information* to resolve syntactic ambiguities, sometimes in conjunction with user-specified precedences (Pettersson and Fritzson 1992; Missura 1997; Goguen et al. 1999; Paulson et al. 2008). One way to accomplish this is to first parse the input using a possibly ambiguous grammar, then type check every parse tree, and finally accept the input if exactly one parse tree is type correct. Such an approach, while possibly costly, can easily be combined with the grammar scheme described in this work. More optimised approaches are possible, though. The parser for Missura's *higher-order mixfix syntax* (1997), aimed at parsing (linear) mathematical notation, is integrated with Hindley-Milner style type inference.

Missura also argues that precedence relations should not have to be total orders, and Heinlein (2004) argues that precedence relations should be partial orders. The language Fortress uses a non-transitive precedence relation, hardcoded in the language's grammar (Allen et al. 2008).

Finally we note that Missura (1997) and Wansbrough (1999) discuss some other approaches to handling mixfix operators, and that it is also possible to support user-defined *binding constructs*, like ∀x ∈ S. P (Missura 1997; Coq Development Team 2009; Paulson et al. 2008).

8   Conclusions

We have presented a simple grammar scheme for expressions containing mixfix operators, and discussed integration of the grammar scheme into the parsing process of a full-fledged programming language implementation.

The simplicity of our approach comes at a price: other methods, like Aasa's (1995), treat more expressions as being precedence correct, and some methods enable programmers to extend the grammar with other forms of expressions, like binding constructs. However, we believe that our approach strikes a nice balance between simplicity and expressiveness. In the future we plan to replace Agda's support for mixfix operators (Norell 2007) with a grammar scheme and an implementation based on this work.

Acknowledgements

We would like to thank Graham Hutton, Wouter Swierstra and the anonymous reviewers for useful feedback.

References

Aasa, A.: Precedences in specifications and implementations of programming languages. Theoretical Computer Science 142(1), 3–26 (1995)

Aasa, A.: User Defined Syntax. PhD thesis, Chalmers University of Technology (1992)

The Agda Team. The Agda Wiki (2009), `http://wiki.portal.chalmers.se/agda/`

Aho, A.V., Sethi, R., Ullman, J.D.: Compilers: Principles, Techniques, and Tools. Addison-Wesley, Reading (1986)

Allen, E., Chase, D., Hallett, J., Luchangco, V., Maessen, J.-W., Ryu, S., Steele Jr., G.L., Tobin-Hochstadt, S., et al.: The Fortress Language Specification, Version 1.0 (2008)

The Coq Development Team. The Coq Proof Assistant Reference Manual, Version 8.2 (2009)

Danielsson, N.A., Altenkirch, T.: Mixing induction and coinduction. Draft (2009)

Floyd, R.W.: Syntactic analysis and operator precedence. Journal of the ACM 10(3), 316–333 (1963)

Frost, R.A., Szydlowski, B.: Memoizing purely functional top-down backtracking language processors. Science of Computer Programming 27(3), 263–288 (1996)

Goguen, J.A., Winkler, T., Meseguer, J., Futatsugi, K., Jouannaud, J.-P.: Introducing OBJ (1999)

Heinlein, C.: C+++: User-defined operator symbols in C++. In: INFORMATIK 2004 – Informatik verbindet, Band 2, Beiträge der 34. Jahrestagung der Gesellschaft für Informatik e.V (GI). Lecture Notes in Informatics, vol. P-51, pp. 459–468 (2004)

Lotfallah, W.B.: Characterizing unambiguous precedence systems in expressions without superfluous parentheses. International Journal of Computer Mathematics 86(1), 1–20 (2009)

McBride, C., Paterson, R.: Applicative programming with effects. Journal of Functional Programming 18, 1–13 (2008)

Milner, R., Tofte, M., Harper, R., MacQueen, D.: The Definition of Standard ML. MIT Press, Cambridge (1997) (revised edition)

Missura, S.A.: Higher-Order Mixfix Syntax for Representing Mathematical Notation and its Parsing. PhD thesis, ETH Zürich (1997)

Norell, U.: Towards a practical programming language based on dependent type theory. PhD thesis, Chalmers University of Technology and Göteborg University (2007)

Norvig, P.: Techniques for automatic memoization with applications to context-free parsing. Computational Linguistics 17(1), 91–98 (1991)

Odersky, M.: The Scala Language Specification, Version 2.7. Programming Methods Laboratory, EPFL, Switzerland. Draft (2009)

Paulson, L.C., Nipkow, T., Wenzel, M.: The Isabelle Reference Manual (2008)

Pettersson, M., Fritzson, P.: A general and practical approach to concrete syntax objects within ML. In: Proceedings of the ACM SIGPLAN Workshop on ML and its Applications (1992)

Peyton Jones, S. (ed.): Haskell 98 Language and Libraries: The Revised Report. Cambridge University Press, Cambridge (2003)

Peyton Jones, S.L.: Parsing distfix operators. Communications of the ACM 29(2), 118–122 (1986)

Sterling, L., Shapiro, E.: The Art of Prolog, 2nd edn., Advanced Programming Techniques. MIT Press, Cambridge (1994)

Wadler, P.: How to replace failure by a list of successes; a method for exception handling, backtracking, and pattern matching in lazy functional languages. In: Jouannaud, J.-P. (ed.) FPCA 1985. LNCS, vol. 201, pp. 113–128. Springer, Heidelberg (1985)

Wansbrough, K.: Macros and preprocessing in Haskell, unpublished manuscript (1999)

Descriptor-Free Representation of Arrays with Dependent Types

Kai Trojahner[1] and Clemens Grelck[2,3]

[1] Institute of Software Technology and Programming Languages
University of Lübeck, Germany
trojahner@isp.uni-luebeck.de
[2] Institute of Informatics
University of Amsterdam, Netherlands
c.grelck@uva.nl
[3] School of Computer Science
University of Hertfordshire, United Kingdom
c.grelck@herts.ac.uk

Abstract. Besides element type and values, a multidimensional array is characterized by the number of axes (rank) and their respective lengths (shape vector). Both properties are essential for bounds checking and to compute linear offsets into heap memory at run time. In order to have an array's rank and shape available at any time during program execution, both are typically kept in an array descriptor that is maintained at run time in addition to the array itself.

In this paper, we propose a different approach: we treat array rank and shape as first-class citizens themselves. Firstly, we use dependent types to reflect structural properties of arrays in the type system. Secondly, we annotate a program with the explicit array properties wherever necessary. This choice not only renders implicit run time array descriptors obsolete, but exposing all rank and shape computations explicitly in intermediate code also allows us to perform extensive compile time optimisation on them. We have implemented the proposed approach in our experimental array language Qube; preliminary experimental results indicate the suitability of the proposed approach.

1 Introduction

Multidimensional arrays as found in APL [1], MATLAB [2], and SAC[3,4] are, apart from the data they contain, characterized by two properties: a *rank* scalar and a *shape vector*. An array's rank denotes the array's number of axes. Its shape vector contains the array's extent along each axis. Thus, for any given array, the length of its shape vector equals its rank.

Array ranks and shape vectors are essential for the evaluation of shape-generic array programs: when we select the element $A_{i,j}$ from a matrix $A : \mathbb{R}^{m \times n}$ stored in row-major order, the offset into the linear memory representation of A is $i * n + j$. Both extents m and n are necessary to check whether the indices i and j range within the array boundaries. In general, not even array rank is a compile

S.-B. Scholz and O. Chitil (Eds.): IFL 2008, LNCS 5836, pp. 100–117, 2011.

time constant. If so, both bound checking and offset computation require to loop over the shape vector and the index vector.

To provide rank and shape vector whenever necessary, language implementations usually associate each array with its respective properties at run time. For example, one-dimensional arrays may be represented as pairs of the form $\langle l, [d_1, ..., d_l] \rangle$ where l denotes the array's length. To the programmer, an array appears as an abstract data type, providing means for obtaining array length and (safely) accessing individual elements. Extending this scheme to truly multidimensional arrays yields tuples $\langle r, [s_1, ..., s_r], [d_1, ..., d_p] \rangle$ where r denotes the rank and $[s_1, ..., s_r]$ the shape vector. As as data type invariant, $p = \Pi_{i=1}^{r} s_i$ must hold for all arrays.

While a descriptor-based run time representation of arrays is intuitive, the information in the descriptors is often redundant. We observe that array programs typically contain relationships between ranks, shapes, and elements of different arrays. For example, the shape-generic function **add** takes two arrays of arbitrary but identical shape and yields yet another array of that shape. The result contains the element-wise sum of the arguments.

```
add a b = gen x < (shape a) with (a.[x] + b.[x]);
```

Through the descriptors of **a** and **b**, rank and shape are passed to the operation twice and returned once more into the calling context through yet another descriptor. Moreover, the expression **shape a** queries the shape vector of **a**: the shape vector is copied from the implicit descriptor of **a** into a newly allocated array whose descriptor merely contains the rank of **a**. As the value of **shape a** is used to specify the shape of the result of **add**, its elements are copied again into the function result's descriptor.

To eliminate such redundancies, we propose a descriptor-free evaluation scheme for multidimensional arrays. The key idea is to use dependent types to capture the array properties symbolically at compile time. We use this information to statically annotate intermediate code with terms representing array properties wherever they are required. Any operation in the intermediate code that needs an array's rank or shape vector is extended to accept this information explicitly through additional arguments. An expression that originally evaluated to an array/descriptor combination, may then evaluate to a mere vector that contains the array's elements. Through this transformation, we emancipate ranks and shape vectors, which are now first-class arrays themselves.

Once all structural properties of arrays and their relationships are represented explicitly in intermediate code, they become subject to program optimisation. For example, dead code removal eliminates superfluous computations of and on structural properties. Likewise, common subexpression elimination avoids repeated computation of identical structural information. Constant folding, algebraic simplification and strength reduction contribute their share to optimise computations on structural array properties.

We have implemented the proposed descriptor-free run time representation of arrays in our functional array language Qube [5]. In essence, Qube is an experimental offspring of the generic functional array language SAC [6]. Unlike SAC,

Qube employs a type system with dependent types to provide static guarantees for the successful evaluation of array programs. Beyond rendering dynamic checks obsolete, the combination of dependent types and the descriptor-free run time representation of arrays, is a particularly fruitful one. Dependent array types allow us to express relationships between the ranks and shapes of argument and result arrays of functions explicitly. It is this information in particular that triggers optimisation both within individual function definitions and across function applications. As a consequence, we can often substantially reduce the number of explicit shape and rank values compared to the number of implicit descriptors in a conventional setting.

The remainder of this paper is organized as follows: Section 2 introduces the basic concepts of Qube by means of a core language; we assign a static semantics to the core language by defining the essential typing rules in Section 3. The dependent types are then used in Section 4 to annotate the program with rank and shape information wherever this information will be required at run time. In Section 5, we define an operational semantics for the annotated language that does not require dynamically looking up array properties. We quantify the impact of our approach by means of a custom benchmark in Section 6. In Section 7, we describe related work in the field before we conclude the paper in Section 8.

2   Array Programming Basics

For our presentation, we define a core language that enhances the λ-calculus with essential array programming features. Figure 1 shows the syntax and an operational semantics of the core language. In addition to the usual variables, λ-abstractions and function applications, the language provides means for array creation, array inspection and some vector arithmetic. The core language employs a call-by-value evaluation regime, i.e. the evaluation of nested expressions always starts with the leftmost-innermost (closed) subexpression.

In the array programming paradigm all values are arrays. Each array is characterized by its *rank* denoting the array's number of axes and a *shape vector* that describes the length of each axis. For example, a vector [1 2 3] has rank 1 and shape [3]; a scalar value, such as 23, has rank 0 and shape [] (the empty vector).

Array values have the form $[|\, q^p \,|\, [s^d]\, |]$ [1] with $p = \text{prod}(s^d)$. The integer vector $[s^d]$ is called the *array descriptor*. It serves as a run time representation of the shape vector. In our notation, the length d of s^d implicitly encodes the array rank. A computing machine, however, must explicitly encode d in some way. The *data vector* q^p contains the array elements in row-major order as a sequence of *quarks*. These are shapeless entities and may thus only occur inside of arrays. Quarks may be primitive values such as the integers c, abstractions $\lambda x.\, t$ mapping arrays to arrays, and tuples of arrays (not discussed in this paper). To ease the notation of scalars, we define $c \equiv [|\, c \,|\, []\, |]$ and $\lambda x.\, t \equiv [|\, \lambda x.\, t \,|\, []\, |]$.

---

[1] We use the notation a^n to denote a sequence $a_1, .., a_n$.

Both the data vector and the array descriptor are essential for the evaluation of array programs. E.g. an application $t\,t'$ can only be reduced according to rule E-APP if t is a scalar array that contains a single λ-abstraction.

The built-in functions $\mathtt{dim}(t)$ and $\mathtt{shape}(t)$ yield the rank and shape vector of t by inspecting the descriptor of their evaluated argument. Similarly, $\mathtt{length}(t)$, if applied to a vector, yields its length as a scalar. The selection $\mathtt{sel}(t_1,t_2)$ obtains the element of t_1 that is located at the position t_2. Evaluating the selection requires that the length of the index vector t_2 equals the rank of t_1 and that t_2 denotes a position inside of t_1. The function $\iota(d, s^d, i^d)$ computes the linear offset of the index vector i^d into the data vector of an array of rank d and shape s^d.

Integer vectors have special significance in array programming as they serve as both index and shape vectors. When t_l is a non-negative integer, $\mathtt{vec}(t_l,t)$ evaluates to a vector of length t_l that contains the scalar t at each index. $\mathtt{cat}(t_1,t_2)$ appends a vector t_2 to a vector t_1. Conversely, vectors are split by the operations $\mathtt{take}$ and $\mathtt{drop}$. For a given vector t of length m and an integer t_n with $0 \le t_n \le m$, $\mathtt{take}(t_n,t)$ and $\mathtt{drop}(t_n,t)$ yield the prefix of t of length t_n and the suffix of t of length $m - n$, respectively.

Linear binary operations such as $+$, $-$, etc. may be applied to both pairs of scalars and pairs of equally sized integer vectors. Thereby, $\tilde{f}$ represents the operation denoted by the symbol f.

The array constructor $[t^p \,|\, [f^d]]$ with $\forall i.f_i > 0$, $p = \mathtt{prod}(f^d)$, and thus $p > 0$ creates a new array of *frame shape* f^d by evaluating the *cell expressions* t_j. When all cells evaluate to arrays of identical shape c^r, the new array's descriptor is $\mathtt{cat}(f^d,c^r)$. Its data vector is the concatenation of the cells' individual elements. For example

$$[\,[|\,1,2\,|\,[2]\,|], \,[|\,1,2\,|\,[2]\,|]\,|\,[2]\,] \;\to\; [|\,1,2,3,4\,|\,[2,2]\,|]$$

An array constructor cannot specify arrays without cells: although an array may not contain any quarks, the descriptor suffix c^r would be unknown.

Arrays with a statically unknown frame shape may be specified using the WITH-loop, an array comprehension inherited from SAC. When t_{fs} evaluates to a positive integer vector, an expression $\mathtt{gen}\; x < t_{fs}\; \mathtt{with}\; t_c$ evaluates to an array constructor of frame shape t_{fs}. The WITH-loop binds the *index vector* x that may appear free in the *cell expression* t_c. Each cell is computed by instantiating t_c such that x is replaced by a vector that denotes the cell's location inside the frame. Using the WITH-loop, we can for example map a function f to an arbitrarily shaped array a:

$$\mathtt{gen}\; x < \mathtt{shape}(a)\; \mathtt{with}\; (f\; \mathtt{sel}(a,x))$$

Note that this specification is not total as a may be an empty array, i.e. its shape vector contains at least one zero, in which case the with-loop evaluates to an ill-formed array constructor without cells.

In this section, we have specified an untyped core language for functional array programming. Each array is represented by both its elements and a descriptor, a run time data structure that describes the array's rank and shape. Descriptors

Syntax

$t ::= [\![\,q^* \,|\, [c^*]\,]\!] \mid x \mid t\,t \mid f(t^+) \mid [\![\,t^+ \,|\, [c^*]\,]\!] \mid \mathtt{gen}\ x < t\ \mathtt{with}\ t$ Terms

$q ::= c \mid \lambda x.\,t$ Quarks

$f ::= \mathtt{dim} \mid \mathtt{shape} \mid \mathtt{length} \mid \mathtt{sel} \mid \vec{f} \mid f_2$ Built-ins

$\vec{f} ::= \mathtt{vec} \mid \mathtt{cat} \mid \mathtt{take} \mid \mathtt{drop}$ Vector ops

$f_2 ::= + \mid - \mid \ldots$ Binary ops

$v ::= [\![\,q^* \,|\, [c^*]\,]\!]$ Array values

Evaluation

$$\frac{t_1 \to t_1'}{t_1\,t_2 \to t_1'\,t_2}\ (\text{E-App1}) \qquad \frac{t_2 \to t_2'}{v_1\,t_2 \to v_1\,t_2'}\ (\text{E-App1})$$

$$[\![\,\lambda x : T.t \,|\, [\,]\,]\!]\ v \to t[x \mapsto v]\ (\text{E-App})$$

$$\frac{t_1 \to t_1'}{f(t_1) \to f(t_1')}\ (\text{E-F1})$$

$$\mathtt{dim}([\![\,q^p \,|\, [c^d]\,]\!]) \to [\![\,d \,|\, [\,]\,]\!]\ (\text{E-Dim})$$

$$\mathtt{shape}([\![\,q^p \,|\, [c^d]\,]\!]) \to [\![\,c^d \,|\, [d]\,]\!]\ (\text{E-Shp})$$

$$\mathtt{length}([\![\,q^n \,|\, [n]\,]\!]) \to [\![\,n \,|\, [\,]\,]\!]\ (\text{E-Len})$$

$$\frac{t_1 \to t_1'}{f(t_1, t_2) \to f(t_1', t_2)}\ (\text{E-F21}) \qquad \frac{t_2 \to t_2'}{f(v_1, t_2) \to f(v_1, t_2')}\ (\text{E-F22})$$

$$\frac{\forall k.\,0 \le i_k < s_k}{\mathtt{sel}([\![\,q^p \,|\, [s^d]\,]\!], [\![\,i^d \,|\, [d]\,]\!]) \to [\![\,q_{\iota(d,s^d,i^d)} \,|\, [\,]\,]\!]}\ (\text{E-Sel})$$

$$\frac{0 \le c_l}{\mathtt{vec}([\![\,c_l \,|\, [\,]\,]\!], [\![\,c \,|\, [\,]\,]\!]) \to [\![\,c, \ldots, c \,|\, [c_l]\,]\!]}\ (\text{E-Vec})$$

$$\frac{0 \le c \le n}{\mathtt{take}([\![\,c \,|\, [\,]\,]\!], [\![\,q^n \,|\, [n]\,]\!]) \to [\![\,q_1, \ldots, q_c \,|\, [c]\,]\!]}\ (\text{E-Take})$$

$$\frac{0 \le c \le n}{\mathtt{drop}([\![\,c \,|\, [\,]\,]\!], [\![\,q^n \,|\, [n]\,]\!]) \to [\![\,q_{c+1}, \ldots, q_n \,|\, [n-c]\,]\!]}\ (\text{E-Drop})$$

$$\mathtt{cat}([\![\,c^m \,|\, [m]\,]\!], [\![\,c'^n \,|\, [n]\,]\!]) \to [\![\,c^m, c'^n \,|\, \mathtt{vec}(t, m\hat{+}n)\,]\!]\ (\text{E-Cat})$$

$$f_2(([\![\,c \,|\, [\,]\,]\!], [\![\,c' \,|\, [\,]\,]\!])) \to [\![\,\tilde{f}_2(c, c') \,|\, [\,]\,]\!]\ (\text{E-Bin})$$

$$f_2(([\![\,c^n \,|\, [n]\,]\!], [\![\,c'^n \,|\, [n]\,]\!])) \to [\![\,\tilde{f}_2(c_1, c_1'), .., \tilde{f}_2(c_n, c_n') \,|\, [n]\,]\!]\ (\text{E-VBin})$$

$$\frac{t_i \to t_i'}{[\![\,t^{i-1}, t_i, t^{p-i} \,|\, [f^d]\,]\!] \to [\![\,t^{i-1}, t_i', t^{p-i} \,|\, [f^d]\,]\!]}\ (\text{E-ArrC})$$

$$[\![\,[\![\,q_1^p \,|\, [c^r]\,]\!], \ldots, [\![\,q_n^p \,|\, [c^r]\,]\!] \,|\, [f^d]\,]\!] \to [\![\,q_1^p, .., q_n^p \,|\, [f^d, c^r]\,]\!]\ (\text{E-Arr})$$

$$\frac{t \to t'}{\mathtt{gen}\ x < t\ \mathtt{with}\ t_c \to \mathtt{gen}\ x < t'\ \mathtt{with}\ t_c}\ (\text{E-GenF})$$

$$\frac{\forall k.\,f_k > 0 \qquad \forall y^d \in \vec{0}..f^d.\ t_{\iota(d,f^d,y^d)} = t_c[x \mapsto [\![\,y^d \,|\, [d]\,]\!]]}{\mathtt{gen}\ x < [\![\,f^d \,|\, [d]\,]\!]\ \mathtt{with}\ t_c \to [\![\,t^p \,|\, [f^d]\,]\!]}\ (\text{E-Gen})$$

Fig. 1. A core language for functional array programming

$$
\begin{array}{lll}
I ::= \texttt{idx} \mid \texttt{idxvec}\ i \mid \{I\ \texttt{in}\ ir\} & & \text{Index sorts} \\
i ::= c \mid x \mid [i^n] \mid \vec{f}(i,i) \mid f_2(i,i) & & \text{Index terms} \\
ir ::= i \mid i.. \mid ..i \mid i..i & & \text{Index ranges} \\[4pt]
T ::= [Q\,|\,t] \mid \texttt{num}\ i \mid \texttt{numvec}\ t\ i & & \text{Array types} \\
Q ::= \bot_Q \mid \texttt{int} \mid S \rightarrow T & & \text{Quark types} \\
S ::= T \mid x :: I \mid x : \texttt{num}\ [\texttt{in}\ ir] \mid x : \texttt{numvec}\ t\ [\texttt{in}\ ir] & & \text{Domain types} \\[4pt]
t ::= ... \mid t\ '\,i & & \text{Terms} \\
q ::= ... \mid \lambda s.\,t & & \text{Quarks} \\
s ::= x : T \mid x :: I \mid x : \texttt{num}\ [\texttt{in}\ ir] \mid x : \texttt{numvec}\ t\ [\texttt{in}\ ir] & & \text{Binders}
\end{array}
$$

Fig. 2. Dependent array types for the core language

are in two ways essential for the evaluation of array programs: First, they are required to check whether a term satisfies the necessary preconditions for further evaluation. Second, they are relevant for computing the result of an evaluation step. Nonetheless, we aim at representing arrays without descriptors.

3 Types

The focus of this paper lies on harnessing type information to evaluate array programs without descriptors. Therefore, our presentation of the type system concentrates on how to gather and represent the necessary information and guarantee orderly evaluation. For a more thorough treatment of the type system, see [5].

Our approach for eliminating run time descriptors relies on extensive use of compile time information about the arrays. We use dependent types to represent not only the element type of an array, but also the array's rank and its shape vector. In the presence of unbounded recursion, type checking of a programming language with dependent types is undecidable [7]. To make type checking decidable, our approach resembles an *indexed type system* [8,9] that only allows types to depend on compile time terms of a specific index language, on which constraints may be resolved statically.

We intend to annotate our programs with the rank and shape information from the array types. This rules out standard indexed types as the indices are only available at compile time. Therefore, we index our family of array types with proper language terms. However, these terms must be of a *singleton type*, i.e. the value of the expression describing an array's shape must be associated with a compile time index. This way, we may put run time terms into programs wherever shape and rank information is required. Yet, we may statically reason about array ranks, shape vectors, and even values by means of a constraint solver.

Fig. 2 shows the extensions we make to the core language. Our index language consists of integer scalars of sort `idx` and integer vectors which belong to a member of the sort family `idxvec` i where i denotes the vector length. Index terms may be variables, integers, vectors of scalars and linear operations applied to index terms. Index vectors may also be formed using the structural operations `vec`, `take`, `drop`, and `cat`. Index sorts can be restricted to specific ranges using the subset notation $\{I \text{ in } ir\}$. A range $a\mathinner{.\,.}b$ denotes all x for which $a \leq x < b$. Both boundaries may be omitted, indicating $\pm\infty$ as the boundaries. Sort checking is decidable if the structural operations allow us to statically decompose structured vectors into atomic vector fragments [5].

The singleton type `num` i characterizes scalar integers whose value is denoted by the index term i. Similarly, the type `numvec` t_l i describes specific integer vectors where t_l is a non-negative `num`. More generally, $[Q\,|\,t]$ is the type of all arrays whose elements have quark type Q and whose shape vector is characterized by the non-negative `numvec` t. By means of subtyping, each `num` i is also an `[int|[]]` and a `numvec` t i is also an `[int|[t]]`.

The bottom quark type is a subtype of all quark types. It serves as a quark type for empty arrays like the empty vector `[| | [0] |]` with type `[⊥Q | [0]]`. Populated arrays may contain primitive data such as integers and functions. Regular functions of type $T \rightarrow T$ map arrays to arrays, whereas the type $x :: I \rightarrow T$ allows us to specify functions whose result type depends on an index. Additionally, functions may depend on singleton arguments: the type $x : \text{num in } ir \rightarrow T$ simultaneously binds an index x in the range ir and a value of type `num` x.

The basic typing rules for quarks and terms are summarized in Fig. 3. Note that through subtyping quarks and terms have multiple types [5].

The type rule T-VAL for non-empty array values $[|\,q^p\,|\,[s^d]\,|]$ checks that each quark q_i has the same quark type Q. For an empty array value without quarks, no precise quark type can be determined. For this reason, rule T-VALE assigns it the bottom quark type $\perp_Q$, which is a subtype of any quark type. In addition to their array types, constant integer scalars and vectors also have more specific constant singleton types according to the rules T-NUM, T-NUMVEC.

The rules T-APP, T-IAPP, T-NAPP, and T-VAPP ensure that only scalar arrays of (dependent) functions can be applied to suitable arguments. The result type of a dependent function application is obtained by replacing occurrences of the bound variable in the co-domain with the concrete argument.

Typing of the array specific operations is shown in Fig. 4. The `dim` and `shape` primitives can be applied to arbitrary arrays and yield singleton types. `length` is only applicable to singleton vectors and yields a scalar singleton. The typing rule T-SEL statically enforces all the necessary preconditions of the selection: the selection vector must be a singleton vector with appropriate length that ranges within the boundaries of the array selected into. A (valid) selection always yields a scalar array but never a singleton.

The vector operations `vec`, `cat`, `take`, and `drop` require appropriate singleton arguments and yield a singleton vector whose index is formed in the same way. Three rules are used to type applications of binary operations: they may be

$$\Gamma \vdash c :_Q \textbf{int} \ (\text{QT-I{\scriptsize NT}})$$

$$\frac{\Gamma,\ x : T_1 \vdash t : T_2}{\Gamma \vdash \lambda x : T_1.t :_Q T_1 \rightarrow T_2} \ (\text{QT-A{\scriptsize BS}})$$

$$\frac{\Gamma,\ x :: I \vdash t : T}{\Gamma \vdash \lambda x :: I.t :_Q x :: I \rightarrow T} \ (\text{QT-IA{\scriptsize BS}})$$

$$\frac{\Gamma,\ x :: \{\textbf{idx in } ir\},\ x : \textbf{num } x \vdash t : T}{\Gamma \vdash \lambda x : \textbf{num in } ir.t :_Q x : \textbf{num in } ir \rightarrow T} \ (\text{QT-NA{\scriptsize BS}})$$

$$\frac{\Gamma \vdash t_l : \textbf{num } i_l \qquad \Gamma,\ x :: \{\textbf{idxvec } i_l \textbf{ in } ir\},\ x : \textbf{numvec } t_l \ x \vdash t : T}{\Gamma \vdash \lambda x : \textbf{numvec } t_l \textbf{ in } ir.t :_Q x : \textbf{numvec } t_l \textbf{ in } ir \rightarrow T} \ (\text{QT-VA{\scriptsize BS}})$$

$$\frac{x : T \in \Gamma}{\Gamma \vdash x : T} \ (\text{T-C{\scriptsize TX}})$$

$$\frac{n > 0 \qquad \forall j.\ \Gamma \vdash q_j :_Q Q}{\Gamma \vdash [\![q^n \mid [s^d] \,]\!] : [Q \mid [s^d]]} \ (\text{T-V{\scriptsize AL}})$$

$$\Gamma \vdash [\![\, \mid [s^d] \,]\!] : [\bot_Q \mid [s^d]] \ (\text{T-V{\scriptsize ALE}})$$

$$\Gamma \vdash [\![c \mid [] \,]\!] : \textbf{num } c \ (\text{T-N{\scriptsize UM}})$$

$$\Gamma \vdash [\![c^n \mid [n] \,]\!] : \textbf{numvec } n \ [c^n] \ (\text{T-N{\scriptsize UMVEC}})$$

$$\frac{\Gamma \vdash t_1 : [T_1 \rightarrow T_2 \mid []] \qquad \Gamma \vdash t_2 : T_1}{\Gamma \vdash t_1 \ t_2 : T_2} \ (\text{T-A{\scriptsize PP}})$$

$$\frac{\Gamma \vdash t : [x :: I \rightarrow T \mid []] \qquad \Gamma \vdash i :: I}{\Gamma \vdash t \ 'i : T[x \mapsto_i i]} \ (\text{T-IA{\scriptsize PP}})$$

$$\frac{\Gamma \vdash t_1 : [x : \textbf{num in } ir \rightarrow T \mid []] \quad \Gamma \vdash t_2 : \textbf{num } i_2 \quad \Gamma \vdash i_2 :: \{\textbf{idx in } ir\}}{\Gamma \vdash t_1 \ t_2 : T[x \mapsto_i i_2][x \mapsto t_2]} \ (\text{T-NA{\scriptsize PP}})$$

$$\frac{\begin{array}{c}\Gamma \vdash t_1 : [x : \textbf{numvec } t_{l1} \textbf{ in } ir \rightarrow T \mid []] \qquad \Gamma \vdash t_{l1} : \textbf{num } i_{l1} \\ \Gamma \vdash t_2 : \textbf{numvec } t_{l1} \ i_2 \qquad \Gamma \vdash i_2 :: \{\textbf{idxvec } i_{l1} \textbf{ in } ir\}\end{array}}{\Gamma \vdash t_1 \ t_2 : T[x \mapsto_i i_2][x \mapsto t_2]} \ (\text{T-VA{\scriptsize PP}})$$

Fig. 3. Basic typing rules

applied to integer scalars (T-B{\scriptsize IN}), yielding another array of the same element type and shape. More interestingly, when applied to (compatible) singletons (T-B{\scriptsize INS}, T-B{\scriptsize INV}), the result is also a singleton whose index is characterized by the application of the operation to the original singletons' indices.

An array constructor with frame shape $[c^n]$ is well-typed if all cells have the same quark type Q and the same shape t_s. The new array then has type $[Q \mid \texttt{cat}([c^n], t_s)]$. In the special case where all cells of a vector are singleton

$$\frac{\Gamma \vdash t : [Q\,|\,t_s] \qquad \Gamma \vdash t_s : \mathtt{numvec}\ t_d\ i_s \qquad \Gamma \vdash t_d : \mathtt{num}\ i_d}{\Gamma \vdash \mathtt{dim}(t) : \mathtt{num}\ i_d} \ \text{(T-Dim)}$$

$$\frac{\Gamma \vdash t : [Q\,|\,t_s] \qquad \Gamma \vdash t_s : \mathtt{numvec}\ t_d\ i_s}{\Gamma \vdash \mathtt{shape}(t) : \mathtt{numvec}\ t_d\ i_s} \ \text{(T-Shape)}$$

$$\frac{\Gamma \vdash t : \mathtt{numvec}\ t_l\ i \qquad \Gamma \vdash t_l : \mathtt{num}\ i_l}{\Gamma \vdash \mathtt{length}(t) : \mathtt{num}\ i_l} \ \text{(T-Length)}$$

$$\frac{\begin{array}{c}\Gamma \vdash t : [Q\,|\,t_s] \qquad \Gamma \vdash t_s : \mathtt{numvec}\ t_d\ i_s \qquad \Gamma \vdash i_d : \mathtt{num}\ i_d \\ \Gamma \vdash t_i : \mathtt{numvec}\ t_d\ i_i \qquad \Gamma \vdash i_i :: \{\mathtt{idxvec}\ i_d\ \mathtt{in}\ \mathtt{vec}(i_d,0)\,..\,i_s\}\end{array}}{\Gamma \vdash \mathtt{sel}(t,t_i) : [Q\,|\,[\,]]} \ \text{(T-Sel)}$$

$$\frac{\Gamma \vdash t_l : \mathtt{num}\ i_l \qquad \Gamma \vdash i_l :: \{\mathtt{idx}\ \mathtt{in}\ 0\,..\} \qquad \Gamma \vdash t : \mathtt{num}\ i}{\Gamma \vdash \mathtt{vec}(t_l,t) : \mathtt{numvec}\ t_l\ (\mathtt{vec}(i_l,i))} \ \text{(T-Vec)}$$

$$\frac{\Gamma \vdash t_1 : \mathtt{numvec}\ t_{l1}\ i_1 \qquad \Gamma \vdash t_2 : \mathtt{numvec}\ t_{l2}\ i_2}{\Gamma \vdash \mathtt{cat}(t_1,t_2) : \mathtt{numvec}\ (t_{l1} + t_{l2})\ (\mathtt{cat}(i_1,i_2))} \ \text{(T-Cat)}$$

$$\frac{\Gamma \vdash t_1 : \mathtt{num}\ i_1 \qquad \Gamma \vdash t_2 : \mathtt{numvec}\ t_{l2}\ i_2 \qquad \Gamma \vdash i_1 :: \{\mathtt{idx}\ \mathtt{in}\ 0\,..\,i_{l2} + 1\}}{\Gamma \vdash \mathtt{take}(t_1,t_2) : \mathtt{numvec}\ t_1\ (\mathtt{take}(i_1,i_2))} \ \text{(T-Take)}$$

$$\frac{\Gamma \vdash t_1 : \mathtt{num}\ i_1 \qquad \Gamma \vdash t_2 : \mathtt{numvec}\ t_{l2}\ i_2 \qquad \Gamma \vdash i_1 :: \{\mathtt{idx}\ \mathtt{in}\ 0\,..\,i_{l2} + 1\}}{\Gamma \vdash \mathtt{drop}(t_1,t_2) : \mathtt{numvec}\ (t_{l2} - t_1)\ (\mathtt{drop}(i_1,i_2))} \ \text{(T-Drop)}$$

$$\frac{\Gamma \vdash t_1 : [\mathtt{int}\,|\,[\,]] \qquad \Gamma \vdash t_2 : [\mathtt{int}\,|\,[\,]]}{\Gamma \vdash f_2(t_1,t_2) : [\mathtt{int}\,|\,[\,]]} \ \text{(T-Bin)}$$

$$\frac{\Gamma \vdash t_1 : \mathtt{num}\ i_1 \qquad \Gamma \vdash t_2 : \mathtt{num}\ i_2}{\Gamma \vdash f_2(t_1,t_2) : \mathtt{num}\ (f_2(i_1,i_2))} \ \text{(T-BinS)}$$

$$\frac{\Gamma \vdash t_1 : [\mathtt{int}\,|\,[\,]] \qquad \Gamma \vdash t_2 : [\mathtt{int}\,|\,[\,]]}{\Gamma \vdash f_2(t_1,t_2) : [\mathtt{int}\,|\,[\,]]} \ \text{(T-Bin)}$$

$$\frac{\Gamma \vdash t_1 : \mathtt{numvec}\ t_{l1}\ i_1 \qquad \Gamma \vdash t_2 : \mathtt{numvec}\ t_{l1}\ i_2}{\Gamma \vdash f_2(t_1,t_2) : \mathtt{numvec}\ t_{l1}\ (f_2(i_1,i_2))} \ \text{(T-BinV)}$$

$$\frac{\forall j.\ \Gamma \vdash t_j : [Q\,|\,t_s]}{\Gamma \vdash [t^p\,|\,[c^n]] : [Q\,|\,\mathtt{cat}([c^n],t_s)]} \ \text{(T-Arr)}$$

$$\frac{\forall j.\ \Gamma \vdash t_j : \mathtt{num}\ i_j}{\Gamma \vdash [t^n\,|\,[n]] : \mathtt{numvec}\ n\ [i^n]} \ \text{(T-ArrNumvec)}$$

$$\frac{\begin{array}{c}\Gamma \vdash t_{fs} : \mathtt{numvec}\ t_{fd}\ i_{fs} \qquad \Gamma \vdash t_{fd} : \mathtt{num}\ i_{fd} \\ \Gamma \vdash i_{fs} :: \{\mathtt{idxvec}\ i_{fd}\ \mathtt{in}\ \mathtt{vec}(i_{fd},0)\,..\} \qquad x \notin \mathcal{FREE}([Q\,|\,t_{cs}]) \\ \Gamma, x :: \{\mathtt{idxvec}\ i_{fd}\ \mathtt{in}\ \mathtt{vec}(i_{fd},0)\,..\,i_{fs}\}, x : \mathtt{numvec}\ t_{fd} \vdash t_c : [Q\,|\,t_{cs}]\end{array}}{\Gamma \vdash \mathtt{gen}\ x < t_{fs}\ \mathtt{with}\ t_c : [Q\,|\,\mathtt{cat}(t_{fs},t_{cs})]} \ \text{(T-Gen)}$$

Fig. 4. Typing rules for array specific language elements

scalars, rule T-ARRNUMVEC gives the array the appropriate singleton vector type. The typing rule T-GEN for the WITH-loop gen $x < t_{fs}$ with t_c verifies that the frame shape t_{fs} is a non-negative vector. For checking the cell expression t_c, the identifier x is bound to both a vector sort that ranges between zero and the frame shape and a singleton vector with exactly that value. If the cell expression then has type $[Q|t_{cs}]$, then the WITH-loop has type $[Q|\mathtt{cat}(t_{fs},t_{cs})]$. The type rule allows WITH-loops with empty frame shapes as these will be enabled by the modified semantics in Section 6.

Type checking rules out all programs that may not satisfy the constraints on ranks, shape vectors, and array values inherent to array programs. Program evaluation may thus entirely dispense with dynamic checks of these constraints. Still, array descriptors are required whenever array properties determine the evaluation result.

4   Array Properties on Demand

By definition, the type of an array $[Q|t_s]$ encodes both the array's quark type Q and its shape vector t_s. As t_s must be a $\mathtt{numvec}$ t_d , its length t_d also denotes the array's rank. Thus, both rank and shape vector are symbolically known at compile time. We annotate the program with these terms wherever array properties will be required for program evaluation. In Section 5 we will define an operational semantics that takes the annotations into account. Ultimately, this allows us to entirely eliminate array descriptors.

Fig. 5 shows the relation $\rightarrow_C$ for statically annotating array programs with the array properties that will be required at run time. The rules are applied exhaustively throughout the program. By virtue of type checking, the premises hold for every well-typed program. They are only required to match the desired type patterns.

The evaluation of function applications and scalar operations does not require any array properties.

The operations $\mathtt{dim}(t)$, $\mathtt{shape}(t)$, and $\mathtt{length}(t)$ yield array properties for which terms may be directly derived from the type of t. Instead of replacing the entire expressions, we merely extend the argument lists in order to maintain the call-by-value semantics. The selection $\mathtt{sel}(t,t_{iv})$ requires both the rank t_d and the shape vector t_s of t to compute the offset into the data vector of t through $\iota(t_d, t_s, t_{iv})$.

The vector construction $\mathtt{vec}(t_l,t)$ and prefix operation $\mathtt{take}(t_l,t)$ do not require additional information at run time as the result lengths are given by the argument t_l itself. However, computing the suffix of a vector with $\mathtt{drop}(t_d,t)$ also requires the length of t. The concatenation operation $\mathtt{cat}(t_1,t_2)$ needs to knokw the lengths of both argument vectors. In contrast, the arguments of well-typed linear vector arithmetic operations must have the same length; we thus only annotate the length of the first vector.

The size of an array defined by an array constructor $[t^p | [c^d]]$ depends on both the static frame shape $[c^d]$ and the size of the array cells. The size of an

$$\frac{t : [Q\,|\,t_s] \qquad t_s : \text{numvec } t_d\ i_s}{\text{dim}(t) \ \rightarrow_C \ \text{dim}(t, t_d)} \ (\text{C-Dim})$$

$$\frac{t : [Q\,|\,t_s]}{\text{shape}(t) \ \rightarrow_C \ \text{shape}(t, t_s)} \ (\text{C-Shape})$$

$$\frac{t : \text{numvec } t_l\ i}{\text{length}(t) \ \rightarrow_C \ \text{length}(t, t_l)} \ (\text{C-Length})$$

$$\frac{t_1 : [Q\,|\,t_{s1}] \qquad t_1 : \text{numvec } t_{d1}\ i_{s1}}{\text{sel}(t_1, t_2) \ \rightarrow_C \ \text{sel}(t_1, t_2, t_{d1}, t_{s1})} \ (\text{C-Sel})$$

$$\frac{t_1 : \text{numvec } t_{l1}\ i_1 \qquad t_2 : \text{numvec } t_{l2}\ i_2}{\text{cat}(t_1, t_2) \ \rightarrow_C \ \text{cat}(t_1, t_2, t_{l1}, t_{l2})} \ (\text{C-Cat})$$

$$\frac{t_2 : \text{numvec } t_{l2}\ i_2}{\text{drop}(t_1, t_2) \ \rightarrow_C \ \text{drop}(t_1, t_2, t_{l2})} \ (\text{C-Drop})$$

$$\frac{t_1 : \text{numvec } t_{l1}\ i_1}{f_2(t_1, t_2) \ \rightarrow_C \ f_2(t_1, t_2, t_{l1})} \ (\text{C-BinV})$$

$$\frac{t_1 : [Q\,|\,t_{1s}] \qquad t_{1s} : \text{numvec } t_{1d}\ i_1}{[t^p\,|\,[c^n]] \ \rightarrow_C \ [t^p\,|\,[c^n]\ \text{of}\ t_{1s}(t_{1d})]} \ (\text{C-Arr})$$

$$\frac{t_{fs} : \text{numvec } t_{fd}\ i_{fs} \qquad t_c : [Q\,|\,t_{cs}] \qquad t_{cs} : \text{numvec } t_{cd}\ i_{cs}}{\text{gen } x < t_{fs} \text{ with } t_c \ \rightarrow_C \ \text{gen } x < t_{fs}(t_{fd}) \text{ of } t_{cs}(t_{cd}) \text{ with } t_c} \ (\text{C-Gen})$$

Fig. 5. Static annotation of the required array properties

array cell is the product of its shape vector. Since all cells must have the same rank and shape, we annotate the constructor with the first cell's rank and shape vector. For the same reason, a WITH-loop $\text{gen } x < t_s$ with t_c is annotated rank and shape vector of the cell expression t_c. As the WITH-loop's frame shape t_s is a vector expression, we also annotate its length.

5   Evaluation of Annotated Array Programs

In this section, we redefine the evaluation relation $\rightarrow$ for well-typed programs such that it uses the property annotations instead of dynamically accessing array descriptors. No dynamic checks are performed as potential run time errors have been ruled out by means of type checking. Fig. 6 shows the modified semantics. We underline the descriptor in an array value $[\![\,q^p\,|\,\underline{[s^d]}\,]\!]$ to indicate that it is a mere compile time attribute that is required for type checking. At run time however, no descriptor will be built.

$$[|\lambda x : T.t|\,\underline{[]}\,|]\ v\ \to\ t[x \mapsto v] \quad \text{(E-APP)}$$

$$[|\lambda x :: I.t|\,\underline{[]}\,|]\ 'i\ \to\ t[x \mapsto_i i] \quad \text{(E-IAPP)}$$

$$[|\lambda x : \mathbf{num}.t|\,\underline{[]}\,|]\ [|c|\,\underline{[]}\,|]\ \to\ t[x \mapsto_i c][x \mapsto [|c|\,\underline{[]}\,|]] \quad \text{(E-NAPP)}$$

$$[|\lambda x : \mathbf{numvec}\ t_l.t|\,\underline{[]}\,|]\ [|c_1,...,c_n|\,\underline{[n]}\,|]$$
$$\to\ t[x \mapsto_i [c_1,...,c_n]][x \mapsto [|c_1,...,c_n|\,\underline{[n]}\,|]] \quad \text{(E-VAPP)}$$

$$\mathbf{dim}(v, v_d)\ \to\ v_d \quad \text{(E-DIM)}$$

$$\mathbf{shape}(v, v_s)\ \to\ v_s \quad \text{(E-SHAPE)}$$

$$\mathbf{length}(v, v_l)\ \to\ v_l \quad \text{(E-LENGTH)}$$

$$\mathbf{sel}(v, v_i, [|c_d|\,\underline{[]}\,|], v_s)\ \to\ [|v_{\iota(c_d, v_s, v_i)}|\,\underline{[]}\,|] \quad \text{(E-SEL)}$$

$$\mathbf{vec}([|c_l|\,\underline{[]}\,|], [|c|\,\underline{[]}\,|])\ \to\ [|\underbrace{c,...,c}_{c_l}|\,\underline{[c_l]}\,|] \quad \text{(E-VEC)}$$

$$\mathbf{cat}(v, w, [|c_v|\,\underline{[]}\,|], [|c_w|\,\underline{[]}\,|])\ \to\ [|v_1,...,v_{c_v}, w_1,...,w_{c_w}|\,\underline{[c_v \hat{+} c_w]}\,|] \quad \text{(E-CAT)}$$

$$\mathbf{take}([|c_t|\,\underline{[]}\,|], v)\ \to\ [|v_1,...,v_{c_t}|\,\underline{[c_t]}\,|] \quad \text{(E-TAKE)}$$

$$\mathbf{drop}([|c_d|\,\underline{[]}\,|], v, [|c_l|\,\underline{[]}\,|])\ \to\ [|v_{c_d+1},...,v_{c_l}|\,\underline{[c_l \hat{-} c_d]}\,|] \quad \text{(E-DROP)}$$

$$f_2([|c_1|\,\underline{[]}\,|], [|c_2|\,\underline{[]}\,|])\ \to\ [|\hat{f_2}(c_1, c_2)|\,\underline{[]}\,|] \quad \text{(E-BINS)}$$

$$f_2(v, w, [|c_l|\,\underline{[]}\,|])\ \to\ [|\hat{f_2}(v_1, w_1),...,\hat{f_2}(v_{c_l}, w_{c_l})|\,\underline{[c_l]}\,|] \quad \text{(E-BINV)}$$

$$[v^p\,|\,[c^n]\ \text{of}\ v_s([|c_d|\,\underline{[]}\,|])]\ \to\ [|v_1^1,..,v_s^1,...,v_p^1,...,v_s^s|\,\underline{[c^n, v_s^1,...,v_s^{cd}]}\,|] \quad \text{(E-ARR)}$$
$$\text{where}\ s = \Pi_{i=1}^{cd} v_s^i$$

$$\frac{\exists k.\ fs_k = 0}{\mathbf{gen}\ x < [|fs^{fd}|\,\underline{[fd]}\,|]\,(fd)\ \text{of}\ cs(cd)\ \text{with}\ t_c\ \to\ [|\ |\,\underline{[fs^{fd}, cs^{cd}]}\,|]} \quad \text{(E-GENE)}$$

$$\frac{\forall k.\ fs_k > 0 \qquad \forall y^{fd} \in \vec{0}..fs^{fd}.\ t_{\iota(fd, fs^{fd}, y^{fd})} = t_c[x \mapsto_i [y^{fd}]][x \mapsto [y^{fd}]]}{\mathbf{gen}\ x < [|fs^{fd}|\,\underline{[fd]}\,|]\,(fd)\ \text{of}\ cs(cd)\ \text{with}\ t_c\ \to\ [t^p\,|\,[fs^{fd}]\ \text{of}\ cs(cd)]} \quad \text{(E-GEN)}$$

Fig. 6. Descriptor-free evaluation of well-typed programs with property annotations

Evaluation of function applications does not require any array properties. The array inspection operations dim, shape, and length have been annotated with terms denoting the sought array properties. They evaluate directly to their second argument, ignoring the inspected array.

The selection blindly fetches the indexed element from the data vector as out-of-bounds accesses cannot occur and the relevant information for computing the linear offset is available. The modified evaluation of the vector operations is similarly straightforward.

Annotated array constructors evaluate to an array value whose size is determined by the static frame shape and the dynamic cell shape vector cs of length cd. All cells will evaluate to arrays of that shape. Thus, the new data vector is formed by copying $\mathbf{prod}(cs)$ quarks from each cell array.

The evaluation rule E-Gen for the with-loop is adjusted to the typed, annotated setting. The substitution of the index vector in the cell expression now takes type indices into account and the annotated cell shape is transcribed to the resulting array constructor. More interestingly, the additional evaluation rule E-GenE specifies that annotated with-loops with empty frame shape are evaluated to empty array values with an appropriate (compile time) descriptor. Hence, we may use with-loops to define arbitrary shape-generic operations even if the frame shape is empty.

6   Experimental Evaluation

We have implemented the proposed descriptor-free evaluation of array programs in our functional array language Qube. Essentially, Qube is an experimental offspring of SaC [6] with a notation similar to that of Haskell. We use Qube to explore how dependent array types can be harnessed to compile verified shape-generic programs into efficient, data-parallel code.

6.1   Implementation

Our language implementation compiles Qube programs into C code, which in turn is compiled into natively executable code using any standard C compiler. The implementation is currently limited to first order functions. For efficiency, we use two array representations: scalars are held on the C run time stack or in registers depending on the C compiler, whereas the data vectors of non-scalar arrays are always allocated on the heap. Automatic memory management relies on the Boehm-Dehmers-Weiser conservative garbage collector [10]. In the future, we would like to replace it with a memory management scheme based on reference counting, since this would allow us to safely perform destructive array updates in our context of immutable arrays [11]. Our compiler performs basic program optimisations, e.g. dead code elimination, constant folding, common subexpression elimination. Furthermore, it avoids the costly creation of with-loop index vectors and index computations as described in [12]. The measurements were performed on an Apple Mac$_{mini}$ with an Intel Core Duo 2 clocked at 2GHz with 4MB L2 Cache and 2GB of RAM. We use GCC version 4.2 as a back-end compiler.

6.2   A Custom Benchmark

Array descriptors add an overhead to each array. To quantify the precise effect of descriptor-free evaluation, we use a custom micro benchmark.

```
add : d : num in 0.. -> s : numvec d in vec(d,0).. ->
      [int|s] -> [int|s] -> [int|s];
add d s a b = gen x < shape a with a.[x] + b.[x];
```

```
void add__0( int d__1, int *s__1, int *a__0, int *b__0, int **add__1) {
  int   flat__5;
  int *flat__7__0;
  int   x__idx__0;
  int   flat__0;
  int   flat__1;
  int   flat__2;

  {
    int i__0;
    flat__5 = 1;
    for (i__0 = 0; i__0 < d__1; i__0++) {
      flat__5 = (flat__5 * s__1[i__0]);
    }
  }

  flat__7__0 = GC_malloc_atomic_ignore_off_page(flat__5 * sizeof(int));

  for (x__idx__0 = 0; x__idx__0 < flat__5; x__idx__0++) {
    flat__0 = b__0[x__idx__0];
    flat__1 = a__0[x__idx__0];
    flat__2 = (flat__0 + flat__1);
    flat__7__0[x__idx__0] = flat__2;
  }
  *add__1 = flat__7__0;
}
```

Fig. 7. The compiled C program for shape-generic array addition

The rank-generic function **add** adds the elements of two equally shaped integer arrays and returns the result. Fig. 7 shows the compiled **Qube** program. It calculates the size of the new array, allocated memory and computes the result with virtually no overhead. To simulate the behaviour outlined in Section 2, we annotated the C program with array descriptors. The modified program thus keeps separate rank scalars and shape vectors for each array. It also has to compute **shape a** by creating a new array that mirrors the shape vector of a. In both programs, scalar arrays are represented as primitive C values. Moreover, both neither perform dynamic constraint checks such as array bounds checks nor index vector computations.

We use **add** to iterate the addition of two matrices of varying size $N \times N$ such that the overall number of scalar additions is roughly $2 * 10^9$. Fig. 8 shows the run time results. The descriptor-free program performs substantially better than the descriptor-based program for small arrays sizes. For matrices larger than 32×32, the overhead of descriptor maintenance becomes less significant and virtually vanishes for arrays larger than 1024×1024. The running times are dominated by memory management: a modified version of the descriptor-free program that destructively updates the first argument performs clearly superior.

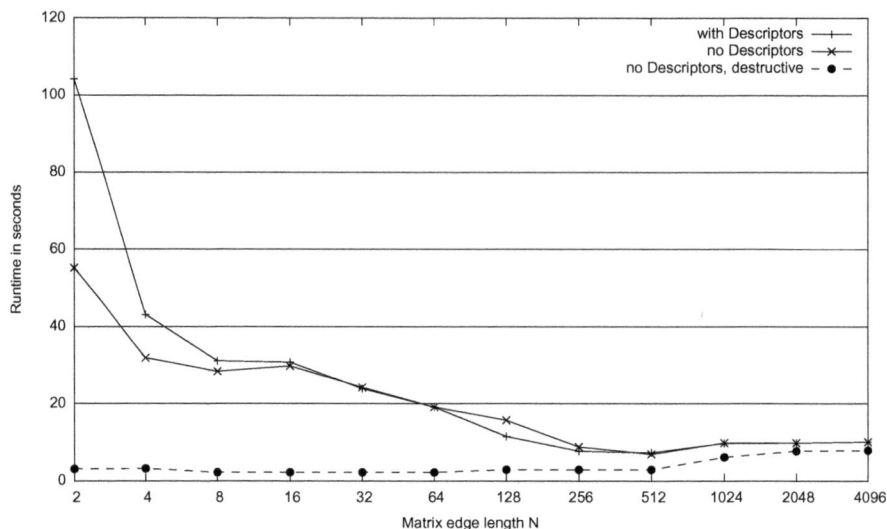

Fig. 8. Run time measurements for $2^{31} \approx 2*10^9$ integer additions organized as element-wise array additions for varying array sizes

Execution times increase for all tested programs once the argument and result arrays become too big for the processor's L2 Cache.

7   Related Work

Many array languages like MATLAB [2], APL [13,1], J [14] or NIAL [15] are interpreted and untyped. These languages are known for offering a plethora of well optimised operators for each array operation supported by the language. They rely on the ability to dynamically access array properties via some form of descriptor.

Static knowledge about the array properties is crucial for compiling array programs into efficient executables. For example in FISH [16], each function f is accompanied by a shape function #f which maps the shape of the argument to the shape of the result. Shape inference proceeds by first inlining all functions and then statically evaluating all shape functions. FISH rejects all programs that contain non-constant array shapes.

The array language SAC uses different types [3] for arrays of statically known shape (e.g. int[10,10]), arrays of statically known rank (but unknown shape) (e.g. int[.,.]), and arrays of unknown rank and shape (e.g. int[*]). A compilation scheme for shape-generic SAC programs has been devised that takes the array types into account to avoid creating run time descriptors whenever possible [17]. To improve the static shape information, the SAC compiler uses a combination of partial evaluation and function specialisation [18]. Recently, we proposed *symbolic array attributes* as a uniform scheme to infer and represent structural information in shape-generic array programs such that it may be used by optimisations [19].

Light-weight dependently typed languages such as Xi and Pfenning's DML [9], Xi's *Applied Type System* [20], and Zenger's *indexed types* [8] are also related to our approach. These allow term-indexing into type families only by means of compile time index terms. As such, these indices cannot replace run time descriptors. In contrast, AGDA [21] and EPIGRAM [22] support types that depend on arbitrary terms but offer no particular support for shape-generic array programming. In his thesis [25], Brady showed how the rich type information in EPIGRAM programs may be used for the compilation into efficient G-machine code. More recently, Swierstra and Altenkirch proposed an AGDA library for specifying locality aware algorithms over distributed arrays [24]. The YNOT project aims at combining dependently typed programming systems with effects [23].

8   Conclusion and Future Work

In this paper, we have proposed a new method for evaluating array programs without annotating arrays with a run time descriptor. Dependent types allow us to represent an expression's rank and shape in the type system. We use this information to statically annotate an intermediate program with array properties wherever these are required for evaluation. Evaluation rules that take the annotations into account entirely dispense with the need for array descriptors. In addition, type checking renders dynamic constraint checks such as array bounds checks superfluous. The compiled programs thus contain very little overhead. Preliminary run time measurements indicate that descriptor-free evaluation can positively influence run time performance, especially when a program deals with many small arrays.

In the future, we would like to further develop the Qube compiler and implement more complex programs to demonstrate our approach. The existing results indicate that a memory management scheme based on reference counting will benefit the evaluation efficiency as it would allow us to often perform array updates destructively. Our general aim is to use the information present in the array types to aggressively optimise array programs. Ultimately, this will allow us to generate more efficient array programs both for sequential and parallel execution.

Acknowledgments. We would like to thank Florian Büther and Markus Weigel for their contributions to implementing Qube. Moreover, we thank Walter Dosch for many interesting discussions on the topic, and last not least the anonymous reviewers for their helpful comments on the draft version of this paper.

References

1. Falkoff, A., Iverson, K.: The Design of APL. IBM Journal of Research and Development 17(4), 324–334 (1973)
2. Moler, C., Little, J., Bangert, S.: Pro-Matlab User's Guide. The MathWorks, Cochituate Place, 24 Prime Park Way, Natick, MA, USA (1987)

3. Scholz, S.B.: Single Assignment C — Efficient Support for High-Level Array Operations in a Functional Setting. Journal of Functional Programming 13(6), 1005–1059 (2003)
4. Grelck, C.: Shared Memory Multiprocessor Support for Functional Array Processing in SAC. Journal of Functional Programming 15(3), 353–401 (2005)
5. Trojahner, K., Grelck, C.: Dependently Typed Array Programs Don't Go Wrong. Technical Report A-08-06, Schriftenreihe der Institute für Informatik/Mathematik University of Lübeck, Lübeck, Germany (2008)
6. Grelck, C., Scholz, S.B.: SAC: A Functional Array Language for Efficient Multithreaded Execution. International Journal of Parallel Programming 34(4), 383–427 (2006)
7. Barthe, G., Coquand, T.: An introduction to dependent type theory. In: Barthe, G., Dybjer, P., Pinto, L., Saraiva, J. (eds.) APPSEM 2000. LNCS, vol. 2395, pp. 1–41. Springer, Heidelberg (2002)
8. Zenger, C.: Indexed Types. Theoretical Computer Science 187(1-2), 147–165 (1997)
9. Xi, H., Pfenning, F.: Eliminating array bound checking through dependent types. In: Proceedings of ACM SIGPLAN Conference on Programming Language Design and Implementation, Montreal, pp. 249–257 (1998)
10. Boehm, H., Demers, A., Shenker, S.: Mostly parallel garbage collection. In: Proceedings of the ACM SIGPLAN 1991 Conference on Programming Languages Design and Implementation. ACM SIGPLAN Notices, vol. 26, pp. 157–164. ACM, New York (1991)
11. Grelck, C., Trojahner, K.: Implicit Memory Management for SAC. In: Grelck, C., Huch, F. (eds.) Proceedings of the 16th International Workshop on Implementation and Application of Functional Languages, IFL, Lübeck, Germany, September 8-10. Technical Report, vol. 0408, pp. 335–348. University of Kiel (2004)
12. Bernecky, R., Herhut, S., Scholz, S.-B., Trojahner, K., Grelck, C., Shafarenko, A.: Index Vector Elimination – Making Index Vectors Affordable. In: Horváth, Z., Zsók, V., Butterfield, A. (eds.) IFL 2006. LNCS, vol. 4449, pp. 19–36. Springer, Heidelberg (2007)
13. Iverson, K.: A Programming Language. John Wiley, New York City (1962)
14. Iverson, K.: J. Introduction and Dictionary. Iverson Software Inc., Toronto (1995)
15. Jenkins, M.: Q'Nial: A Portable Interpreter for the Nested Interactive Array Language Nial. Software Practice and Experience 19(2), 111–126 (1989)
16. Jay, C.B., Steckler, P.A.: The Functional Imperative: Shape! In: Hankin, C. (ed.) ESOP 1998. LNCS, vol. 1381, pp. 139–153. Springer, Heidelberg (1998)
17. Kreye, D.: A Compilation Scheme for a Hierarchy of Array Types. In: Arts, T., Mohnen, M. (eds.) IFL 2002. LNCS, vol. 2312, pp. 18–35. Springer, Heidelberg (2002)
18. Grelck, C., Scholz, S.-B., Shafarenko, A.: A Binding Scope Analysis for Generic Programs on Arrays. In: Butterfield, A., Grelck, C., Huch, F. (eds.) IFL 2005. LNCS, vol. 4015, pp. 212–230. Springer, Heidelberg (2006)
19. Trojahner, K., Grelck, C., Scholz, S.-B.: On optimising shape-generic array programs using symbolic structural information. In: Horváth, Z., Zsók, V., Butterfield, A. (eds.) IFL 2006. LNCS, vol. 4449, pp. 1–18. Springer, Heidelberg (2007)
20. Xi, H.: Applied Type System (extended abstract). In: Berardi, S., Coppo, M., Damiani, F. (eds.) TYPES 2003. LNCS, vol. 3085, pp. 394–408. Springer, Heidelberg (2004)

21. Norell, U.: Towards a practical programming language based on dependent type theory. PhD thesis. PhD thesis, Chalmers University of Technology, Göteborg, Sweden (2007)
22. McBride, C.: Epigram: Practical programming with dependent types. In: Advanced Functional Programming, pp. 130–170 (2004)
23. Nanevski, A., Morrisett, G., Birkedal, L.: Polymorphism and Separation in Hoare Type Theory. In: International Conference on Functional Programming, pp. 62–73. ACM Press, New York (2006)
24. Swierstra, W., Altenkirch, T.: Dependent types for distributed arrays. In: Achten, P., Koopman, P., Morazán, M. (eds.) Trends in Functional Programming, vol. 9. Intellect Books (2008)
25. Brady, E.: Practical Implementation of a Dependently Typed Functional Programming Language. PhD thesis, Department of Computer Science, University of Durham, Durham, UK (2005)

Collected Size Semantics
for Functional Programs over Lists*

Olha Shkaravska, Marko van Eekelen, and Alejandro Tamalet

Institute for Computing and Information Sciences
Radboud University Nijmegen

Abstract. This work introduces collected size semantics of strict functional programs over lists. The collected size semantics of a function definition is a multivalued size function that collects the dependencies between every possible output size and the corresponding input sizes. Such functions annotate standard types and are defined by conditional rewriting rules generated during type inference.

We focus on the connection between the rewriting rules and lower and upper bounds on the multivalued size functions, when the bounds are given by piecewise polynomials. We show how, given a set of conditional rewriting rules, one can infer bounds that define an indexed family of polynomials that approximates the multivalued size function.

Using collected size semantics we are able to infer non-monotonic and non-linear lower and upper polynomial bounds for many functional programs. As a feasibility study, we use the procedure to infer lower and upper polynomial size-bounds on typical functions of a list library.

1 Introduction

Estimating heap consumption is an active research area as it becomes more and more of an issue in many applications, e.g. distributed computing and programming for small devices like smart cards, mobile phones or embedded systems.

This work explores typing support for checking output-on-input size dependencies for function definitions (functions for short) in a strict functional language. Knowing lower and upper bounds of these dependencies one can apply *amortisation* [12] to check and infer tight non-linear bounds on heap consumption [17]. Size dependencies are presented via *multivalued size functions* defined by conditional multiple-choice rewriting rules generated during type inference. These functions are used to annotate types. Since one is mostly interested in lower and upper bounds for size functions, we establish connections between the rewriting rules and size bounds. We focus on piecewise polynomial bounds, i.e., bounds that can be described by a finite number of polynomials. Given a set of conditional multiple-choice rewriting rules, we show how to infer lower and upper bounds that define an indexed family of polynomials. Such a family fully

---

* This work is part of the AHA project [17] which is sponsored by the Netherlands Organisation for Scientific Research (NWO) under grant nr. 612.063.511.

S.-B. Scholz and O. Chitil (Eds.): IFL 2008, LNCS 5836, pp. 118–137, 2011.

covers the size function induced by the rewriting rules in the sense that for each input, there is a polynomial in the family that describes the size of the output.

We work with strict functions over *matrix-like* lists of lists, i.e., every nested list must have the same length. (It is possible to omit this restriction by allowing higher-order size functions. This is a subject of our nearest-future work.) We allow higher-order functions only when the size of the output depends just on zero-order arguments.

This work continues a series of papers where we have studied output-on-input polynomial size dependencies, in which the polynomials are not necessary monotonic. In [15] we designed a type system where each type is annotated with a single polynomial size expression. It allows to type function definitions where the size of the output depends on the sizes of the inputs, but not on their values. For instance, append: $L_n(\alpha) \times L_m(\alpha) \rightarrow L_{n+m}(\alpha)$, whereas delete (which deletes, from a list, the first occurrence of an element if it exists) does not have a type in that system since it may or may not delete an element. We also developed a test-based annotation inference procedure for that system in [18].

To get a global idea of the results of this paper, consider again the function delete. Its collected size semantics can be expressed by the multivalued function $f_{\text{delete}}(n) = \{n, \max_0(n-1)\}$, with $\max_0(n) = \max(0, n)$, where n denotes the length of the input list. Our type system allows to express and infer such multi-valued size functions in the form of rewriting rules. For instance, $\vdash f_{\text{delete}}(0) \rightarrow 0$ and $n \geq 1 \vdash f_{\text{delete}}(n) \rightarrow n-1 \mid 1 + f_{\text{delete}}(n-1)$, where "$\vdash$" denotes a logical entailment and "$\mid$" denotes "multiple-choice rewriting". However, a user often prefers to deal with size functions in *closed form*, i.e. without recursion, like $f(n) = \{n, \max_0(n-1)\}$, or with their lower and upper bounds. The problem of obtaining closed forms for rewriting rules does not have a general solution. We study how to approximate a closed-form solution with an indexed family of piecewise polynomials, if such an approximation exists. For f_{delete} we can infer the family $\{\max_0(n-i)\}_{0 \leq i \leq 1}$, which precisely describes it.

Let $\bar{n}$ denote a vector of variables of the form $(n_1, \ldots, n_k)$. The inference procedure is based on the well-known fact that a polynomial p of degree d is defined by a finite number of points of the form $\{(\bar{n}_i, p(\bar{n}_i))\}_{i=0}^{d}$, that determine a system of linear equations w.r.t. the polynomial coefficients. It takes the following parameters: the *degree* d of polynomial lower and upper bounds of the size function, an *initial point* $\bar{n}^0$ and a *step* to obtain the next point. Using these parameters, the procedure generates the points lying on the bounds. For instance, for delete, we choose degree 1, initial point $n^0 = 1$ and step 1. Then the procedure generates the test points $\bar{n}^i$. In the example it generates $n^0 = 1$, $n^1 = 2$. Next, the rewriting rules are used to calculate the sets $f(\bar{n}^i)$. For delete we obtain $f(n^0) = \{0, 1\}$ and $f(n^1) = \{1, 2\}$. The procedure picks up the minimal and maximal values from each of the set $f(\bar{n}^i)$ and computes the coefficients of the lower and upper polynomial bounds as the solutions of two corresponding linear systems. In the example, the lower bound $p_{\min}(n) = n - 1$ is computed from the nodes $\{(1, 0), (2, 1)\}$, and the upper bound $p_{\max}(n) = n$

from $\{(1, 1), (2, 2)\}$. The obtained bounds $p_{\min}$ and $p_{\max}$ define an indexed family of polynomials, which may be presented, for instance, as $\{p_{\min}(\overline{n}) + i\}_{i=0}^{\delta(\overline{n})}$, where $\delta(\overline{n}) = p_{\max}(\overline{n}) - p_{\min}(\overline{n})$. The procedure depends on user-defined parameters (an initial point, a step, a degree). The consequences of a bad choice of parameters is that the bound will not be tight or they may even be incorrect. Checking if a given indexed family of polynomials approximates a given function is shown to be similar to type checking types annotated with indexed families of polynomials [14].

The rest of this paper is organised as follows. In Section 2 we define the programming language and in Section 3 its size-aware type system. Section 3 also defines the semantics of program values w.r.t. zero-order types and the operational semantics of the language. We give an inference procedure for families of polynomials that approximate multivalued size functions and discuss examples in Section 4. In Section 5 we discuss the feasibility of applying the analysis to a typical list library. Related work is discussed in Section 6. Section 7 draws conclusions and gives directions to future work. The technical report [13] gives more examples of checking and inference in detail.

2   Language

The type system is designed for a strict functional language over integers and (polymorphic) lists. Algebraic data types could be added as we did in [16]. Language expressions are defined by the following grammar:

$Basic\ b ::= c \mid$ unop x $\mid$ x binop y $\mid$ Nil $\mid$ Cons(z, l) $\mid$ f($g_1, \ldots, g_l, z_1, \ldots, z_k$)
$Expr\ e ::= b \mid$ if x then e_1 else e_2
  $\mid$ let z $= b$ in e_1
  $\mid$ match l with $\mid$ Nil $\Rightarrow e_1$
          $\mid$ Cons(z_{hd}, l_{tl}) $\Rightarrow e_2$
  $\mid$ letfun f($g_1, \ldots, g_l, z_1, \ldots, z_k$) $= e_1$ in e_2

where c ranges over integer and boolean constants False and True, x and y denote program variables of integer and boolean types, l ranges over lists, z denotes a program variable of zero-order type, g ranges over higher-order program variables, unop is a unary operation, either $-$ or $\neg$, binop is one of the integer or boolean binary operations, and f denotes a function name. Variables may be decorated with sub- and superscripts.

The syntax distinguishes between zero-order let-binding of variables and higher-order letfun-binding of functions. In a function body, the only free program variables are its parameters. We prohibit head-nested let-expressions and restrict subexpressions in function calls to variables to make type checking straightforward. Program expressions of a general form may be equivalently transformed into expressions of this form. We consider this language as an intermediate language where a more user friendly language may be compiled into.

3   Type System

We consider a type system constituted from zero-order and higher-order types and typing rules corresponding to program constructs. Size annotations are multivalued numerical functions $f \colon \mathcal{R}^k \to 2^{\mathcal{R}}$ that represent lengths of finite lists and arithmetic operations over these lengths. $\mathcal{R}$ can be any numerical ring; its choice influences decidability of type checking and the set of well-typed programs.

Zero-order types are assigned to program values, which are integers, booleans and finite lists. The list type is annotated by a multivalued size function:

$$Types \; \tau ::= \mathsf{Int} \mid \mathsf{Bool} \mid \alpha \mid \mathsf{L}_{f(\overline{n})}(\tau),$$

where α is a type variable and $\overline{n}$ is a collection of size variables. The multivalued size functions f in our type system are defined by conditional rewriting rules. For example, consider a function insert that inserts an element z into a list l if and only if there is no element in l related to z by g.

insert(g, z, l) =
  match l with | Nil $\Rightarrow$ let l' = Nil in Cons(z, l')
               | Cons(hd, tl) $\Rightarrow$ if g(z, hd) then l else
                                    let l'' = insert(g, z, tl) in Cons(hd, l'')

The corresponding size rewriting system is

$$\vdash f_{\mathsf{insert}}(0) \to 1$$
$$n \geq 1 \vdash f_{\mathsf{insert}}(n) \to \; n \mid 1 + f_{\mathsf{insert}}(n-1)$$

The type of insert is $(\alpha \times \alpha \to \mathsf{Bool}) \times \alpha \times \mathsf{L}_n(\alpha) \to \mathsf{L}_{f_{\mathsf{insert}}(n)}(\alpha)$. It is desirable to find closed forms for functions defined by such rewriting rules. In this work we are interested in the cases where closed-form solutions (or approximations of the solutions) are definable as indexed families of piecewise polynomials. For instance, a closed-form solution for f_{insert} is $\{n+i\}_{0 \leq i \leq 1}$.

The sets $TV(\tau)$ and $SV(\tau)$ of type and size variables of a type τ are defined inductively in the obvious way. Note that $SV(\mathsf{L}_0(\tau)) = \emptyset$, since all empty lists of the same underlying type represent the same data structure. For instance, $\mathsf{L}_0(\mathsf{L}_m(\mathsf{Int}))$ represent the same structure as $\mathsf{L}_0(\mathsf{L}_0(\mathsf{Int}))$.

Zero-order types without type variables and size variables are *ground types*:

$$Ground \, Types \; \tau^{\bullet} ::= \tau \text{ such that } SV(\tau) = \emptyset \wedge TV(\tau) = \emptyset$$

The semantics of ground types is defined in Section 3.1. Here we give some examples: Int, $\mathsf{L}_5(\mathsf{Bool})$, $\mathsf{L}_{f_{\mathsf{insert}}(2)}(\mathsf{Bool})$ with $\mathcal{R} = \mathsf{Int}$ are ground types, whereas α, $\mathsf{L}_{n+5}(\mathsf{Int})$ and $\mathsf{L}_{f_{\mathsf{insert}}(n)}(\mathsf{Bool})$ with non-specified n are not. Examples of inhabitants of ground types are [True, True] and [False, True, True] for $\mathsf{L}_{f_{\mathsf{insert}}(2)}(\mathsf{Bool})$.

Let τ° denote a zero-order type where size expressions are all size variables or constants, like, e.g., $\mathsf{L}_n(\alpha)$. Function types are then defined inductively:

$$Function \, Types \quad \tau^f ::= \tau_1^f \times \ldots \times \tau_{k'}^f \times \tau_1^{\circ} \times \ldots \times \tau_k^{\circ} \to \tau_0$$

where k' may be zero (i.e. the list $\tau_1^f, \ldots, \tau_{k'}^f$ is empty) and $SV(\tau_0)$ contains only size variables of $\tau_1^{\circ}, \ldots, \tau_k^{\circ}$. Consider, for instance, the function definition for filter : $(\alpha \to \mathsf{Bool}) \times \mathsf{L}_n(\alpha) \to \mathsf{L}_{f_{\mathsf{filter}}(n)}(\alpha)$

filter(g, l) =
  match l with | Nil ⇒ Nil
             | Cons(hd, tl) ⇒ if g(hd) then let l' = filter(g, tl) in Cons(hd, l')
                             else filter(g, tl)

The size function f_{filter} is defined by

$$\vdash f_{\text{filter}}(0) = 0$$
$$n \geq 1 \vdash f_{\text{filter}}(n) = 1 + f_{\text{filter}}(n-1) \mid f_{\text{filter}}(n-1)$$

The closed-form solution for f_{filter} is $\{i\}_{0 \leq i \leq n}$.

A context Γ is a mapping from zero-order variables to zero-order types. A signature Σ is a mapping from function names to function types. The definition of $SV(-)$ is straightforwardly extended to contexts:

$$SV(\Gamma) = \bigcup_{z \in dom(\Gamma)} SV(\Gamma(z))$$

3.1   Semantics of Zero-order Types

In our semantic model, the purpose of the heap is to store lists. Therefore, a heap is a finite collection of locations ℓ that can store list elements. A location is the address of a cons-cell consisting of a head field hd, which stores a list element, and a tail field tl, which contains the location of the next cons-cell of the list, or the NULL address. Formally, a program value is either an integer or boolean constant, a location or the null-address and a heap is a finite partial mapping from locations and fields into program values:

$$
\begin{array}{llll}
Address & \mathbf{adr} ::= \ell \mid \text{NULL} & \ell \in Loc \\
Val & v \quad ::= c \mid \mathbf{adr} & c \in \text{Int} \cup \text{Bool} \\
Heap & h \quad : \quad Loc \rightharpoonup \{hd, tl\} \rightharpoonup Val
\end{array}
$$

We will write $h.\ell.hd$ and $h.\ell.tl$ for the results of applications $h\,\ell\,hd$ and $h\,\ell\,tl$, which denote the values stored in the heap h at the location ℓ at its fields hd and tl, respectively. Let $h.\ell.[hd := v_h, \ tl := v_t]$ denote the heap equal to h everywhere but in ℓ, which at the hd-field of ℓ gets the value v_h and at the tl-field of ℓ gets the value v_t.

The semantics w of a program value v with respect to a specific heap h and a *ground type* $\tau^{\bullet}$ is a set-theoretic interpretation given via the four-place relation $v \models_{\tau^{\bullet}}^{h} w$. Integer and boolean constants interpret themselves, and locations are interpreted as non-cyclic lists:

$$
\begin{array}{ll}
c & \models_{\text{Int} \cup \text{Bool}}^{h} c \\
\text{NULL} & \models_{\mathsf{L}_{f(\overline{n}_0)}(\tau^{\bullet})}^{h} [\,] \quad \textit{iff} \ 0 \in f(\overline{n}_0) \\
\ell & \models_{\mathsf{L}_{f(\overline{n}_0)}(\tau^{\bullet})}^{h} w_{hd} :: w_{tl} \ \textit{iff} \ \ell \in dom(h), \\
& \qquad\qquad h.\ell.hd \models_{\tau^{\bullet}}^{h|_{dom(h)\setminus\{\ell\}}} w_{hd}, \\
& \qquad\qquad h.\ell.tl \models_{\mathsf{L}_{f(\overline{n}_0)-1}(\tau^{\bullet})}^{h|_{dom(h)\setminus\{\ell\}}} w_{tl}
\end{array}
$$

where $h|_{dom(h)\setminus\{\ell\}}$ denotes the heap equal to h everywhere except in ℓ, where it is undefined.

It is easy to establish a natural connection between the size functions in a ground list type and the length of a chain of cons-cells that "implements" its inhabitant in a heap. The length is defined by the function:

$$length : Heap \rightharpoonup Address \rightharpoonup \mathcal{N}$$
$$length_h(\text{NULL}) = 0 \qquad length_h(\ell) = 1 + length_{h|_{dom(h) \setminus \{\ell\}}}(h.\ell.tl)$$

Note that the function $length_h(-)$ does not take sharing into account, in the sense that the actual total size of allocated shared lists is less than the sum of their lengths. Thus, the sum of the lengths of the lists provides an upper bound on the amount of memory actually allocated.

Lemma 1 (Consistency of model relation)
   The relation $\text{adr} \models^h_{L_{f(\overline{n}_0)}(\tau\bullet)} w$ *implies that* $length_h(\text{adr}) \in f(\overline{n}_0)$.

The proof is done by induction on the relation $\models$.

3.2   Operational Semantics of Program Expressions

The operational semantics is standard. It extends the semantics from [15] with higher-order functions.

   We introduce a *frame store* as a mapping from program variables to program values. This mapping is maintained when a function body is evaluated. Before evaluation of the function body starts, the store contains only the actual parameters of the function. During evaluation, the store is extended with the variables introduced by pattern matching or let-constructs. These variables are eventually bound to the actual parameters. Thus there is no access beyond the current frame. Formally, a frame store s is a finite partial map from variables to values, *Store* $s: ProgramVars \rightharpoonup Val$.

   Using heaps and a frame store and maintaining a mapping $\mathcal{C}$ of *closures*, from function names to the bodies of the function definitions, the operational semantics of program expressions is defined inductively in the usual way. Here we give some of the rules as examples. The full operational semantics may be found in the technical report [13].

$$\frac{c \in \text{Int} \cup \text{Bool}}{s;\, h;\, \mathcal{C} \vdash c \rightsquigarrow c;\, h} \text{ OSConst} \qquad \frac{}{s;\, h;\, \mathcal{C} \vdash z \rightsquigarrow s(z);\, h} \text{ OSVar}$$

$$\frac{h.s(\mathsf{l}).hd = v_{hd} \qquad h.s(\mathsf{l}).tl = v_{tl} \qquad s[\mathsf{hd} := v_{hd}, \mathsf{tl} := v_{tl}];\, h;\, \mathcal{C} \vdash e_2 \rightsquigarrow v;\, h'}{s;\, h;\, \mathcal{C} \vdash \text{match } \mathsf{l} \text{ with } |\text{ Nil} \Rightarrow e_1 \qquad \rightsquigarrow v;\, h' \qquad\qquad |\text{ Cons(hd, tl)} \Rightarrow e_2} \text{ OSMatch-Cons}$$

3.3   Typing Rules

A typing judgement is a relation of the form $D, \Gamma \vdash_\Sigma e : \tau$. Informally, it means that with the set of constraints D in the zero-order variable context Γ the expression e has type τ where the signature Σ contains type assumptions for all

124   O. Shkaravska, M. van Eekelen, and A. Tamalet

called functions. The set D of disequations and inclusions is relevant only when a rule for pattern-matching is applied. When the nil-branch is entered on a list $\mathsf{L}_{f(\overline{n})}(\alpha)$, then D is extended with $0 \in f(\overline{n})$. When the cons-branch is entered, then D is extended with $n' \geq 1$, $n' \in f(\overline{n})$, where n' is a fresh size variable in D.

Given types $\tau = \mathsf{L}_{f_1(\overline{n})}(\ldots \mathsf{L}_{f_k(\overline{n})}(\alpha) \ldots)$ and $\tau' = \mathsf{L}_{f_1'(\overline{n})}(\ldots \mathsf{L}_{f_k'(\overline{n})}(\alpha) \ldots)$, let the entailment $D \vdash \tau \to \tau'$ abbreviate the collection of rules that (conditionally) rewrite $f_i(\overline{n})$ to $f_i'(\overline{n})$:

$$D \vdash f_1(\overline{n}) \to f_1'(\overline{n})$$
if there exists a positive value in $f_1'(\overline{n})$ then $\quad D \vdash f_2(\overline{n}) \to f_2'(\overline{n})$
if there exist positive values in $f_1'(\overline{n})$, $f_2'(\overline{n})$ then $\quad D \vdash f_3(\overline{n}) \to f_3'(\overline{n})$
...

if there exist positive values in $f_1'(\overline{n}), \ldots, f_{k-1}'(\overline{n})$ then $D \vdash f_k(\overline{n}) \to f_k'(\overline{n})$

For instance, the entailment $n \geq 2 \vdash \mathsf{L}_{f_1(n)}(\mathsf{L}_{f_2(n)}(\alpha)) \to \mathsf{L}_{n-1}(\mathsf{L}_{n^2}(\alpha))$ abbreviates the rules $n \geq 2 \vdash f_1(n) \to n - 1$ and $n \geq 2 \vdash f_2(n) \to n^2$. However, the entailment $n = 1 \vdash \mathsf{L}_{f_1(n)}(\mathsf{L}_{f_2(n)}(\alpha)) \to \mathsf{L}_{n-1}(\mathsf{L}_{n^2}(\alpha))$ abbreviates the single rule $n = 1 \vdash f_1(n) = n - 1$. The rule $n = 1 \vdash f_2(n) \to n^2$ is not present because $f_1(1) = 0$ and thus the outer list must be empty.

The typing judgement relation is defined by the following rules:

$$\frac{}{D, \Gamma \vdash_\Sigma c : \mathsf{Int}} \text{ IConst} \qquad \frac{}{D, \Gamma \vdash_\Sigma b : \mathsf{Bool}} \text{ BConst}$$

$$\frac{D \vdash \tau' \to \tau}{D, \Gamma, z : \tau \vdash_\Sigma z : \tau'} \text{ Var} \qquad \frac{D \vdash \tau' \to \mathsf{L}_0(\tau)}{D, \Gamma \vdash_\Sigma \mathsf{Nil} : \tau'} \text{ Nil}$$

$$\frac{D \vdash \tau' \to \mathsf{L}_{f(\overline{n})+1}(\tau_2) \qquad D \vdash \tau_2 \to \tau_1}{D, \Gamma, hd : \tau_1, tl : \mathsf{L}_{f(\overline{n})}(\tau_2) \vdash_\Sigma \mathsf{Cons}(hd, tl) : \tau'} \text{ Cons}$$

$$\frac{\Gamma(x) = \mathsf{Bool} \quad D, \Gamma \vdash_\Sigma e_t : \tau_1 \quad D, \Gamma \vdash_\Sigma e_f : \tau_2}{D, \Gamma \vdash_\Sigma \text{ if } x \text{ then } e_t \text{ else } e_f : \tau} \text{ If}$$

$$\frac{z \notin dom(\Gamma) \quad D, \Gamma \vdash_\Sigma e_1 : \tau_z \quad D, \Gamma, z : \tau_z \vdash_\Sigma e_2 : \tau}{D, \Gamma \vdash_\Sigma \text{ let } z = e_1 \text{ in } e_2 : \tau} \text{ Let}$$

$$\frac{D, 0 \in f(\overline{n}), \Gamma, l : \mathsf{L}_{f(\overline{n})}(\tau) \vdash_\Sigma e_{\mathsf{Nil}} : \tau' \quad hd, tl \notin dom(\Gamma)}{D, n' \geq 1 \in f(\overline{n}), \Gamma, hd : \tau, l : \mathsf{L}_{f(\overline{n})}(\tau), tl : \mathsf{L}_{f(\overline{n})-1}(\tau) \vdash_\Sigma e_{\mathsf{Cons}} : \tau'}{D; l : \mathsf{L}_{f(\overline{n})}(\tau) \vdash_\Sigma \begin{array}{l} \text{match } l \text{ with } | \text{ Nil} \Rightarrow e_{\mathsf{Nil}} \\ \qquad\qquad\quad | \text{ Cons}(hd, tl) \Rightarrow e_{\mathsf{Cons}} \end{array} : \tau'} \text{ Match}$$

where $n' \notin SV(D)$. Note that if in the MATCH-rule f is single-valued, then the statements in the nil and cons branches are $f(\overline{n}) = 0$ and $f(\overline{n}) \geq 1$, respectively.

$$\frac{\begin{array}{c} \Sigma(f) = \tau_1^f \times \ldots \times \tau_{k'}^f \times \tau_1^\circ \times \cdots \times \tau_k^\circ \to \tau_0 \\ \Sigma(g_1) = \tau_1^f, \ldots, \Sigma(g_{k'}) = \tau_{k'}^f \\ z_1 : \tau_1^\circ, \ldots, z_k : \tau_k^\circ \vdash_\Sigma e_1 : \tau_0 \quad D; \Gamma \vdash_\Sigma e_2 : \tau' \end{array}}{D; \Gamma \vdash_\Sigma \text{letfun } f(g_1, \ldots, g_{k'}, z_1, \ldots, z_k) = e_1 \text{ in } e_2 : \tau'} \text{ LetFun}$$

$$\Sigma(f) = \tau_1^f \times \ldots \times \tau_{k'}^f \times \tau_1^\circ \times \ldots \times \tau_k^\circ \to \tau_0$$

$$\Sigma(g_i) \text{ is an instance of the type } \tau_i^f;$$

$$\frac{D \vdash \tau \to \sigma(\tau_0) \qquad D \vdash C(\tau_1, \ldots, \tau_k)}{D, \Gamma, z_1 : \tau_1, \ldots, z_1 : \tau_k \vdash_\Sigma f(g_1, \ldots, g_{k'}, z_1, \ldots, z_k) : \tau} \text{ FunApp}$$

The function application rule computes a substitution σ from the formal size variables to the actual size expressions, and a set C of equations collecting restrictions on the actual input types. These restrictions are of the form $\tau \equiv \tau'$ abbreviating equality of the corresponding underlying types and size functions. The equation $\tau \equiv \tau'$ belongs to C if τ and τ' are actual types corresponding to the same formal type. As an example of such an equivalence consider a call to a function scalarprod : $\mathsf{L}_m(\mathsf{Int}) \times \mathsf{L}_m(\mathsf{Int}) \to \mathsf{Int}$. Due to the occurrence of m in both arguments the actual parameters $\mathsf{l} : \tau$ and $\mathsf{l}' : \tau'$ corresponding to the same formal type $\mathsf{L}_m(\mathsf{Int})$ must have equal sizes. To see how the substitution σ is applied, consider a formal size parameter m with $\sigma(m) = f'(\overline{n})$. Then

$$\sigma\left(\mathsf{L}(\ldots \mathsf{L}_{f(m)}(\ldots \mathsf{L}(\alpha) \ldots) \ldots)\right) = \mathsf{L}(\ldots \mathsf{L}_{f(f'(\overline{n}))}(\ldots \mathsf{L}(\alpha) \ldots) \ldots) .$$

Now we illustrate with an example how the typing rules are used to construct rewriting rules for multivalued size functions. Consider a function rel that produces all pairs of elements from two argument lists that are related to each other according to a given predicate. For instance rel$(>, [2, 3, 5], [2, 3]) = [[3, 2], [5, 2], [5, 3]]$. This function calls an auxiliary function rel_pairs, that given a single element z and a list, produces the list of all pairs (z, z') of the related elements, where z' runs over the list. The definitions for rel and rel_pairs are

rel$(g, l_1, l_2) = $ match l_1 with | Nil $\Rightarrow$ Nil
                              | Cons(hd, tl) $\Rightarrow$ append(rel_pairs(g, hd, l_2), rel(g, tl, l_2))

and rel_pairs$(g, z, l) = $ match l with | Nil $\Rightarrow$ Nil
                                    | Cons(hd, tl) $\Rightarrow$ if g(z, hd) then
                                              Cons(Cons(z, Cons(hd, Nil)), rel_pairs(g, z, tl))
                                              else rel_pairs(g, z, tl)

The types are $(\alpha \to \alpha \to \mathsf{Bool}) \times \mathsf{L}_n(\alpha) \times \mathsf{L}_m(\alpha) \to \mathsf{L}_{f_{rel_1}}(\mathsf{L}_{f_{rel_2}}(\alpha))$ and $(\alpha \to \alpha \to \mathsf{Bool}) \times \alpha \times \mathsf{L}_m(\alpha) \to \mathsf{L}_{f_{rel\_pairs_1}}(\mathsf{L}_{f_{rel\_pairs_2}}(\alpha))$, respectively. We want to construct rewriting rules for $f_{rel\_pairs_1}$ and $f_{rel\_pairs_2}$. We apply typing rules in the backward style to the body of rel_pairs. For the sake of convenience, below in the typing judgements, we list only the relevant variables of the context.

1. We want to infer $f_{rel\_pairs_1}$ and $f_{rel\_pairs_2}$ such that

   $z : \alpha, l : \mathsf{L}_n(\alpha) \vdash_\Sigma e_{rel\_pairs} : \mathsf{L}_{f_{rel\_pairs_1}}(\mathsf{L}_{f_{rel\_pairs_2}}(\alpha))$

2. We start applying the match-rule since e_{rel_pairs} is given by a pattern-matching. We obtain

   Nil-branch: $n = 0 \vdash_\Sigma$ Nil : $\mathsf{L}_{f_{rel\_pairs_1}}(\mathsf{L}_{f_{rel\_pairs_2}}(\alpha))$

   Cons-branch: $n \geq 1$; $z : \alpha, l : \mathsf{L}_n(\alpha) \vdash_\Sigma e' : \mathsf{L}_{f_{rel\_pairs_1}}(\mathsf{L}_{f_{rel\_pairs_2}}(\alpha))$

where e' is the if-expression in the cons-branch.

3. Since the expression in the nil-branch is just Nil, we apply the nil-rule and obtain $n = 0 \vdash \mathsf{L}_{f_{\mathsf{rel\_pairs}_1}}(\mathsf{L}_{f_{\mathsf{rel\_pairs}_2}}(\alpha)) \to \mathsf{L}_0(\tau_0)$ that according to the definition of $D \vdash \tau \to \tau'$ reduces to $n = 0 \vdash f_{\mathsf{rel\_pairs}_1}(n) \to 0$.

4. Apply the if-rule to the expression e' in the cons-branch to obtain that $\mathsf{L}_{f_{\mathsf{rel\_pairs}_1}}(\mathsf{L}_{f_{\mathsf{rel\_pairs}_2}}(\alpha)) \to \tau_1 \mid \tau_2$, where

$n \geq 1;\ \mathsf{z}\!:\alpha, \mathsf{hd}\!:\alpha, \mathsf{tl}\!:\mathsf{L}_{n-1}(\alpha) \vdash_\Sigma \mathsf{Cons}(\mathsf{Cons}(\mathsf{z}, \mathsf{Cons}(\mathsf{hd}, \mathsf{Nil})), \mathsf{rel\_pairs}(\mathsf{g}, \mathsf{z}, \mathsf{tl})): \tau_1$
$n \geq 1;\ \mathsf{z}\!:\alpha,\ \mathsf{tl}\!:\mathsf{L}_{n-1}(\alpha) \vdash_\Sigma \mathsf{rel\_pairs}(\mathsf{g}, \mathsf{z}, \mathsf{tl}): \tau_2$

Note, that the expression in the true-branch abbreviates the chain of let-bindings:

let $z_1 =$ Nil in let $z_2 =$ Cons(hd, z_1) in let $z_3 =$ Cons(z, z_2) in
    let $z_4 =$ rel_pairs(g, z, tl) in Cons(z_3, z_4)

Let $e_{\mathsf{body}_1}, \ldots, e_{\mathsf{body}_4}$ denote the let-bodies corresponding to the let-bindings of $z_1, \ldots, z_4$, respectively.

5. Applying the let-rule to z_1-binding gives

$\mathsf{let}_1:\quad n \geq 1 \vdash_\Sigma \mathsf{Nil}: ?\tau^1$
$\mathsf{body}_1: n \geq 1;\ z_1\!:?\tau^1, \ldots \vdash_\Sigma e_{\mathsf{body}_1}: \tau_1$

6. Applying the nil-rule to the let-branch instantiates $?\tau^1$ with $\mathsf{L}_0(?\tau^{10})$, so we obtain $n \geq 1;\ z_1\!: \mathsf{L}_0(?\tau^{10}), \ldots \vdash_\Sigma e_{\mathsf{body}_1}: \tau_1$.

7. Applying the let-rule to z_2-binding gives

$\mathsf{let}_2:\quad n \geq 1; \mathsf{hd}\!:\alpha, z_1\!: \mathsf{L}_0(?\tau^{10}) \vdash_\Sigma \mathsf{Cons}(\mathsf{hd}, z_1): ?\tau^2$
$\mathsf{body}_2: n \geq 1;\ z_2\!:?\tau^2, \ldots \vdash_\Sigma e_{\mathsf{body}_2}: \tau_1$

8. Applying the cons-rule to the let-branch instantiates $?\tau^2$ with $\mathsf{L}_1(\alpha)$, so we obtain $\mathsf{body}_2: n \geq 1;\ z_2\!: \mathsf{L}_1(\alpha), \ldots \vdash_\Sigma e_{\mathsf{body}_2}: \tau_1$.

9. Similarly, applying the let- and cons-rules for z_3-binding gives

$\mathsf{body}_3: n \geq 1;\ z_3\!: \mathsf{L}_2(\alpha), \ldots \vdash_\Sigma e_{\mathsf{body}_3}: \tau_1$

10. Applying the let- and funapp-rules for z_4-binding gives

$\mathsf{body}_4: n \geq 1;\ z_3\!: \mathsf{L}_2(\alpha), z_4\!: \mathsf{L}_{f_{\mathsf{rel\_pairs}_1}(n-1)}(\mathsf{L}_{f_{\mathsf{rel\_pairs}_2}(n-1)}(\alpha)) \vdash_\Sigma \mathsf{Cons}(z_3, z_4): \tau_1$

11. Applying the cons-rule gives $n \geq 1 \vdash \tau_1 \to \mathsf{L}_{f_{\mathsf{rel\_pairs}_1}(n-1)+1}(\mathsf{L}_{f_{\mathsf{rel\_pairs}_2}(n-1)}(\alpha))$ and $n \geq 1 \vdash f_{\mathsf{rel\_pairs}_2}(n-1) \to 2$.

12. Applying the function application rule in the false-branch gives $n \geq 1 \vdash \tau_2 \to \mathsf{L}_{f_{\mathsf{rel\_pairs}_1}(n-1)}(\mathsf{L}_{f_{\mathsf{rel\_pairs}_2}(n-1)}(\alpha))$.

13. Recalling the multiple-choice-rewriting side condition from the application of the if-rule we obtain

$n \geq 1 \vdash \mathsf{L}_{f_{\mathsf{rel\_pairs}_1}(n)}(\mathsf{L}_{f_{\mathsf{rel\_pairs}_2}(n)}(\alpha)) \to$
$\quad \mathsf{L}_{f_{\mathsf{rel\_pairs}_1}(n-1)+1}(\mathsf{L}_{f_{\mathsf{rel\_pairs}_2}(n-1)}(\alpha)) \mid \mathsf{L}_{f_{\mathsf{rel\_pairs}_1}(n-1)}(\mathsf{L}_{f_{\mathsf{rel\_pairs}_2}(n-1)}(\alpha))$

that abbreviates

$n \geq 1 \qquad\qquad\qquad\qquad\qquad \vdash\ f_{\mathsf{rel\_pairs}_1}(n) \to f_{\mathsf{rel\_pairs}_1}(n-1) + 1 \mid$
$\qquad\qquad\qquad\qquad\qquad\qquad\qquad\qquad f_{\mathsf{rel\_pairs}_1}(n-1)$
$n' \in f_{\mathsf{rel\_pairs}_1}(n-1) + 1,\ n' \geq 1,\ n \geq 1 \vdash\ f_{\mathsf{rel\_pairs}_2}(n) \to f_{\mathsf{rel\_pairs}_2}(n-1)$
$n' \in f_{\mathsf{rel\_pairs}_1}(n-1),\ n' \geq 1,\ n \geq 1 \qquad \vdash\ f_{\mathsf{rel\_pairs}_2}(n) \to f_{\mathsf{rel\_pairs}_2}(n-1)$

Recall that $\vdash f_{\mathsf{rel\_pairs}_1}(0) \to 0$ and $n \geq 1 \vdash f_{\mathsf{rel\_pairs}_2}(n-1) \to 2$ due to the nil-rule in the nil-branch and the last cons-rule respectively. So, combining this altogether gives

$$\vdash f_{\mathsf{rel\_pairs}_1}(0) \to 0$$
$$n \geq 1 \vdash f_{\mathsf{rel\_pairs}_1}(n) \to f_{\mathsf{rel\_pairs}_1}(n-1) + 1 \mid f_{\mathsf{rel\_pairs}_1}(n-1)$$
$$n \geq 0 \vdash f_{\mathsf{rel\_pairs}_2}(n) \to 2$$

Similarly we obtain rewriting rules for the multivalued size functions for rel:

$$\vdash f_{\mathsf{rel}_1}(0, m) \to 0$$
$$n \geq 1 \vdash f_{\mathsf{rel}_1}(n, m) \to f_{\mathsf{rel\_pairs}_1}(m) + f_{\mathsf{rel}_1}(n-1, m)$$
$$n \geq 1 \vdash f_{\mathsf{rel}_2}(n, m) \to f_{\mathsf{rel\_pairs}_2}(m)$$

3.4 Semantics of Typing Judgements (soundness)

The set-theoretic semantics of typing judgements is formalised later in this section as the soundness theorem, which is defined by means of the following two predicates. One indicates if a program value is *valid* with respect to a certain heap and a ground type. The other does the same for sets of values and types, taken from a frame store and a ground context $\Gamma^\bullet$:

$$Valid_{\mathsf{val}}(v, \tau^\bullet, h) \quad = \exists_w[\ v \models^h_{\tau^\bullet} w\ ]$$
$$Valid_{\mathsf{store}}(vars, \Gamma^\bullet, s, h) = \forall_{\mathsf{z} \in vars}[\ Valid_{\mathsf{val}}(s(\mathsf{z}), \Gamma^\bullet(\mathsf{z}), h)\ ]$$

Let a valuation ϵ map size variables to concrete sizes (numbers from the ring $\mathcal{R}$) and an instantiation η map type variables to ground types:

$$Valuation \quad \epsilon : \quad Size\,Variables \to \mathcal{R}$$
$$Instantiation \quad \eta : \quad Type\,Variables \to \tau^\bullet$$

Valuations and instantiations distribute over types and size functions in the following way: $\eta\epsilon((\mathsf{L}_{f(\overline{n})}(\tau))) = \mathsf{L}_{f(\epsilon(\overline{n}))}(\eta(\epsilon(\tau)))$.

Now, stating the soundness theorem is straightforward. Informally, it states that assuming that the context zero-order variables are *valid*, i.e. indeed point to lists of the sizes mentioned in the input types, then the result in the heap will be *valid*, i.e. of the size indicated in the output type.

Theorem 1 (Soundness). *For any store s, heaps h and h', closure $\mathcal{C}$, expression e, value v, context Γ, quantifier-free formula D, signature Σ, type τ, size valuation ϵ, and type instantiation η such that*

- *the expression e terminates with the value v, i.e. in terms of operational semantics the relation $s; h; \mathcal{C} \vdash e \rightsquigarrow v; h'$ holds,*
- *$D, \Gamma \vdash_\Sigma e : \tau$ is a node in the derivation tree for some function body,*
- *$dom(s) = dom(\Gamma)$,*
- *$D(\epsilon(\overline{n}))$ holds, where $\overline{n}$ is the set of size variables from $dom(\Gamma \cup D)$,*
- *$Valid_{\mathsf{store}}(dom(s), \eta(\epsilon(\Gamma)), s, h)$ holds,*

then the return value v is valid according to its return type τ, i.e.

$$Valid_{\mathsf{val}}(v, \eta(\epsilon(\tau)), h')$$

holds.

Proof. The proof is done by induction on the size of the derivation tree for the operational-semantic judgement. For the sake of convenience we abbreviate $D(\epsilon(\overline{n}))$ to D_ϵ, $\eta(\epsilon(\tau))$ to $\tau_{\eta\epsilon}$ and $\eta(\epsilon(\Gamma))$ to $\Gamma_{\eta\epsilon}$. One can easily check by induction that $TV(\tau) \subseteq TV(\Gamma)$. Fix a valuation $\epsilon\colon SV(\Gamma)\cup SV(D) \rightarrow \mathcal{R}$, and a type instantiation $\eta\colon TV(\Gamma) \rightarrow \tau^\bullet$ such that the assumptions of the lemma hold. We must show that $Valid_{\mathsf{val}}(v, \tau_{\eta\epsilon}, h')$ holds. The full proof is given in the technical report [13]. Below, we consider only the most interesting case: the cons-branch of matching.

OSMatch-Cons: In this case $e = \mathsf{match}\ \mathsf{l}\ \mathsf{with}\ |\ \mathsf{Nil} \Rightarrow e_1\ |\ \mathsf{Cons(hd, tl)} \Rightarrow e_2$ for some l, hd, tl, e_1 and e_2. The typing context has the form $\Gamma = \Gamma' \cup \{\mathsf{l}\colon \mathsf{L}_{f(\overline{n})}(\tau')\}$ for some Γ', τ' and f. From the operational semantics we know that $h.s(\mathsf{l}).hd = v_{hd}$ and $h.s(\mathsf{l}).tl = v_{tl}$ for some v_{hd} and v_{tl}, that is $s(\mathsf{l}) \neq$ NULL. Due to the validity of $s(\mathsf{l})$ and Lemma 1, there exists $n_0 \geq 1 \in f(\epsilon(\overline{n}))$. From the validity $s(\mathsf{l}) \models^h_{\mathsf{L}_{f(\epsilon(\overline{n}))}(\tau'_{\eta\epsilon})} w_{hd} : w_{tl}$ the validities of v_{hd} and v_{tl} follow: $v_{hd} \models^h_{\tau'_{\eta\epsilon}} w_{hd}$, $v_{tl} \models^h_{\mathsf{L}_{f_\epsilon(\overline{n})-1}(\tau'_{\eta\epsilon})} w_{tl}$.

From $Valid_{\mathsf{store}}(dom(s), \Gamma_{\eta\epsilon}, s, h)$ and the results above, we obtain

$$Valid_{\mathsf{store}}(dom(s'), \Gamma_{\eta\epsilon},\ \mathsf{l}\colon \mathsf{L}_{f(\epsilon(\overline{n}))}(\tau'_{\eta\epsilon}),\ \mathsf{hd}\colon \tau'_{\eta\epsilon},\ \mathsf{tl}\colon \mathsf{L}_{f(\epsilon(\overline{n}))-1}(\tau'_{\eta\epsilon}), s', h)$$

where $s' = s[\mathsf{hd} := v_{hd}][\mathsf{tl} := v_{tl}]$. From the typing rule for e we obtain that

$$D, n_0 \geq 1 \in f(\overline{n});\ \Gamma',\ \mathsf{l}\colon \mathsf{L}_{f(\epsilon(\overline{n}))}(\tau'_{\eta\epsilon}),\ \mathsf{hd}\colon \tau'_{\eta\epsilon},\ \mathsf{tl}\colon \mathsf{L}_{f(\epsilon(\overline{n}))-1}(\tau'_{\eta\epsilon}) \vdash_\Sigma e_2 : \tau_{\eta\epsilon}$$

With $\epsilon' = \epsilon[n_0 := length_h(s(\mathsf{l}))]$ the induction hypothesis yields

$$Valid_{\mathsf{store}}(dom(s'), \left\{ \begin{array}{l} \Gamma'_{\eta\epsilon}\ \cup \\ \{\mathsf{l}\colon \mathsf{L}_{f(\epsilon'(\overline{n}))}(\tau'_{\eta\epsilon'}), \\ \mathsf{hd}\colon \tau'_{\eta\epsilon'}, \\ \mathsf{tl}\colon \mathsf{L}_{f(\epsilon'(\overline{n}))-1}(\tau'_{\eta\epsilon'})\} \end{array} \right\}, s\left[\begin{array}{l} \mathsf{hd} := v_{hd}, \\ \mathsf{tl} := v_{tl} \end{array} \right], h) \implies$$

$$Valid_{\mathsf{val}}(v, \tau_{\eta\epsilon'}, h').$$

Now from the induction hypothesis and the fact that $n_0 \notin SV(\tau)$ (and thus, $\tau_{\eta\epsilon} = \tau_{\eta\epsilon'}$), we have $Valid_{\mathsf{val}}(v, \tau_{\eta\epsilon}, h')$.

$\square$

4   Approximation of Multivalued Size Functions

In practice, size functions in closed forms, like $f(n) = \{n, n+1\}$ for insert, are preferable to ones in the form of rewriting rules. However, inference of closed forms is a hard problem. Instead, we propose to infer their approximations given by indexed families of piecewise polynomials.

Definition. *A family $\{g(\overline{n}, \overline{\imath})\}_{Q(\overline{n}, \overline{\imath})}$ of piecewise polynomials, where $Q(\overline{n}, \overline{\imath})$ is a quantifier-free first-order arithmetic predicate, approximates a multivalued*

function f if and only if for all $\overline{n}$ in the domain of f, $f(\overline{n}) \subseteq \{g(\overline{n}, \overline{\imath})\}_{Q(\overline{n}, \overline{\imath})}$.
In other words, for all $m \in f(\overline{n})$, there exists $\overline{\imath}$ such that $m = g(\overline{n}, \overline{\imath})$ and the predicate $Q(\overline{n}, \overline{\imath})$ holds.

Given a multivalued size function in the form of rewriting rules, the inference procedure first generates a candidate approximating family and then checks if it indeed approximates the function.

4.1   Inferring a Candidate Approximating Family of Polynomials

To give an idea behind the interactive procedure that infers approximating families of piecewise polynomials, we start with a simple example. We show how to infer candidate polynomial lower and upper bounds for the size function of insert and how to construct an approximating family from it. Recall the size rewriting system for insert:

$$\vdash f_{\mathsf{insert}}(0) \to 1$$
$$n \geq 1 \vdash f_{\mathsf{insert}}(n) \to n \mid 1 + f_{\mathsf{insert}}(n-1)$$

Assume that $p_{\min}$ and $p_{\max}$ are linear, that is, that they are of the form $a_{\min}n + b_{\min}$ and $a_{\max}n + b_{\max}$, respectively. We want to find the coefficients $a_{\min}$, $b_{\min}$, $a_{\max}$, $b_{\max}$ (as we did in [15] for strict polynomial (single-valued) size functions, where the lower and upper bounds were equal). To reconstruct $p_{\min}$, one needs to know two points on its graph, and the same holds for $p_{\max}$. Take $n = 1$ and $n = 2$. Evaluating the rewriting rules gives $f_{\mathsf{insert}}(1) = \{1, 2\}$ and $f_{\mathsf{insert}}(2) = \{2, 3\}$. Pick up the minimal values from $f_{\mathsf{insert}}(1)$ and $f_{\mathsf{insert}}(2)$ and assume that they are the output of $p_{\min}$ for those inputs, i.e., that the graph of $p_{\min}$ contains the points $(1, 1)$ and $(2, 2)$. Similarly, pick up the maximal values from $f_{\mathsf{insert}}(1)$ and $f_{\mathsf{insert}}(2)$ and assume that $p_{\max}$ contains $(1, 2)$ and $(2, 3)$. We obtain two systems of equations, for $a_{\min}$, $b_{\min}$ and $a_{\max}$, $b_{\max}$, respectively:

$$\begin{cases} a_{\min} + b_{\min} = 1 \\ 2a_{\min} + b_{\min} = 2 \end{cases} \qquad \begin{cases} a_{\max} + b_{\max} = 2 \\ 2a_{\max} + b_{\max} = 3 \end{cases}$$

Solving these linear systems we get $a_{\min} = 1$, $b_{\min} = 0$ and $a_{\max} = 1$, $b_{\max} = 1$. Thus, we reconstruct the expressions for $p_{\min}(n) = n$ and $p_{\max}(n) = n + 1$, and the approximating family $p_{\min}(n) + i$, where $0 \leq i \leq \delta(n)$ with $\delta(n) = p_{\max}(n) - p_{\min}(n) = 1$. The rest of the job is to check whether this reconstruction approximates the solution of the rewriting rules. We discuss it in Section 4.2.

It is easy to see that we have inferred accurate bound for insert, i.e. the *greatest lower* and the *lowest upper* bounds for the multivalued size function. Moreover, given any $n \geq 1$, there is an evaluation path for $f_{\mathsf{insert}}(n)$ that evaluates to $p_{\min}(n)$, and there is a path that evaluates to $p_{\max}(n)$. It explains the choice of the *step*=1: it is enough to take two consecutive natural numbers to generate the systems of equations for the coefficients of the linear lower and upper bounds.

The bounds for insert are one-variable and the systems of linear equations w.r.t. the polynomial coefficients are trivially consistent if one chooses different testing size values, in the example $n = 1$ and $n = 2$. The reason for this is that the matrix of such a system has a 1-variable non-zero *Vandermonde* determinant. In the multivariate case, say s variables, the consistency of the systems for $p_{\min}$ and $p_{\max}$ (for which the corresponding multivariate Vandermonde determinant is non-zero) depends on a more involving condition. If the testing values, i.e. the points in an s-dimensional space, lie in a so called *Node Configuration A* (**NCA** configuration [8]), the systems for $p_{\min}$ and $p_{\max}$ have unique solutions, and thus the polynomials are uniquely defined.

We describe an **NCA** configuration for the case $s = 2$ in detail. Let d be the degree of a polynomial and N_d^2 denote the amount of its coefficients. A set W of N_d^2 points on a plane lie in a *2-dimensional **NCA** configuration* if there exist lines $\gamma_1, \ldots, \gamma_{d+1}$ in the space $\mathcal{R}^2$, such that $d+1$ points of W lie on γ_{d+1}, d points of W lie on $\gamma_d \setminus \gamma_{d+1}$, ..., and finally 1 point of W lies on $\gamma_1 \setminus (\gamma_2 \cup \ldots \cup \gamma_{d+1})$. The simplest example of an **NCA** configuration on a plane is a "triangle" of points, where $d+1$ different points lie on the line $y = 1$, d points lie on the line $y = 2,...,$ and 1 point lies on the line $y = d + 1$. For instance, with $d = 2$ a two variable polynomial has $N_2^2 = \binom{2+2}{2} = 6$ coefficients, hence we pick up 6 points: $(1, 1), (2, 1), (3, 1), (1, 2), (2, 2)$ and $(1, 3)$.

For dimensions $s > 2$ this configuration is formulated inductively, using the notion of a hyperplane [8]. Since the definition itself is technically involved, we just give an example of an **NCA** for 3 variables ($s = 3$) and degree $d = 2$. To define a polynomial of three variables of degree 2 one needs to know $N_2^3 = \binom{2+3}{3} = 10$ coefficients, hence we need to place 10 points:

1. on the plane $x = 0$ take the "triangle" of $N_2^2 = 6$ points that lies in the 2-dimensional **NCA**, say $(0, 0, 0)$, $(0, 0, 1)$, $(0, 0, 2)$, $(0, 1, 0)$, $(0, 1, 1)$, $(0, 2, 0)$,
2. on the plane $x = 1$ take the "triangle" of $N_1^2 = 3$ points that lies in the 2-dimensional **NCA**, say $(1, 0, 0)$, $(1, 0, 1)$, $(1, 1, 0)$,
3. on the plane $x = 2$ take the point $(2, 0, 0)$.

Now we give a general procedure for inferring lower and upper polynomial bounds from a given system of size rewriting rules.

INPUT: The degrees $d_{\min}, d_{\max}$ of hypothetical upper and lower bounds, s size variables, $\bar{n} = (n_1, .., n_s)$, initial test points $w_{\min}^0 = \bar{n}_{\min}^0$, $w_{\max}^0 = \bar{n}_{\max}^0$, steps $\epsilon_{\min}, \epsilon_{\max}$ and the system G of size rewriting rules.

OUTPUT: A lower $p_{\min}$ and an upper $p_{\max}$ bound or the proposal to repeat the procedure for higher degrees and/or other $w_{\min}^0, w_{\max}^0, \epsilon_{\min}, \epsilon_{\max}$.

PROCEDURE: 1. According to the initial points and steps, pick up N_d^s points $w = (n_1, \ldots, n_s)$ in the s-dimensional space that lie in **NCA** configuration; let they constitute the sets $W_{\min}$. Similarly, generate $W_{\max}$.

2. For any $w^i \in W_{\min}$ compute the set $f_{i,\,\min} = f(w^i)$.
    Similarly, compute $f_{j,\,\max}$ for any $w^j \in W_{\max}$.
3. For any f_i (f_j) pick up its minimal $f_i^{\min}$ (maximal $f_j^{\max}$) values.
4.1. Interpolate $p_{\min}$ using the points $(w_i, f_i^{\min})$ by solving
    the system of linear equations w.r.t. its coefficients.
4.2. Interpolate $p_{\max}$ using the points $(w_j, f_i^{\max})$ by
    solving the system of linear equations w.r.t. its coefficients.
5. Check whether the family $\{p_{\min}(\overline{n}) + i\}_{0 \le i \le (p_{\max}(\overline{n}) - p_{\min}(\overline{n}))}$
    approximates the multivalued function defined by G.
5.1. If "yes": stop and output $p_{\min}$ and $p_{\max}$.
5.2. If "not": pick up other parameters d, $w_{\min}^0$, $w_{\max}^0$, $\epsilon_{\min}$, $\epsilon_{\max}$

The choice of the parameters $w_{\min}^0$, $w_{\max}^0$, $\epsilon_{\min}$, $\epsilon_{\max}$ is crucial. Based on them, the procedure generates the points $(w, f(w))$. A bad choice of parameters has one of two consequences: either no bounds will be detected even if they exist, or loose bounds will be inferred. The first happens when $W_{\min}$ (resp., $W_{\max}$) are constructed in such a way that there is no bound $p_{\min}$ (resp., $p_{\max}$) such that its graph contains all points from $W_{\min}$ (resp., $W_{\max}$). Consider, for instance, a function divtwo: $L_n(\alpha) \to L_{f(n)}(\alpha)$ that takes a list of length n and returns a list of length $n/2$ if n is even, and $(n-1)/2$, if n is odd. The rewriting rules for the size function are $f(0) \to 0$, $f(1) \to 0$, $n \ge 2 \vdash f(n) \to f(n-2) + 1$. Take $d = 1$, $n_{\min,\max}^0 = 0$, $\epsilon_{\min,\max} = 1$. Then $f(0) = f(1) = 0$. There is no linear upper bound that contains both, $(0,0)$ and $(1,0)$, points since output type $L_0(\alpha)$ is rejected by the checker. Still, linear bounds can be obtained if suitable parameters are provided. Take e.g. $n_{\min}^0 = 3$, $n_{\max}^0 = 2$, $\epsilon_{\min,\max} = 2$. Then $f(3) = 1$, $f(5) = 2$ and $p_{\min}(n) = (n-1)/2$, similarly $f(2) = 1$, $f(4) = 2$ and $p_{\max}(n) = n/2$.

Inferring rough lower (upper) bound happens when the graph of some lower (upper) bound does contain all points $W_{\min}$ (resp., $W_{\max}$), but the bound itself is rough. For instance, this happens when $n^0 = 0$ for insert. Then $f(0) = 1$, $f(1) = \{1,2\}$, so the inferred $p_{\min}(n) = 1$.

The examples above show that users should choose the parameters based on common sense and their intuitive knowledge about the functions under considerations. We recommend not to include the base-of-recursion sizes into sets of test points since these cases are usually "non-typical".

Adaptations for inferring families of piecewise polynomials are possible. The user hints the inference system on which areas P_i she assumes different pieces of polynomial bounds. Different parameters must be provided for each piece.

As a more elaborated example, consider the inference procedure for the function rel (defined in Section 3.3). The inferred size rewriting system is:

$$\vdash f_{rel_1}(0, m) \to 0$$
$$n \ge 1 \vdash f_{rel_1}(n, m) \to f_{rel\_pairs_1}(m) + f_{rel_1}(n-1, m) \qquad n \ge 1 \vdash f_{rel_2}(n, m) \to f_{rel\_pairs_2}(m)$$

We show how to infer the family $\{i\}_{0 \le i \le nm}$. A quadratic polynomial $q(n, m) = a_{20}n^2 + a_{02}m^2 + a_{11}nm + a_{10}n + a_{01}m + a_{00}$ of two variables has 6 coefficients, so to define the polynomial one needs to know 6 points (n_i, m_i, q_i) on the graph of q. The coefficients are computed as the solution of the system of linear equations

$q_i = a_{20}n_i^2 + a_{02}m_i^2 + a_{11}n_im_i + a_{10}n_i + a_{01}m_i + a_{00}$, where $1 \le i \le 6$. For instance, one can take the points (n,m) from $\{(1,1),(2,1),(3,1),(1,2),(2,2)(1,3)\}$. Then, the linear system w.r.t. the coefficients of q has the form

$$
\begin{aligned}
a_{20} + a_{02} + a_{11} + a_{10} + a_{01} + a_{00} &= q(1,1) \\
4a_{20} + a_{02} + 2a_{11} + 2a_{10} + a_{01} + a_{00} &= q(2,1) \\
9a_{20} + 3a_{02} + 3a_{11} + 3a_{10} + a_{01} + a_{00} &= q(3,1) \\
a_{20} + 4a_{02} + 2a_{11} + a_{10} + 2a_{01} + a_{00} &= q(1,2) \\
4a_{20} + 4a_{02} + 4a_{11} + 2a_{10} + 2a_{01} + a_{00} &= q(2,2) \\
a_{20} + 9a_{02} + 3a_{11} + a_{10} + 3a_{01} + a_{00} &= q(1,3)
\end{aligned}
$$

To reconstruct $p_{\min}$ and $p_{\max}$, consider all possible evaluation paths for f_{rel} at these points, using the fact that for any fixed n,m there is only finite number of indices j satisfying $0 \le j \le m$.

$$
\begin{aligned}
f_{\mathrm{rel}}(1,1) &= j + 0 &&= \{0,1\} \\
f_{\mathrm{rel}}(2,1) &= j + f_{\mathrm{rel}}(1,1) = \{0,1,2\} \\
f_{\mathrm{rel}}(3,1) &= j + f_{\mathrm{rel}}(2,1) = \{0,1,2,3\} \\
f_{\mathrm{rel}}(1,2) &= j + 0 &&= \{0,1,2\} \\
f_{\mathrm{rel}}(2,2) &= j + f_{\mathrm{rel}}(1,2) = \{0,1,2,3,4\} \\
f_{\mathrm{rel}}(1,3) &= j + 0 &&= \{0,1,2,3\}
\end{aligned}
$$

Thus, for the coefficients of $p_{\max}$ one has the system

$$
\begin{aligned}
a_{20} + a_{02} + a_{11} + a_{10} + a_{01} + a_{00} &= 1 \\
4a_{20} + a_{02} + 2a_{11} + 2a_{10} + a_{01} + a_{00} &= 2 \\
9a_{20} + 3a_{02} + 3a_{11} + 3a_{10} + a_{01} + a_{00} &= 3 \\
a_{20} + 4a_{02} + 2a_{11} + a_{10} + 2a_{01} + a_{00} &= 2 \\
4a_{20} + 4a_{02} + 4a_{11} + 2a_{10} + 2a_{01} + a_{00} &= 4 \\
a_{20} + 9a_{02} + 3a_{11} + a_{10} + 3a_{01} + a_{00} &= 3
\end{aligned}
$$

The solution is $(0,0,1,0,0,0)$, so $p_{\max}(n,m) = nm$. The system for $p_{\min}$ has all zeros on its right hand side, thus $p_{\min} = 0$. The inferred family is indeed $\{i\}_{0 \le i \le nm}$, which approximates the multivalued size function $f_{\mathrm{rel}1}$.

4.2   Checking If a Family Approximates a Size Function

Checking an inferred family is similar to type checking types annotated with families of piecewise polynomials directly [14]. In that type system, for instance, the output type of insert is $\mathsf{L}_{n+i}^{0 \le i \le 1}(\alpha)$.

We show that, *given a multivalued size function and some indexed family of piecewise polynomials, there is a set of first-order arithmetic entailments such that their satisfiability implies that the family approximates the size function.* Such predicates are obtained by substituting indexed families of polynomials, which are to be checked as approximations, for the corresponding multivalued-function symbols in the rewriting rules. For instance, verifying whether the family $\{n+i\}_{0 \le i \le 1}$ approximates $f_{\mathrm{insert}}(n)$ reduces to checking the entailments

$$n = 0 \qquad\qquad \vdash 1 = n+?i \wedge 0 \leq ?i \leq 1$$
$$n \geq 1 \qquad\qquad \vdash n = n+?i \wedge 0 \leq ?i \leq 1$$
$$n \geq 1, 0 \leq j \leq 1 \vdash 1 + (n-1) + j = n+?i \wedge 0 \leq ?i \leq 1$$

Checking succeeds by instantiating $?i$ to 1, 0 and j, respectively. Substitution of an indexed family of polynomials $\{g(\overline{n}, \overline{i})\}_{Q(\overline{n},\overline{i})}$ for a multivalued-function symbol f is defined in the usual way. Let an arithmetic expression $\varepsilon(\overline{n}, \overline{i})$ contain size variables $\overline{n}$, indices $\overline{i}$ (such that $Q(\overline{n}, \overline{i})$), symbols $+$, $-$, $*$ and symbols of multivalued functions. Examples of $\varepsilon(\overline{n}, \overline{i})$ are $1 + f_{\mathsf{insert}}(n-1)$, $f_{\mathsf{insert}}(n-2) + f_{\mathsf{insert}}(n-1)$ and $f_{\mathsf{rinsert}}(m-1, n) + i$, with $0 \leq i \leq 1$. Substituting the family $\{n+i\}_{0 \leq i \leq 1}$, for f_{insert} in the first expression results in $1 + n - 1 + i = n + i$. In the second expression it gives $n - 2 + i_1 + n - 1 + i_2 = 2n - 3 + i_1 + i_2$, where $0 \leq i_1, i_2 \leq 1$. The substitution $\{n+j\}_{0 \leq j \leq m}$, for $f_{\mathsf{rinsert}}(m-1, n)$ in the third expression results in $n + j + i$ with $0 \leq j \leq m-1$ and $0 \leq i \leq 1$.

We generalise substitution to types $\tau = \mathsf{L}_{\varepsilon_1}^{Q_1(\overline{n},\overline{i}_1)}(\ldots \mathsf{L}_{\varepsilon_k}^{Q_k(\overline{n},\overline{i}_k)}(\alpha)\ldots)$, which annotated by indexed families of expressions, in the natural way:
$$[\tau] = \mathsf{L}_{[\varepsilon_1]}^{Q_1'(\overline{n},\overline{i}_1,\overline{j}_1)}(\ldots \mathsf{L}_{[\varepsilon_k]}^{Q_k'(\overline{n},\overline{i}_k,\overline{j}_k)}(\alpha)\ldots)$$
To construct predicates to check candidate approximations, one also needs the notion of subtyping for types annotated by indexed families of piece-wise polynomials directly [14]. Examples of subtypings in those type system are $\vdash \mathsf{L}_{n+i}^{0 \leq i \leq 1}(\alpha) \preccurlyeq \mathsf{L}_{n+i}^{0 \leq i \leq 2}(\alpha)$ and $n = 0 \vdash \mathsf{L}_n(\mathsf{L}_i^{0 \leq i \leq 2}(\alpha)) \preccurlyeq \mathsf{L}_n(\mathsf{L}_2(\alpha))$. Let

$$T = \mathsf{L}_{g^1(\overline{n},\overline{i}^1)}^{Q^1(\overline{n},\overline{i}^1)}(\ldots \mathsf{L}_{g^k(\overline{n},\overline{i}^k)}^{Q^k(\overline{n},\overline{i}^k)}(\alpha)\ldots)$$
$$T' = \mathsf{L}_{g'^1(\overline{n},\overline{j}^1)}^{Q'^1(\overline{n},\overline{j}^1)}(\ldots \mathsf{L}_{g'^k(\overline{n},\overline{j}^k)}^{Q'^k(\overline{n},\overline{j}^k)}(\alpha)\ldots)$$

Then $D \vdash T' \preccurlyeq T$ holds if and only if

$$\forall \overline{n}\, \overline{j}^1.\ D(\overline{n}) \wedge Q'^1(\overline{n}, \overline{j}^1) \implies \exists\, \overline{i}^1.g'^1(\overline{n}, \overline{j}^1) = g^1(\overline{n}, \overline{i}^1) \wedge Q^1(\overline{n}, \overline{i}^1)$$

and if, moreover, there exists $\overline{j}^1$ such that $D(\overline{n}) \wedge Q'^1(\overline{n}, \overline{j}^1)$ and $g'^1(\overline{n}, \overline{j}^1) \geq 1$ then

$$D \vdash \mathsf{L}_{g'^2(\overline{n},\overline{j}^2)}^{Q'^2(\overline{n},\overline{j}^2)}(\ldots \mathsf{L}_{g'^k(\overline{n},\overline{j}^k)}^{Q'^k(\overline{n},\overline{j}^k)}(\alpha)\ldots) \preccurlyeq \mathsf{L}_{g^2(\overline{n},\overline{i}^2)}^{Q^2(\overline{n},\overline{i}^2)}(\ldots \mathsf{L}_{g^k(\overline{n},\overline{i}^k)}^{Q^k(\overline{n},\overline{i}^k)}(\alpha)\ldots)$$

Let $\tau = \mathsf{L}_{f_1}(\ldots \mathsf{L}_{f_s}(\alpha))$ and $D \vdash \tau \to \tau'$. To check if a family $\{g_\imath(\overline{n}, \overline{i}_\imath)\}_{Q(\overline{n},\overline{i}_\imath)}$ approximates $f_\imath$, for all $1 \leq \imath \leq s$. one uses the following lemma.

Lemma 2 (Checking). *Let $[\phi_l](\overline{n}, \overline{j}_l)$, with $1 \leq l \leq t$, approximate multivalued-function symbols $\{\phi_1(\overline{n}), \ldots, \phi_t(\overline{n})\}$ that occur τ' but not in τ. Let $[\tau]$ and $[\tau']$ be obtained by substituting $g_\imath$ and $[\phi_l]$ for the corresponding function symbols $f_\imath$ and ϕ_l. Then $D \vdash [\tau'] \preccurlyeq [\tau]$ implies that $\{g(\overline{n}, \overline{i}_\imath)\}_{Q(\overline{n},\overline{i}_\imath)}$ approximates $f_\imath$, where $1 \leq \imath \leq s$.*

Proof. By induction on the length of the rewriting chain for an arbitrary $\imath$, fixing some $m \in f_\imath(\overline{n})$.

As an example, checking whether $\{i\}_{0 \leq i \leq nm}$ approximates $f_{1,\text{rel}}$ reduces to checking the entailments

$$n = 0 \qquad\qquad\qquad \vdash 0 =?i \wedge 0 \leq?i \leq nm$$
$$n \geq 1,\ 0 \leq j' \leq m,\ 0 \leq j \leq (n-1)m \vdash j' + j =?i \wedge 0 \leq?i \leq nm$$

The decidability problem of checking whether an indexed family of piecewise polynomials approximates a given multivalued size function is treated similarly to the decidability of type checking for the system annotated with such families directly [14]. In particular, checking is decidable when function definitions satisfy the syntactical condition from [15] and output approximations are finite families of polynomials. Also, checking is decidable for indexed families of piecewise linear polynomials with indices delimited by linear predicates.

5   Feasibility of Analysing of a Typical List Library

As a small feasibility study, we applied our analysis to a typical list library, The functions were adapted from Hugs' list library, version September 2006. Since we have an intermediate language we first needed to make some assumptions.

Firstly, we assume strict semantics, which means that we cannot deal with infinite lists. Hence functions like repeat were omitted. Secondly, it must be possible to translate the function into our language. Our type system requires that inner lists all have the same length, which is not the case for a general version of e.g. concat. This restriction may be removed in a future version of our work. Thirdly, we ignore classes of types like Eq and Ord and we write the functions uncurried. Finally, we write *interface types* where the family is given as an annotation that can be inferred directly from the set of term rewriting rules as shown above. Annotations in interface types are approximations studied in Section 4.

Many functions (like head, null, length, elem, notElem, and, or, any, all, sum, product, maximum, minimum, isPrefix, isSuffix, isInfix, and atIndex) do not return lists and thus they are analysable but not interesting from the size dependency point of view. E.g., the type for length is $\mathsf{L}_n(\alpha) \to \mathsf{Int}$.

The family of fold functions are parametric on the type of the result and hence not suitable for our analysis. Even an specialised version that returns lists would still be out of the scope of our analysis because the length of the output would depend on the length of the list returned by the high-order parameter.

Other functions (like append, tail, init, map, reverse and sort, and restricted versions of concat and union) are shapely, i.e. they have an exact polynomial size function. These functions are typable in the type systems developed in [15,16]. Of these functions we only give the type of append: $\mathsf{L}_n(\alpha) \times \mathsf{L}_m(\alpha) \to \mathsf{L}_{n+m}(\alpha)$.

Some functions have a precise size dependency but they need $\max_0$ or they have first-order arguments, and thus they cannot be handled by our previous systems. Now we can type them as follows:

intersperse : $\alpha \times \mathsf{L}_n(\alpha) \to \mathsf{L}_{\max_0(2*n-1)}(\alpha)$
scanl   : $(\alpha \times \beta \to \alpha) \times \alpha \times \mathsf{L}_n(\beta) \to \mathsf{L}_{n+1}(\alpha)$
scanl1   : $(\alpha \times \alpha \to \alpha) \times \mathsf{L}_n(\alpha) \to \mathsf{L}_n(\alpha)$

For functions with a multivalued size function, an indexed family of polynomials is needed to express the possible output sizes. Several functions have a list of size n among their arguments and perform some filtering of the elements, returning a list of length at most n, i.e., $\mathsf{L}_i^{0 \leq i \leq n}(\alpha)$. The functions takeWhile, dropWhile, filter, findIndices, elemIndices, nub and nubBy fall in this category.

Probably more interesting are the types of the functions that may delete some elements. delete and deleteBy take a list of size n and return a list with maybe one element less: $\mathsf{L}_{\max_0(n-i)}^{0 \leq i \leq 1}(\alpha)$; deleteFirstBy and $(\backslash\backslash)$ take a list of size n and a list of size m and delete at most m elements from the first list: $\mathsf{L}_{\max_0(n-i)}^{0 \leq i \leq m}(\alpha)$; finally, given lists of size n and m, intersect and intersectBy return a list of length at most $\min(n, m)$: $\mathsf{L}_i^{0 \leq i \leq \max_0(n, \max_0(n-m))}(\alpha)$.

Adding algebraic data types to our language, many other functions could be analysed. There are, of course, functions whose sized types cannot be expressed in our type system or our procedure cannot deal with them. Our type system cannot express types where the size of the output depends on a higher-order parameter (this is the case for concatMap). Furthermore, we cannot express types where the size of the result depends on the *value* of the arguments, i.e., the size cannot be determined statically (like unfoldr).

6   Related Work

This research extends our work [15,18,16] about shapely function definitions that have a single-valued, exact input-output polynomial size functions. Our non-monotonic framework resembles [2] in which the authors describe *monotonic* resource consumption for Java bytecode by means of Cost Equation Systems (CESs), which are similar to, but more general than recurrence equations. CESs express the cost of a program in terms of the size of its input data. In a further step, a closed-form solution or upper bound can sometimes be found by using existing Computer Algebra Systems, such as *Maple* and *Mathematica*. This work is continued by the authors in [1], where mechanisms for solving and upper bounding CESs are studied. However, they do not consider non-monotonic size functions.

Our approach is related to size analysis with polynomial quasi-interpretations [6,3]. There, a program is interpreted as a *monotonic* polynomial extended with the max operation. For instance, Cons(hd, tl) is interpreted as $T + 1$, where T is a numerical variable abstracting tl. Using such interpretations one obtains upper monotonic-polynomial bounds for size functions. The main difference with our approach is that we are interested in non-monotonic lower and upper bounds. In particular, we may infer the size function $(n - m)^2$ for sqdiff : $\mathsf{L}_n(\alpha) \times \mathsf{L}_m(\alpha) \rightarrow \mathsf{L}_{(n-m)^2}(\alpha)$ (in this simple example the tight lower and upper bounds coincide), see e.g. [18]. To our knowledge, non-monotonic quasi-interpretations have not been studied for size analysis, but only for proving termination [10]. In this work one considers some unspecified algorithmically decidable classes of non-negative and negative polynomials and introduces abstract variables for the rest.

The EmBounded project aims to identify and certify resource-bounded code in *Hume*, a domain-specific high-level programming language for real-time embedded systems. In his thesis, Pedro Vasconcelos [19] uses abstract interpretation to automatically infer linear approximations of the sizes of recursive data types and the stack and heap of recursive functions written in a subset of *Hume*.

Several papers have studied programming languages with *implicit computational complexity* properties [9,5]. This line of research is motivated both by the perspective of automated complexity analysis and by fundamental goals, in particular to give natural characterisations of complexity classes, like PTIME or PSPACE. Resource analysis may be performed within a *Proof Carrying Code* framework. In [4] the authors introduce resource policies for mobile code to be run on smart devices. Policies are integrated into a proof-carrying code architecture. Two forms of policies are used: *guaranteed policies* which come with proofs and *target policies* which describe limits of the device.

7 Conclusions and Future Work

This paper presents a size-aware type system that describes multivalued size functions expressing the dependency between the sizes of inputs and the output size of a function definition. It allows to approximate multivalued output size functions via indexed *non-monotonic* polynomials augmented with the $\max_0$ operation. This feature greatly increases the applicability of our earlier size analysis, which was limited to exact sizes. The extra expressibility comes at a cost: we have crossed the border of decidability. However, this does not make the analysis infeasible in practice.

Our next step will be to extend our prototype implementation, available via `www.aha.cs.ru.nl`, to cope with different output sizes and apply it in some case studies. After that, as part of the AHA project, we will transfer our size analysis results to the world of imperative programs.

References

1. Albert, E., Arenas, P., Genaim, S., Puebla, G.: Automatic Inference of Upper Bounds for Recurrence Relations in Cost Analysis. In: Alpuente, M., Vidal, G. (eds.) SAS 2008. LNCS, vol. 5079, pp. 221–237. Springer, Heidelberg (2008)
2. Albert, E., Arenas, P., Genaim, S., Puebla, G., Zanardini, D.: Cost Analysis of Java Bytecode. In: De Nicola, R. (ed.) ESOP 2007. LNCS, vol. 4421, pp. 157–172. Springer, Heidelberg (2007)
3. Amadio, R.M.: Synthesis of max-plus quasi-interpretations. Fundamenta Informaticae 65(1-2), 29–60 (2004)
4. Aspinall, D., MacKenzie, K.: Mobile Resource Guarantees and Policies. In: Barthe, G., Grégoire, B., Huisman, M., Lanet, J.-L. (eds.) CASSIS 2005. LNCS, vol. 3956, pp. 16–36. Springer, Heidelberg (2006)
5. Atassi, V., Baillot, P., Terui, K.: Verification of Ptime Reducibility for System F Terms: Type Inference in Dual Light Affine Logic. Logical Methods in Computer Science 3(4) (2007)

6. Bonfante, G., Marion, J.-Y., Moyen, J.-Y.: Quasi-interpretations, a way to control resources. Theoretical Computer Science (2005)
7. Campbell, B.: Space Cost Analysis Using Sized Types. PhD thesis, School of Informatics, University of Edinburgh (2008)
8. Chui, C.K., Lai, M.-J.: Vandermonde determinants and lagrange interpolation in R^s. Nonlinear and Convex Analysis, 23–35 (1987)
9. Gaboardi, M., Marion, J.-Y., Rocca, S.R.D.: A logical account of PSPACE. In: Proceedings of the 35th ACM SIGPLAN-SIGACT Symposium on Principles of Programming Languages POPL 2008, San Francisco, January 10-12, pp. 121–131 (2008)
10. Hirokawa, N., Middeldorp, A.: Polynomial interpretations with negative coefficients. In: Buchberger, B., Campbell, J. (eds.) AISC 2004. LNCS (LNAI), vol. 3249, pp. 185–198. Springer, Heidelberg (2004)
11. Hofmann, M., Jost, S.: Static prediction of heap space usage for first-order functional programs. SIGPLAN Not. 38(1), 185–197 (2003)
12. Okasaki, C.: Purely Functional Data Structures. Cambridge University Press, Cambridge (1998)
13. Shkaravska, O., van Eekelen, M., Tamalet, A.: Collected size semantics for functional programs. Technical Report ICIS-R08021, Radboud University Nijmegen (November 2008)
14. Shkaravska, O., van Eekelen, M., Tamalet, A.: Polynomial size complexity analysis with families of piecewise polynomials. Technical Report ICIS-R08020, Radboud University Nijmegen (November 2008)
15. Shkaravska, O., van Kesteren, R., van Eekelen, M.: Polynomial Size Analysis of First-Order Functions. In: Rocca, S.R.D. (ed.) TLCA 2007. LNCS, vol. 4583, pp. 351–366. Springer, Heidelberg (2007)
16. Tamalet, A., Shkaravska, O., van Eekelen, M.: Size Analysis of Algebraic Data Types. In: Morazán, M. (ed.) Selected Papers of the 9th International Symposium on Trends in Functional Programming (TFP 2008). Intellect Publishers (2008) (to appear)
17. van Eekelen, M., Shkaravska, O., van Kesteren, R., Jacobs, B., Poll, E., Smetsers, S.: AHA: Amortized Heap Space Usage Analysis. In: Morazán, M. (ed.) Selected Papers of the 8th International Symposium on Trends in Functional Programming (TFP 2007), New York, USA, pp. 36–53. Intellect Publishers, UK (2007)
18. van Kesteren, R., Shkaravska, O., van Eekelen, M.: Inferring static non-monotonically sized types through testing. In: Proceedings of 16th International Workshop on Functional and (Constraint) Logic Programming (WFLP 2007), Paris, France. ENTCS, vol. 216C, pp. 45–63 (2007)
19. Vasconcelos, P.B.: Space Cost Analysis Using Sized Types. PhD thesis, School of Computer Science, University of St. Andrews (August 2008)

Embedding a Functional Hybrid Modelling Language in Haskell

George Giorgidze and Henrik Nilsson

Functional Programming Laboratory
School of Computer Science
University of Nottingham
United Kingdom
{ggg,nhn}@cs.nott.ac.uk

Abstract. In this paper we present the first investigation into the implementation of a Functional Hybrid Modelling language for non-causal modelling and simulation of physical systems. In particular, we present a simple way to handle connect constructs: a facility for composing model fragments present in some form in most non-causal modelling languages. Our implementation is realised as a domain-specific language embedded in Haskell. The method of embedding employs quasiquoting, thus demonstrating the effectiveness of this approach for languages that are not suitable for embedding in more traditional ways. Our implementation is available on-line, and thus the first publicly available prototype implementation of a Functional Hybrid Modelling language.

1 Introduction

Functional Hybrid Modelling (FHM) [21,22] is a new approach to designing *non-causal modelling languages* [4]. This class of languages is intended for modelling and simulation of systems that can be described by Differential Algebraic Equations (DAEs). Examples primarily include *physical systems*, such that electrical (see Figure 1), mechanical, hydraulic, and thermal systems. But any domain where models can be expressed in terms of DAEs, or any combination of such domains, is fine. *Non-causal* refers to treating equations as being *undirected*: an equation can be used to solve for any of the variables occurring in it. This is in contrast to *causal* modelling languages where equations are restricted to be *directed*: only known variables on one side of the equal sign, and only unknown variables on the other. Consequently, in a causal language, an equation is effectively little more than a (possibly parallel) assignment statement.

The main advantage of the causal languages is that simulation is relatively straightforward thanks to equations being directed. The advantages of the non-causal languages over the causal ones include that models are more *reusable* (as the equations can be used in many ways) and more *declarative* (as the modeller can focus on *what* to model, worrying less about *how* to model it to enable simulation) [4]. Modelica [18] is a prominent, state-of-the-art representative of the class of non-causal modelling and simulation languages.

S.-B. Scholz and O. Chitil (Eds.): IFL 2008, LNCS 5836, pp. 138–155, 2011.
© Springer-Verlag Berlin Heidelberg 2011

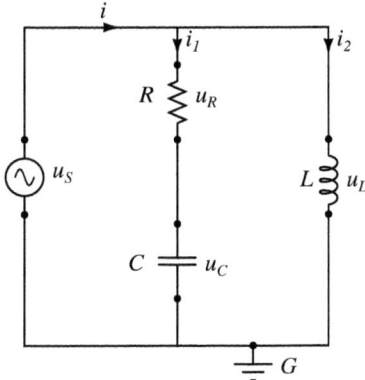

Fig. 1. A simple electrical circuit

However, current non-causal languages have their drawbacks. For example, the language designs tend to be relatively complex, being based around class systems inspired by object-oriented programming languages[1]. Modelling support for *hybrid systems* (systems that exhibit both continuous and discrete dynamic behaviour) is often not very declarative. To facilitate efficient simulation, the languages are designed on the assumption that the model is translated into simulation code once and for all. This limits the possibilities for describing *structurally dynamic systems*, where the structure evolve over time through the addition or removal of components, and in particular *highly* structurally dynamic systems, where the number of structural configurations (the *modes*) is large, unbounded, or impossible to determine in advance.

The idea of FHM is to enrich a purely functional language with a few key abstractions for supporting hybrid, non-causal modelling. By leveraging the abstraction power of the functional host language, much of the scaffolding of current non-causal modelling languages becomes redundant, and it becomes possible to describe highly structurally dynamic systems [21]. Our hypothesis is that the FHM approach will result in non-causal modelling languages that are relatively simple, have clear, purely declarative semantics, and, aided by this, advance the state of the art by supporting e.g. highly structurally dynamic systems, thus addressing the problems of current non-causal designs.

FHM is inspired by Functional Reactive Programming (FRP) [8,26], in particular Yampa [20,12]. Yampa is an *Embedded Domain-Specific Language* (EDSL) [11]. The host language is Haskell, and the central domain-specific abstraction is the *signal function*: first-class functions on signals (time-varying values). In a dynamic systems setting, signal functions are essentially directed differential equations on signals. Yampa further provides *switch constructs* that are capable

---

[1] Indeed, non-causal languages are often referred to as *object-oriented modelling languages*, even though they do not feature central object-oriented concepts like mutable objects and methods.

of switching between signal functions during simulation. Yampa thus supports *causal* modelling of highly structurally dynamic systems [6,5,10].

The key insight of FHM is that *non-causal* modelling can be supported by enriching a functional language with first-class *signal relations*: relations on signals described by undirected differential equations. While the idea of FHM is not predicated on an embedded implementation, we are currently pursuing an EDSL approach for FHM to enable us to focus on research problems related to non-causal modelling as opposed to functional language implementation.

This paper contributes at two levels: firstly to the area of design and implementation of declarative, non-causal modelling languages; secondly, and more generally, to the area of EDSLs. Specifically:

- We present the first implementation of *Hydra*[2], a language following the FHM approach. The present implementation covers all key aspects of the continuous[3] part of the FHM paradigm.
- We describe how to translate *connect constructs*, a facility for composing model fragments present in most non-causal modelling languages, into equations in the FHM setting. Our method is simpler than in other non-causal languages like Modelica [18], although it remains to be seen to what extent our approach can be used outside of FHM.
- We show how *quasiquoting* [16] makes a convenient embedded implementation of a non-causal modelling language possible, thus extending the EDSL approach to a new class of languages and further demonstrating the effectiveness of quasiquoting for embedding domain-specific languages, as pioneered by Mainland et al. [17]. This approach is particularly relevant for languages that are sufficiently different from the host language that more conventional methods of embedding, such as combinator libraries [11], are a poor fit.

The rest of this paper is organised as follows: In Section 2 we outline fundamental concepts of FHM and Hydra. In Section 3 we implement Hydra as a domain-specific language embedded in Haskell. Section 4 considers related work. Finally, we discuss future work in Section 5, notably support for highly structurally dynamic hybrid systems, and give conclusions in Section 6.

2   Fundamental Concepts of FHM and Hydra

2.1   Signals and Signal Functions

Before turning to FHM, let us review two central concepts of Yampa: *signals* and *signal functions*. Conceptually, a *signal* is a time-varying value; i.e., a function from time to a value of some type α:

$$Signal \; \alpha \approx Time \rightarrow \alpha$$

---

[2] The source code of the prototype is publicly available on-line (http://cs.nott.ac.uk/~ggg/) under the open source BSD license.

[3] E.g., structurally dynamic systems are not supported at present.

Time is continuous, and is represented as a non-negative real number. The type parameter α specifies the type of values carried by the signal. A *signal function* can be thought of as a function from signal to signal:

$$SF\ \alpha\ \beta \approx Signal\ \alpha \rightarrow Signal\ \beta$$

However, signal functions are abstract, and to ensure that they are realisable, they are additionally required to be *temporally causal*: The output of a signal function at time t is uniquely determined by the input signal on the interval $[0, t]$.

Signal functions are *first class entities* in Yampa. Signals, however, are not: they only exist indirectly through the notion of a signal function. Programming in Yampa consists of defining signal functions compositionally using Yampa's library of primitive signal functions and a set of combinators. The first class nature of signal functions enables programming of highly structurally dynamic systems using Yampa's switching combinators [20].

2.2 Signal Relations

FHM generalises the notion of signal functions to *signal relations*. A signal relation is simply a relation on signals. Stating that some signals are in a particular relation to each other imposes *constraints* on those signals. Assuming these constraints can be satisfied, this allows some of the signals to be determined in terms of the others depending on which signals are known and unknown in a given context. That is, signal relations are non-causal, unlike signal functions where the knowns and unknowns (inputs and outputs) are given a priori. Like signal functions in Yampa, signal relations are first class entities in Hydra.

Because a product of signals, say *Signal* α and *Signal* β, is isomorphic to a signal of the product of the carried types, in this case *Signal* (α, β), unary signal relations actually suffice for handling signal relations of any arity. We thus introduce the type *SR* α for a signal relation on a signal of type α.

An ordinary relation can be seen as a predicate that decides whether some given values are related or not. The same is of course true for signal relations:

$$SR\ \alpha \approx Signal\ \alpha \rightarrow Bool$$

Solving a relation thus means finding a signal that satisfies the predicate. As an example, equality is a binary signal relation:

$$(=) :: SR\ (\alpha, \alpha)$$
$$(=)\ s \approx \forall\ t.fst\ (s\ t) \equiv snd\ (s\ t)$$

Hydra adopts the following syntax for defining signal relations (inspired by the arrow notation [24]):

sigrel *pattern* **where** *equations*

The pattern binds *signal variables* that scope over the equations that follow. The equations are DAEs stated using *signal relation application* (the operator $\diamond$). Signal relation application is how the constraints embodied by a signal relation are imposed on particular signals:

$$sr \diamond s$$

Equations must be well typed. In this example, if sr has type $SR\ \alpha$, s must have type $Signal\ \alpha$. Additionally, Hydra provides a more conventional-looking syntax for equality between signals. For example: $a * x + b = 0$ is equivalent to $(=) \diamond (a * x + b, 0)$.

2.3   The Hydra Syntax

The abstract syntax of Hydra is given below. The aspects that have not yet been discussed, such as flow variables and the connect construct, are covered in the following sections. Note that, because Hydra is implemented as an embedded language, we are able to reuse Haskell for the functional part, as described in Section 3.

$\langle SigRel \rangle ::=$ `sigrel` $\langle Pattern \rangle$ `where` $\{$ $\langle ListEquation \rangle$ $\}$
$\langle Pattern \rangle ::= \langle PatNameQual \rangle \langle Identifier \rangle$
$\qquad \mid \quad (\langle ListPattern \rangle)$
$\langle ListPattern \rangle ::= \epsilon$
$\qquad \mid \quad \langle Pattern \rangle$
$\qquad \mid \quad \langle Pattern \rangle , \langle ListPattern \rangle$
$\langle PatNameQual \rangle ::= \epsilon$
$\qquad \mid \quad$ `flow`
$\langle Equation \rangle ::= \langle SigRel \rangle <> \langle Expr \rangle$
$\qquad \mid \quad \langle Expr \rangle = \langle Expr \rangle$
$\qquad \mid \quad$ `connect` $\langle Identifier \rangle \langle Identifier \rangle \langle ListIdentifier \rangle$
$\langle ListEquation \rangle ::= \epsilon$
$\qquad \mid \quad \langle Equation \rangle$
$\qquad \mid \quad \langle Equation \rangle ; \langle ListEquation \rangle$
$\langle ListIdentifier \rangle ::= \epsilon$
$\qquad \mid \quad \langle Identifier \rangle \langle ListIdentifier \rangle$
$\langle Expr \rangle ::= \langle Expr \rangle \langle Expr \rangle$
$\qquad \mid \quad \langle Expr \rangle + \langle Expr \rangle$
$\qquad \mid \quad \langle Expr \rangle - \langle Expr \rangle$
$\qquad \mid \quad \langle Expr \rangle * \langle Expr \rangle$
$\qquad \mid \quad \langle Expr \rangle / \langle Expr \rangle$
$\qquad \mid \quad \langle Expr \rangle \hat{\ } \langle Expr \rangle$
$\qquad \mid \quad - \langle Expr \rangle$
$\qquad \mid \quad \langle Identifier \rangle$
$\qquad \mid \quad \langle Integer \rangle$
$\qquad \mid \quad \langle Double \rangle$
$\qquad \mid \quad (\langle ListExpr \rangle)$
$\langle ListExpr \rangle ::= \epsilon$
$\qquad \mid \quad \langle Expr \rangle$
$\qquad \mid \quad \langle Expr \rangle , \langle ListExpr \rangle$

Instead of semicolons and curly braces, the modeller can use layout syntax in the same way as in Haskell. All examples in this paper use layout. We used the BNF Converter [25], a compiler front-end generator taking a labelled BNF grammar as input, to generate the lexer and parser of Hydra.

3   Embedding Hydra

In this section we implement Hydra as a domain-specific language embedded in Haskell. The method of embedding is inspired by Mainland et al. [17] and employs quasiquoting [16].

3.1   Why Quasiquoting?

Because of the non-causal nature of Hydra, an implementation needs the ability to manipulate models symbolically; e.g., to solve parts of models symbolically, to transform models into a form suitable for numerical simulation, and to compile models to efficient simulation code. This suggests a *deep embedding* where embedded language terms are represented as Abstract Syntax Trees (ASTs) [13,7,1].

One way to achieve this is to design a combinator library for building ASTs representing the embedded language terms. However, the use of combinators implies that the domain-specific syntax fundamentally needs to conform to the syntax of Haskell. While this can work really well in many cases (thanks to clever use of overloading, carefully crafted infix operators, and the like), the result is not always satisfying. Indeed, this observation has lead to proposals for syntactic extensions of Haskell, such as the arrow notation [24], to allow certain kinds of combinator libraries to be used in a more convenient way.

Hydra is an example of a language that does not quite fit with Haskell's syntax (or established extensions like the arrow syntax). Designing a clean combinator library without sacrificing certain aspects of the desired syntax, or introducing distracting "syntactic noise", proved to be hard. Instead, we opted to use *quasiquoting*, a meta-programming feature provided by Glasgow Haskell Compiler (GHC) as of version 6.10, which allows us to use almost exactly the syntax we want at the cost of having to provide our own parser. This parser takes a string in the domain-specific concrete syntax and returns the corresponding AST, additionally allowing for ASTs resulting from evaluating Haskell expressions to be "spliced in" where needed. Our embedding of Hydra thus allows a modeller to use a syntax that is very close to that proposed in earlier FHM-related publications [21,22].

This embedding technique clearly separates embedded language terms (in our case, non-causal Hydra models) from host language terms (in our case, the genuine Haskell expressions). Specifically, signal variables in Hydra are clearly separated from Haskell variables, which is important as signal variables must only be used in a **sigrel** abstraction.

3.2   The Haskell Embedding

Let us introduce the Haskell embedding of Hydra by modelling the circuit in Figure 1. We first define a *twoPin* model: a signal relation that captures the common behaviour of electrical components with two connectors (see Figure 2):

> *twoPin* :: *SigRel*
> *twoPin* = [**$hydra**|
>   **sigrel** ((**flow** p_i, p_v), (**flow** n_i, n_v), u) **where**
> $p_v - n_v = u$
> $p_i + n_i = 0$
> |]

The signal variables p_i and p_v represent the current into the component and the voltage at the positive pin. The signal variables n_i and n_v represent the current into the component and the voltage at the negative pin. The signal variable u represents the voltage drop across the electrical component. Signal variables in the **sigrel** pattern qualified as **flow** are called *flow* signal variables. Signal variables without any qualifier are called *potential* signal variables. The distinction between flow and potential variables is central to the meaning of the **connect** construct as discussed in Section 3.3.

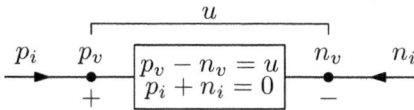

Fig. 2. An electrical component with two connectors

The symbols [**$hydra**| and |] are the quasiquotes. At compile time, GHC applies the user-defined parsing function named in the opening quote to the text between the quotes. Here, the function is called *hydra*. It has type *String* → *SigRel* and parses the concrete version of the Hydra syntax defined in Section 2.3. Values of type *SigRel* are ASTs representing Hydra signal relations. This enables the embedded Hydra compiler to process them symbolically and ultimately compile them into simulation code.

We can now use *twoPin* to define a model for a resistor parametrised with respect to the resistance. Note that a parametrised model simply is an ordinary function returning a signal relation:

> *resistor* :: *Double* → *SigRel*
> *resistor* r = [**$hydra**|
>   **sigrel** ((**flow** p_i, p_v), (**flow** n_i, n_v)) **where**
> $twoPin$ ◇ ((p_i, p_v), (n_i, n_v), u)
> r * p_i = u
> |]

Expressions between dollar signs are *antiquoted* Haskell expressions. All variables in antiquoted expressions must be in the Haskell scope. Using this technique, a modeller can splice in Haskell expressions in the Hydra models.

The current implementation only allows antiquoting of Haskell expressions of type *SigRel* in the left hand side of signal relation applications and of type *Double* in signal expressions. The result spliced in to the left in a signal relation application is thus an entire AST representing a signal relation, as required by the abstract syntax (see Section 2.3). Antiquoted expressions must have the correct type, i.e *SigRel* and *Double* respectively. Type-incorrect, antiquoted expressions are detected by GHC at compile time.

In this case, note how antiquoting is used to splice in a copy of the *twoPin* model; that is, its equations are *reused* in the context of the resistor model. Alternatively, this can be viewed as defining the resistor model by extending the *twoPin* model with an equation that characterises the specific concrete electrical component, in this case Ohm's law.

To clearly see how *twoPin* contributes to the definition of *resistor*, let us consider what happens when the resistor model is *flattened* as part of flattening of a complete model, a transformation that is described in detail in Section 3.4. Intuitively, flattening can be understood as "inlining" of applied signal relations. Thus, the arguments of a signal relation application is substituted into the body of the applied signal relation, and the entire application is then replaced by the instantiated signal relation body. In our case, the result of flattening the signal relation *resistor* 10 is:

sigrel $((\textbf{flow } p_i, p_v), (\textbf{flow } n_i, n_v))$ **where**
$$p_v - n_v = u$$
$$p_i + n_i = 0$$
$$10 * p_i = u$$

Models for an inductor, a capacitor, a voltage source and a ground are defined similarly:

$inductor :: Double \rightarrow SigRel$
$inductor\ l = [\textbf{\$hydra}|$
    sigrel $((\textbf{flow } p_i, p_v), (\textbf{flow } n_i, n_v))$ **where**
        $\$twoPin\$ \diamond ((p_i, p_v), (n_i, n_v), u)$
        $\$l\$ * der\ p_i = u$
$|]$
$capacitor :: Double \rightarrow SigRel$
$capacitor\ c = [\textbf{\$hydra}|$
    sigrel $((\textbf{flow } p_i, p_v), (\textbf{flow } n_i, n_v))$ **where**
        $\$twoPin\$ \diamond ((p_i, p_v), (n_i, n_v), u)$
        $\$c\$ * der\ u = p_i$
$|]$
$vSourceAC :: Double \rightarrow Double \rightarrow SigRel$
$vSourceAC\ v\ f = [\textbf{\$hydra}|$

```
    sigrel ((flow p_i, p_v), (flow n_i, n_v)) where
       $twoPin$ ◇ ((p_i, p_v), (n_i, n_v), u)
       u = $v$ * sin (2 * $π$ * $f$ * time)
 |]
ground :: SigRel
ground = [$hydra|
    sigrel (flow p_i, p_v) where
       p_v = 0
 |]
```

3.3 Non-causal Connections

To facilitate composition of signal relations, Hydra provides a Modelica-inspired **connect** construct. Using this, a complete model for the circuit of Figure 1 can be defined as follows:

```
simpleCircuit :: SigRel
simpleCircuit = [$hydra|
    sigrel (flow i, u) where
       $vSourceAC 1 1$ ◇ ((acp_i, acp_v), (acn_i, acn_v))
       $resistor 1$      ◇ ((rp_i, rp_v), (rn_i, rn_v))
       $inductor 1$      ◇ ((lp_i, lp_v), (ln_i, ln_v))
       $capacitor 1$     ◇ ((cp_i, cp_v), (cn_i, cn_v))
       $ground$          ◇ (gp_i, gp_v)

       connect acp_i rp_i lp_i
       connect acp_v rp_v lp_v
       connect rn_i cp_i
       connect rn_v cp_v
       connect acn_i cn_i ln_i gp_i
       connect acn_v cn_v ln_v gp_v

       i = acp_i
       u = acp_v - acn_v
 |]
```

Note how the above code is a direct textual representation of how the components are connected in the example circuit.

In the setting of Hydra, the **connect** construct is just syntactic sugar with the following rules[4]:

- The special keyword **connect** takes two or more signal variables.
- A signal variable may not appear in more than one connect statement.
- Connection of flow signal variables with potential signal variables is not allowed.

---

[4] These rules may be relaxed in the future to allow connection of, for example, aggregated signal variables.

For connected flow variables, sum-to-zero equations are generated. In the electrical domain, this corresponds to Kirchhoff's current law. For potential variables, equality constraints are generated. In the electrical domain, this asserts that the voltage at connected pins is equal. The connect constructs of *simpleCircuit* are thus expanded to the following equations:

$$acp_i + rp_i + lp_i = 0$$
$$acp_v = rp_v = lp_v$$
$$rn_i + cp_i = 0$$
$$rn_v = cp_v$$
$$acn_i + cn_i + ln_i + gp_i = 0$$
$$acn_v = cn_v = ln_v = gp_v$$

Note that the notion of flows and potentials are common to many physical domains. For example, the Modelica standard library employs connections for electrical, hydraulic, and mechanical applications, among others.

In Hydra, the expansion of connect constructs into the sum-to-zero and equality constraints is straightforward. In particular, note that all signal variables are counted positively in the sum to zero equations. This is different from Modelica [18] where a special "rule of signs" is used to determine which flow variables go with a plus sign and which go with a minus sign. Hydra obviates the need for a rule of signs by treating flow signal in signal relation applications specially, thus keeping the generation of connection equations simple. The idea is to consider a flow variable in a **sigrel** pattern as two variables, one internal and one external, related by the equation

$$i = -i'$$

where i is the internal variable and i' is the external variable. This way, flows are always directed from an interface into a component, as it were, making it possible to always count flows into connection nodes as being positive.

3.4   Model Flattening

Once the quasiquoting has been processed and the **connect** constructs translated into equations, the model is turned into a single system of equations through a process called *flattening*. This is accomplished by substituting the arguments of signal relation applications into the body of the applied signal relation. The following example illustrates the process. It also shows how flow variables are handled.

$$par :: SigRel \rightarrow SigRel \rightarrow SigRel$$
$$par\ sr1\ sr2 = [\mathbf{\$hydra}|$$
   sigrel $((\mathbf{flow}\ p_i, p_v), (\mathbf{flow}\ n_i, n_v))$ **where**
      $\$sr1\$ \diamond ((p1_i, p1_v), (n1_i, n1_v))$
      $\$sr2\$ \diamond ((p2_i, p2_v), (n2_i, n2_v))$

      connect $p_i\ p1_i\ p2_i$

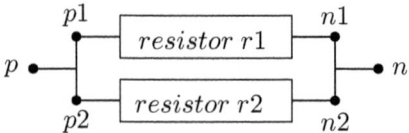

Fig. 3. Two resistors connected in parallel

       connect p_v $p1_v$ $p2_v$
       connect n_i $n1_i$ $n2_i$
       connect n_v $n1_v$ $n2_v$
|]

The function *par* takes two models of electrical components and returns a model where these components are connected in parallel. We use this function to model the component in Figure 3 and show that:

$$par\ (resistor\ r1)\ (resistor\ r2) \equiv resistor\ ((r1 * r2)\ /\ (r1 + r2))$$

First we perform the substitution of function arguments:

$par\ (resistor\ r1)\ (resistor\ r2) = [\$\mathbf{hydra}|$
    sigrel $((\mathbf{flow}\ p_i, p_v), (\mathbf{flow}\ n_i, n_v))$ **where**
       $\$resistor\ r1\$ \diamond ((p1_i, p1_v), (n1_i, n1_v))$
       $\$resistor\ r2\$ \diamond ((p2_i, p2_v), (n2_i, n2_v))$

       connect p_i $p1_i$ $p2_i$
       connect p_v $p1_v$ $p2_v$
       connect n_i $n1_i$ $n2_i$
       connect n_v $n1_v$ $n2_v$
|]

We then generate connection equations and unfold the signal relation applications:

$par\ (resistor\ r1)\ (resistor\ r2) = [\$\mathbf{hydra}|$
    sigrel $((\mathbf{flow}\ p_i, p_v), (\mathbf{flow}\ n_i, n_v))$ **where**
       $\$twoPin\$ \diamond ((-p1_i, p1_v), (-n1_i, n1_v), u1)$
       $\$r1\$ * (-p1_i) = u1$

       $\$twoPin\$ \diamond ((-p2_i, p2_v), (-n2_i, n2_v), u2)$
       $\$r2\$ * (-p2_i) = u2$

       $p_i + p1_i + p2_i = 0$
       $p_v\ \ = p1_v$
       $p1_v = p2_v$
       $n_i + n1_i + n2_i = 0$
       $n_v\ \ = n1_v$
       $n1_v = n2_v$
|]

By further unfolding of signal relation applications we get:

$par\ (resistor\ r1)\ (resistor\ r2) = [\textbf{\$hydra}|$
    $\textbf{sigrel}\ ((\textbf{flow}\ p_i, p_v), (\textbf{flow}\ n_i, n_v))\ \textbf{where}$
        $p1_v - n1_v = u1$
        $(-(-p1_i)) + (-(-n1_i)) = 0$
        $\$r1\$ * (-p1_i) = u1$

        $p2_v - n2_v = u2$
        $(-(-p2_i)) + (-(-n2_i)) = 0$
        $\$r2\$ * (-p2_i) = u2$

        $p_i + p1_i + p2_i = 0$
        $p_v\ \ = p1_v$
        $p1_v = p2_v$
        $n_i + n1_i + n2_i = 0$
        $n_v\ \ = n1_v$
        $n1_v = n2_v$
$|]$

We note that $u = u1 = u2 = p_v - n_v$ and simplify:

$par\ (resistor\ r1)\ (resistor\ r2) = [\textbf{\$hydra}|$
    $\textbf{sigrel}\ ((\textbf{flow}\ p_i, p_v), (\textbf{flow}\ n_i, n_v))\ \textbf{where}$
        $p_v - n_v = u$
        $p1_i + n1_i = 0$
        $\$r1\$ * (-p1_i) = u$
        $p2_i + n2_i = 0$
        $\$r2\$ * (-p2_i) = u$
        $p_i + p1_i + p2_i = 0$
        $n_i + n1_i + n2_i = 0$
$|]$

Solving and eliminating the variables $p1_i$, $n1_i$, $p2_i$ and $n2_i$ yields:

$par\ (resistor\ r1)\ (resistor\ r2) = [\textbf{\$hydra}|$
    $\textbf{sigrel}\ ((\textbf{flow}\ p_i, p_v), (\textbf{flow}\ n_i, n_v))\ \textbf{where}$
        $p_v - n_v = u$
        $p_i\ + n_i\ = 0$
        $\$(r1 * r2)\ /\ (r1 + r2)\$ * p_i = u$
$|]$

This is what we expected. This example also demonstrated how the first class nature of signal relations enables us to define a signal relation parametrised over other signal relations. Such models are called *higher-order non-causal models*. Broman et al. provide other motivating examples for the use of this modelling technique [3].

3.5   Simulating Hydra Models

Figure 4 illustrates the stages involved in compiling Haskell-embedded Hydra models into executable simulation code.

In the first stage, GHC is used to compile the Haskell-embedded Hydra models into the executable program. GHC first transforms all quasiquoted Hydra models into the ASTs, then type checks the Haskell program, and finally produces the executable binary.

In the second stage, the executable program is run. This compiles the Hydra ASTs into a single Modelica class. The executable internally performs type checking of the models, desugars connection statements, flattens the top level signal relation and translates it to Modelica code. For example, this type checking ensures that the type of an applied signal relation and the signal it is applied to agree. Separate type checking is necessary, because we have chosen not to embed Hydra's type system into Haskell's type system. GHC's Haskell type checking phase only guarantees that Hydra's signal relations are syntactically correct.

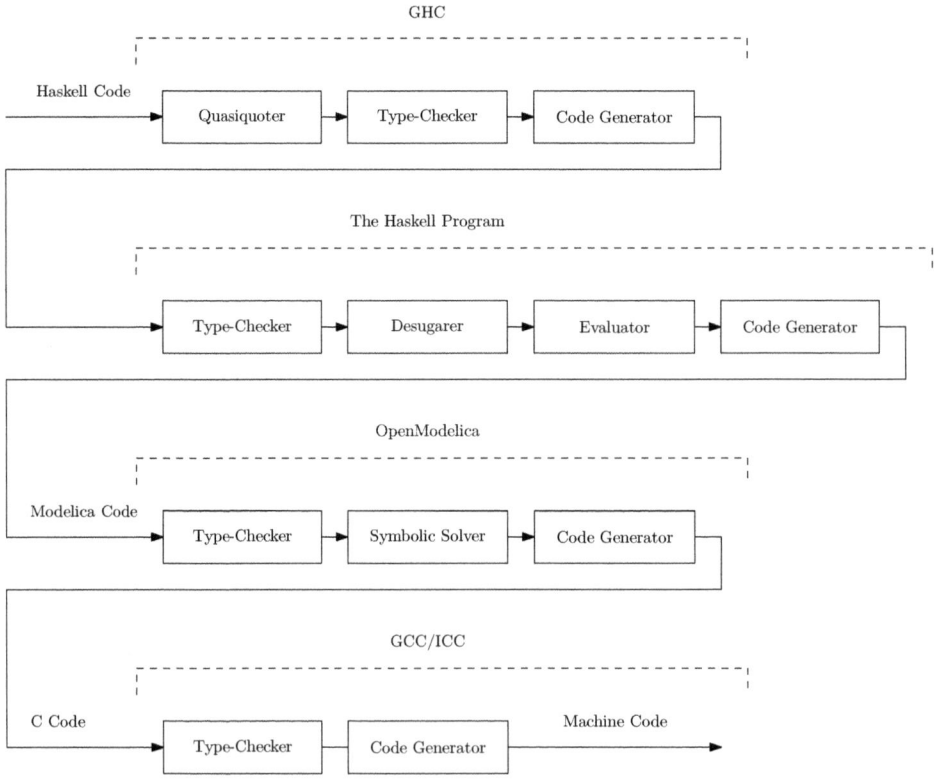

Fig. 4. The translation process in the prototype implementation from Haskell-embedded Hydra models to executable simulation code

This is well known issue in meta-programming using quasiquoting [16]. Because the type errors are detected before the start of the simulation, this is not a major drawback.

In the third phase, the OpenModelica compiler [9] is invoked to compile the generated Modelica code into the C code that then in the forth phase is compiled into the executable binary using the GNU C compiler. Finally, the actual simulation can be carried out by running this last executable.

4   Related Work

4.1   Flask

The implementation of Hydra is directly inspired by recent work on Flask [17]. Flask is a domain-specific language embedded in Haskell for programming applications for *sensor networks*: collections of devices with very limited computational and memory resources. The authors note that FRP is a suitable programming model for programming such networks. However, currently available Haskell embeddings cannot be used in this domain because that would necessitate running a Haskell run-time system. Such run-time systems are too large and heavy for typical sensor network nodes.

Flask thus uses a different embedding approach. Haskell is only used for meta-programming, not for running the actual programs. This is accomplished through quasiquoting. Haskell is used to manipulate program fragments written in the object language, which can be either Red, a restricted subset of Haskell where all functions are total and memory allocation is bounded, or nesC, a dialect of C used for programming sensor networks. NesC is provided for easy integration with existing sensor network code. The terms in the object-languages are composed using FRP-inspired combinators.

A Flask program is first compiled into the nesC code. This code is then compiled using the nesC compiler that generates code ready to be deployed on sensor network nodes. This embedding approach caught our attention as it allows for embedding of languages that are far removed from the host language, clearly separates the embedded language from the host language, and makes it possible to employ standard compiler technology to handle parsing, type checking, and code generation.

4.2   Modelling Kernel Language

Broman [2] is developing Modelling Kernel Language (MKL) that is intended to be a core language for non-causal modelling languages (e.g. Modelica). Broman takes a functional approach to non-causal modelling, which is similar to the FHM approach [21]. One of his main goal is to provide formal semantics of the core language. Currently, the formal semantics of MKL is based on an untyped λ-calculus.

Similarly to Hydra, MKL provides a λ-abstraction for defining functions and an abstraction similar to **sigrel** for defining non-causal models. Both functions and non-causal models are first class entities in MKL. This enables higher-order non-causal modelling. The similarity of the basic abstractions leads to a very similar modelling style in both languages.

However, there are a number of differences as well. MKL introduces a special notion of *connector* to state non-causal connections. This is not the case in Hydra where the connect construct works on signal variables. As a result, both the syntax and the semantics (generation of connection equations) of the connection constructs of the two languages differ. In particular, in the formal semantics of MKL the λ-calculus is extended with *effectful* constructs to handle non-causal connections; i.e., functions in MKL have an effect and are not pure. In contrast, functions in Hydra are pure and non-causal connections are also handled in a purely functional manner. Broman's ultimate goal, though, is to provide a pure, declarative surface language for modelling.

4.3   FHM at Yale

Work on FHM has also been carried out at Yale by Hai Liu under the supervision of Paul Hudak [15]. This work is mostly complementary to ours, focusing on describing the *dynamic semantics* of FHM, including structural changes. Additionally, Liu developed a type system for FHM with a strict separation between ordinary variables and signal variables. This type system thus has some similarities to the arrow calculus [14], but note that Liu's work is earlier by a few years. This similarity is to be expected as FHM was inspired by Yampa which is based on arrows, and as the distinction between ordinary variables and arrow-bound variables is second nature to anyone who has programmed using Paterson's arrow syntax [24].

4.4   Non-causal Modelling and Simulation of Hybrid Systems

As one of the goals of Hydra is to support hybrid modelling, we will briefly survey some of the most closely related work in that area.

MOSILA is an extension of the Modelica language that supports the description of structural changes using object-oriented statecharts [23]. This enables modelling of structurally dynamic systems. However, the statechart approach implies that all structural modes must be specified in advance. This means that MOSILA does not support highly structurally dynamic systems.

Sol is a Modelica-like language [27]. It introduces language constructs which enable the description of systems where objects are dynamically created and deleted, with the aim of supporting modelling of highly structurally dynamic systems. At the time of writing, this work is in its very early stages and the design and implementation of the language has not yet been completed.

5   Future Work

In Section 3 we demonstrated the embedding into Haskell of Hydra, an FHM language that supports modelling with first class signal relations. The next major step is to design and implement switching combinators capable of switching between signal relations during the simulation. This will make modelling of highly structurally dynamic systems possible. However, there are number of challenges that needs to be overcome, such as state transfer during switches and simulation code generation for highly structurally dynamic systems [21,22].

We also aim to investigate domain-specific type system aspects related to solvability of systems of equations and consistency of models in the presence of structural dynamism. The goal is to provide as many static guarantees at compile time as possible [19].

We intend to pursue our current implementation approach based on embedding and quasiquoting in our future work on extending Hydra as we have found this approach quick and flexible from an implementation perspective, while also allowing models to be written with very little syntactic "embedding noise". However, note that neither the FHM framework, nor Hydra, are predicated on this implementation approach. Ultimately, a stand-alone implementation may be the way to go.

6 Conclusions

In this paper, we showed how to realise the basic FHM notion of a signal relation and language constructs for composing signal relations into complete models as a domain-specific, deep, embedding in Haskell. We used quasiquoting, as pioneered by Mainland et al. [17], to achieve this, motivated by the fact that the syntax of the embedded language is quite far removed from Haskell, and a desire to avoid as much "syntactic embedding noise" as possible. We think quasiquoting is a promising approach for domain-specific embeddings as it, in addition to the usual benefits of embedded language implementations, allows standard compilation technology to be applied for analysis and code generation, something which can can be essential for performance reasons.

The main contribution of this paper is the first investigation into the implementation of the fundamental aspects of an FHM language. The paper is supported by the publicly available prototype implementation. It enables physical modelling with first class signal relations and can model and simulate systems with static structure. Support of highly structurally dynamic hybrid systems is the subject of future work, together with other topics outlined in Section 5.

Acknowledgements. This work was supported by EPSRC grant EP/D064554/1. Thanks to the anonymous referees for many useful suggestions. We would also like to thank Neil Sculthorpe and Zurab Khetsuriani for their helpful comments and feedback.

References

1. Augustsson, L., Mansell, H., Sittampalam, G.: Paradise: a two-stage DSL embedded in Haskell. In: ICFP 2008: Proceeding of the 13th ACM SIGPLAN International Conference on Functional Programming, pp. 225–228. ACM, New York (2008)

2. Broman, D.: Flow lambda calculus for declarative physical connection semantics. Technical Reports in Computer and Information Science No. 1. LIU Electronic Press (2007)

3. Broman, D., Fritzson, P.: Higher-order acausal models. In: Proceedings of the 2nd International Workshop on Equation-Based Object-Oriented Languages and Tools, Paphos, Cyprus, pp. 59–69. LIU Electronic Press (2008)

4. Cellier, F.E.: Object-oriented modelling: Means for dealing with system complexity. In: Proceedings of the 15th Benelux Meeting on Systems and Control, Mierlo, The Netherlands, pp. 53–64 (1996)

5. Cheong, M.H.: Functional programming and 3D games. BEng thesis, University of New South Wales, Sydney, Australia (November 2005)

6. Courtney, A., Nilsson, H., Peterson, J.: The Yampa arcade. In: Proceedings of the 2003 ACM SIGPLAN Haskell Workshop (Haskell 2003), Uppsala, Sweden, pp. 7–18. ACM Press, New York (2003)

7. Elliott, C., Finne, S., de Moor, O.: Compiling embedded languages. Journal of Functional Programming 13(2) (2003); Updated version of paper by the same name that appeared in SAIG 2000 proceedings

8. Elliott, C., Hudak, P.: Functional reactive animation. In: Proceedings of ICFP 1997: International Conference on Functional Programming, pp. 163–173 (June 1997)

9. Fritzson, P., Aronsson, P., Pop, A., Lundvall, H., Nystrom, K., Saldamli, L., Broman, D., Sandholm, A.: OpenModelica - a free open-source environment for system modeling, simulation, and teaching. In: 2006 IEEE International Symposium on Computer-Aided Control Systems Design, pp. 1588–1595 (October 2006)

10. Giorgidze, G., Nilsson, H.: Switched-on Yampa. In: Hudak, P., Warren, D.S. (eds.) PADL 2008. LNCS, vol. 4902, pp. 282–298. Springer, Heidelberg (2008)

11. Hudak, P.: Modular domain specific languages and tools. In: Proceedings of Fifth International Conference on Software Reuse, pp. 134–142 (June 1998)

12. Hudak, P., Courtney, A., Nilsson, H., Peterson, J.: Arrows, robots, and functional reactive programming. In: Jeuring, J., Jones, S.L.P. (eds.) AFP 2002. LNCS, vol. 2638, pp. 159–187. Springer, Heidelberg (2003)

13. Leijen, D., Meijer, E.: Domain specific embedded compilers. In: Proceedings of the 2nd Conference on Domain-Specific Languages, pp. 109–122. ACM Press, New York (1999)

14. Lindley, S., Wadler, P., Yallop, J.: The arrow calculus, functional pearl (2008), http://homepages.inf.ed.ac.uk/wadler/topics/links.html

15. Liu, H.: CS690 report of FHM. Available from Computer Science, Yale University (May 2005)

16. Mainland, G.: Why it's nice to be quoted: Quasiquoting for Haskell. In: Haskell 2007: Proceedings of the ACM SIGPLAN Workshop on Haskell Workshop, pp. 73–82. ACM, New York (2007)

17. Mainland, G., Morrisett, G., Welsh, M.: Flask: Staged functional programming for sensor networks. In: Proceedings of the Thirteenth ACM SIGPLAN International Conference on Functional Programming (ICFP 2008), Victoria, British Columbia, Canada. ACM Press, New York (2008)

18. The Modelica Association. Modelica – A unified object-oriented language for physical systems modeling: Language Specification version 3.0 (September 2007), http://www.modelica.org/documents/ModelicaSpec30.pdf

19. Nilsson, H.: Type-based structural analysis for modular systems of equations. In: Fritzson, P., Cellier, F., Broman, D. (eds.) Proceedings of the 2nd International Workshop on Equation-Based Object-Oriented Languages and Tools, Paphos, Cyprus. Linköping Electronic Conference Proceedings, vol. 29, pp. 71–81. Linköping University Electronic Press (July 2008)
20. Nilsson, H., Courtney, A., Peterson, J.: Functional reactive programming, continued. In: Proceedings of the 2002 ACM SIGPLAN Haskell Workshop (Haskell 2002), Pittsburgh, Pennsylvania, USA, pp. 51–64. ACM Press, New York (2002)
21. Nilsson, H., Peterson, J., Hudak, P.: Functional Hybrid Modeling. In: Dahl, V. (ed.) PADL 2003. LNCS, vol. 2562, pp. 376–390. Springer, Heidelberg (2002)
22. Nilsson, H., Peterson, J., Hudak, P.: Functional hybrid modeling from an object-oriented perspective. In: Fritzson, P., Cellier, F., Nytsch-Geusen, C. (eds.) Proceedings of the 1st International Workshop on Equation-Based Object-Oriented Languages and Tools. Linköping Electronic Conference Proceedings, vol. 24, pp. 71–87. Linköping University Electronic Press (2007)
23. Nytsch-Geusen, C., Ernst, T., Nordwig, A., Schwarz, P., Schneider, P., Vetter, M., Wittwer, C., Nouidui, T., Holm, A., Leopold, J., Schmidt, G., Mattes, A., Doll, U.: MOSILAB: Development of a modelica based generic simulation tool supporting model structural dynamics. In: Proceedings of the 4th International Modelica Conference, Hamburg, Germany, pp. 527–535 (2005)
24. Paterson, R.: A new notation for arrows. In: Proceedings of the 2001 ACM SIGPLAN International Conference on Functional Programming, Firenze, Italy, pp. 229–240 (September 2001)
25. Pellauer, M., Forsberg, M., Ranta, A.: BNF Converter: Multilingual front-end generation from labelled BNF grammars. Technical report, Computing Science at Chalmers University of Technology and Gothenburg University (September 2004)
26. Wan, Z., Hudak, P.: Functional reactive programming from first principles. In: Proceedings of PLDI 2001: Symposium on Programming Language Design and Implementation, pp. 242–252 (June 2000)
27. Zimmer, D.: Introducing Sol: A general methodology for equation-based modeling of variable-structure systems. In: Proceedings of the 6th International Modelica Conference, Bielefeld, Germany, pp. 47–56 (2008)

Obsidian:
A Domain Specific Embedded Language
for Parallel Programming of Graphics Processors

Joel Svensson, Mary Sheeran, and Koen Claessen

Chalmers University of Technology, Göteborg, Sweden

Abstract. We present a domain specific language, embedded in Haskell, for general purpose parallel programming on GPUs. Our intention is to explore the use of *connection patterns* in parallel programming. We briefly present our earlier work on hardware generation, and outline the current state of GPU architectures and programming models. Finally, we present the current status of the *Obsidian* project, which aims to make GPU programming easier, without relinquishing detailed control of GPU resources. Both a programming example and some details of the implementation are presented. This is a report on work in progress.

1 Introduction

There is a pressing need for new and better ways to program parallel machines. Graphics Processing Units (GPUs) are one kind of such parallel machines that provide a lot of computing power. Modern GPUs have become extremely interesting for *general purpose* programming, i.e. computing functions that have little or nothing to do with graphics programming.

We aim to develop high-level methods and tools, based on functional programming, for low-level general purpose programming of GPUs. The methods are high-level because we are making use of common powerful programming abstractions in functional programming, such as higher-order functions and polymorphism. At the same time, we still want to provide control to the programmer on important low-level details such as how much parallelism is introduced, and memory layout. (These aims are in contrast to other approaches to GPU programming, where the programmer expresses the intent in a high-level language, and then lets a smart compiler try to do its best.)

Based on our earlier work on structural hardware design, we plan to investigate whether or not a *structure-oriented programming style* can be used in programming modern GPUs. We are developing Obsidian, a domain specific language embedded in Haskell. The aim is to make extensive use of higher order functions capturing *connection patterns*, and from these compact descriptions to generate code to run on the GPUs. Our hardware-oriented view of programming also leads us to investigate the use of algorithmic ideas from the hardware design community in parallel programming.

S.-B. Scholz and O. Chitil (Eds.): IFL 2008, LNCS 5836, pp. 156–173, 2011.

In the rest of the paper, we first briefly review our earlier work on hardware description languages (Sect. 2), and introduce the GPU architecture we are working with (Sect. 3). After that, we describe the current status of the language Obsidian, and show examples (Sect. 4) and experimental results (Sect. 5). Obsidian is currently very much work in progress; we discuss motivations and current shortcomings (Sect. 6) and future directions (Sect. 7).

2   Connection Patterns for Hardware Design and Parallel Programming

Connection patterns that capture common ways to connect sub-circuits into larger structures have been central to our research on functional and relational languages for hardware design. Inspired by Backus' FP language, Sheeran's early work on μFP made use of *combining forms* with geometric interpretations [23]. This approach to capturing circuit regularity was also influenced by contact with designers of regular array circuits in industry – see reference [24] for an overview of this and much other work on functional programming and hardware design.

Later work on (our) Ruby considered the use of binary relations, rather than functions in specifying hardware [13]. Lava builds upon these ideas, but also gains much in expressiveness and flexibility by being embedded in Haskell [1,5]. The user writes what look like circuit descriptions, but are in fact circuit *generators*. Commonly used *connection patterns* are captured by higher order functions.

For example, an important pattern is parallel prefix or scan. Given inputs $[x_0, x_1 \ldots x_{n-1}]$, the prefix problem is to compute each $x_0 \circ x_1 \circ \ldots \circ x_j$ for $0 \leq j < n$, for $\circ$ an associative, but not necessarily commutative, operator. For example, the prefix sum of [1..10] is [1,3,6,10,15,21,28,36,45,55]. There is an obvious sequential solution, but in circuit design one is often aiming for a circuit that exploits parallelism, and so is faster (but also larger). In a construction attributed to Sklansky, one can perform the prefix calculation by first, recursively, performing the prefix calculation on each half of the input, and then combining (via the operator) the last output of the first of these recursive calls with each of the outputs of the second. For instance, to calculate the prefix sum of [1..10], one can compute the prefix sums of [1..5] and [6..10], giving [1,3,6,10,15] and [6,13,21,30,40], respectively. The final step is to add the last element of the output of the first recursive call (15) to each element of the output of the second.

To express the construction in Lava, we make use of two connection patterns. `two :: ([a] -> [b]) -> [a] -> [b]` applies its component to the top and bottom halves of the input list, concatenating the two sub-lists that result from these applications. Thus, `two (sklansky plus)` applied to [1..10] gives [1,3,6,10,15,6,13,21,30,40]. Left-to-right serial composition has type `(a -> b) -> (b -> c) -> a -> c` and is written as infix `->-`. The description of the construction mixes the use of connection patterns, giving a form of reuse, with the naming of "wires".

```
sklansky :: ((t, t) -> t) -> [t] -> [t]
sklansky op [a] = [a]
sklansky op as = (two (sklansky op) ->- sfan) as
  where
    sfan as = a1s ++ a2s'
      where
        (a1s,a2s) = splitAt ((length as + 1) 'div' 2) as
        a2s'      = [op(last a1s,a) | a <- a2s]

*Main> simulate (sklansky plus) [1..10]
[1,3,6,10,15,21,28,36,45,55]
```

Lava supports simulation, formal verification and netlist generation from definitions like this. Circuit descriptions are *run* (in fact symbolically evaluated) in order to produce an intermediate representation, which is in turn written out in various formats (for fixed size instances). So this is an example of *staged programming* [26].

The Sklansky construction is one way to implement parallel prefix, and there are many others, see for instance Hinze's excellent survey [11]. Those who develop prefix algorithms suitable for hardware implementation use a standard notation to represent the resulting networks. Data flows from top to bottom and the least significant input is at top left. Black dots represent operators. For example, Figure 1 shows the recursive Sklansky construction for 32 inputs.

In this work, we plan to investigate the use of connection patterns, and more generally an emphasis on *structure*, in parallel programming. We have chosen to target GPUs partly because of available expertise among our colleagues at Chalmers, and partly because reading papers about General Purpose GPU (GPGPU) programming gave us a sense of déjà vu. Programs are illustrated graphically, and bear a remarkable resemblance to circuit modules that we have generated in the past using Lava. We see an opportunity here, as there is an extensive literature, going back to the 1960s, about implementing algorithms on silicon that may provide clues about implementing algorithms on GPUs. This literature does not seem to have yet been scrutinised by the Data Parallel Programming or GPGPU communities. This is possibly because GPUs are moving

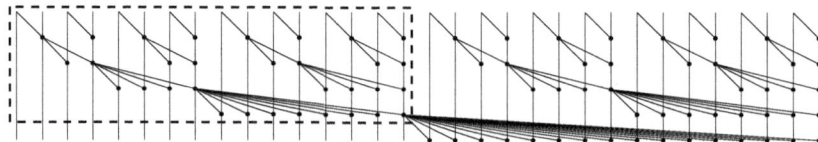

Fig. 1. The Sklansky construction for 32 inputs. It recursively computes the parallel prefix for each half of the inputs (corresponding to the use of **two** in the definition) and then combines the last output of the lower (left) half with each of the outputs of the upper (right) half. The dotted box outlines the recursive call on the lower half of the inputs.

closer to simply being data parallel machines, and so work on library functions has taken inspiration from earlier work on Data Parallel Programming, such as Blelloch's NESL [2]. But some of the restrictions from the early data parallel machines no longer hold today; for instance broadcasting a value to many processors was expensive in the past, but is much easier to do on modern GPUs. So a construction like Sklansky, which requires such broadcasting, should now be reconsidered, and indeed we have found it to give good results in our initial experiments (writing directly in CUDA). In general, it makes sense to spread the net beyond the standard data parallel programming literature when looking for inspiration in parallel algorithm design. We plan to explore the use of "old" circuit design ideas in programming library functions for GPUs.

Below, we briefly review modern GPUs and a standard programming model.

3   Graphics Processing Units, Accessible High Performance Parallel Computing

In the development of microprocessors, the addition of new cores is now the way forward, rather than the improvement of single thread performance. Graphics processing units (GPUs) have moved from being specialised graphics engines to being suitable to tackle applications with high computational demands. For a recent survey of the hardware, programming methods and tools, and successful applications, the reader is referred to [20]. Figure 2, taken from that paper, and due to NVIDIA, shows the architecture of a modern GPU from NVIDIA. It contains 16 multiprocessors, grouped in pairs that share a texture fetch unit (TF in the figure). The texture fetch unit is of little importance when using the GPU for general purpose computations. Each multiprocessor has 8 stream processors (marked SP in the figure). These stream processors has access to 16kB of shared memory.

See reference [20] for information about the very similar AMD GPU architecture. We have used the NVIDIA architecture, but developments are similar at AMD. Intel's Larrabee processor points to a future in which each individual core is considerably more powerful than in today's GPUs [22].

The question of how to program powerful data-parallel processors is likely to continue to be an interesting one. Unlike for current multicore machines, the question here is how to keep a large number of small processors productively occupied. NVIDIA's solution has been to develop the architecture and the programming model in parallel. The result is called CUDA – an extension of C designed to allow developers to exploit the power of GPUs. Reference [17] gives a very brief but illuminating introduction to CUDA for potential new users. The idea is that the user writes small blocks of straightforward C code, which should then run in thousands or millions of threads. We borrow the example from the above introduction. To add two $N \times N$ matrices on a CPU, using C, one would write something like

```
// add 2 matrices on the CPU:
void addMatrix(float *a, float *b, float *c, int N)
{
  int i, j, index;
  for (i = 0; i < N; i++) {
    for (j = 0; j < N; j++) {
      index = i + j * N;
      c[index]=a[index] + b[index];
    }
  }
}
```

In CUDA, one writes a similar C function, called a *kernel*, to compute one element of the matrix. Then, the kernel is invoked as many times as the matrix has elements, resulting in many threads, which can be run in parallel. A predefined structure called `threadIdx` is used to label each of these many threads, and can be referred to in the kernel.

```
// add 2 matrices on the GPU (simplified)
__global__ void addMatrix(float *a,float *b, float *c, int N)
{
  int i= threadIdx.x;
  int j= threadIdx.y;
  int index= i + j * N;
  c[index]= a[index] + b[index];
}

void main()
{
  // run addMatrix in 1 block of NxN threads:
  dim3 blocksize(N, N),
  addMatrix<<<1, blocksize>>>(a, b, c, N);
}
```

Here, a two dimensional *thread block* of size $N \times N$ is created.

CUDA uses *barrier synchronisation* and *shared memory* for introducing communication between threads. Contents of shared memory (16kB per multiprocessor in the architecture shown in Figure 2) is visible to all threads in a thread block. It is very much faster to access this shared memory than to access the global device memory. We shall see later that Obsidian provides users with both shared and global arrays, giving the user control over where data is to be stored.

Since many threads are now writing and reading from the same shared memory, it is necessary to have a mechanism that enables the necessary synchronisation between threads. CUDA provides a barrier synchronisation mechanism called `__syncthreads()`. Only when all threads in a block have reached this barrier can any of them proceed. This allows the programmer to ensure safe access to the shared memory for the many threads in a thread block.

Now, a *grid* is a collection of thread blocks. Each thread block runs on a single multiprocessor, and the CUDA system can schedule these individual blocks in

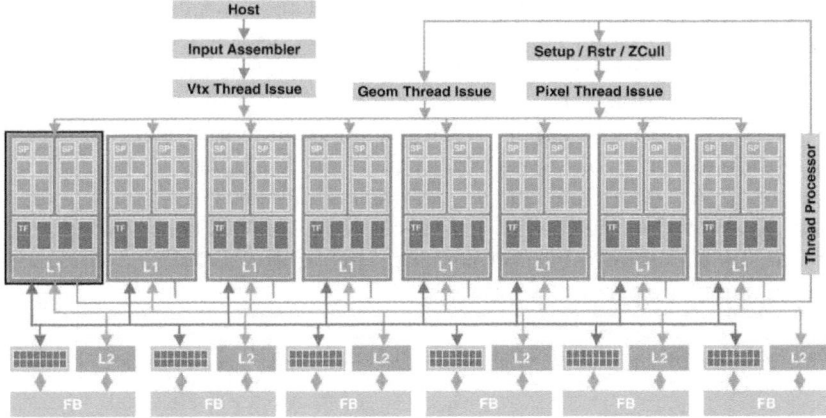

Fig. 2. The NVIDIA 8800GTX GPU architecture, with 8 pairs of multiprocessors. Diagram courtesy of NVIDIA.

order to maximise the use of GPU resources. A complete program then consists not only of the kernel definitions, but also of code, to be run on the CPU, to launch a kernel on the GPU, examine the results and possibly launch new kernels. In this paper, we will not go into details about how kernels are coordinated, but will concentrate on how to write individual kernels, as this is the part of Obsidian that is most developed. In Obsidian, we write code that looks like the Lava descriptions in section 2, and we generate CUDA code like that shown above. This is a considerably more complex process than the generation of netlists in Lava.

4   Obsidian: A Domain Specific Embedded Language for GPU Programming

To introduce Obsidian, we consider the implementation of a parallel prefix kernel. The implementation bears a close resemblance to the Lava implementation from section 2:

```
sklansky :: (Choice a, Syncable (Arr s a)) =>
             (a -> a -> a) -> Arr s a -> W (Arr s a)
sklansky op arr
    | len arr == 1 = return arr
    | otherwise = (two (sklansky op) ->- sfan ->- sync) arr
    where sfan arr = do
             (a1,a2) <- halve arr
             let m = len a1
                 c = a1 ! (fromInt (m-1))
             a2' <- fun (op c) a2
             conc (a1,a2')
```

The most notable differences between the two implementations are that Obsidian functions are monadic and that a datatype `Arr` is used where Haskell lists are used in Lava. The pattern matching on the list used in Lava is here replaced by guards. The function `len :: Arr s a -> Int` gives the length of the array. These differences lead to a slightly different programming style.

The Obsidian version of the `sklansky` function implements the sought recursive parallel prefix algorithm, but it contains no information about where in the memory hierarchy the intermediate results are to be held. The following program uses `sklansky` from above but turns it into a concrete kernel that computes all the partial sums of an array of integers:

```
scan_add_kernel :: GArr IntE -> W (GArr IntE)
scan_add_kernel = cache ->- sklansky (+) ->- wb ->- sync
```

The function `cache` specifies that if the array is stored it should be stored in the on-chip shared memory. Actually storing an array is done using the `sync` function, which functionally is the identity function, but has the extra effect of synchronising all processes after writing their data in shared memory, such that they can exchange intermediate results. Using `sync` here allows for computations or transformations to be performed on the data as it is being read in from global device memory. In the `scan_add_kernel` above this means that the first `sklansky` stage will be computed with global data as input, putting its result into shared memory. A kernel computing the same thing but using the memory differently can be implemented like this:

```
scan_add_kernel2 :: GArr IntE -> W (GArr IntE)
scan_add_kernel2 = cache ->- sync ->- sklansky (+) ->- wb ->-
                   sync
```

Here the array is first stored into shared memory. The `sklansky` stages are then computed entirely in shared memory. The write-back function, `wb`, works in a very similar way but specifies that the array should be moved back into the global memory.

Now, `scan_add_kernel` can be launched on the GPU from within a GHCI session using a function called `execute`:

```
execute :: ExecMode -> (GArr (Exp a) -> W (GArr (Exp b)) ->
           [Exp a] -> IO [Exp b]
```

Here `ExecMode` can be either `GPU` for launching the kernel on the GPU or `EMU` for running it in emulation mode on the system's CPU. Below is the result[1] of launching the scan kernel on example input:

```
*Main> execute GPU scan_add_kernel [1..256]
[0,1,3,6,10,15, ... ,32131,32385,32640]
```

---

[1] The output has been shortened to fit on a line.

Beyond the combinators described so far, we have experimented with combinators and permutations needed for certain iterative sorting networks. Amongst these are **evens** that applies a function to each pair of elements of an array. Together with **rep** that repeats a computation a given number of times and a permutation called **riffle** a shuffle exchange network can be defined:

```
shex n f = rep n (riffle ->- evens f ->- sync)
```

The shuffle exchange network can be used to implement a merger useful in sorters.

4.1   Implementation

As seen in the examples, an Obsidian program is built from functions between arrays. These arrays are of type **Arr s a**. There are also type synonyms **GArr** and **SArr** implemented as follows:

```
data Arr s a = Arr (IxExp ->  a, Int)
type GArr a = Arr Global a
type SArr a = Arr Shared a
```

In Obsidian an array is represented by a function from indices to values and an integer giving the length of the array.

In most cases the **a** in **Arr s a** will be of an expression type:

```
data DExp = LitInt Int
          | LitBool Bool
          | LitFloat Float
          | BinOp Op2 DExp DExp
          | UnOp  Op1 DExp
          | If DExp DExp DExp
          | Variable Name
          | Index DExp DExp
            deriving(Eq,Show)
```

The above expressions are dynamic in the sense that they can be used to represent values of **Int**, **Float** and **Bool** type. This follows the approach from Compiling Embedded Languages [9]. However, to obtain a typed environment in which to operate, phantom types are used.

```
type Exp a = E DExp

type IntE   = Exp Int
type FloatE = Exp Float
type BoolE  = Exp Bool
type IxExp  = IntE
```

As an example consider the program:

```
add_one :: GArr IntE -> W (GArr IntE)
add_one = fun (+1) ->- sync
```

This program adds 1 to each element of an array of integers. The function `fun` has type `(a -> b) -> Arr s a -> Arr s b`. `fun` performs for arrays what `map` does for lists. The `sync` function used in the example has the effect that the array being synced upon is written to memory. At this point the type of the array determines where in memory it is stored. An array of type `SArr` will end up in the *shared memory* (which is currently 16KB per multi-processor). In this version of Obsidian it is up to the programmer to make sure that the array fits in the memory. An array of type `GArr` ends up in the global device memory, roughly a gigabyte on current graphics cards. Using `sync` can have performance implications since it facilitates sharing of computed values.

To generate CUDA code from the Obsidian program `add_one`, it is applied to a symbolic array of a given concrete length (in this example 256 elements):

```
input :: GArr IntE
input = mkArray (\ix -> (index (variable "input") ix)) 256
```

Applying `fun (+1)` to this input array results in an array with the following indexing function:

```
(\ix -> (E (BinOp Add (Index (Variable "input") ix) (LitInt 1))))
```

At the code generation phase this function is evaluated using a variable representing a thread Id. The result is an expression looking as follows:

```
E (BinOp Add (Index (Variable "input") (Variable "tid")) (LitInt 1))
```

This expression is a direct description of what is to be computed.

Importantly, the basic library functions can be implemented using the `Arr s a` type and thus be applicable both to shared and global arrays. The library function `rev` that reverses an array is shown as an example of this:

```
rev :: Arr s a -> W (Arr s a)
rev arr = let n = len arr
          in  return $ mkArray (\ix -> arr ! ((n - 1) - ix)) n
```

The function `rev` uses `mkArray` to create an array whose indexing function reverses the order of the elements of the given array `arr`. The Obsidian program `rev ->- sync` corresponds[2] to the following lines of C code:

```
arrx[ThreadIdx.x] = arry[n - 1 - ThreadIdx.x];
__syncthreads();
```

When an Obsidian function, such as the `scan_add_kernel` from the previous section, is run, two data structures are accumulated into a monad called `W`. The first is intermediate code `IC` and the second a symbol table. The `W` monad is a writer monad extended with some extra functionality for generating identifier names and to maintain the symbol table. You can think of the `W` monad as:

---

[2] In the real IC `arrx` and `arry` are replaced by identifiers generated in the `W` monad.

```
type W a = WriterT (IxExp -> IC) (State (SymbolTable,Int)) a
```

The IC used here is just a list of statements, (less important statements have been removed to save space (...)). The IC contains a subset of CUDA. In this version of Obsidian not much more than the **Synchronize** and assignment statements of CUDA are used.

```
data Statement = Synchronize
               | DExp ::= DExp
               -- used later in code generation
               | IfThenElse BoolE [Statement] [Statement]
                 deriving (Show,Eq)

type IC = [Statement]
```

The symbol table is a mapping from names to types and sizes:

```
type SymbolTable = Map Name (Type,Int)
```

Information needs to be stored into the SymbolTable whenever new intermediate arrays are created. We have chosen to put this power in the hands of the programmer using the **sync** function. The **sync** function is overloaded for a number of different array types:

```
class Syncable a where
    sync :: a -> W a
    commit :: a -> W a
```

The types of the **sync** and the related **commit** function are shown in the class declaration above. To illustrate what **sync** does, one instance of its implementation is shown:

```
instance TypeOf (Exp a) => Syncable (GArr (Exp a)) where
    sync arr = do
      arr' <- commit arr
      write $ \ix -> [Synchronize]
      return arr'
    commit arr = do
      let n = len arr
      var  <- newGlobalArray (typeOf (arr ! (E (LitInt 0)))) n
      write $ \ix -> [(unE (index var ix)) ::= unE (arr ! ix)]
      return $ mkArray (\ix -> index var ix) n
```

The **sync** function commits its argument array and thereafter writes [Synchronize] into the W monad. To see what this means, one should also look at the **commit** function, in which a new array is created of the same size and type as the given array. In the next step, an assignment statement is written into W monad (added to the intermediate code). It assigns the values computed in the given array to the newly created array. From the intermediate code and

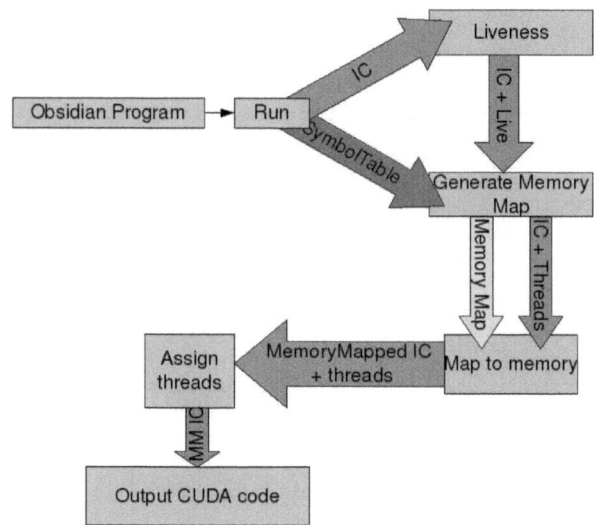

Fig. 3. Steps involved in generating CUDA C code from Obsidian description. The boxes represent functions and the arrows represent data structures.

the symbol table accumulated into the W monad, C code is generated following a procedure outlined in figure 3.

The first step depicted in the figure is the running the Obsidian program. This builds two data structures IC and SymbolTable. The IC goes through a simple liveness analysis where for each statement information about what data elements, in this case arrays, are alive at that point is added. An array is alive if it is used in any of the following statements or if it is considered a result of the program. The result of this pass is a new *IC* where each statement also has a set of names pointing out arrays that are alive at that point.

```
type ICLive = [(Statement, Set Name)]
```

Now, the symbol table together with the ICLive object is used to lay out the arrays in memory. Arrays that had type SArr are assigned storage in the shared memory and arrays of type GArr in Global memory. The result of this stage is a *Memory Map*. This is a mapping from names to positions in memory. The picture also shows that another output from this stage is intermediate code annotated with thread information, call it ICT. This is now done in a separate pass over the IC but it could be fused with the memory mapping stage, saving a pass over the IC. The ICT is just a list of statements and the number of threads assigned to compute them:

```
type ICT = [(Statement,Int)]
```

This enables the final pass over the IC to move thread information into the actual IC as conditionals. The resulting IC is used to output CUDA code.

To illustrate this, the code generated from a simple Obsidian program is shown. The example is very artificial and uses sync excessively in order to create more intermediate arrays :

```
rev_add :: GArr IntE -> W (GArr IntE)
rev_add = rev ->- sync ->- fun (+1) ->- sync
```

Figure 4 shows the CUDA C code generated from the rev_add program. Here it is visible how intermediate arrays are assigned memory in global memory. The global memory is pointed to by gbase:

```
__global__ static void rev_add(int *source0,char *gbase){
extern __shared__ char sbase[] __attribute__ ((aligned(4)));
const int tid = threadIdx.x;
const int n0 __attribute__ ((unused)) = 256;
((int *)(gbase+0))[tid] = source0[((256 - 1) - tid)];
__syncthreads();
  ((int *)(gbase+1024))[tid] = (((int *)(gbase+0))[tid] + 1);
__syncthreads();
```

Fig. 4. Generated CUDA code

The code in figure 4 does however not show how the ICT is used in assigning work to threads. To show this a small part of the generated CUDA code from the scan_add_kernel is given in figure 5. Notice the conditional if (tid < 128). This line effectively shuts down half of the threads. It can also be seen here how shared memory is used, pointed to by sbase. Moreover, from the line with (63 < 64) ? ... it becomes clear that there is room for some obvious optimisations.

```
 __syncthreads();
 if (tid < 128){
   ((int *)(sbase+1520))[tid] = ((tid < 64) ?
   ((tid < 64) ?
   ((int *)(sbase+496))[tid] :
   ((int *)(sbase+752))[(tid - 64)]) :
   (((63 < 64) ?
   ((int *)(sbase+496))[63] :
   ((int *)(sbase+752))[(63 - 64)]) + ((tid < 64) ?
   ((int *)(sbase+496))[tid] :
   ((int *)(sbase+752))[(tid - 64)])));
 }
```

Fig. 5. A small part of the CUDA code generated from the recursive implementation of the Sklansky parallel prefix algorithm.

5 Results

Apart from the parallel prefix algorithm shown in this paper we have used Obsidian to implement sorters. For the sorters, the generated C code performs quite well. One periodic sorting network, called *Vsort*, implemented in Obsidian in the style of the sorters presented in reference [6], has a running time of 95μsecs for 256 elements (the largest size that we can cope with in a single kernel). This running time can be compared to the 28μsecs running time of the bitonic sort example supplied with the CUDA SDK. However, for 256 inputs, bitonic sort has a depth (counted in number of comparators between input and output), of 36 compared to Vsort's 64. So we feel confident that we can make a sorter that improves considerably on our Vsort by implementing a recursive algorithm for which the corresponding network depth is less. (We implemented the periodic sorter in an earlier version of the system, in which recursion was not available.) The point here is not to be as fast as hand-crafted library code, but to come close enough to allow the user to quickly construct short readable programs that give decent performance. The results for sorting are promising in this respect. Sadly, the results for the Sklansky example are rather poor, and we will return to this point in the following section.

The programs reported here were run on an NVIDIA 8800GTS and timed using the CUDA profiler.

6 Discussion

6.1 Our Influences

As mentioned above, our earlier work on Lava has provided the inspiration for the combinator-oriented or hardware-like style of programming that we are exploring in Obsidian. On the other hand, the *implementation* of Obsidian has been much influenced by Pan, an embedded language for image synthesis developed by Conal Elliot [7]. Because of the computational complexity of image generation, C code is generated. This C code can then be compiled by an optimising compiler. Many ideas from the paper "Compiling Embedded Languages", describing the implementation of Pan have been used in the implementation of Obsidian [9].

6.2 Related Work on GPU and GPGPU Programming Languages

We cannot attempt an exhaustive description of GPU programming languages here, but refer the reader to a recent PhD thesis by Philipp Lucas, which contains an enlightening survey [16]. Lucas distinguishes carefully between languages (such as CG and HLSL) that aim to raise the level of abstraction at which graphics-oriented GPU programs are written, and those that attempt to abstract the entire GPU, and so must also provide a means to express the placing of programs on the GPU, feeding such programs with data, reading the results back to the CPU, and so on, as well as deciding to what extent the programmer should be involved in stipulating those tasks. In the first group of graphics-oriented languages, we include PyGPU and Vertigo. PyGPU is a language for image processing embedded in Python [15]. PyGPU uses the introspective abilities of Python and thus bypasses the need to implement new loop structures and conditionals for the embedded language. In Python it is possible to access the bytecode of a function and from that extract information about loops and conditionals. Programs written in PyGPU can be compiled and run on a GPU. Vertigo is another embedded language by Conal Elliot [8]. It is a language for 3D graphics that targets the DirectX 8.1 shader model, and can be used to describe geometry, shaders and to generate textures.

The more general purpose languages aim to abstract away from the graphics heritage of GPUs, and target a larger group of programmers. The thesis by Lucas presents CGiS, an imperative data-parallel programming language that targets both GPUs and SIMD capable CPUs – with the aim being a combination of a high degree of abstraction and a close resemblance to traditional programming languages [16]. BrookGPU (which is usually just called Brook) is a classic example of a language [3] designed to raise the level of abstraction at which GPGPU programming is done. It is an extension of C with embedded kernels, aimed at arithmetic-intense data parallel computations. C is used to declare streams[3], CG/HLSL (the lower level GPU languages) to declare kernels, while function calls to a runtime library direct the execution of the program. Brook had significant impact in that it raised the level of abstraction at which GPGPU programming can be done. The language Sh also aimed to raise the level of abstraction at which GPUs were programmed [19]. Sh was an embedded language in C++, so our work is close in spirit to it. Sh has since evolved into the RapidMind development platform [18], which now supports multicores and Cell processors as well as GPUs. The RapidMind programming model has arrays as first class types. It has been influenced by functional languages like NESL and SETL, and its program objects are pure functions. Thus it supports both functional and imperative styles of programming. A recent PhD thesis by Jansen asserts that there are some problems with RapidMind's use of macros to embed the GPU programming language in C++, including the inability to pass kernels (or shader programs) as classes [12]; the thesis proposes GPU++ and claims improvement over previous approaches, particularly through the exploitation of automatic partitioning of the programs onto the available GPU hardware, and through compiler optimisations that improve runtime performance.

Microsoft's Accelerator project moves even closer to general purpose programming by doing away with the kernel notion and simply expressing programs in a data parallel style, using functions on arrays [27]. Data Parallel Haskell [4] incorporates Nested Data Parallelism in the style of NESL [2] into Haskell. GPUGen, like Obsidian, aims to support GPGPU programming from Haskell [14]. It works by translating Haskell's intermediate language, Core, into CUDA, for collective data operations such as scan, fold and map. The intention is to plug GPUGen

---

[3] Brook is referred to as a "stream processing" language, but this means something different from what the reader might expect: a stream in this context is a possibly multi-dimensional array of elements, each of which can be processed separately, in parallel.

into the Nested Data Parallel framework of the Glasgow Haskell Compiler. Our
impression is that we wish to expose considerably more detail about the GPU to
the programmer, but we do not yet have sufficient information about GPUGen to
be able to do a more complete comparison. Finally, we mention the Spiral project,
which develops methods and tools for automatically generating high performance
libraries for a variety of platforms, in domains such a signal processing, multiplication and sorting [21]. The tuning of an algorithm for a given platform is expressed
as an optimisation problem, and the domain specific mathematical structure of
the algorithm is used to create a feedback-driven optimiser. The results are indeed impressive, and we feel that the approach based on an algebra of what we
would call combinators will interest functional programmers. We hope to experiment with similar search and learning based methods, having applied similar ideas
in the simpler setting of arithmetic data-path generation in Lava.

6.3   Lessons Learned so Far in the Project

Our first lesson has been the gradual realisation that a key aspect of a usable
GPU programming language that exposes details of the GPU architecture to the
user is the means to express where and when data is placed in and read from the
memory hierarchy. We are accustomed, from our earlier experience in hardware
design, to describing and generating networks of communicating components –
something like data-flow graphs. We are, however, unused to needing to express
choices about the use of the various levels in a memory hierarchy. We believe that
we need to develop programming idioms and language support for this. It seems
likely, too, that such idioms will not be quite as specific to GPU programming as
other aspects of our embedded language development. How to deal with control
of access to a memory hierarchy in a parallel system seems to be a central
problem that must be tackled if we are to develop better parallel programming
methods in general. A typical example of a generic approach to this problem
is the language Sequoia, which aims to provide programmers with a means to
express how the memory hierarchy is to be used, where a relatively abstract
description of the platform, viewed as a tree of processing nodes and memories,
is a parameter [10]. Thus, programmers should write very generic code, which can
be compiled for many different platforms. This kind of platform independence
is not our aim here, and we would like to experiment with programming idioms
for control of memory access for the particular case of a CPU plus some form of
highly parallel co-processor that accelerates some computations.

A second lesson concerns ways to think about synchronisation on the GPU. We
naively assumed that `sync` would have nice compositional behaviour, but we have
found that in reality one can really only sync at the top level. The reason why the
CUDA code generated from the `sklanky` example works poorly on the GPU is
that it uses `syncs` in a way that leads to unwanted serialisation of computations.
Looking at our generated code, we see that it may be possible to make major improvements by being cleverer about the placement of `syncs`. For instance, the semantics of `two` guarantees that the two components act on distinct data, and this
can be exploited in the placing of `syncs` in the generated code.

Finally, we have found that we need to think harder about the two levels of abstraction: writing the kernels themselves and kernel coordination. This paper concerned the kernel level. We do not yet have a satisfactory solution to the question of how best to express kernel coordination. This question is closely related to that about how to express memory use.

7   Future Work

The version of Obsidian described here is at a very experimental stage. The quality of the C code generated needs to improve to get performance on par with the previous version. The previous version however, was very limited in what you could express. This older version is described in [25]. There is a clear opportunity to perform classic compiler optimisations on the IC formed by running an Obsidian program. Currently this is not done at all.

Ways to describe the coordination of kernels in code that is still short and sweet are also needed. Some experiments using methods similar to Lava's netlist generation have been performed, but the resulting performance is not yet satisfactory. In CUDA, Kernel coordination is in part described in the actual kernel code. Kernels decide which parts of the given data to use. As future work we will approach the kernel coordination problem at a lower more CUDA-like level. We will, of necessity, need to develop programming idioms or combinators that express how data is placed in the memory hierarchy. The isolation of this as a central question is one of the more unexpected and interesting results of the project. Right now work is focused on developing combinators that are more clever in their treatment of syncs. This leads to new data structures that allow the merging of syncs. This new approach seems to make efficient implementations of combinators such as two possible.

8   Conclusion

Obsidian provides a good interface for experimenting with algorithms on GPUs. The earlier version described in [25] showed that it is possible to generate efficient CUDA code from the kind of high level descriptions we are interested in. For the kernel level, the work in progress described in this paper enhances the expressive power of Obsidian, extending the range of algorithms that can be described, as well as the degree of control exercised by the user. Future work will concentrate on improving the performance of the resulting applications, as well as on support for the kernel coordination level.

References

1. Bjesse, P., Claessen, K., Sheeran, M., Singh, S.: Lava: Hardware Design in Haskell. In: International Conference on Functional Programming, ICFP, pp. 174–184. ACM, New York (1998)
2. Blelloch, G.E.: NESL: A Nested Data-Parallel Language. Technical Report CMU-CS-95-170, CS Dept., Carnegie Mellon University (April 1995)

172   J. Svensson, M. Sheeran, and K. Claessen

3. Buck, I., Foley, T., Horn, D., Sugerman, J., Fatahalian, K., Houston, M., Hanrahan, P.: Brook for GPUs: Stream computing on graphics hardware. In: SIGGRAPH (2004)
4. Chakravarty, M.M.T., Leshchinskiy, R., Jones, S.P., Keller, G., Marlow, S.: Data parallel haskell: a status report. In: DAMP 2007: Proceedings of the 2007 Workshop on Declarative Aspects of Multicore Programming, pp. 10–18. ACM Press, New York (2007)
5. Claessen, K.: Embedded Languages for Describing and Verifying Hardware. PhD thesis, Chalmers University of Technology (2001)
6. Claessen, K., Sheeran, M., Singh, S.: The design and verification of a sorter core. In: Margaria, T., Melham, T.F. (eds.) CHARME 2001. LNCS, vol. 2144, pp. 355–369. Springer, Heidelberg (2001)
7. Elliott, C.: Functional images. In: The Fun of Programming. "Cornerstones of Computing" series, Palgrave (March 2003)
8. Elliott, C.: Programming graphics processors functionally. In: Proceedings of the 2004 Haskell Workshop. ACM Press, New York (2004)
9. Elliott, C., Finne, S., de Moor, O.: Compiling embedded languages. Journal of Functional Programming 13(2) (2003)
10. Fatahalian, K., Knight, T.J., Houston, M., Erez, M., Horn, D.R., Leem, L., Park, J.Y., Ren, M., Aiken, A., Dally, W.J., Hanrahan, P.: Sequoia: Programming the memory hierarchy. In: Proceedings of the 2006 ACM/IEEE Conference on Supercomputing (2006)
11. Hinze, R.: An algebra of scans. In: Kozen, D. (ed.) MPC 2004. LNCS, vol. 3125, pp. 186–210. Springer, Heidelberg (2004)
12. Jansen, T.C.: GPU++ An Embedded GPU Development System for General-Purpose Computations. PhD thesis, Technische Universitäat München and Forschungsinstitut caesar in Bonn (2007)
13. Jones, G., Sheeran, M.: Circuit design in Ruby. In: Staunstrup, J. (ed.) Formal Methods for VLSI Design, pp. 13–70. North-Holland, Amsterdam (1990)
14. Lee, S.: Bringing the power of gpus to haskell. Slides from Galois Tech. Talk (September 2008)
15. Lejdfors, C., Ohlsson, L.: Implementing an embedded GPU language by combining translation and generation. In: SAC 2006: Proceedings of the 2006 ACM Symposium on Applied Computing, pp. 1610–1614. ACM, New York (2006)
16. Lucas, P.: CGiS: High-Level Data-Parallel GPU Programming. PhD thesis, Saarland University, Saarbrücken (January 2008)
17. Luebke, D.: CUDA: Scalable parallel programming for high-performance scientific computing. In: 5th International Symposium on Biomedical Imaging: From Nano to Macro, ISBI 2008, pp. 836–838. IEEE, Los Alamitos (2008)
18. McCool, M.D.: Data-Parallel Programming on the Cell BE and the GPU using the RapidMind Development Platform. In: GSPx Multicore Applications Conference (October 2006)
19. McCool, M.D., Qin, Z., Popa, T.S.: Shader Metaprogramming. In: SIGGRAPH/Eurographics Graphics Hardware Workshop (September 2002)
20. Owens, J.D., Houston, M., Luebke, D., Green, S., Stone, J.E., Phillips, J.C.: GPU Computing. Proceedings of the IEEE 96(5), 879–899 (2008)
21. Püschel, M., Moura, J.M.F., Johnson, J., Padua, D., Veloso, M., Singer, B., Xiong, J., Franchetti, F., Gacic, A., Voronenko, Y., Chen, K., Johnson, R.W., Rizzolo, N.: SPIRAL: Code Generation for DSP Transforms. Proceedings of the IEEE special issue on Program Generation, Optimization, and Adaptation V93(2), 232–275 (2005)

22. Seiler, L., Carmean, D., Sprangle, T., Forsyth, D., Abrash, M., Dubey, P., Junkins, S., Lake, A., Sugerman, J., Cavin, R., Espasa, R., Grochowski, E., Juan, T., Hanrahan, P.: Larrabee: A Many-Core x86 Architecture for Visual Computing. ACM Transactions on Graphics (2008)
23. Sheeran, M.: muFP, A Language for VLSI Design. In: LISP and Functional Programming, pp. 104–112. ACM, New York (1984)
24. Sheeran, M.: Hardware design and functional programming: a perfect match. Journal of Universal Computer Science 11(7), 1135–1158 (2005)
25. Svensson, J.: An embedded language for data-parallel programming. Master's thesis, Göteborg University (2008),
    http://www.cs.chalmers.se/~ms/JoelMScThesis.pdf
26. Taha, W.: A gentle introduction to multi-stage programming. In: Lengauer, C., Batory, D., Blum, A., Vetta, A. (eds.) Domain-Specific Program Generation. LNCS, vol. 3016, pp. 30–50. Springer, Heidelberg (2004)
27. Tarditi, D., Puri, S., Oglesby, J.: Accelerator: Using Data Parallelism to Program GPUs for General-Purpose Uses. In: Proceedings of the 12th International Conference on Architectural Support for Programming Languages and Operating Systems (2006)

A Library for Processing Ad hoc Data in Haskell
Embedding a Data Description Language

Yan Wang and Verónica Gaspes

Halmstad University
{yan.wang,veronica.gaspes}@hh.se

Abstract. Ad hoc data formats, i.e. semistructured non-standard data formats, are pervasive in many domains that need software tools — bioinformatics, demographic surveys, geophysics and network software are just a few. Building tools becomes easier if parsing and other standard input-output processing can be automated. Modern approaches for dealing with ad hoc data formats consist of domain specific languages based on type systems. Compilers for these languages generate data structures and parsing functions in a target programming language in which tools and applications are then written. We present a monadic library in Haskell that implements a data description language. Using our library, Haskell programmers have access to data description primitives that can be used for parsing and that can be integrated with other libraries and application programs without the need of yet another compiler.

1 Introduction

Imagine your favorite online travel agency dealing with data from many sources: airlines, train companies, car rental companies, hotels and maybe some more. It has to understand all these formats for which parsers and converters have to be programmed. Moreover, as the agency comes to serve more companies this work has to be done again for new data formats. It is most likely that these companies have legacy data formats that have not been upgraded to XML or other standardized formats for which tools exist. Furthermore, these data formats frequently evolve over time, leave some fields unused or use them for new purposes etc, making some of the data seem erroneous according to the latest version of the format. This scenario is not at all unique. In bioinformatics, demographic applications, geophysics applications, network traffic monitoring, web servers logs, etc, most of the data formats are *ad hoc*, i.e., semistructured non-standard data formats. Typical tools programmed for ad hoc data sources of this kind include generating reports, exporting data to other formats, collecting statistics and reporting errors in input data.

We came across a similar problem when designing a domain specific language for the implementation of protocol stacks. Packet formats are often described in packet specifications. The physical organization, the dependencies among field contents and the constraints over the values of some fields are provided using a combination of figures and explanations. In protocol implementations there are

S.-B. Scholz and O. Chitil (Eds.): IFL 2008, LNCS 5836, pp. 174–191, 2011.
© Springer-Verlag Berlin Heidelberg 2011

no traces of this. Instead, references to fragments of a buffer are interspersed all over the code implementing a protocol. These fragments are converted to and from network format; bit operations are used to determine the value of the fields that need to be checked, etc.

Parser generators are very good at describing data formats specified by context free grammars. However, for ad hoc data they have been found lacking. In most ad hoc formats some of the fields depend on the values of other fields. Using parser generators these dependencies are usually dealt with in the actions specified together with the grammar rules and are thus not part of the format specification. Also, parser generators support error handling, but this becomes part of the parser. In the case of ad hoc formats it is desirable to leave error handling to other tools as it is often the case that erroneous data has to be processed anyway. Finally, ad hoc formats are needed also for binary data.

Modern approaches for describing ad hoc data formats are data description languages[12,3,5]. These are domain specific languages with constructs based on dependent type systems. Compilers for these languages generate libraries in some target programming language. These libraries include types, parsing functions and tools like pretty printing that can be used to build more advanced tools. This is very good: one description is used to generate several utilities automatically. On the other hand, extensions with new constructs and the creation of more tools require in most of the cases modifications to the compiler – the exception being PADS/ML for which a generic mechanism is provided [4].

This paper describes a library implementing a data description language embedded in Haskell that facilitates dealing with ad hoc data formats. With our approach, both the data description and the rest of the tools are Haskell programs. The library is based on the Data Description Calculus (DDC) [6], which we briefly present in Section 2. In Section 3 we present our DDC library, constructed in the style of monadic parser combinators [9]. In Section 4 we show how to integrate a data description with other tools by using pretty printing as an example. In Section 5 we explore performance, and in Section 6 we discuss related work, before the final conclusions. The contributions of this work are as follows:

- A rich collection of parser combinators for ad hoc data formats. Both physical layout, field dependencies and semantic constraints can be expressed.
- Built-in error detection and collection that does not halt the parsing process. This can be used for generating precise error messages and statistics, including positions and causes, both syntactical and semantic.
- Ways of extending the library with new primitive parsers, using type classes.
- Suggestions for extending the library with additional tools.

2   The Data Description Calculus

Recently, the essentials of data description languages have been formalized in the Data Description Calculus (DDC) [6]. It uses types from a polymorphic, dependent type theory to describe various forms of ad hoc data. What we report in this paper is an implementation of this calculus as an embedded language in Haskell. In order to motivate our choices later on, we briefly present the calculus. We explain only a few constructs by giving small examples and explaining the semantic functions for these cases.

In DDC, data formats are described using types according to the syntax shown in Figure 1. Base types $C(e)$ are variations of types of the target language[1], for example strings or integers, parameterized by an expression e in the target language. The expression is used to specify simple properties of a data field, such as its length in number of characters or the number of bits in the representation. This expression can be a variable that can be used to refer to the value of a previous field in the data format. For imposing more semantic constraints on a data field there is the constraint type $\{x : \tau \mid e\}$ where the expression e from the target language can refer to x, the value of the data field. For putting together fields there is the dependent sum type $\Sigma x : \tau_1.\tau_2$. The variable x can be used in τ_2 to refer to the value of the first field. In this way the value of a field can influence some aspect of another one, for example its length: $\Sigma x : Int.String(x)$.

$$\tau = C(e) \mid \{x : \tau \mid e\} \mid \Sigma x : \tau.\tau \mid \tau + \tau \mid \tau \& \tau \mid \texttt{compute}(e) \mid \texttt{absorb}(\tau) \mid \ldots$$

Fig. 1. The syntax of DDC

For each type τ the semantics prescribes three interpretations:

1. $[\![\tau]\!]_\text{P}$ maps τ into a parsing function in the target language. The parsing functions return pairs $([\![\tau]\!]_\text{REP}, [\![\tau]\!]_\text{PD})$.
2. $[\![\tau]\!]_\text{REP}$ maps τ into a type in the target language for the in-memory representation of the data.
3. $[\![\tau]\!]_\text{PD}$ maps τ into a type in the target language for a parse descriptor where error information can be collected during parsing. This meta data is interesting when parsing ad hoc data because usually sources have to be dealt with in spite of being erroneous and in some cases applications are even meant for the collection and analysis of errors.

Some short illustrations should help clarify how to use the constructs of DDC and the role of the three interpretations.

- $C(e)$, with a type C and an expression e of the target language, can be used to describe physical layouts. For example, strings of a given length $String(20)$; or ending in a particular character $String(';')$. Likewise, it can describe integers that use a number of digits $Int(3)$; or are represented by a number of bits $BitInt(8)$. For these types, $[\![\ ]\!]_\text{REP}$ is an atomic type in the target language, like `String` or `Integer`. The function $[\![\ ]\!]_\text{P}$ takes care of the constraint provided by the expression during parsing.
- $\Sigma x : \tau_1.\tau_2$ is the construct for dependent pairs. It can be used to constrain fields with the values of previous fields, as in $\Sigma x : BitInt(8).String(x)$. The parsing function provided by $[\![\ ]\!]_\text{P}$ deals with the two fields in sequence using

---

[1] The target language is the language for which tools are generated, it is a parameter for the calculus.

$[\![\tau_1]\!]_P$ first, and then using the result of type $[\![\tau_1]\!]_{REP}$ when the remaining input is parsed according to $[\![\tau_2]\!]_P$. $[\![\ \ ]\!]_{REP}$ is the pair $([\![\tau_1]\!]_{REP}, [\![\tau_2]\!]_{REP})$.

- $\{x:\tau|e\}$ expresses constraints on a field, for example $\{x:Int(3)|x > 38\}$. The constraint itself is given as a boolean expression e in the target language that depends on values x of type $[\![\tau]\!]_{REP}$. The parsing function parses according to $[\![\tau]\!]_P$ and then checks whether the calculated value of type $[\![\tau]\!]_{REP}$ satisfies e. The parse descriptor $[\![\tau]\!]_{PD}$ indicates whether the value satisfies the condition or not.
- $\text{compute}(e:\sigma)$ can be used to output a value in the parsing function (the value of e) without a corresponding field in the input.
- $\text{absorb}(\tau)$ deals with data that is important for parsing, for example a separator, but becomes uninteresting as output. The parser parses according to $[\![\tau]\!]_P$ and discards the output.

As Fisher et al. argue in [6], there are many parallels between DDC and parser combinators [9]. For example there is a clear relation between the parsing function for Σ types and the monadic sequence combinator. We exploit this in our library using rich monadic combinators for parsing and generating error information. However, DDC constructs focus on ad hoc formats and describe data formats using types rather than grammars, so the combinators are rather different. Another difference is the inclusion of parser descriptors in the result of parsing instead of the generation of errors.

3   A Haskell Embedding

We present an embedding of the DDC in Haskell as a library of ad hoc data parser combinators. Our combinators follow closely the structure of the type constructors of DDC. Our embedding works by implementing the interpretation of DDC types as parsing functions (see Section 2 for an informal explanation). Both the representation type and the parse descriptor associated to each DDC type are implemented in the return type of our combinators. By embedding the constructors of DDC in this manner, our library is easily extensible: ad hoc data descriptions are ordinary Haskell terms, and we have full access to existing Haskell libraries.

We identify each type τ in the calculus with the parsing function $[\![\tau]\!]_P$ introduced in Section 2. Parsing functions compute values of the representation type $[\![\tau]\!]_{REP}$ and in doing so also update meta data corresponding to the parse descriptor $[\![\tau]\!]_{PD}$. Therefore, we have introduced a data type representing a parser for type τ:

```
AdhocParser t a
```

In this type, t is the type of tokens in the input source and a is the type of the result. The type of parse descriptors is not a parameter and is described in more detail in Section 3.4.

Briefly, our library consists of a collection of primitive parsers and parser combinators with a monadic interface that correspond to the combinators for constructing types in DDC. We first give a flavor of our library using an example.

3.1   An Introductory Example

The following is a description of a network address format using our library:

```
webserver =
  orp ipaddress dnsname
ipaddress =
  countp (charequal ".")
         bottom
         (int_range 0 255)
         4
dnsname =
  seqp (charequal ".")
       (charequal " ")
       (stringendsat (\x -> x=="."||x==" "))
       false
```

A network address is either an IP address, or a DNS name. An IP address is a sequence of 4 integers separated by ".". Each integer should lie between 0 and 255. Similarly, a DNS name is a sequence of strings, separated by "." and ended by " ". The sample records could for instance be *"www.hh.se ... ..."* or *"194.47.12.29 ... ..."*.

The two alternatives are put together using **orp**. **Ipaddress** is a sequence with a fixed length 4 which is specified using **countp**. The elements of the sequence are separated by "." (**charequal** "."). There is no terminator (**bottom**) to signal the end of the sequence. Each element is an integer within an interval (**int_range** 0 255). **Dnsname** is a sequence with no predefined length, thus it is specified using a more general combinator **seqp** with the separator ".", the terminator " ", the description of the elements: strings ended by either "." or " ", and a trivial boolean-valued function **false**, i.e., _ -> False, to specify no extra termination condition.

3.2   Primitive Parsers

For the primitive DDC types *unit* and *bottom* our library includes two primitive parsers:

```
unit :: AdhocParser t ()
```

that consumes no input and returns nothing. It also produces a parse descriptor indicating no error. The parser for *bottom*

```
bottom :: AdhocParser t ()
```

neither consumes input nor returns a result, but the parse descriptor indicates the error count and the error code.

The implementation of primitive parsers for the base types $C(e)$ depends on both C and e. In DDC, C can be any type from the target language (also Haskell in our case). In order to provide for ways of adding more base types, we have introduced a type class **Basetype**.

```
class Basetype t a where
  readTokens :: [t] -> Maybe a
  fromTokens :: [t] -> (Maybe a, Offset)
```

A pair of types t and a for the input tokens and the result value respectively, is an instance of Basetype if we can transform a chunk of tokens into a value and consume valid tokens as far as possible for building a value.

There are three kinds of expressions (e) which are the most commonly used: $()$ for no extra information, $(e :: Int)$ for values described using e tokens and $(e :: t)$ for values ending with token e. In our library there is a parser for each of these.

For the base type $C()$, we have defined base: it parses an input stream by eagerly reading valid tokens. It requires t and a to be an instance of Basetype.

```
base :: (Basetype t a) => AdhocParser t a
```

For the base type $C(n :: Int)$, we have defined baselen that parses data consuming exactly n tokens.

```
baselen :: (Basetype t a) => Int -> AdhocParser t a
```

For the base type $C(e :: t)$, we have defined baseend that consumes a sequence of tokens until the terminating token e.

```
baseend :: (Basetype t a, Eq t) => t -> AdhocParser t a
```

We can easily use readTokens and fromTokens to built other variants with different kinds of e for $C(e)$. For example, the parser

```
baseendsat :: (Basetype t a) => (t -> Bool) -> AdhocParser t a
```

consumes a sequence of tokens until the terminating token satisfies the supposed condition.

With the primitive parsers for base types, it is straightforward to define parsers for Haskell types. After instantiating BaseType with the type of tokens t and the desired type of values a, only the signatures for parsers have to be provided. We illustrate this by implementing parsers for $Int()$, $Int(n)$ and $Int(e)$ in the case of a character input stream. We have to specify how a sequence of Char can be translated into a value of type Int by implementing readTokens, and what is a legal Char stream for type Int by implementing fromTokens:

```
instance Basetype Char Int where
  readTokens [] = Nothing
  readTokens ts = if (all isDigit ts) then Just (read ts)
                                      else Nothing
  fromTokens ts = (readTokens ts', len)
    where ts' = takeWhile isDigit ts
          len = length ts'
```

Finally, we just give a type signature for each parser:

```
int :: AdhocParser Char Int
int = base

intlen :: Int -> AdhocParser Char Int
intlen = baselen

intend :: Char -> AdhocParser Char Int
intend = baseend
```

3.3 Parser Combinators

Parser combinators follow DDC type constructors. However, thanks to higher-order functions and recursive types in Haskell, we need not define combinators for the abstraction type $\lambda x.\tau$, the application type τe, and the fix point type $\mu\alpha.\tau$. We present the implementation of the other types of DDC.

– The dependent sum combinator **sigmap** corresponds to the dependent sum type $\Sigma x : \tau_1.\tau_2$ in DDC.

```
sigmap :: AdhocParser t a ->          -- [[τ₁]]ₚ
          (a -> AdhocParser t b) ->   -- [[τ₂(x)]]ₚ
          AdhocParser t (a,b)         -- [[Σ x : τ₁.τ₂]]ₚ
```
$$-- \;[\![\tau_1]\!]_\mathsf{P}$$
$$-- \;[\![\tau_2(x)]\!]_\mathsf{P}$$
$$-- \;[\![\Sigma \; x : \tau_1.\tau_2]\!]_\mathsf{P}$$

sigmap p q combines the parsers p and q sequentially in which q may refer to the parsing result of p. For example, in DDC we would use $\Sigma x : Char().String(x)$ to describe a sequence of characters started and terminated by a same character. Using our library combinator *sigmap*, we write

```
xstringx = sigmap char stringend
```

– The choice combinator **orp** corresponds to the sum type $\tau_1+\tau_2$ in DDC, which is used to describe a data source with values of type either τ_1 or alternatively τ_2.

```
orp :: AdhocParser t a ->          -- [[τ₁]]ₚ
       AdhocParser t b ->          -- [[τ₂]]ₚ
       AdhocParser t (Either a b)  -- [[τ₁ + τ₂]]ₚ
```

orp p q first tries p. If p succeeds, it returns the value of type **Left** a. If p fails, it goes back to the starting point of the input stream to apply q and returns the value of type **Right** b. For example, in DDC we would use $String("September") + String("Sep")$ and with our library we write

```
sep = orp (stringequals "September")
          (stringequals "Sep")
```

– The intersection combinator **andp** implements the intersection type $\tau_1 * \tau_2$, which is used to describe data source whose value matches both τ_1 and τ_2.

```
andp :: AdhocParser t a ->      -- ⟦τ₁⟧ₚ
         AdhocParser t b ->      -- ⟦τ₂⟧ₚ
         AdhocParser t (a,b)     -- ⟦τ₁ * τ₂⟧ₚ
```

`andp p q` is parameterized by two underlying parsers `p` and `q`. It advances the input stream by employing both `p` and `q` from the same starting point and ending at the maximum offsets of two parsers. The final parsed result is a pair built by the two results returned by `p` and `q`. If and only if both parsers succeed on the input stream, the whole parser succeeds. For example,

```
num = andp (intlen 4) (floatlen 6)
```

is a parser that accepts strings starting with four characters to build an integer and six characters to build a float. Assume that the input stream is "1234.0...", it results in (1234, 1234.0). Since the maximum offset of two underlying parsers is 6, the remaining input stream is "...".

– The constrain combinator `constrainp` implements the constrained type $\{x : \tau | e\}$, which is used to impose conditions on data fields. This combinator has type

```
constrainp :: (a -> Bool) ->        -- e
               AdhocParser t a ->    -- ⟦τ⟧ₚ
               AdhocParser t a       -- ⟦{x:τ|e}⟧ₚ
```

`constrainp f p` is parameterized by a single underlying parser `p` and a boolean-valued function `f`. The parsing result of `p` is checked according to `f`. If the imposed constraint is not satisfied, the semantic error is recorded in the parse descriptor. For example,

```
int_range a b = constrainp (\x -> x>=a && x<=b) int
```

is a parser that accepts strings starting with an integer value produced by the parser `int`. The value should lie between `a` and `b`. If it is outside the range, the result is anyway the integer read and an error code `Err` indicating semantical error is recorded in the parse descriptor.

– The sequence combinator `seqp` implements the array type $\tau seq(\tau_s, e, \tau_t)$, which is the type used to describe data source formed as a sequence of fields of type τ.

```
seqp :: AdhocParser t sep ->      -- ⟦τ_s⟧ₚ
         AdhocParser t term  ->   -- ⟦τ_t⟧ₚ
         AdhocParser t a  ->      -- ⟦τ⟧ₚ
         ([a] -> Bool)  ->        -- e
         AdhocParser t [a]        -- ⟦τ seq (τ_s, e, τ_t)⟧ₚ
```

`seqp ts tt te f` has four parameters: `ts` is the parser for the separator found between elements, `tt` is the parser for the terminator of the sequence, `te` is the parser for each element in the sequence and `f` is a boolean-valued function which examines the parsed sequence to determine whether the sequence has completed before reaching the terminator. In the example,

```
arr = seqp charends ","
           charends "."
           int
           (\ls -> length ls == 10)
```

`","` is the array separator, `"."` is the array terminator, the length of the result array should not be greater than 10 and the elements of array are parsed with `int`. If the given input is a string *"1,2,3,4,5,6,7,8,9,10,11,12"*, resulting value is a list `[1,2,3,4,5,6,7,8,9,10]` `::` `[Int]`. If the input is *"1,2,3,4,5.6,7,8,9,10,11,12"*, the result is a list `[1,2,3,4,5]` instead.

The last argument of the parser is examined after each element is read to see whether the parsing should end: execution becomes very expensive. Because testing for length is so common, we provide a parser `countp` that calculates the length incrementally

```
countp :: AdhocParser t sep ->
          AdhocParser t term  ->
          AdhocParser t a   ->
          Int  ->
          AdhocParser t [a]
```

- The compute combinator `computep` implements the compute type *compute(e)*, which allows us to include a value in the output that does not appear in the data source.

```
computep :: a ->                    -- e
            AdhocParser t a  -- [[compute(e)]]ₚ
```

`computep e` does not do any parsing, but returns the computation result of e without parsing errors. In the example,

```
c = computep (2+3)
```

no matter what the input stream is, it results in **5**.

- The absorb combinator `absorbp` implements the type $absorb(\tau)$, which is used to parse and discard the result

```
absorbp :: AdhocParser t a ->  -- [[τ]]ₚ
           AdhocParser t ()     -- [[absorb(τ)]]ₚ
```

`absorbp p` simply applies the underlying parser p, but ignores the parsed result. In the example

```
xstringx' = absorbp xstringx
```

if `xstringx` parses successfully, the parser `xstringx'` will result in `()`. If `xstringx` fails, `xstringx'` fails as well.

- The scan combinator `scanp` implements the type $scan(\tau)$, which is used to scan the input stream for data that makes the underlying parser succeed.

```
scanp :: Offset ->
         AdhocParser t a ->           -- [[τ]]ₚ
         AdhocParser t (Maybe a)      -- [[scan(τ)]]ₚ
```

`scanp maxoffset p` is parameterized by a predefined maximum scan-offset `maxoffset` and the underlying parser `p`. It attempts to apply `p`, if it fails, it moves on one more token and tries it again until it reaches the scan-offset `maxoffset`. For example,

```
scanxstring = scanp 100 xstringx
```

tries at most 100 times to find a string started and terminated by the same character.

3.4   Implementation

The type `AdhocParser` has been implemented using [9] as a guideline.

```
newtype AdhocParser t a
  = P ((([t], PD) -> (Either String a, [t],PD)))
```

Parsers are functions that transform a stream of input tokens of type `[t]` paired with the current parser descriptor of type `PD` into a tuple containing the resulting data representation of type `a`, the remaining unconsumed tokens of type `[t]` and the updated parse descriptor of type `PD`.

`AdhocParser` is actually a combination of the usual `Parser Monad` with the `Error` and `State Monads`. The monadic sequencer `>>=` can be considered as a combinator and the do-notation achieves a programming style mimicking the records or structures provided in some conventional languages. We make `AdhocParser t a` an instance of the `MonadPlus` class for backtracking. We encapsulate the result into the `Either Monad` to handle parsing failure gracefully. We use `Right` to indicate success or success with error and `Left` to indicate failure. We deal with parse descriptors as states and thus make `AdhocParser t a` an instance of the `MonadState` class.

For parse descriptors we use the type `PD`

```
newtype PD = MkPD Int ErrCode Span Body
```

that corresponds closely to how parse descriptors are defined in the DDC:

$$pd = pd\_hdr * pd\_body$$
$$pd\_hdr = int * errcode * span$$

It stores the detected error information for corrupted input streams including an error count of type `Int`, an error code of type `ErrCode`, a span of type `Span`, and a parse descriptor body of type `Body`. The error count for a parse accumulates the error counts from its subcomponents and itself. The error code specifies the degree of success of a parser, i.e., success (`Ok`), success with errors (`Err`) or failure (`Fail`). The span is a pair of offsets which indicate the start and end points in the input stream for the current parser. The body for a parse descriptor puts together the descriptors from its underlying parsers. For example, the parse descriptor body for an array has type `Seq Int [PD]` including the number of element errors and parse descriptors of its elements.

```
newtype ErrCode = Ok | Err | Fail
type Span = (Offset, Offset)
data Body = Unit
          | Pair PD PD
          | Or (Either PD PD)
          | Constrain PD
          | Seq Int [PD]
          | Scan (Maybe (Int,PD))
          | Struct [PD]
```

4   Adding Tools

One of the advantages of *embedding* a domain specific language is that terms of the language are just ordinary terms in the host language. In our case, since combinator parsers are written and used within Haskell as well as the rest of the application that uses our library, we are able to use existing Haskell libraries seamlessly. So far we have seen that, by using our library, programmers only need to put effort into describing the formats of their ad hoc data to get parsers for free. In this section, we show how to add another tool by using existing Haskell libraries. However, the instance we will show here is not the only case. For example, it is straightforward to build an error reporter by inspecting the parse descriptor and producing error messages.

4.1   Pretty Printing

A frequent need when dealing ad hoc data is to make sources readable. This can be achieved by displaying the data in a suitable layout. Our basic idea is to process the parsing result using Haskell's pretty-printing library [8]. Since the type of the representation result shows enough information of the built-in structures for ad hoc data, we can convert the representation result to a *pretty document* of type `Doc` with a specific layout according to its type. To do so we introduced a type class `Prettytype`.

```
class Prettytype a where
  pprint :: a -> Doc
```

It is straightforward to make a type an instance of `Prettytype`. We have instantiated some base types. For example, we use a standard document generator `double` to make `Double` an instance.

```
instance Prettytype Double where
  pprint = double
```

We have provided instances for some advanced types, which might result from the ad hoc data parser combinators. For example, the representation result of the parser `seqp` has type `[]`. We use a document combinator `cat` to instance it.

```
instance (Prettytype a) => Prettytype [a] where
  pprint xs = cat (map pprint xs)
```

Users can express their preferred layout by instantiating with custom types. For example,

```
data Date = Date Int Int Int
instance Prettytype Date where
  pprint (Date y m d) = pprint y <>
                        (char '.') <>
                        (pprint $ f m) <>
                        (char '.') <>
                        pprint d
    where f m = case m of
                  1 -> pprint "Jan"
                  2 -> pprint "Feb"
                  ... ...
```

We have defined a function which takes an ad hoc parser and an ad hoc stream as input and generates a *pretty document* for the further processing.

```
adhocpprinter :: (Prettytype a) => AdhocParser t a -> [t] -> Doc
```

5   Practical Considerations

In this section, we compare our library to two other approaches: using a traditional parsing library, Parsec, and using a data description language that generates C code, PADS/C. We wish to demonstrate the utility of our library with respect to three criteria: execution time of the resulting parsing functions, conciseness of the specifications, and the ability to collect error information. For the purpose of our evaluation, we built a realistic test scenario related to the motivating example from our domain of interest, i.e., communication protocols. The application is a packet sniffer used for network troubleshooting and analysis. Its functionality is to intercept and display TCP/IP packets being transmitted or received over the Ethernet network. Its main task is to interpret a raw buffer into a well-formed packet according to the packet format of different protocols and the structure of protocol stack. We implemented the TCP/IP packet parser using Parsec, PADS/C, and our library.

To make sure all the experiments work on the same input, we use the packet capture library pcap [2] to capture and dump raw network traffic from a live connection into logs for further processing. The logs were loaded with different sizes from 0 to 1,000 packets. The size of each packet is between 54 to 1514 bytes. One sample already-captured packet record (hexadecimal digits) looks as follows:

005056F975DD000C29EA09AE08060001080006040002000C29EA09AEC0A81780
005056F975DDC0A81702
000C29EA09AE005056F975DD08004500002C454200008006CA78D1558193C0A8
17800050801F103B2CCCD2387D516012FAF065130000020405B40000

Data sources described with ad hoc data formats frequently contain errors. In our scenario, for example, errors might be caused by disturbances in the network. To evaluate execution time when processing erroneous data, we built another suite of logs. They are similar to the previous ones but with randomly injected one single bit-flip error per packet.

5.1 Performance

We compared the execution time of a parser built using our library and one using Parsec combinators. We used GHC 6.8.1 with -O2 and carried out all experiments on the same computer running Windows XP with a 1.73GHz processor and 1GB RAM. Each experiment was repeated 3 times and the lowest value was taken.

Figure 2 shows the execution time results where the X-axis shows the size of the log in bytes and the Y-axis shows the execution time in seconds. Our library performs as well as Parsec for the error-free logs. In the case of logs with errors, the Parsec parser runs very fast since it fails at the first unrecoverable error, while our parser continues to work. It is also worth comparing the performance of our parser for logs without errors and for logs with errors. The difference is accounted for by the time needed to construct the parse descriptor.

5.2 Lines of Code

Table 1 shows the lines of code for equivalent Parsec, PADS/C and our own packet parsers. Our parser and the PADS/C description have approximately the same size which is more than 30 lines shorter than the Parsec parser. The expected gain in code length is primarily because of the extra code that has to

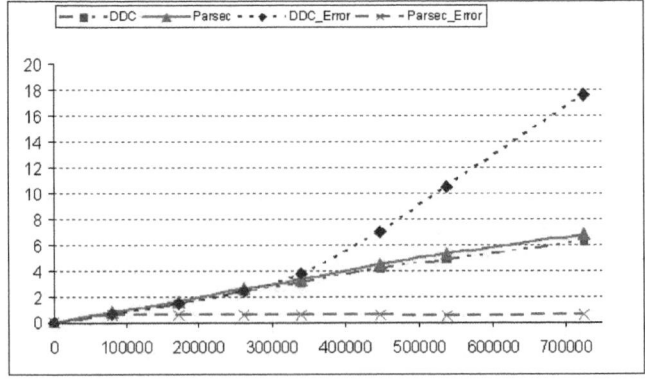

Fig. 2. Execution time results

Table 1. Lines of code results

	Parsec	PADS/C	Our library
Lines of code	135	98	101

Table 2. Code for expressing constraints and physical layout

| Parsec | ```
type MyState = [(SourcePos, SourcePos)]
hexDigitN :: Int -> GenParser Char MyState Int
hexDigitN 0 = return 0
hexDigitN n =
...
constrain :: (a -> Bool) -> GenParser Char MyState a
                         -> GenParser Char MyState a
constrain f p =
  do pos1 <- getPosition
     p_value <- p
     if (f p_value)
        then return p_value
        else do pos2 <- getPosition
                state1 <- getState
                setState ((pos1,pos2):state1)
                return p_value
ipv4packet =
  do ...
     ihl <- constrain (>=5) (hexDigitN 1)
     ...
``` |
| PADS | ```
Ptypedef Puint8_FW(:1:) ihl_t:
ihl_t x => {x>=5}
``` |
| DDC | ```
ipv4packet =
  do ...
     ihl <- constrainp (>=5) (intlen 1)
     ...
``` |

be written in Parsec to handle semantic constraints and physical layout. Table 2 illustrates how we chose to deal with constraints in Parsec and compare it with the PADS/C code and ours. The case we look at is the field for the length of an IP packet header, ihl: an integer value described with 4 bits(1 hexadecimal digit in the case of logs) and with a value of at least 5.
```

- **Physical layout**

  In Parsec, the parser for integer values can not be parameterized to specify physical layout. Thus we have to define a special function `hexDigitN` to build an integer from a chunk of hexadecimal digits. This has to be done for all other cases where the physical layout is needed. In PADS/C, there are primitives for expressing almost all the frequently used data formats, e.g., `Puint8_FW(:1:)` is an unsigned 8-bit integer described in 1 character. In our library, we also cover the most frequent cases, e.g., `intlen 1` is an integer described in 1 character, and we provide means for extending the library with new primitive parsers including physical layout(see Section 3.2).

- **Constraints**

  In order to deal with semantic constraints in Parsec, we also have to put some effort. Since `GenParser` is a `State Monad`, we first introduce state `MyState` to record the positions of errors, and then update the state during parsing. Of course, more effort would be put in for more precise error reporting. In contrast, both PADS/C and our library include primitives for dealing with constraints.

5.3   Error Detection

Ad hoc data processing needs extensive error handling and good parser error messages. Our parser is able to accurately report syntactical errors i.e., physical layout mismatching as well as semantic errors i.e., constraint violations. Let us reuse the example of Section 5.2. Suppose that there are two contiguous packets containing errors as follows: one has an illegal character on the `ihl` field, and one does not satisfy the condition on this field. Since the syntactical error is unrecoverable, our parser skips the remaining part of the first packet and continues to parse the second one. Meanwhile, it records error information into its parse descriptor. Then we can produce an error message with the precise position and the cause of errors as well as the unexpected input from the data source by inspecting the parse descriptor from the outermost layer to the innermost layer.

```
success with error:
<sequence error>
record 1 <baselen type error> <(31,31)> unexpected input:
...09AE08004>>>H<<<00164464...
record 2 <constraint error> <(31,31)> unexpected input:
...75DD08004>>>3<<<0005DC42...
```

Similarly, PADS/C gives:

```
warning: Error [in Puint8_FW_read]: at record 1 at byte 31
         Invalid ASCII character encoding of a number
[record 1]...09AE08004>>>H<<<00164464...
warning: Error [in ihl_t_read]: at record 2 at byte 31:
         Typedef constraint error
[record 2]...75DD08004>>>3<<<0005DC42...
```

In contrast, Parsec halts parsing and discards the remaining part of the input. It can only report the first error:

```
Left (line 1, column 31):
unexpected "H"
expecting hexadecimal digit
```

6   Related Work

Ad hoc data formats have been in the focus of tool developers for a long time. Unix provides a number of utilities that can be pipelined to form filters. Scripting languages are often used to put together parsing utilities. The problem with this kind of approaches is that they do not result in a description of the data format in the program and are thus difficult to keep consistent with implementations and are of no use when changes are made to the data format.

Modern approaches are instead based on domain specific languages used to define the formats. These languages are based on dependent types and are compiled to different kind of processing tools in some target programming languages.

PACKETTYPES [12] is used to write programmatic descriptions of network protocol packet formats. From these descriptions, a compiler can generate parsers and other tools for packet processing in C. To our knowledge, [12] were the first to use types for packet specifications. There is only one basic type, *bit*, and type constructors for repetition and sequencing. In order to cope with data dependency, fields are allowed to have *attributes* that can be referred to in restriction clauses. There are also ways for overlaying a packet specification in another specification's field — typically in the payload field for layered protocols.

DataScript [3] uses a language of types to describe and manipulate binary data formats and generates libraries in Java. However, it addresses a very specific domain and has been tested to deal with Java byte code. Furthermore, it assumes that the data is error-free, i.e., if an error is detected, parsing needs to halt.

The PADS project [1] has produced a family of data description languages [5] that are used as sources to generate C (PADS/C) and ML (PADS/ML). The languages offer a wider range of basic types, recursive definitions and full blown type dependencies. The compiler generates a type and a parsing function for each type. For base types and type constructors, the target types are fixed. Changing this requires changes to the compiler, as does the addition of new base types. The embedded language we have implemented has clear advantages precisely in this matter. A difficulty with PADS/C is that the compiler has to be modified in order to add tools. This has been recently remedied for PADS/ML [4] taking advantage of the expressiveness of ML's module system.

Parsec [11] is a monadic parser combinator library for Haskell. It is able to process thousands of lines per second making it suitable for industrial-strength purposes. Our library is similar to Parsec in many respects. In both cases, parser combinators are provided to build more advanced parsers, e.g., union, choice, sequence, etc. However our application domain differs from Parsec's that addresses context-sensitive, infinite look-ahead grammars, while we target ad hoc data formats. Our library provides combinators for expressing physical layout, semantic constraints and field dependencies. We also generate parse descriptors that record information about errors in the sources that can be used by the applications.

The Pickler library [10] is a combinator library implemented in Haskell. It builds picklers and unpicklers to convert data from an internal representation (e.g., a Haskell data type) into to external data format (e.g., a stream of bytes) back and forth. There are some similarities with our work. In both cases the programmer describes data formats by composing primitives using combinators, rather than writing tools like parsers and picklers by hand. The pickler combinators tie together the pickling and unpickling actions in a single value, i.e., a value of type a is interpreted to *pickle* and *unpickle* functions respectively, while our DDC library produces an internal representation and a parser descriptor. The primitives and combinators in [10] are analogous to our ad hoc data descriptors. However, since [10] has a separate goal on a different scale, it does neither describe the physical layout and semantic properties nor does it include dependencies.

7   Conclusions and Further Work

We have presented an embedding of the Data Description Calculus in Haskell. It provides us with a domain specific language for describing ad hoc data formats while having access to a complete programming language for building tools and applications. The descriptions are parsing functions with a monadic interface and are thus easy to use together with other libraries in Haskell. We have organized our embedding in such a way that it is easy to extend with new primitive combinators. For doing so we made use of type classes. We have also presented an example showing how to integrate other tools and comparing our embedded language with another domain specific language with a similar semantics.

There are many things we would like to do after testing our library more extensively. We would like to add some useful primitive types that occur frequently in many domains, like dates and IP addresses. We would like to extend it with some standard tools like error statistics, generation of XML schemas, generation of abstract syntax trees, etc.

We are convinced that there is a lot of work to do regarding the implementation. For example, we have only implemented a straightforward version of backtracking and this might need to be revised for efficiency considerations. We are also interested in studying how we could add rewrite rules to GHC to improve execution time.

Beyond, we believe that our library might be an excellent setting for tools that discover the data formats from examples and generate data descriptions automatically [7]. Furthermore, we are intrigued by the connections between the DDC and the theory of formal languages.

Acknowledgment

We want to thank John Hughes for insightful comments and suggestions.

References

1. Pads, `http://www.padsproj.org` ([Online]; accessed June 22, 2008)
2. Pcap, `http://www.tcpdump.org/pcap.htm` ([Online]; accessed October 10, 2008)
3. Back, G.: DataScript - A specification and scripting language for binary data. In: Batory, D., Blum, A., Taha, W. (eds.) GPCE 2002. LNCS, vol. 2487, pp. 66–77. Springer, Heidelberg (2002)
4. Fernández, M.F., Fisher, K., Foster, J.N., Greenberg, M., Mandelbaum, Y.: A Generic Programming Toolkit for PADS/ML: First-Class Upgrades for Third-Party Developers. In: Hudak, P., Warren, D.S. (eds.) PADL 2008. LNCS, vol. 4902, pp. 133–149. Springer, Heidelberg (2008)
5. Fisher, K., Gruber, R.: Pads: a domain-specific language for processing ad hoc data. In: PLDI 2005: Proceedings of the 2005 ACM SIGPLAN Conference on Programming Language Design and Implementation, pp. 295–304. ACM Press, New York (2005)
6. Fisher, K., Mandelbaum, Y., Walker, D.: The next 700 data description languages. In: POPL 2006, pp. 2–15. ACM Press, New York (2006)
7. Fisher, K., Walker, D., Zhu, K.Q., White, P.: From dirt to shovels: fully automatic tool generation from ad hoc data. In: POPL 2008, pp. 421–434. ACM, New York (2008)
8. Hughes, J.: The design of a pretty-printing library. In: First International Spring School on Advanced Functional Programming Techniques-Tutorial Text, pp. 53–96. Springer, London (1995)
9. Hutton, G., Meijer, E.: Monadic parsing in Haskell. Journal of Functional Programming 8(4), 437–444 (1998)
10. Kennedy, A.J.: Pickler combinators. Journal of Functional Programming 14(6), 727–739 (2004)
11. Leijen, D., Meijer, E.: Parsec: Direct style monadic parser combinators for the real world. Tech. Rep. UU-CS-2001-27, Department of Computer Science, Universiteit Utrecht (2001)
12. McCann, P.J., Chandra, S.: Packet types: Abstract specification of network protocol messages. SIGCOMM Comput. Commun. Rev. 30(4), 321–333 (2000)

iEditors:
Extending **iTask** with Interactive Plug-ins

Jan Martin Jansen[1], Rinus Plasmeijer[2], and Pieter Koopman[2]

[1] Faculty of Military Sciences,
Netherlands Defence Academy, Den Helder, the Netherlands
[2] Institute for Computing and Information Sciences (ICIS),
Radboud University Nijmegen, the Netherlands
`jm.jansen.04@nlda.nl`, {`rinus,pieter`}`@cs.ru.nl`

Abstract. The iTask library of Clean enables the user to specify web-enabled workflow systems on a high level of abstraction. Details like client-server communication, storage and retrieval of state information, HTML generation, and web form handling are all handled automatically. Using only standard HTML web browser elements also has a disadvantage: it does not offer the same level of interaction as we are used to from desktop applications. Browser plug-ins can fill this gap. They make it possible to extend web-applications with interactive functionality like the making of drawings. In this paper we explain how plug-ins can be nicely integrated in the iTask system. A special feature of the integration is the possibility for a plug-in to use Clean functions as call-back mechanism for the handling of events. These call-backs can be handled on the server as well as on the client. As a result we are now able to create interactive iTask applications (iEditors) using plug-ins like graphical editors. Although complicated, distributed multi-user applications can be created in this way, reasoning about the program remains easy since all code is generated from one and the same source: the high-level iTask specification in Clean.

1   Introduction

The internet has become an important platform for the deployment of applications. Despite this popularity, for an application programmer it is still hard to write web applications. To overcome this, the iData [18] and iTask [19] toolkits have been developed. They enable the development of web applications at a high level of abstraction, where the programmer can focus on the essence of the application without having to deal with web details like HTML generation and client-server communication. An iData application automatically generates output (HTML) and automatically handles user changes made in an HTML form. The iTask system adds the concept of tasks to iData. An iTask application can be considered as a structured collection of tasks to be performed by one or more users. In iTask specifications the flow of control and information between tasks can be expressed. To enhance the performance of iTask applications, the possi-

S.-B. Scholz and O. Chitil (Eds.): IFL 2008, LNCS 5836, pp. 192–211, 2011.

bility to handle tasks at the client side of a web application was added. For this the SAPL interpreter [20] was extended to a full Clean interpreter [9].

iData and iTask make use of standard HTML elements. In many cases these standard elements do not suffice for the creation of desktop-like applications. Browser plug-ins can be used to overcome this. Examples of plug-ins are media players for playing music and movies and Java Applets that offer the possibility to run Java programs at the client side of web applications.

When developing a web application using a plug-in the programmer has to deal with the following issues:

1. How to include the plug-in in the web application?
2. How to load relevant data into the plug-in?
3. How to transfer relevant data from the plug-in to the server application?
4. How to do specific processing for the plug-in (e.g, event handling for editors)?

For the inclusion of plug-ins in web applications, standard solutions in HTML exist. The other issues are mostly handled on an ad hoc basis, depending on the kind of application developed.

In this paper we focus on a more systematic solution for the last three issues. The focus is on the inclusion of Java Applet plug-ins [6,23] into iTask applications using generic [8] programming techniques. The presented techniques are not restricted to Java Applets alone but can also be used for communication with other kinds of plug-ins like advanced text editors (e.g. fckeditor [10]). For incorporating plug-ins into iTasks, a generic (read: poly-typical) framework is developed. The benefits for an application programmer are:

– A plug-in can be used with a minimum of programming effort and use of specific interface code. Generic functions take care of the conversion of Clean to Java data and back. They also take care of the communication between web-application and plug-in;
– One can define call-backs for the plug-in in Clean which can be handled either on server or client. Server handling can be used for executing more time consuming functions and client handling can be used for events requiring a quick response like mouse-event handling; For client side evaluation of call-backs the SAPL interpreter is used;
– Plug-in tasks behave like ordinary iTasks. If a suitable plug-in already exists, the application programmer only has to define Clean types (matching the content and event types of the plug-in), similarly to what is needed for ordinary iTasks. In order to include a plug-in into an iTask application only two interface functions are needed. For Java Applets the interface with plug-ins is encapsulated into a generic Java class.

We will call an iTask plug-in with Clean call-backs an iEditor. The technical contributions are:

– The seamless integration of plug-in tasks in the iTask formalism. This is realized by specializing the generic HTML generation and data update functions, in a completely transparent way for the application programmer;

- The use of Clean and SAPL dynamics [24] for realizing fine grained control over call-back function handling. Clean expressions are serialized at the server side, moved to the client side and executed there (this requires a referential transparent formalism). In this way it is possible to move entire computations from server to client in a dynamic way;
- A generic way to exchange data between Clean and Java. On the Clean side this is realized by standard generic print and parse functions. On the Java side this is realized by the Java reflection [14] mechanism.

The structure of this paper is as follows. In Section 2 we start with a short survey of the iTask system and architecture. In Section 3 we discuss the issues to be dealt with for including plug-ins in iTask and we give an example of the use of iEditors. Section 4 discusses the implementation of iEditors. In Section 5 we present a generic framework for the exchange of data between Clean and Java. In Section 6 we discuss some alternative uses and implementations of the techniques we developed. Section 7 compares our solution with other approaches that use client-side processing. Finally, we end with some concluding remarks in Section 8.

2   The iTask Toolkit

The iTask toolkit [19] is a web-based combinator library written in the lazy, purely functional programming language Clean. It can be used to implement powerful web-applications like online shops, etc. We briefly repeat the most important characteristics of iTask. A task in iTask can be a basic task or a combination of tasks:

- A basic task is created by the `editTask` function, which turns an element of an arbitrary data type into an editable web form. User edits of the form lead to automatic updates of the underlying data type;
- Task combinators enable the combination of tasks. Combinators are used to control the flow of processing and data from one task to another. Tasks can be performed sequentially, in parallel and distributed over several users. New tasks can dynamically depend on the results of previous tasks.

In the original iTask architecture all processing is done at the server side of the application and all user actions lead to a complete update of the web-page the user is editing. In [20] we showed how we can update sub-tasks in web pages and reduce the overhead of client-server communication in iTask applications by adding Ajax [5] and client side evaluation of tasks. The plug-in extensions discussed in this paper extend the set of basic tasks with powerful interactive tasks. This is done in a way that does not restrict the way in which tasks can be combined with combinators.

2.1   The Architecture of iTask Applications

The architecture (see Fig. 1) of iTask applications is representative for web applications based on the Ajax philosophy (web 2.0 applications [5,17], [25] gives details about web development with Ajax). It has the following characteristics:

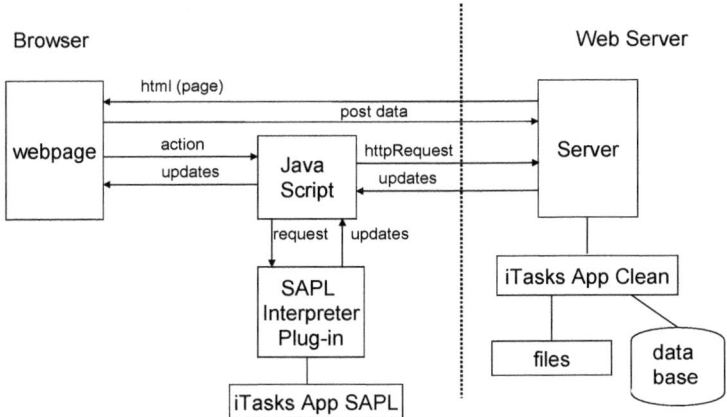

Fig. 1. The architecture of an iTask Application

- An iTask application consists of two images. A server executable running in native code at the server side of the application and a client side image running in the SAPL (Simple Application Programming Language) interpreter that is integrated in the web browser as a plug-in;
- Both the server and client images are generated from one single source programmed in Clean. From this source the server executable and a client SAPL program are generated by the Clean compiler. Both the Clean executable and the SAPL source comprise the complete iTask program. Tasks can be handled either at the server or the client. In principle, it is even possible to run the complete application (all tasks) at the client, except for the storage and retrieval of information in files and data bases;
- The server application initially generates a complete HTML page (web form) that is displayed in the client browser;
- User actions in the web form can be handled as normal post messages by the server or as an `httpRequest` by either client or server. In the first case a complete new HTML page is generated. In the second case it should be decided in JavaScript whether a request to either server or client application must be made. As result of the request a (partial) update of the web-page is made;
- The JavaScript at the client side is generic (the same for all iTask programs). JavaScript acts as an intermediary between client and server and client and SAPL interpreter. It takes care of updating the page with results from the server or client and it transforms user actions in the forms into calls for server or client application.

The use of JavaScript is a characteristic of all Ajax-based applications, but in our case the JavaScript functions are only a means for passing requests and results between the server application, client application and web-page. All application related programming is done in Clean. In this paper we extend this architecture with plug-in communication.

2.2   The **SAPL** Interpreter and **Clean-SAPL** Dynamics

To execute tasks and Clean functions at the client-side, we need a Clean platform there. This is realized by making a plug-in version of the SAPL interpreter
[9] and a Clean to SAPL compiler. By using a Java Applet for the interpreter,
client-side Clean processing becomes available for all major internet browsers.
The interpreter, originally realized in C, was re-implemented as a Java Applet
with a performance penalty of less than 40%. This means that this interpreter is
still considerably faster than other interpreters like GHCi, Helium and Hugs (see
[9]). We also constructed a Clean to SAPL compiler, supporting the full Clean
language. The generated SAPL code can be loaded into the SAPL interpreter at
start-up of web applications. Loading times of SAPL and client program (exclud-
ing the time needed to load the Java virtual machine) are comparable to that of
web pages including JavaScripts of about 1000 lines.

A special feature of the SAPL interpreter is that we can use a dedicated form
of Clean dynamics [24] for it. With dynamics it is possible to serialize a Clean
expression (closure) to a string, store the string somewhere, retrieve the string at
a later moment, turn it into a Clean expression again and execute it. We extended
the dynamics features of Clean in such a way that it is also possible to serialize
an expression in a Clean executable and de-serialize it in the SAPL interpreter
(running the corresponding SAPL program), and execute the expression there.
This is a powerful feature because it makes it possible to migrate execution
of a Clean program from server to client. In this paper we use this feature for
executing call-back functions at the client side.

2.3   Examples of **iTask** Applications

To give an idea of the iTask system, we give some small examples. Creating
a basic task in iTask is simple. With the `editTask` function one can turn an
element of an arbitrary data type into a task. As a result an editor for the data
type element is created residing in a web form. A user edit action of this form
results in an automatic update of the data type that can be further processed by
the remainder of the iTask application. `editTask` has two arguments: the name
of the button that the user should press to end the task and the initial value of
the editor. Here two examples of the use of this function are given: `simpleInt`
creates an editor for an integer while `simplePerson` creates an editor for an
element of type **Person**. We also give the definition of the type **Person**.

```
simpleInt :: Task Int
simpleInt = editTask "Ok" createDefault

:: Person = { name         :: String
            , e_mail       :: String
            , dateOfBirth  :: HtmlDate
            , gender       :: Gender
            }
:: Gender = Female | Male
```

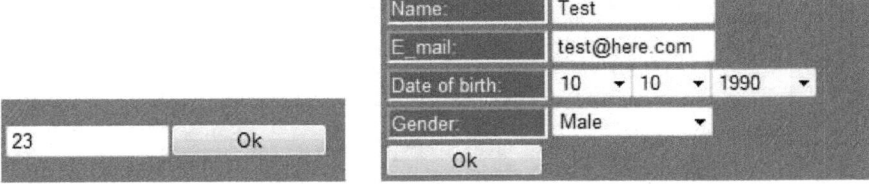

Fig. 2. editTask for Int (left) and Person (right)

```
simplePerson :: Task Person
simplePerson = editTask "Ok" createDefault
```

Fig. 2 shows the resulting editors created when respectively **simpleInt** and **simplePerson** are called. Note we use **createDefault** for the initial value of the editors. The fields in the form now get default values generated by the system using generic functions.

The 'simple' examples just create a form to be filled in by a single user, yielding a value of the corresponding type. In the following example a combinator is used to let two users perform tasks after each other:

```
addMultiUserTask :: Task Int
addMultiUserTask
=           0  @:: editTask "Ready" 0
  =>> λv → 1  @:: editTask "Ready" 0
  =>> λw → 0  @:: editTask "Result" (v+w),
```

User 0 (a login procedure binds a user to a unique id) has to enter a number, then user 1 has to enter a second number, then user 0 gets the sum of the numbers, but can still edit the result.

=>> is the iTask equivalent of the monadic 'bind' operator. n @:: task assigns task to user n.

3   iEditor: Plug-ins in iTask

Plug-ins are used for features that are not supported by standard HTML constructs like interactive drawing, complex text editing and animations. Plug-ins have to be installed by the user of the browser. Once this is done, they can be loaded by special HTML constructs. The use of plug-ins however, complicates the development of web applications. The developer has to take care that the plug-in is initialized and that the data needed by the plug-in is passed to it. In some cases, data from the plug-in has to be passed back to the web application or events occurring in the plug-in have to be handled by the web applications (e.g. mouse events).

In this section we introduce iEditor, an extension to iTask for the integration of plug-ins and give an example of its use.

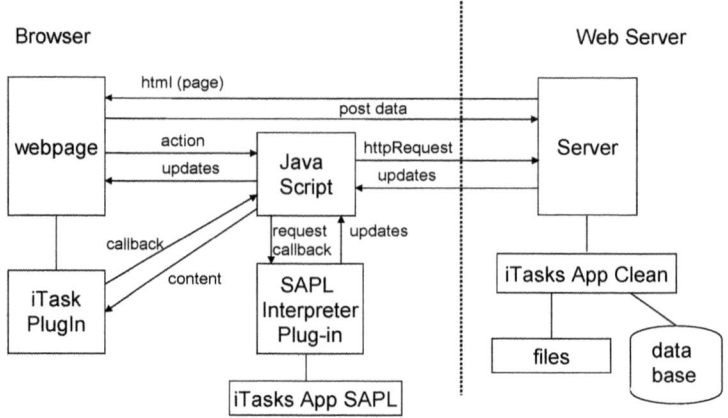

Fig. 3. The architecture of iTask with plug-ins

3.1   The iTask Architecture Including iEditors

In Fig. 3 we show the adapted iTask architecture for including iEditors. The extensions with respect to the standard iTask architecture (Fig. 1) are:

- The plug-in is part of a web-page. This means that the initial web-page should contain an HTML representation of the plug-in;
- All communication with a plug-in must be done via JavaScript functions. This is the standard way of communication with plug-ins. All popular plug-ins can be accessed from JavaScript and can call JavaScript functions. Although it is possible to communicate directly with Java Applets from the SAPL interpreter, we use the indirection via JavaScript to obtain a uniform interface that can also be used for non-Java plug-ins;
- For call-backs from the plug-in, the JavaScript function handling them has to decide where the calls should be made: either server or client.

3.2   The PlugIn Wrapper Type

In a basic iTask an element of a data type is turned into an editable HTML form by the function editTask and the result of editing the form is automatically turned into an updated instance of this data type. We want to maintain this interface for iEditors. More concretely, the information exchanged with a plug-in must also be represented by a data type and the use of the plug-in should lead to an updated instance of this data type. Because editTask has no means of distinguishing a data type intended for a plug-in from any other data type and also because we need information about how to load and display the plug-in, we have to wrap the content data type into a special PlugIn data type. For this wrapper type we can now make a specific implementation of the editTask function.

```
::PlugIn ct et st = {plugininfo     :: PlugInInfo,
                     content        :: ct,
                     events         :: [et],
                     state          :: st,
                     callback       :: [et] (ct,st) → (ct,st),
                     isServerEvent  :: et → Bool}
```

The wrapper type contains all information needed for the creation of the plug-in (the right HTML code). It also contains all information needed to enable communication from plug-in to JavaScript and vice versa. PlugIn has three type parameters ct, et and st:

- ct is the type of the content to be exchanged with the plug-in;
- et is the type of the events that can occur in the plug-in;
- st is the type of the state that must be maintained between calls of the call-back. This type is not visible to the plug-in itself, but only to the call-back function that handles events from the plug-in.

The fields in the PlugIn type have the following meaning:

- plugininfo: information for constructing the HTML representation of the plug-in: how to load the plug-in, its size and other initializing parameters (see the example in Section 3.4);
- content: content of the plug-in. This field contains the initial content of the plug-in and after the plug-in is ready it contains the result of the plug-in;
- events: generated events that have to be processed by the call-back function;
- state: value of the state to be maintained between call-back calls;
- callback: call-back function that handles the generated events;
- isServerEvent: indication where events have to be handled.

The call-back function takes the generated events, the current content and state as input and returns a new content and state. The content is passed back to the plug-in. The state is maintained for the next call of the call-back. The call-back function is automatically called from the plug-in whenever an event occurs. On the plug-in side there should be data types where the content and event types can be mapped on (more details in Section 4). Mismatches will lead to the generation of exceptions on either Clean or plug-in side.

For indicating where events have to be handled, the user must specify the function isServerEvent. If this function returns True for an event, this event is handled on the server; if it returns False, the event is handled on the client.

From the iTask point of view an iEditor is just another editor for a data type (the content field). All other information in the PlugIn type is only there for enabling the creation of the iEditor and for doing processing (event handling) for the plug-in (invisible at the iTask level). For plug-ins not requiring event processing, the events, state and callback fields can be filled with stubs.

3.3 Interface Functions for a Plug-in

For exchanging information between the iTask program and the plug-in two interface functions (one for the plug-in and one for JavaScript) are needed:

```
setContent(String content)
doPlugInCall(String pluginid, String content, String events)
```

setContent should be implemented by the plug-in and must be callable from
JavaScript. doPlugInCall is a JavaScript function and must be called by the
plug-in. pluginid is a unique id, identifying the plug-in (there can be more
than one plug-in). The content and events arguments are serialized versions
of the corresponding Clean datatypes (see Sections 3.4 and 4). For Java Applets
we provide a generic Java class that takes care of the communication between
plug-in and iTask program (see Section 5).

For other plug-ins there are two possibilities. Either the plug-in should be
adapted by wrapping code that supports these functions, or special interface
code can be written in JavaScript taking care of the conversion of Clean data to
data compatible with that of the plug-in. Often, this interface code can be used
for a whole class of similar plug-ins.

3.4   A Graphical Editor Plug-in for iTask

We now look at an example of the inclusion of an iEditor in iTask: a simple
graphical editor. We assume, we have created a Java Applet plug-in that is
capable of displaying simple graphics (lines, ovals, rectangles, etc.) and that can
generate events for mouse and button actions. The processing of events depends
on what kind of graphical editor we want to make (vector graphics, diagrams,
etc.). It is possible to create a dedicated plug-in for each kind of editor, but by
using Clean for doing event handling we can adapt the behavior of the application
by only changing the Clean source, without the need to adapt the plug-in. The
key idea is that mouse and button events are passed to the web-application by
a call-back function call. The call-back function can either be executed on the
server by the Clean executable or on the client by the SAPL version of the Clean
application. For each type of event, the programmer can choose where it must
be handled.

We give the (almost) complete Clean source code for this editor. We start with
the data types:

```
::GraphObject  = GraphLine Int Int Int Int | GraphOval Int Int Int Int |
                 GraphRect Int Int Int Int | GraphPolyLine [Pnt]        |
                 GraphButton String
::Pnt          = Pnt Int Int

::GraphEvent   = MouseDown Int Int | MouseDrag Int Int |
                 MouseUp   Int Int | ButtonEvent String

::GraphState   = NewLine | NewPolyLine | NewRect | NewOval
```

In the application a drawing is represented by a list of GraphObject. We distinguish several types of figures and simple buttons (for the sake of simplicity we
combined figures and buttons in one type). GraphEvent represents the events
that can occur. We distinguish mouse (down, up, drag) and button events.

The Ints represent the x and y position of the mouse event We assume that the plug-in is capable of displaying elements of GraphObject and that it turns events into elements of GraphEvent. The plug-in should have matching types for GraphObject and GraphEvent. The transformation of elements of these types onto each other is done automatically (see Section 4 and 5). GraphState is a state data type maintaining that part of the state that is not passed to the plug-in, but that is needed by the call-back function. In this example it maintains the type of the figure to be drawn at a mouse down event.

The task definition is given by:

```
graphtask :: Task (PlugIn [GraphObject] GraphEvent GraphState)
graphtask =   editTask "Ready" graphplugin
```

The initialization of the plug-in is given by:

```
graphplugin :: PlugIn [GraphObject] GraphEvent GraphState
graphplugin = {plugininfo     = grapheditapplet,
               content        = initpicture,
               events         = [],
               state          = NewLine,
               callback       = doEvents,
               isServerEvent  = isMouseUp}

isMouseUp (MouseUp _ _) = True
isMouseUp             _  = False

grapheditapplet = AppletPlugIn {id      = "drawplugin",
                                archive = "drawapplet.jar",
                                code    = "drawapplet/maincanvas.class",
                                width   = 500,
                                height  = 200}

initpicture = [GraphButton "Line",      GraphButton "PolyLine",
               GraphButton "Rectangle", GraphButton "Oval"]
```

graphplugin contains the initialization of the plug-in. We see that all events are handled on the client except MouseUp events. As a consequence, the server side PlugIn data type is updated at every MouseUp. grapheditapplet contains the information needed for generating the HTML representation of the plug-in: the Applet id, the codebase and main class, its width and height. Finally, we see that the initial picture only contains the buttons.

Events occurring in the plug-in, are handled by the doEvents function:

```
doEvents ::    [GraphEvent] ([GraphObject], GraphState) →
                            ([GraphObject], GraphState)

doEvents [ButtonEvent "Line":evs]  (figs,_)
= doEvents                    evs  (figs,NewLine)

doEvents [MouseDown x y:evs]        (figs,NewLine)
= doEvents              evs         ([GraphLine x y x y:figs],NewLine)
```

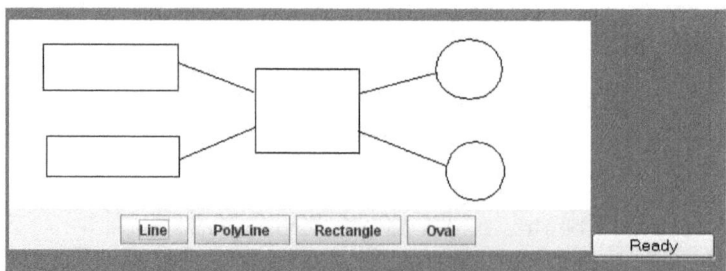

Fig. 4. Screen shot of the drawing application

```
doEvents [MouseDrag x y:evs]         ([GraphLine v w _ _: figs],a)
= doEvents              evs          ([GraphLine v w x y: figs],a)

doEvents [e:evs] (figs,a) = doEvents evs (figs,a) // ignore other events
doEvents []      (figs,a) =              (figs,a) // return result
```

Here only the code for Line is shown, Rectangle, PolyLine and Oval are handled in a similar way. Fig. 4 shows a screen shot of the application.

The user can stop editing by clicking the 'Ready' button. The current content and state are now made available to the remainder of the iTask application.

A multi-user graphical editor. To show that the plug-in task simply behaves like a normal iTask we give a small variation of **graphtask** analogous to the multi-user example from Section 3:

```
graphtask :: Task (PlugIn [GraphObject] GraphEvent GraphState)
graphtask =               0 @:: editTask "0 Ready" graphplugin
             =>> λv → 1 @:: editTask "1 Ready" v
             =>> λw → 0 @:: editTask "Result" w
```

Two users are involved in this example. User 0 makes an initial drawing. The result is passed to user 1, who can further edit the drawing. If this task is ready the result is passed back to user 0 who can continue editing.

For this application the programmer only has to specify the (content, state and event) types and the call-back function needed for handling events. The plug-in iTask behaves like an ordinary iTask. All communication with the plug-in is handled in a way that is transparent for the programmer.

It is also possible to wrap several plug-ins into one task. For example: editTask "Ready" (graphplugin,texteditplugin) wraps two editors together into one form. The editors are displayed next to each other.

4   Implementation of iEditors

From the example it is clear that the use of iEditors is straightforward for the application programmer and that, from the iTask point of view, an iEditor is just another editor. In the implementation we face a number of challenges (to answer questions 1 to 4 from Section 1):

- How to fit the plug-in into the iData/iTask architecture?
- How to exchange data between server, plug-in and client?
- How to invoke call-back functions from plug-in for server and client?

4.1 Fitting a Plug-in into the iTask Architecture

The HTML representation of the plug-in is generated as part of the initial iTask web-page. This is realized by making a specialized implementation of the generic gForm [18] function that is part of the implementation of editTask and that is responsible for the generation of the web form. The resulting HTML also contains the initial content of the plug-in and all other information needed by the plug-in and by the JavaScript functions that interact with the plug-in. This adapted gForm is generic and works for all plug-ins.

4.2 Data Exchange between Client, Plug-in and Server

For data exchange between plug-in, server and client Clean program we use the generic print and parse functions on the Clean side (on server and client). As a consequence the plug-in must have a (generic) way to parse and unparse the strings representing the event and content data types. In Section 5 we discuss how this is realized for Java.

Although we have the same Clean program running at both the server and client side, the internal representations of data types are completely different. Therefore we also use the generic print and parse functions for the exchange of data between the Clean programs at server and client side.

All communication between server, client and plug-in is done using JavaScript functions, similar to what is done for Ajax and client side handling of iTask tasks (see [20]). These functions are generic in the sense that they do not depend on the specific plug-in. The JavaScript functions are responsible for passing data from plug-in to server and client and vice-versa, but also for making the call-back and deciding where the call-back must be handled. The addition of plug-ins only requires one extra JavaScript function to handle all communication from the plug-in with client and server Clean programs:

```
doPlugInCall(String pluginid, String content, String events)
```

This function can both handle the final result from a plug-in and the call-backs generated by the plug-in. The first argument is the unique ID of the plug-in (there can be more than one plug-in and they all use this JavaScript function). The second argument is the serialized version of the current content of the plug-in. The third argument is a serialized version of the list of the events that must be processed (this list is empty in case the plug-in just wants to synchronize its content with the server program). The JavaScript function takes care of either updating the server program with the content of the plug-in or by making the call-back to client or server program (see Section 4.3).

For updating its content the plug-in should implement the following function:

`setContent(String content)`

The argument is again a (serialized) string representation of the content. This function is called from JavaScript. It is custom for plug-ins to support function calls from JavaScript.

4.3 Handling Call-Backs

Call-backs can be made to either client or server. The plug-in makes the call-back by calling the (generic) Javascript function `doPlugInCall` with the serialized content and events as arguments. The JavaScript function determines whether the call must be handled on the server or the client by executing the `isServerEvent` function for the event in the SAPL interpreter. For the server case, the `PlugIn` data type is updated in a similar way as for an ordinary update for iData [18]. The implementation of `editTask` makes use of the generic function `gUpd` for updating the data type with the result of a user edit action. For the `PlugIn` data type a specialized version of `gUpd` is made that applies the call-back function to its arguments before updating the `PlugIn` data structure with the result. Finally, the HTML representation of the plug-in is re-generated with the new content.

We could use the same strategy for the client side (the full Clean program is available). But we must do it in a much more efficient way, because the overhead of finding out for which task the update is intended can be large. We can do it more efficiently because we have an interpreter available that can execute an arbitrary Clean expression. We use this to directly execute the call-back function call and use the result to make a direct update of the content of the plug-in. In this way we short-circuit the use of `gUpd` and the whole iTask machinery needed for finding out which task is updated [19]. This optimization is absolutely necessary for events needing immediate response like mouse drag events.

For making the direct call-back on the client we use Clean-SAPL dynamics (see Section 2.2). For this, the serialized call-back function is stored in the plug-in HTML representation. Not only is the call-back function itself serialized, but the `isServerEvent` function and the parse and unparse functions for the arguments (content, state and events) are also serialized. The last is necessary because the arguments are passed to the call-back as serialized strings from the plug-in via the `doPlugInCall` function and the result must be passed back in serialized form too.

In the actual call-back, it is first checked if the event is really intended for the client by applying the `isServerEvent` function to the deserialized event. If not, the server call-back is made as described above. Otherwise the call-back and parse and unparse functions are all de-serialized, the arguments are parsed, the call-back is applied, and the result state and content are unparsed again. The content is handed back to the plug-in directly (via `setContent`) and the state is maintained in the HTML representation of the plug-in.

Note that we cannot handle all call-backs at the client side. Processing intensive call-backs and call-backs requiring information from data bases or files should be handled on the server side.

4.4   Evaluation of Efficiency of Handling Call-Backs

In the graphical editor application we used the call-back function to handle mouse down and drag events by the SAPL interpreter. Mouse drag events often occur in quick sequences (in the order of 10-15 events per second). The whole call-back machinery was capable of keeping track of these events on an Intel 1.6 GHz Core Duo 2 machine (using only one core). Attempts to handle the drag events by the server lead to a browser hang-up due to a client-server communication overload. Of course, the (de)serialization of data types takes a significant amount of time and is a limiting factor in the amount of events that can be handled. Native implementations (without the need to (de)serialize) can easily handle up to ten times as much events.

5   Implementation for **Java** Applets

Java Applets [6,23] are an important class of plug-ins. All modern web browsers offer the possibility of Applet plug-ins. In this way it is possible to incorporate complex Java applications into web pages. We already used the Java Applet mechanism for loading the SAPL interpreter at the client side of iTask for handling client tasks and call-backs. Although Java Applets can offer rich functionality they are less popular, because communicating with them must be handled in an ad-hoc manner, making it difficult to integrate them with the remainder of a web application (see also [21]). By using the iTask plug-in techniques, we have a generic strategy which simplifies the communication with Java Applets. To include a Java Applet in an iTask application we have to deal with the following issues:

 – We have to find a way to map Clean types on corresponding Java data types;
 – We have to take care that we offer the interface needed for communication with JavaScript.

5.1   Mapping **Clean** and **Java** Data Types onto Each other

In order to exchange information between a Clean and Java application there must be a way to transfer Clean data to Java data and back. To save the programmer from writing boilerplate data transformation code we included generic code in Clean and Java to handle this data transformation. Not all Clean and Java data types can be mapped onto each other. For a Java class the member fields are (currently) restricted to the following types:

 – primitive types: (`int`,`long`,`float`,`double`,`boolean`,`char`);
 – the `String` type;
 – all subtypes of `List` (they are all mapped on a Clean list);
 – other Java classes with members that obey these rules.

A class may be a subclass of another class or implement an interface, but all superclasses must obey the rules mentioned above. Other (container) types, like Map and arrays are not (yet) allowed. For these classes an ad-hoc mapping must be made (like is done for List).

From the Clean point of view, the automatic conversion of Clean data types to Java types is restricted to first order data types that can be described by standard Algebraic Data Types. Records are not allowed yet, but they can be easily added. If a Clean type is mapped onto a Java type hierarchy the fields of the Clean type should match the union of all fields in the class hierarchy in the order of the hierarchy (fields of superclass before fields of subclass).

More formally, consider the following algebraic data type definition in Clean:

```
::typename t1 .. tk = C1 t11 .. t1n_1 | .. | Cm tm1 .. tmn_m
```

t1..tk are type parameters, C1..Cm constructor names and tik type names or type parameters. This type definition corresponds to the following Java interface and m Java classes:

```
interface typename {}
class<t1,..,tk> C1 implements typename {t11 a11; .. t1n_1 a1n_1;}
...
class<t1,..,tk> Cm implements typename {tm1 am1; .. tmn_m amn_m;}
```

Each constructor is represented by a separate Java class with as name the constructor name and with as fields the arguments of the constructor (with names aik) with their type. As an example, the Clean type GraphObject from Section 3 corresponds to the following Java classes:

```
interface GraphObject {}
class GraphLine implements GraphObject {int x, y, v, w;}
class GraphRect implements GraphObject {int x, y, v, w;}
class GraphOval implements GraphObject {int x, y, v, w;}
class GraphPolyLine implements GraphObject {List<Pnt> points;}
class GraphButton implements GraphObject {String name;}

class Pnt {int x, y;}
```

It is possible to generate a corresponding Clean data type definition from an existing Java class (hierarchy) using generic Java functions. Otherwise the programmer has to take care that matching types at Clean and Java side exist, as we did in our graphics editor example. Once corresponding data types exist, the conversion of data is done automatically.

For the actual conversion of data we use the standard generic print and parse functions at the Clean side (gPrint and gParse) and reflection [14] on the Java side.

5.2   Java Applet Plug-in Interface

To further simplify the communication between Java plug-in and Clean iTask application, the Java class CleanJavaCom is offered. This class contains member functions that can be used for parsing and unparsing Java objects and functions for handling the communication with the JavaScript interface. The CleanJavaCom class is generic and can be used in every Java Applet to be used as plug-in in an iTask application.

```
class CleanJavaCom<CT,ET> {
  private String writeClassToString(Object object)   {...}
  private Object readClassFromString(String inp)      {...}
  public CT getContent() {...}
  public void setContent(String ser_content) {...}
  public void handleEvents(List<ET> events) {...}
  ...
}
```

The class is parametrised by the Java versions of the content (CT) and event (ET) types.

- writeClassToString generates a string representation of an object that exactly fits the Clean representation;
- readClassFromString parses a string representation generated by gPrint to the corresponding Java object;
- getContent is called to obtain the content by the remainder of the Applet;
- setContent is called from JavaScript to set the content. The content string is de-serialized by a call to readClassFromString. The result can now be obtained by the remainder of the applet by a call of getContent;
- handleEvents is called by the Applet after one (or more) event(s) have occurred. This function takes care of serializing the content and events and calling the doPlugInCall function in JavaScript. JavaScript should pass back the result by a call of setContent. If the plug-in only wants to synchronize its content with the iTask server application it should call doEvents with an empty event list.

In the implementation of writeClassToString and readClassFromString the Java reflection mechanism is used.

6 Discussion

Plug-ins must have matching types for the content and event types. For Java we implemented a generic way to convert the serialized content and event types to Java data structures and back. Not all plug-in types offer the possibility to do this conversion in a generic way. An alternative is to use generic functions in Clean for generating a representation the plug-in can deal with and for parsing back the results. An example is the use of XML [2]. Java has the XMLEncoder and XMLDecoder classes for generating and parsing XML representations of data types. For us, a more interesting alternative is the use of JSON (JavaScript Object Notation) [1]. This has as an advantage that we can also exchange data with JavaScript and a large number of other formalisms. Like string serialization, it allows for a lightweight implementation with little overhead. We already started to implement generic generation and parsing of JSON data in Clean and we will use this for future implementations.

Other alternatives are the use of CORBA [16] or the Java Native Interface [12] for exchanging data between Clean and the plug-in. Examples can be found in [15,21,4]. For us, these approaches are too heavyweight to be used at the client side in the SAPL interpreter.

The idea of attaching an event handler to an editor is not restricted to plug-in tasks. Call-back functions can also be attached to other basic iTask editors. The call-back can be used to check the content of the editor before sending it back to the server and give the user feedback in case something is wrong or to reformat the content before displaying it again. Because the full power of Clean is available at the client side there are no restrictions to the call-back functions that can be defined. In this way, the concept of iEditors can be extended to arbitrary iTask editors. To implement this, we can either use a wrapper type like `PlugIn` or introduce a special combinator in iTask like the one used for assigning users to tasks (see Section 2).

7   Related Work

In this paper we extended the iTask toolkit with a generic framework for the inclusion of plug-ins, with the possibility to make calls from the plug-in to Clean functions that can be executed on either client or server. We are not aware of any other functional system that has these features. However, there are functional approaches for handling web pages using the same formalism for server and client side processing. Most of them compile to JavaScript for client side execution. An example of this approach is Hop [22,13]. Hop is a dedicated web programming language and its syntax is HTML-like. In Hop it is also possible to specify a complete web application without the (direct) use of JavaScript. Hop uses two compilers, one for compiling the server side program and one for compiling the client-side part. The client side part is only used for executing the user interface. The application essentially runs on the client and may call services on the server. Hop uses syntactic constructions for indicating client and server part code. It is build on top of the Scheme programming language. In our case we do not have to extend Clean, but can write the entire web application in Clean itself. In [13] it is shown that a reasonably good performance for the client side functions in Hop can be obtained. For us, compiling to JavaScript is no option because Clean is lazy. Instead we use the SAPL interpreter, which also has competitive performance as was shown in [9] and the graphics editor application.

Links [3] and its extension formlets is a functional language-based web programming language. Links compiles to JavaScript for rendering HTML pages, and SQL to communicate with a back-end database. A Links program stores its session state at the client side. In a Links program, the keywords `client` and `server` force a top-level function to be executed at the client or server respectively. In Links, processes can be spawned and these processes can communicate via message passing. Client-server communication is implemented using

Ajax technology, like we do. In the iData and iTask toolkits, forms are generated generically for every data type, whereas in Links and Formlets these need to be coded by the programmer.

The Flapjax language [11] is an implementation of functional reactive programming in JavaScript, with features comparable to those of Hop. Both are designed to create intricate web applications. In Flapjax, Hop and Formlets processing is directly attached to web form handling, which is comparable to the use of call-backs in iEditors.

A much more restricted approach has been implemented in Curry [7]: only a very restricted subset of Curry is translated to JavaScript to handle client side verification code fragments only.

Summarizing the main differences with the other approaches are:

- iTask/iEditor applications are just plain Clean applications, where web forms are generated from data types. The other approaches define dedicated web languages where processing is attached to web forms;
- We can use the full Clean functionality at the client side because the SAPL interpreter offers a full Clean platform. The other approaches rely on compilation to JavaScript with, in many cases, restrictions on the functions that can be compiled to JavaScript;
- Clean-SAPL dynamics offers a generic and flexible way to attach call-back handling to web forms and plug-ins. Where the other approaches use static annotations to indicate whether functions have to be executed on either client or server, in our approach this can be decided dynamically, depending on the events to be processed.

8   Conclusions

Plug-ins are often an essential part of more interactive web applications. In this paper we discussed a generic way for including plug-ins in iTask applications. All communication between iTask application and plug-in is on the level of exchanging and updating data types, which is entirely consistent with the normal way iTask works. Plug-in tasks behave like ordinary tasks. No adaptations of iTask were necessary to incorporate them, only a specialization of the gForm and gUpd functions for the PlugIn type.

An important feature is that plug-ins can use Clean functions, which can be executed on either server or client, for event handling. This gives the programmer fine-grained control over the behavior of the plug-in without the need to adapt the plug-in itself. In this way, we can keep the plug-in to its essence and use Clean for all processing not involving the specialities of the plug-in.

Information exchange between server, client and plug-in is realized with the use of generic (un)parsing of data types. For efficient client side event handling a combination of Clean-SAPL dynamics and generic (un)parsing is used. With Clean-SAPL dynamics it is possible to move the execution of arbitrary Clean expressions from server to client. This turns out to be a powerful feature that can also be used for attaching client side functions to arbitrary web forms.

For Java Applets, a straightforward to use generic class is provided that handles all interaction of the plug-in with Clean including the conversion of data types and the forwarding of call-backs. Plug-ins of other type should implement a simple JavaScript interface and the (de)serialization of the data types used for the exchange of information.

We have maintained the declarative approach of the iTask toolkit. Server and client programs and all call-back handling functions are generated from an annotated, single-source specification with a low burden on the programmer because the system itself switches automatically between client and server side evaluation of tasks and call-backs when this is necessary. The iTask system integrates all mentioned technologies in a truly transparent and declarative way.

References

1. Introducing JSON, http://www.json.org (visited March 2009)
2. Bray, T., Paoli, J., Sperberg-Macqueen, C.: Extensible Markup Language (XML) 1.0 (w3c recommendation). Technical Report (1998), http://www.w3.org/TR/1998/REC-xml-19980210
3. Cooper, E., Lindley, S., Wadler, P., Yallop, J.: Links: Web programming without tiers. In: de Boer, F.S., Bonsangue, M.M., Graf, S., de Roever, W.-P. (eds.) FMCO 2006. LNCS, vol. 4709, pp. 266–296. Springer, Heidelberg (2007)
4. Evans, E., Rogers, D.: Using Java applets and CORBA for multi-user distributed applications. IEEE Internet Computing 1, 43–55 (1997)
5. Garrett, J.: Ajax: A new approach to web applications, 2005, http://www.adaptivepath.com/ideas/essays/archives/000385.php (visited March 2009)
6. Gosling, J., Joy, B., Steele, G.: The Java Language Specification. Sun Microsystems (1996)
7. Hanus, M.: Putting declarative programming into the web: Translating Curry to JavaScript. In: Proc. of the 9th International ACM SIGPLAN Conference on Principle and Practice of Declarative Programming (PPDP 2007), pp. 155–166. ACM Press, New York (2007)
8. Hinze, R.: A new approach to generic functional programming. In: Proceedings of the 27th Annual ACM SIGPLAN-SIGACT Symposium on Principles of Programming Languages (January 2000)
9. Jansen, J.M., Koopman, P., Plasmeijer, R.: Efficient interpretation by transforming data types and patterns to functions. In: Nilsson, H. (ed.) Proceedings Seventh Symposium on Trends in Functional Programming, TFP 2006, Nottingham, UK, The University of Nottingham, April 19-21. Trends in Functional Programming, vol. 7. Intellect Publisher (2006)
10. Knabben, F.C.: FCK editor (2003), http://www.fckeditor.net (visited March 2009)
11. Krishnamurthi, S.: The Flapjax site (2007), http://www.flapjax-lang.org (visited March 2009)
12. Liang, S.: Java Native Interface: Programmer's Guide and Reference. Addison-Wesley Longman Publishing Company, Amsterdam (1999)
13. Loitsch, F., Serrano, M.: Hop client-side compilation. In: Trends in Functional Programming, TFP 2007, New York, pp. 141–158, Interact (2008)
14. McCluskey, G.: Using Java reflection (1998), http://java.sun.com/developer/technicalArticles/ALT/Reflection/index.html (visited March 2009)

15. Meijer, E., Finne, S.: Lambada: Haskell as a better Java. In: Proceedings of the 2000 Haskell Workshop, Montreal, Canada (2000)
16. OMG: Object Management Group. The Common Object Request Broker: Architecture and SpecificationRevision 2.0 (1996),
    `http://www.omg.org/corba-e/index.htm` (visited March 2009)
17. Paulson, L.D.: Building Rich Web Applications with Ajax. Computer 38(10), 14–17 (2005)
18. Plasmeijer, R., Achten, P.: The implementation of iData. In: Butterfield, A., Grelck, C., Huch, F. (eds.) IFL 2005. LNCS, vol. 4015, pp. 106–123. Springer, Heidelberg (2006)
19. Plasmeijer, R., Achten, P., Koopman, P.: iTasks: Executable specifications of interactive work flow systems for the web. In: Ramsey, N. (ed.) Proceedings of the 2007 ACM SIGPLAN International Conference on Functional Programming, ICFP 2007, Freiburg, Germany, October 1-3, pp. 141–152. ACM, New York (2007)
20. Plasmeijer, R., Jansen, J.M., Koopman, P., Achten, P.: Declarative Ajax and client side evaluation of workflows using iTasks. In: Principles and Practice of Declarative Programming, PPDP 2008, Valencia, Spain (2008)
21. Reinke, C.: Towards a haskell/Java connection. In: Hammond, K., Davie, T., Clack, C. (eds.) IFL 1998. LNCS, vol. 1595, pp. 203–219. Springer, Heidelberg (1999)
22. Serrano, M., Gallesio, E., Loitsch, F.: Hop: a language for programming the web 2.0. In: ACM SIGPLAN Conference on Object-Oriented Programming, Systems, Languages, and Applications (OOPSLA 2006), Portland, Oregon, USA, October 22-26, pp. 975–985 (2006)
23. Sun Microsystems. Release notes for the next-generation Java Plug-In technology (2008), `http://jdk6.dev.java.net/plugin2` (visited March 2009)
24. van Weelden, A.: Putting Types To Good Use. PhD thesis, Radboud University Nijmegen, the Netherlands (2007)
25. W3 Schools. Ajax tutorial (2008), `http://w3schools.com/ajax/default.asp`

An Executable and Testable Semantics for iTasks

Pieter Koopman, Rinus Plasmeijer, and Peter Achten

Nijmegen Institute for Computing and Information Sciences,
Radboud University Nijmegen, The Netherlands
{pieter,rinus,p.achten}@cs.ru.nl

Abstract. The iTask system is an easy to use combinator library for specifying dynamic data dependent workflows in a very flexible way. The specified workflows are executed as a multi-user web-application. The implementation of the iTask system is fairly complicated. Hence we cannot use it for reasoning about the semantics of workflows in the iTask system. In this paper we define an executable semantics that specifies how workflows react on events generated by the workers executing them. The semantics is used to explain iTasks and to reason about iTasks. Based on this semantics we define a mathematical notion of equivalence of tasks and show how this equivalence for tasks can be approximated automatically. Advantages of this executable semantics are: it is easy to validate the semantics by interactive simulation; properties of the semantics can be tested by our model-based test system G∀st. G∀st can test a large number of properties within seconds. These tests appeared to be a good indication about the consistency of the specified semantics and equivalence relation for tasks. The automatic testing of properties was very helpful in the development of the semantics. The contribution of this paper is a semantics for iTasks as well as the method used to construct this operational semantics.

1 Introduction

The iTask system [10] is an experimental toolkit to specify data dependent dynamic workflows in a flexible and concise way by a set of combinators. The iTask system supports workers executing the specified tasks by a web-based interface. Typical elementary user tasks in this system are filling in forms and pressing buttons to make choices. The elementary tasks are implemented on top of the iData system [9]. Based on an input the iTask system determines the new task that has to be done and updates the interface in the browser. Arbitrary complex tasks are created by combining (elementary) tasks. The real power of data dependent tasks is provided by the monadic bind operator that contains a *function* to generate the next task based on the value produced by the previous task.

The iTask implementation executes the tasks, but has to cope with many other things at the same time: e.g. i/o to files and database, generation of the multi-user web interface, client/server evaluation of tasks, and exception handling. The iTask system uses generic programming to derive interfaces to files, databases and web-browsers for data types. The combination of these things makes the implementation of iTasks much too complicated to grasp the semantics. To overcome

S.-B. Scholz and O. Chitil (Eds.): IFL 2008, LNCS 5836, pp. 212–232, 2011.
© Springer-Verlag Berlin Heidelberg 2011

these problems we develop a high level operational semantics for iTasks in this paper. This semantics is used to explain the behavior of the iTask system, and to reason about the desired behavior of the system. In the future we will use this semantics as model to test the real iTask implementation with our model-based test tool G∀st. A prerequisite for model-based testing is an accurate model of the desired behavior. Making a model with the desired properties is not easy. Such a model is developed, validated, and its properties are tested in this paper.

In this paper we provide a basic rewrite semantics for iTasks as well as a number of useful notions to reason about tasks, such as *needed events* and *equivalence* of tasks. The semantics of many other workflow systems is based on Petri-nets [11], actor-oriented directed graphs (including some simple higher order constructs) [7], or abstract state machines (ASM) [6]. Neither of these alternatives is capable to express the flexibility covered by the dynamic generation of tasks of the monadic bind operation of the iTask system. As usual we omit many details in the semantics to express the meaning of the basic iTask combinators as clearly as possible. The semantics is expressed in the functional programming language Clean instead of the more common Scott Brackets, denotational semantics, or horizontal bar style, structural operational semantics a la Plotkin. The close correspondence between semantics and functional programs goes back at least to [8]. Expressing the operational semantics in a FPL is as concise as in Scott Brackets style. Using a functional programming language as carrier of the specification of the semantics has a number of advantages: **1)** the type system performs basic consistency checks on the semantics; **2)** the semantics is executable; **3)** using the iTask system it is easy to validate the semantics by interactive simulation; **4)** using the model-based test tool G∀st [5] it is possible to express properties about the semantics and equivalence of task concisely, and to test these properties fully automatically. Although the semantics is executable, it is not an iTask system itself. The semantics is a model of the real system, it lacks for instance a frontend (user interface) as well as a backend (e.g. interface to a database).

Especially the ability to express properties of the specified semantics and to test them automatically appears to be extremely convenient in the development of the semantics and associated notions described in this paper. An alternative, more traditional, approach would be to define a semantics in a common mathematical style, state properties in logic, and formally prove these properties. It would be wise to use a proof assistant like COQ [13] or SPARKLE [3] in proving the properties, this would require a transformation of the semantics to the language of the proof assistant. In the past we have used this approach for the iData system [1]. In such a mathematically based approach it is much harder to experiment with different formulations of the semantics and to get the system consistent after a change. Proving a property of a new version of the semantics typical takes some days of human effort where testing the same property is done in seconds by a computer. When we have a final version of the semantics obtained in this way, we can decide to prove (some of) the tested properties in order to obtain absolute confidence in their correctness.

In section 2 we show how we model iTasks and the effect of applying an input
to a task. In this section we also define useful notions about subtasks, such as
when they are enabled or needed. In section 3 we define the equivalence of tasks
and how the equivalence of tasks can be determined in two different ways. Some
important properties of the semantics of iTasks are given in section 4, we also
show how these properties can be tested fully automatically. Testing properties
of the semantics increases the confidence that we have specified the semantics of
iTasks right. In the future we will use this semantics for model-based testing of
the real iTask implementation, this will increase the confidence that the system
obeys the semantics. Finally there is a discussion.

2   A Semantics for iTasks

In the original iTask system a task is a state transformer of the strict and unique
Task State TSt. The required uniqueness of the task state (to guarantee single
threaded use of the state in a pure functional language) is in Clean indicated by
the type annotation *. The type parameter a indicates the type of the result.
This result is returned by the task when it is completely finished.

:: Task a := *TSt $\rightarrow$ *(a,*TSt)   // an iTask is state transition of type TSt

Hence, a Task of type a is a function that takes a unique task state TSt as
argument and produces a unique tuple with a value of type a and a new unique
task state. In this paper we consider only one basic task: the edit task.

editTask :: String a $\rightarrow$ Task a | iData a

The function editTask takes a string and a value of type a as arguments and
produces a task a under the context restriction that the type a is in the type
class iData. The class iData is used to create a web based editor for values of
this type. Here we assume that the desired instances are defined.

The editTask function creates a task editor to modify a value of the given
type, and adds a button with the given name to finish the task. A user can
change the value as often as she wants. The task is not finished until the button
is pressed. There are predefined editors for all basic data types. For other data
types an editor can be derived using Clean's generic programming mechanism
[2], or a tailor-made editor can be defined for that type.

In this paper we focus on the following basic iTask combinators to compose
tasks.

```
return              :: a                        → Task a      | iData a
(>>=) infixl 1   :: (Task a) (a→Task b)  → Task b      | iData b
(-||-) infixr 3  :: (Task a) (Task a)    → Task a      | iData a
(-&&-) infixr 4  :: (Task a) (Task b)    → Task (a,b) | iData a & iData b
```

The combinators **return** and **>>=** are the usual monadic *return* and *bind*. The
return combinator transforms a value in a task yielding that value immediately.
The bind combinator is used to indicate a sequence of tasks. The expression

t >>= u indicates that first task t must be done completely. When this is done, its result is given to u in order to create a new task that is executed subsequently.

The expression t -||- u indicates that both iTasks can be executed in *any* order and *interleaved*, the combined task is completed *as soon as* any subtask is done. The result is the result of the task that completes first, the other task is removed from the system. The expression t -&&- u states that both iTasks must be done in any order (interleaved), the combined task is completed when *both* tasks are done. The result is a tuple containing the results of both tasks.

All these combinators are higher order functions manipulating the complex task state TSt. This higher order function based approach is excellent for constructing such a library in a flexible and type safe way. However, if we want to construct a program with which we can reason about iTasks, higher order functions are rather inconvenient. In a functional programming language like Haskell or Clean it is not possible to inspect which function is given as argument to a higher order function. The only thing we can do with such a function given as argument is applying it to arguments. In a programming context this is exactly what one wants to do with such a function. In order to specify the semantics of the various iTask combinators however, we need to know which operator we are currently dealing with. This implies that we need to replace the higher order functions by a *representation* that can be handled instead. We replace the higher order functions and the task state TSt by the algebraic data type ITask. We use infix constructors for the or-combinator, .||., and the and-combinator, .&&., in order to make the representation similar to the corresponding infix combinators -||- and -&&- from the original iTask library.

```
:: ITask
    = EditTask      ID       String  BVal         // an editor
    | .||. infixr 3 ITask    ITask                // OR-combinator
    | .&&. infixr 4 ITask    ITask                // AND-combinator
    | Bind          ID       ITask   (Val→ITask)  // sequencing-combinator
    | Return        Val                           // return the value

:: Val  = Pair Val Val  | BVal BVal
:: BVal = String String | Int Int   | VOID
```

Instances of this type ITask are called *task trees*. Without loss of generality we assume here that all editors return a value of a basic type (BVal). In the real iTasksystem editors can be used with every (user defined) data type. Using only these basic values in the semantics makes it easier to construct a type preserver simulator (see section 5). Since the right-hand side of the sequencing operator Bind is a normal function, this model has here the same rich expressibility as the real iTask system.

In order to write ITasks conveniently we introduce two abbreviations. For the monadic Bind operator we define an infix version. This operator takes a task and a function producing a new task as arguments and adds a default id to the Bind constructor.

($\Rightarrow$) **infixl** 1 :: ITask (Val$\rightarrow$ITask) $\rightarrow$ ITask
($\Rightarrow$) t f = Bind id1 t f

For convenience we introduce also the notion of a button task. It executes the given iTask after the button with the given label is pressed. A button task is composed of a VOID editor and a Bind operator ignoring the result of this editor.

ButtonTask i s t = EditTask i s VOID $\Rightarrow$ λ_ $\rightarrow$ t

Any executable form of iTasks will show only the button of a VOID editor. Since the Type of the edited value must be preserved, it cannot be changed.

2.1   Task Identification

The task to be executed is composed of elementary subtasks. These subtasks can be changed by events in the generated web-interface, like entering a value in a text-box or pushing a button. In order to link these events to the correct subtask we need an identification mechanism for subtasks. We use an automatic system for the identification of subtasks. Neither the worker, nor the developer of task specification has to worry about these identifications. The fact that the iTask system is in principle a multi-user system implies that there are multiple views on the task. Each worker can generate events independently of the other workers. The update of the task tree can generate new subtasks as well as re-move subtasks of other workers. This implies that the id's of subtasks must be persistent and that newly generated subtasks cannot reuse old id's. For these reasons the numbering system has to be more advanced than just a numbering of the nodes. The semantics in this paper ignores the multi-user aspect of the semantics, but the numbering system is able to handle this (just as the real iTask system).

Tasks are identified by a list of integers. These task identifications are used similar to the sections in a book. On top level the tasks are assigned integer numbers starting at 0. In contrast to sections, the least significant numbers are on the head of the list rather than on the tail. The data type used to represent these task identifiers, ID, is just a list of integers.

:: ID = ID [Int]

next :: ID $\rightarrow$ ID
next (ID [a:x]) = ID [a+1:x]

Whenever a task is replaced by its successor the id is incremented by the function next. For every id, i, we have that next i $\neq$ i. In this way we distinguish inputs for a task from inputs to its successor. The function splitID generates a list of task identifiers for subtasks of a task with the given id. This function adds two numbers to the identifier, one number for the subtask and one number for the version of this subtask. If we would use the same number for both purposes, one application of the function next would incorrectly transform the identification of the current subtask to that of the next subtask.

```
splitID :: ID → [ID]
splitID (ID i) = [ID [0,j:i] \\ j ← [0..]]
```

These identifiers of subtasks are used to relate inputs to the subtasks they belong to. The function nmbr is used to assign fresh and unique identifiers to a task tree.

```
nmbr :: ID ITask → ITask
nmbr i (EditTask _ s v) = EditTask i s v
nmbr i (t .||. u)      = nmbr j t .||. nmbr k u where [j,k:_] = splitID i
nmbr i (t .&&. u)      = nmbr j t .&&. nmbr k u where [j,k:_] = splitID i
nmbr i (Bind _ t f)    = Bind k (nmbr j t) f   where [j,k:_] = splitID i
nmbr i t=:(Return _)   = t
```

By convention we start numbering with id1 = ID [0] in this paper.

2.2 Events

The inputs for a task are called *events*. This implies that the values of input devices are not considered as values that change in time, as in FRP (Functional Reactive Programming). Instead changing the value of an input device generates an event that is passed as an argument to the event handling function. This function will generate a new state and a new user interface.

An event is either altering the current value of an editor task or pressing the button of such an editor. At every stage of running an iTask application, several editor tasks can be available. Hence many inputs are possible. Each event contains the id of the task to which it belongs as well as additional information about the event, the EventKind.

```
:: Event     = Event ID EventKind | Refresh
:: EventKind = EE BVal | BE
```

The event kind EE (*E*ditor *E*vent) indicates a new basic value for an editor. A *B*utton *E*vent BE signals pressing the button in an editor indicating that the user finished editing.

Apart from these events there is a Refresh event. In the actual system it is generated by each refresh of the user-interface. In the real iTask system this event has two effects: 1) the task is normalized; and 2) an interface corresponding to the normalized task is generated. In the semantics we only care about the normalization effect. *Normalization* of a task is done by applying the Refresh event to the task. Although this event is ignored by all elementary subtasks it has effects on subtasks that can be rewritten without user events. For instance, the task editTask "ok" 1 -||- return 5 is replaced by return 5. Similarly the task return 7 >>= editTask "ok" is replaced by editTask "ok" 7 We elaborate on normalization in the next section.

2.3 Rewriting Tasks Given an Event

In this section we define a rewrite semantics for iTasks by defining how a task tree changes if we apply an event to the task. Because we want an executable

```
instance @. ITask Event                                                    1
where                                                                      2
  (@.) (EditTask i n v) (Event j (EE w)) | i=j = EditTask (next i) n w      3
  (@.) (EditTask i n v) (Event j BE)     | i=j = Return (BVal v)            4
  (@.) (t .||. u) e  = case t @. e of                                      5
                       t=:(Return _) = t                                   6
                       t = case u @. e of                                  7
                           u=:(Return _)  = u                              8
                           u              = t .||. u                       9
  (@.) (t .&&. u) e  = case (t @. e, u @. e) of                            10
                       (Return v, Return w) = Return (Pair v w)            11
                       (t, u)               = t .&&. u                     12
  (@.) (Bind i t f) e = case t @. e of                                     13
                        Return v = normalize i (f v)                       14
                        t        = Bind i t f                              15
  (@.) t e = t                                                             16
```

Fig. 1. The basic semantics of iTasks

semantics rewriting is defined by an operator @., pronounced as *apply*. We define
a class for @. in order to be able to overload it, for instance with the application
of a list of events to a task.

class (@.) **infixl** 9 a b :: a b → a

Given a task tree and an event, we can compute the new task tree representing
the task after handling the current input. This is handled by the most important
instance of the operator @. for ITask and Event listed in figure 1. It is assumed
that the task is properly numbered and normalized, and that the edit events
have the correct type for the editor.

This semantics shows that the ids play a dominant role in the rewriting of
task trees. An event only has an effect on a task with the same id. Edit tasks
can react on button events (line 4) as well as edit events (line 3). Line 14 shows
why the Bind operator has an id. Events are never addressed to this operator,
but the id is used to normalize (and hence number) the new subtask that is
dynamically generated by f v if the left-hand side task is finished. All events
that are not enabled are ignored (line 16). All other constructs pass the events
to their subtasks and check if the root of the task tree can be rewritten after the
reduction of the subtasks. The recursive call with @. e on line 13 can only have
an effect when the task was not yet normalized, in all other situations applying
the event has no effect.

A properly numbered task tree remains correctly numbered after reduction.
Editors that receive a new value get a new number by applying the function
next to the task identification number. The numbering scheme used guarantees
that this number cannot occur in any other subtask. If the left left-hand task of
the bind-operator is rewritten to a normal form a new task tree is generated by
f v. The application of normalize (next i) to this tree guarantees that this tree

is well formed and properly numbered within the surrounding tree. This implies that applying an event repeatedly to a task has at most once an effect.

The handling of events for a task tree is somewhat similar to reduction of combinator systems or in the λ-calculus. An essential difference of such a reduction system with the task trees considered here is that all needed information is available inside a λ-expression. The evaluation of task trees needs the event as additional information.

Event sequences are handled by the following instance of the apply operator:

```
instance @. t [e] | @. t e where (@.) t es = foldl (@.) t es
```

Normalization. A task t is *normalized* (or *well formed*) iff t @. Refresh = t. The idea is that all reductions in the task tree that can be done without a new input should have been done. In addition we require that each task tree considered is properly numbered (using the algorithm nmbr in section 2.1). In the definition of the operator @. we assume that the task tree given as argument is already normalized. Each task can be normalized and properly numbered by applying the function normalize1 to that task.

```
normalize :: ID ITask → ITask
normalize i t = nmbr i (t @. Refresh)

normalize1 :: ITask → ITask
normalize1 t = normalize id1 t
```

Enabled Subtasks. All editor tasks that are currently part of the task tree are *enabled*, which implies that they can be rewritten if the right events are supplied. The subtasks that are generated by the function on the right-hand side of a Bind construct are **not** enabled, even if we can predict exactly what subtasks will be generated. Events accepted by the enabled subtasks are called *enabled events*, this is the set of events that have an effect on the task when it is applied to such an event. Consider the following tasks:

```
t1 = EditTask id1 "b" (Int 1) .&&. EditTask id2 "c" (Int 2)
t2 = EditTask id1 "b" (Int 1) .||. EditTask id2 "c" (Int 2)
t3 = ButtonTask id1 "b" (EditTask id2 "c" (Int 3))
t4 = ButtonTask id1 "b" t4
t5 = EditTask id1 "b" (Int 5) ⇒ λv.ButtonTask id2 "c" (Return (Pair v v))
t6 = EditTask id1 "b" (Int 6) ⇒ λv.t6
t7 v p = EditTask id1 "ok" v ⇒ λr=:(BVal w).if (p w) (Return r) (t7 w p)
```

In t1 and t2 all integer and button events with identifier id1 and id2 are enabled. In t3 and t4 only the event Event id1 BE is enabled. In t5, t6 and t7 all integer and button events with identifier id1 are enabled. All other events can only be processed after the button event for the task with id1 on the left-hand side of the bind operator.

Task t4 rewrites to itself after a button event. In t6 the same effect is reached by a bind operator. The automatic numbering system guarantees that the tasks obtain another `id` after applying the enabled button events. Task `t7` is parameterized with a basic value and a predicate on such a value, and terminates only when the worker enters a value satisfying the predicate. This simple example shows that the bind operator is more powerful than just sequencing fixed tasks. In fact any function of type `Val`→`ITask` can be used there.

Normal Form. A task is in *normal form* if it has the form `Return v` for some value `v`. A task in normal form is not changed by applying any event. The function `isNF :: ITask` → `Bool` checks if a task is in normal form. In general a task tree does not have a unique normal form. The normal form obtained depends on the events applied to that task. For task `t2` above the normal form of `t2 @. Event id1 BE` is `Return (BVal (Int 1))` while `t2 @. Event id2 BE` is `Return (BVal (Int 2))`. The recursive tasks `t4` and `t6` do not have a normal form at all.

Needed Events. An event is *needed* in task `t` if the subtask to which the event belongs is enabled and the top node of the task tree `t` cannot be rewritten without that event.

In task `t1` above the events `Event id1 BE` and `Event id2 BE` are needed. Task `t2` has no needed event. This task can evaluate to a normal form by applying either `Event id1 BE` or `Event id2 BE`. As soon as one of these events is applied, the other task disappears. In `t3` only `Event id1 BE` is needed, the event `Event id2 BE` is not enabled. Similarly, in `t4`, `t5` and `t6` (only) the event `Event id1 BE` is needed.

For an edit-task the button-event is needed. Any number of edit-events can be applied to an edit-task, but they are not needed. For the task `t1 .&&. t2` the needed events is the sum of the needed events of `t1` and the needed events of `t2`. For a monadic bind the only needed events are the needed events of the left hand task. The needed events of a task `t` are obtained by `collectNeeded`. To ensure that needed events are collected in a normalized task we apply `normalize1` before scanning the task tree. In the actual iTask system the task is normalized by the initial refresh event and needs no new normalization ever after. In the task `t1 .||. t2` non of the events is needed, the task can is finished as soon as the task `t1` or the task `t2` is finished. Normalization is only include here to ensure that the task is normalized in every application of this function.

```
collectNeeded :: ITask → [Event]
collectNeeded t = col (normalize1 t)
where
  col (EditTask id n v) = [Event id BE]
  col (t1 .&&. t2)      = col t1 ++ col t2
  col (Bind id t f)     = col t            // no events from f
  col _                 = []               // Return and the OR-combinator
```

In exactly the same spirit `collectButtons` collects all enabled button events in a task tree, and `collect` yields all enabled button events plus the enabled edit events containing the current value of the editors. The list of events is needed for the simulation of the task discussed in section 5.

An event is *accepted* if it causes a rewrite in the task tree, i.e. the corresponding subtask is enabled. A sequence of events is accepted if each of the events causes a rewrite when the events are applied in the given order. This implies that an accepted sequence of events can contain events that are not needed, or even not enabled in the original tree. In task t2 the button event with id1 and id2 are accepted, also the editor event Event id1 (EE (Int 42)) is accepted. All these events are enabled, but neither of them is needed. The task t5 accepts the sequence [Event id1 BE, Event id2 BE]. The second event is not enabled in t5, but applying Event id1 BE to t5 enables it.

Value. The *value* of a task is the value returned by the task if we repeatedly press the left most button in the task until it returns a value. This implies that the value of task t1 is Pair (Int 1) (Int 2), the value of t2 is Int 1 since buttons are pressed from left to right. The value of t3 is Int 3 and the value of t5 is Pair (Int 5) (Int 5). The value of t4 and t6 is undefined. Since a task cannot produce a value before all needed events are supplied, we can apply all needed events in one go (there is no need to do this from left to right).

For terminating tasks the value can be computed by inspection of the task tree, there is no need to do the actual rewrite steps as defined by the @. operator. For nonterminating tasks the value is undefined, these tasks will never return a value. The class val determines the value by inspection of the data structure.

```
class val a :: a → Val
```

```
instance val BVal where val v = BVal v
instance val Val   where val v = v
instance val ITask
where
    val (EditTask i n e)    = val e
    val (Return v)          = val v
    val (t .||. u)          = val t    // priority for the left subtask
    val (t .&&. u)          = Pair (val t) (val u)
    val (Bind i t f)        = val (f (val t))
```

The value produced is always equal to the value returned by the task if the user presses all needed buttons and the leftmost button if there is no needed button. The property pVal in section 4 states this and testing does not reveal any problems with this property.

The value of a task can change after applying an edit event. For instance the value of task EditTask id1 "ok" (BVal (Int 2)) is BVal (Int 2). After applying Event id1 (BVal (Int 7)) to this task the value is changed to BVal (Int 7).

Type. Although all values that can be returned by a task are represented by the type Val, we occasionally want to distinguish several families of values within this type. This type is not the data type Val used in the representation of tasks, but the type that the corresponding tasks in the real iTask system would have. We assign the type *Int* to all values of the form Int i. All values of the form String s have type *String*. If value v has type v and value w has type w then the value Pair v w has type *Pair v w*. The types allowed are:

$$Type = Int \mid String \mid VOID \mid Pair\ Type\ Type$$

To prevent the introduction of yet another data type we represent the types yielded by tasks in this paper as instance of `Val`. The type *Int* is represented by `Int` 0 and the type *String* is represented as `String` "". We define a class `type` to determine types of tasks.

```
:: Type := Val
class type a :: a → Type
```

Instances of this class for `Val` and `ITask` are identical to the instances of `val` defined in section 2.3. Only the instance for `BVal` is slightly different:

```
instance type BVal
where
    type (Int i)    = BVal (Int 0)
    type (String s) = BVal (String "")
    type VOID       = BVal VOID
```

3   Equivalence of Tasks

Given the semantics of iTasks we can define equivalence of tasks. Informally we want to consider two tasks equivalent if they have the same semantics. Since we can apply infinitely many update events to each task that contains an editor we cannot determine equivalence by applying all possible input sequences. Moreover, tasks containing a bind operator also contain a function and the equivalence of functions is in general undecidable. iTasks are obviously Turing complete and hence equivalence is also for this reason known to be undecidable. It is even possible to use more general notions of equivalence, like tasks are equivalent if they can be used to do the same job. Hence, developing a useful notion of equivalence for tasks is nontrivial.

In this paper we will develop a rather strict notion of equivalence of tasks: tasks t and u are equivalent if they have an equal value after all possible sequences of events and at each intermediate state the same events are enabled. Since the identifications of events are invisible for the workers using the iTask system, we allow that the lists of events applied to t and u differ in the event identifications. The strings that label the buttons in t and u do not occur in the events, hence it is allowed that these labels are different for equivalent tasks.

First we introduce the notion of *simulation*. Informally a task u can simulate a task t if a worker can do everything with u that can be done with t. It is very well possible that a worker can do more with u than with t. The notation $t \preccurlyeq u$ denotes that u can simulate t. Technically we require that: **1)** for each sequence of accepted events of t there is a corresponding sequence of events accepted by u; **2)** the values of the tasks after applying these events is equal; and **3)** after applying the events, all enabled events of t have a matching event in u. Two events are equivalent, $e_1 \cong e_2$, if they differ at most in their identification.

$$t \preccurlyeq u \equiv \forall i \in \text{accept}(t).\exists j \in \text{accept}(u).i \cong j \land val(t\,@.\,i) = val(u\,@.\,j)$$
$$\land collect(t\,@.\,i) \subseteq collect(u\,@.\,j)$$

The notion $t \preccurlyeq u$ is not symmetrical, it is very well possible that u can do much more than t. As an example we have that for all tasks t and u that are not in normal form $t \preccurlyeq t.||.u$, and $t \preccurlyeq u.||.t$. If one of the tasks is in normal form it has shape $\mathtt{Return\ v}$, after normalization the task tree $u.||.t$ will have the value $\mathtt{Return\ v}$ too. Any task can simulate itself $t \preccurlyeq t$, and an edit task of any basic value $\mathtt{v}$ can simulate a button task that returns that value: $\mathtt{ButtonTask\ id1}$ $\mathtt{"b"\ (Return\ (BVal\ v))} \preccurlyeq \mathtt{EditTask\ id2\ "ok"\ v}$. In general we have $t.||.t \npreccurlyeq t$: for instance if t is an edit task, in $t.||.t$ we can put a new value in one of the editors and produce the original result by pressing the $\mathtt{ok}$ button in the other editor, the task t cannot simulate this. The third requirement in the definition above is included to ensure that $t.||.t \npreccurlyeq t$ also holds for tasks with only one button $\mathtt{ButtonTask\ id1\ "b1"\ (BVal\ (Int\ 36))}$.

Two tasks t and u are considered to be *equivalent* iff t simulates u and u simulates t.

$$t \cong u \equiv t \preccurlyeq u \wedge u \preccurlyeq t$$

This notion of equivalence is weaker then the usual definition of bisimulation [12] since we do not require equality of events, but just equivalency. Two editors containing a different value are not equivalent. There exist infinitely many event sequences such that these editors produce the same value. But for the input sequence consisting only of the button event, they produce a different value.

Since each task can simulate itself ($t \preccurlyeq t$), any task is equivalent to itself: $t \cong t$. If t and u are tasks that are not in normal form we have $t.||.u \cong u.||.t$. Consider the following tasks:

```
u1 = ButtonTask id1 "b1" (Return (BVal (Int 1)))
u2 = EditTask id2 "b2" (Int 1)
u3 = EditTask id2 "b3" (Int 2)
u4 = EditTask id2 "b4" (String "Hi")
u5 = u1 .||. u2
u6 = u2 .||. u1
u7 = u2 .&&. u4
u8 = u4 .&&. u2
u9 = u2 ⇒ λv.Return (BVal (Int 1))
u10 = u2 ⇒ λx.u4 ⇒ λy.Return (Pair x y)
```

The trivial relations between these tasks are $u_i \preccurlyeq u_i$ and $u_i \cong u_i$ for all u_i. The nontrivial relations between these tasks are: $u1 \preccurlyeq u2$, $u1 \preccurlyeq u5$, $u1 \preccurlyeq u6$, $u1 \preccurlyeq u9$, $u2 \preccurlyeq u5$, $u2 \preccurlyeq u6$, $u5 \preccurlyeq u6$, $u6 \preccurlyeq u5$, $u10 \preccurlyeq u7$, $u10 \preccurlyeq u8$, and $u2 \cong u9$, $u5 \cong u6$. Note that $u7 \ncong u8$ since the tasks yield another value.

Due to the presence of functions in the task expressions it is in general undecidable if one task simulates another or if they are equivalent. However, in many situations we can decide these relations between tasks by inspection of the task trees that determine the behavior of the tasks.

3.1   Determining the Equivalence of Task Trees

The equivalence of tasks requires an equal result for all possible sequences of accepted events. Even for a simple integer edit task there are infinitely many sequences of events. This implies that checking equivalence of tasks by applying all possible sequences of events is in general impossible.

In this section we introduce two algorithms to approximate the equivalence of tasks. The first algorithm, section 3.2, is rather straightforward and uses only the enabled events of a task tree and the application of some of these events to approximate equivalence. The second algorithm, section 3.3 is somewhat more advanced and uses the structure of the task trees to determine equivalence whenever possible.

We will use a four valued logic as for the result:

`:: Result = Proof | Pass | CE | Undef`

The result `Proof` corresponds to `True` and indicates that the relation is known to hold. The result `CE` (for *Counter Example*) is equivalent to `False`, the relation does not hold. The result `Pass` indicates that functions are encountered during the scanning of the trees. For the values tried the properties holds. The property might hold for all other values, but it is also possible that there exists inputs to the tasks such that the property does not hold. The value `Undef` is used as result of an existential quantified property ($\exists w.P\ x$) where no proof is found in the given number of test cases; the value of this property is undefined [5]. This type `Result` is a subset of the possible test results handled by the test system G∀st. For these results we define disjunction ('or', ∨), conjunction ('and', ∧), and negation ('not', ¬) with the usual binding power and associativity. In addition we define the type conversion from Boolean to results and the weakening of a result which turns `Proof` in `Pass` and leaves the other values unchanged.

```
class (∨) infixr 2 a b :: a b → Result    // a OR b
class (∧) infixr 3 a b :: a b → Result    // a AND b

instance ¬ Result                          // negation

toResult :: Bool → Result                  // type conversion
toResult b = if b Proof CE

pass :: Result → Result                    // weakens result to at most Pass
pass r = r ∧ Pass
```

For ∨ and ∧ we define instances for all combinations of `Bool` and `Result` as a straightforward extension of the corresponding operation on Booleans.

3.2   Determining Equivalence by Applying Events

In order to compare `ITasks` we first ensure that they are normalized and supply an integer argument to indicate the maximum number of reduction steps. The value of this argument N is usually not very critical. In our tests 100 and 1000 steps usually gives identical (and correct) results. The function `equivalent` first checks if the tasks are returning currently the same value. If both tasks need inputs we first check **1)** if the tasks have the same type, **2)** if the tasks currently offer the same number of buttons to the worker, **3)** if the tasks have the same number of needed buttons, and **4)** if the tasks offer equivalent editors. Whenever either of these conditions does not hold the tasks t and u cannot be equivalent. When these conditions hold we check equivalence recursively after applying events. If there are needed events we apply them all in one go, without these events the tasks cannot produce a normal form. If the tasks have no needed events we apply all combinations of button events and check if one of these combinations makes the tasks equivalent. We need to apply all combinations of events since all button events are equivalent. All needed events can be applied in one go since they are needed in order to reach a normal form and the order of applying needed events is always irrelevant. If there are edit tasks enabled, length et>0, in the task the result is at most Pass. This is achieved by applying the functions pass or id.

```
equivOper :: ITask ITask → Result
equivOper t u = equivalent N (normalize1 t) (normalize1 u)

equivalent :: Int ITask ITask → Result
equivalent n (Return v) (Return w) = v = w
equivalent n (Return v) _ = CE
equivalent n _ (Return w) = CE
equivalent n t u
  | n≤0
    = Pass
    = if (length et>0) pass id
      (type t = type u ∧ lbt = lbu  ∧ lnt = lnu ∧ sort et = sort eu
      ∧ if (lnt>0)
          (equivalent (n-lnt) (t @. nt) (u @. nu))
          (exists N [equivalent n (t @. i) (u @. j)\\(i,j)←diag2 bt bu]))
where
    bt  = collectButtons t; nt  = collectNeeded t
    bu  = collectButtons u; nu  = collectNeeded u
    et  = collectEdit t;    eu  = collectEdit u
    lnt = length nt; lnu = length nu; lbt = length bt; lbu = length bu
```

The function exists checks if one of the first N values is Pass or Proof.

```
exists :: Int [Result] → Result
exists n []    = CE
exists 0 1     = Undef
exists n [a:x] = a ∨ exists (n-1) x
```

In this approach we do not apply any edit events. It is easy to design examples of tasks where the current approximation yields Pass, but applying some edit events reveals that the tasks are actually not equivalent (e.g. t = EditTask id1 (BVal (Int 5)) and t ⇒ Return (BVal (Int 5))). We obtain a better approximation of the equivalence relation by including some edit events in the function equivalent. Due to space limitations and to keep the presentation as simple as possible we have not done this here.

3.3 Determining Equivalence of Tasks by Comparing Task Trees

Since the shape of the task tree determines the behavior of the task corresponding to that task tree, it is tempting to try to determine properties like $t \preccurlyeq u$ and $t \cong u$ by comparing the shapes of the trees for u and t. For most constructs in the trees this works very well. For instance it is much easier to look at the structure of the tasks EditTask id1 "ok" (BVal (Int 5)) and EditTask id2 "done" (BVal (Int 5)) to see that they are equivalent, than approximating equivalence of these tasks by applying events to these tasks and comparing the returned values. In this section we use the comparison of task trees to determine equivalence of tasks. The function eqStruct implements this algorithm.

There are a number of constructions that allow different task trees for equivalent tasks. These constructs require special attention in the structural comparison of task trees:

1. The tasks ButtonTask id1 "b" (Return v) .&&. Return w and ButtonTask id1 "b" (Return (Pair v w)) are equivalent for all basic values v and w. This kind of equivalent tasks with a different task tree can only occur if one of the branches of .&&. is in normal form and the other is not. On lines 9, 16 and 17 of the function eqStruct there are special cases handling this. The problem is handled by switching to a comparison by applying events, very similar to the equivalent algorithm in the previous section. The function equ takes care of applying events and further comparison.

2. The choice operator .||. should be commutative, $(\texttt{t.||.u} \simeq \texttt{u.||.t})$, and associative $((\texttt{t.||.u}).\texttt{||.v} \simeq \texttt{t.||.(u.||.v)})$. In order to guarantee this, eqStruct collects all adjacent or-tasks in a list and checks if there is a unique mapping between the elements of those list such that the corresponding subtasks are equivalent (using eqStruct recursively). The implementation of the auxiliary functions is straightforward.

3. The Bind construct contains real functions, hence there are many ways to construct equivalent tasks with a different structure. For instance, we have that any task t is equivalent to the task $\texttt{t} \Rightarrow \texttt{Return}$, or slightly more advanced: s.&&.t is equivalent $(\texttt{t .\&\&. s}) \Rightarrow \lambda(\texttt{Pair x y}) \rightarrow \texttt{Return (Pair y x)}$ for all tasks s and t.

   The function eqStruct checks if the left-hand sides and the obtained right-hand sides of two bind operators are equivalent. If they are not equivalent the tasks are checked for equivalence by applying inputs, see line 13-15.

The eqStruct algorithm expects normalized task trees. The operator $\simeq$ takes care of this normalisation.

class $(\simeq)$ **infix** 4 a :: a a $\rightarrow$ Result   // *is arg1 equivalent to arg2?*

instance $\simeq$ ITask **where** $(\simeq)$ t u = eqStruc N (normalize1 t) (normalize1 u)

If the structures are not equal, but the task might be event equal we switch to applying inputs using the function equ. This function is very similar to the function equivalent in the previous section. The main difference is that the function `equ` always switches to `eqStruct` instead of using a recursive call. If a structural comparison is not possible after applying an event, the function `eqStruct` will switch to `equ` again.

```
eqStruc :: Int ITask ITask → Result                                          1
eqStruc 0 t u = Pass                                                         2
eqStruc n (Return v)        (Return w)        = v ≃ w                        3
eqStruc n (Return v)        _                 = CE                          4
eqStruc n _                 (Return w)        = CE                          5
eqStruc n (EditTask _ _ e) (EditTask _ _ f) = e ≃ f                         6
eqStruc n s=:(a .&&. b)    t=:(x .&&. y)                                    7
  = eqStruc (n-1) a x ∧ eqStruc (n-1) b y ∨                                 8
    ((inNF a || inNF b || inNF x || inNF y) ∧ equ n s t)                    9
eqStruc n s=:(a .||. b)    t=:(x .||. y)                                   10
  = eqORn n (collectOR s) (collectOR t)                                    11
eqStruc n s=:(Bind i a f) t=:(Bind j b g)                                  12
  = eqStruc (n-1) a b ∧ eqStruc (n-2) (f (val a)) (g (val b)) ∨ equ n s t  13
eqStruc n s=:(Bind _ _ _) t                   = equ n s t                  14
eqStruc n s                t=:(Bind _ _ _) = equ n s t                     15
eqStruc n s=:(a .&&. b)    t                = (inNF a||inNF b) ∧ equ n s t  16
eqStruc n s                t=:(x .&&. y)    = (inNF x||inNF y) ∧ equ n s t  17
eqStruc n s                t                = CE                           18
```

This uses instances of $\simeq$ for basic values (`BVal`) and values (`Val`). For these instances no approximations are needed. The line 10 and 11 implements the commutativity of the operator `.||.`: `collectOR` produces a list of all subtasks glued together with this operator, and `eqORn` determines if these lists of subtasks are equivalent in some permutation. The definitions are a direct generalization of the ordinary equality $=$.

A similar approach can be used to approximate the simulation relation $\precsim$.

Property `pEquiv` in the next section states that both notions of equivalence yield equivalent results, even if we include edit events. Executing the associated tests indicate no problems with this property. This test result increases the confidence in the correct implementation of the operator $\simeq$. Since $\simeq$ uses the structure of the tasks whenever possible, it is more efficient than `equivOper` that applies events until the tasks are in normal form. The efficiency gain is completely determined by the size and contents of the task tree, but can be significant. It is easy to construct examples with an efficiency gain of one order of magnitude or more.

4 Testing Properties of iTasks

Above we mentioned a number of properties of iTasks and their equivalency like $\forall\, s, t \in$ iTask.`s.||.t` $\simeq$ `t.||.s`. Although we designed the system such that these properties should hold, it is good to verify that the properties do hold indeed. Especially during the development of the system many versions are created in order to find a concise formulation of the semantics and an effective check for equivalence.

Creating formal proofs for all properties for all those versions of the semantics during its development is completely infeasible. Assuming that all well-typed versions of the semantics are correct is much to optimistic. We used the automatic test system G∀st to check the semantic functions presented here with a set of desirable properties. For instance the above property can be stated in G∀st as:

```
pOr :: GITask GITask → Property
pOr x y = normalize1 (t.||.u) ≃ normalize1 (u.||.t)
where t = toITask x; u = toITaskT (type t) y
```

The arguments of such a property are treated by the test system as universal quantified variables over the given types. The test system generates test values of these types using the generic class ggen. Since some ITask constructs contain a function, we use an additional data type, GITask, to generate the desired instances. We follow exactly the approach as outlined in [4]. The type GITask contains cases corresponding to the constructors in ITask, for button tasks, for tasks of the form t ⇒ Return, and for some simple recursive terminating tasks. For pOr we need to make sure the tasks t and u have the same type since we combine them with an or-operator. The conversion by toITask from the additional type GITasks used for the generation to ITasks takes care of that.

After executing 23 tests G∀st produces the first counterexample that shows that this property does not hold for t = Return (BVal (Int 0)) and u = Return (Pair (BVal (Int 0)) (BVal (Int 0))). Using the semantics from figure 1 it is clear that G∀st is right, our property is too general. A correct property imposes the condition that t and u are not in normal form:

```
pOr2 x y = notNF [t,u] ==> normalize1 (t.||.u) ≃ normalize1 (u.||.t)
where t = toITask x; u = toITaskT (type t) y
```

In the same way we can show that t.||.t ≇ t for tasks that are not in normal form (p2) and test the associativity of the .||. or operator (p3).

```
p2 :: GITask GITask → Property
p2 x y = notNF [s,t] ==> (s.||.t)≇t
where s = toITask x; t = toITaskT (type s) y
```

```
p3 :: GITask GITask GITask → Property
p3 x y z = (s .||. (t .||. u))≃((s .||. t) .||. u)
where s = toITask x; t = toITaskT (type s) y; u = toITaskT (type s) z
```

In total we have defined over 70 properties to test the consistency of the definitions given in this paper. We list some representative properties here. The first property states that needed events can be applied in any order. Since there are no type restrictions on the type t we can quantify over ITasks directly.

```
pNeeded :: ITask → Property
pNeeded t = (λj. t @. i ≃ t @. j) For perms i where i = collectNeeded t
```

In this test the fragment For perms i indicates an additional quantification over all j in perms i. The function perms :: [x] → [[x]] generates all permutations of the given list. In logic this property would have been written as $\forall t \in$ ITask, $\forall j \in$ perms (collectNeeded t). t @. (collectNeeded t) ≃ t @. j.

The next property states that both approximations of equivalence discussed in the previous section produce equivalent results.

```
pEquiv :: ITask ITask → Property
pEquiv t u = (equivOper t u) ≃ (t≃u)
```

The type of a task should be preserved under reduction. In the property pType also events that are not well typed will be tested. Since we assume that all events are well typed (the edit events have the same type as the edit task they belong to), it is better to use pType2 where the events are derived from the task t.

```
pType :: ITask → Property
pType t = (λi.type t = type (t @. i)) For collect t
```

```
pType2 :: ITask → Property
pType2 t = pType t For collect t
```

The phrase For collect t indicates that for testing these properties the events are collect from the task tree rather then generated systematically by G∀st. However the tasks to be used in the test are generated systematically by G∀st.

The property pVal states that the value of a task obtained by the optimized function val is equal to the value of the task obtained by applying events obtained by collectVal until it returns a value. The function collectVal returns all needed events and the leftmost events if these are no needed events.

```
pVal :: ITask → Property
pVal t = val t = nf t
where
    nf (Return v) = v
    nf t = nf (t @. collectVal t)
```

The definitions presented in this paper pass all stated properties. On a normal laptop (Intel core2 Duo (using only one of the cores), 1.8 GHz) it takes about 7 seconds to check all defined properties with 1000 test cases for each property. This is orders of magnitude faster and more reliable then human inspection, which is on its turn much faster than a formal proof (even if it is supported by a state of the art tool). Most of these properties are very general properties, like the properties shown here. Some properties however check specific test cases that are known to be tricky, or revealed problems in the past. If there are problems with one of the properties, they are usually spotted within the first 50 test cases generated. It appears to be extremely hard to introduce flaws in the system that are not revealed by executing these tests. For instance omitting one of the special cases in the function eqStruct is spotted quickly. Hence testing the consistency of the system in this way is an effective and efficient way to improve the confidence in its consistency.

5   Discussion

In this paper we give a rewrite semantics for iTasks. Such a semantics is necessary to reason about iTasks and their properties, it is also well suited to explain their behavior. In addition we defined useful notions about iTasks and stated properties related to them. The most important notion is the *equivalence* of tasks.

Usually the semantics of workflow systems is based on Petri nets, abstract state machines, or actor-oriented directed graphs. Since the iTask system allows arbitrary functions to generate the continuation in a sequence of tasks (the monadic bind operator), such an approach is not flexible enough. To cope with the rich possibilities of iTasks our semantics incorporates also a function to determine the continuation of the task after a `Bind` operator.

We use the functional programming language Clean as carrier for the semantical definitions. The tasks are represented by a data structure. The effect of supplying an input to such a task is given by an operator modifying the task tree. Since we have the tasks available as data structure we can easily extract information from the task, like the events needed or accepted by the task. A typical case of the operator @. (apply) that specifies the semantics is:

(@.) (EditTask i n e) (Event j BE) | i=j = Return (BVal e)

In the more traditional Scott Brackets style this alternative is written as:

$$\mathcal{A} [\![EditTask\ i\ n\ e]\!]\ (Event\ j\ BE) = Return\ (BVal\ e), \text{ if } i = j$$

Our representation has the same level of abstraction and has as advantages that it can be checked by the type system and executed (and hence simulated and tested).

Having the task as a data structure it is easy to create an editor and simulator for tasks using the iTask library. Editing and simulating tasks is helpful to validate the semantics. Although simulating iTasks provides a way to interpret the given task, the executable semantics is not intended as an interpreter for iTasks. In an interpreter we would have focused on a nice interface and efficiency, the semantics focusses on clearness and simplicity.

Compared with the real iTask system there are a number of important simplifications in our ITask representation. **1)** Instead of arbitrary types, the ITasks can only yield elements of type Val. The type system of the host language is not able to prevent type errors within the ITasks. For instance it is possible to combine a task that yields an integer, BVal (Int i), with a task yielding a string, BVal (String s), using an .||. operator. In ordinary iTasks it is type technically not possible (and semantically not desirable) to combine tasks of type Task Int with Task String using a -||- operator. Probably GADTs would have helped us to enforce this condition in our semantical representation. **2)** The application of a task to an event does not yield an HTML-page that can be used as GUI for the iTask system. In fact there is no notion at all of HTML output in the ITask system. **3)** There is no way to access files or databases in the ITask system. **4)** There is no notion of workers and assigning subtasks to them. **5)** There is no difference between client site and server site evaluation of tasks. **6)** There is only one workflow process which is implicit. In the real iTask system additional processes can be created dynamically. **7)** The exception handling from the real iTask system is missing in this semantics.

Adding these aspects would make the semantics more complicated. We have deliberately chosen to define a concise system that is as clear as possible.

Using the model-based test system it is possible to test the stated properties fully automatically. We maintain a collection of over 70 properties and test them with one push of a button. Within seconds we do known if the current version of the system obeys all properties stated. This is extremely useful during the development and changes of the system. Although the defined notions of equivalence are in general undecidable, the given approximation works very well in practice. Issues in the semantics or properties are found very quickly (usually within the first 100 test cases). We attempted to insert deliberately small errors in the semantics that are not detected by the automatic tests, but we failed miserably.

In the near future we want to test with G∀st if the real iTask system obeys the semantics given in this paper. In addition we want to extend the semantics in order to cover some of the important notions omitted in the current semantics, for instance task execution in a multi-user workflow system. When we are convinced about the quality and suitability of the extended system we plan to prove some of the tested properties. Although proving properties gives more confidence in the correctness, it is much more work then testing. Testing with a large number of properties has shown to be an extremely powerful way to reveal inconsistencies in the system.

Acknowledgement. We thank the anonymous referees and the shephard for their suggestions to improve this paper.

References

1. Achten, P., van Eekelen, M., de Mol, M., Plasmeijer, R.: An Arrow based semantics for interactive applications. In: Morazán, M. (ed.) Preliminary Proceedings of the 8th Symposium on Trends in Functional Programming, TFP 2007, New York, NY, USA, April 2-4 (2007)
2. Alimarine, A., Plasmeijer, R.: A generic programming extension for clean. In: Arts, T., Mohnen, M. (eds.) IFL 2002. LNCS, vol. 2312, pp. 168–186. Springer, Heidelberg (2002)
3. de Mol, M., van Eekelen, M., Plasmeijer, R.: The mathematical foundation of the proof assistant Sparkle. Technical Report ICIS-R07025, Institute for Computing and Information Sciences, Radboud University Nijmegen, The Netherlands (November 2007)
4. Koopman, P., Plasmeijer, R.: Automatic testing of higher order functions. In: Kobayashi, N. (ed.) APLAS 2006. LNCS, vol. 4279, pp. 148–164. Springer, Heidelberg (2006)
5. Koopman, P., Plasmeijer, R.: Fully Automatic Testing with Functions as Specifications. In: Horváth, Z. (ed.) CEFP 2005. LNCS, vol. 4164, pp. 35–61. Springer, Heidelberg (2006)
6. Lee, S.-Y., Lee, Y.-H., Kim, J.-G., Lee, D.C.: Workflow system modeling in the mobile healthcare B2B using semantic information. In: Gervasi, O., Gavrilova, M.L., Kumar, V., Laganá, A., Lee, H.P., Mun, Y., Taniar, D., Tan, C.J.K. (eds.) ICCSA 2005. LNCS, vol. 3481, pp. 762–770. Springer, Heidelberg (2005)

232   P. Koopman, R. Plasmeijer, and P. Achten

7. Ludäscher, B., Altintas, I., Berkley, C., Higgins, D., Jaeger, E., Jones, M., Lee, E., Tao, J., Zhao, Y.: Scientific workflow management and the Kepler system. Concurrency and Computation: Practice & Experience 18, 2006 (2005)
8. Nielson, H.R., Nielson, F.: Semantics with applications: a formal introduction. John Wiley & Sons, Inc., Chichester (1992)
9. Plasmeijer, R., Achten, P.: iData for the world wide web – programming interconnected web forms. In: Hagiya, M. (ed.) FLOPS 2006. LNCS, vol. 3945, pp. 242–258. Springer, Heidelberg (2006)
10. Plasmeijer, R., Achten, P., Koopman, P.: iTasks: executable specifications of interactive work flow systems for the web. In: Proceedings of the 12th International Conference on Functional Programming, ICFP 2007, Freiburg, Germany, October 1-3, pp. 141–152. ACM Press, New York (2007)
11. Russell, N., ter Hofstede, A., van der Aalst, W.: newYAWL: specifying a workflow reference language using coloured Petri nets. In: Proceedings of the 8th 2007 (2007)
12. Stirling, C.: The joys of bisimulation. In: Brim, L., Gruska, J., Zlatuška, J. (eds.) MFCS 1998. LNCS, vol. 1450, pp. 142–151. Springer, Heidelberg (1998)
13. T.C.D. Team The Coq proof assistant reference manual, version 7.0 (1998), urlhttp://pauillac.inria.fr/coq/doc/main.html

Monatron: An Extensible
Monad Transformer Library

Mauro Jaskelioff

Functional Programming Laboratory
University of Nottingham

Abstract. Monads are pervasive in functional programming. In order
to reap the benefits of their abstraction power, combinator libraries for
monads are necessary. Monad transformers provide the basis for such
libraries, and are based on a design that has proved to be successful.
In this article, we show that this design has a number of shortcomings
and provide a new design that builds on the strengths of the traditional
design, but addresses its problems.

1 Introduction

The power of functional languages lies, to a great extent, in their ability to name
and reuse programming idioms [6]. This power is often realised in the form of
combinator libraries, which consist of a collection of idioms commonly found in
the library's application area. Programmers can reuse these idioms and combine
them to obtain programs which, since they are assembled from correct parts, are
likely to be correct.

Monads [15,18] are the standard abstraction for modelling programs with
computational effects such as state, exceptions and continuations. These effects
are usually associated with imperative languages but, with the help of monads,
they can be elegantly modelled in a functional language [11]. However, obtaining
a monad which models several combined effects can be difficult. Moreover, since
monads must satisfy certain coherence conditions, the programmer is faced with
the task of verifying these conditions. Obtaining combined effects can be made
much easier with a good combinator library for monads. But, what are the
properties that make a library good?

A good library should be *expressive*, in the sense that the exposed interface
should be enough to obtain the desired combinations, without the need to look
at the internals of the library. Since new applications might bring additional
requirements, a library should be *extensible*. The semantics of the combinators
should be *predictable* and, ideally, with no corner cases. These features help the
programmer to abstract from low-level implementation details, and to think in
terms of high-level idioms. Finally, a library should strive to be *efficient* and
portable.

Combinator libraries for monads are built from modular components called
monad transformers [14]. Current monad transformer libraries, such as mtl [4],

S.-B. Scholz and O. Chitil (Eds.): IFL 2008, LNCS 5836, pp. 233–248, 2011.
© Springer-Verlag Berlin Heidelberg 2011

have been very successful in providing useful combinators for constructing monads. However, they have a number of shortcomings. Because the lifting of operations through monad transformers is done on a case-by-case basis, there is no guarantee that the liftings are uniform (Section 3.1) and it makes extending the library cumbersome (Section 3.2). Moreover, the lifting overloading mechanism produces shadowing of operations (Section 3.3), and relies essentially on non-portable features (Section 3.4).

The main contribution of this paper is the design of Monatron, a monad transformer library that addresses the issues discussed above (Section 4). Its implementation (Section 5) builds on the strengths of existing monad transformer libraries and incorporates some new ideas on liftings of operations [9] that are based on solid theoretical principles. Although these lifting of operations have been implemented by the author in the library mmtl[1], the implementation of mmtl closely followed the design in existing libraries and, as consequence, still suffered from some of their problems. The desire to eliminate these problems motivated the design of the Monatron [8] library.

The organization of the paper is as follows: in Section 2 we explain how to construct complex monads using monad transformers. In Section 3 we explain some issues raised by the current design, and in Section 4 we introduce a new design that addresses these issues. The implementation of the design is carried out in Section 5 and in Section 6 we conclude.

2   Combining Monads

Monads provide an extremely useful abstraction for computational effects. In Haskell, monads are given by instances of the following type class:

class Monad m **where**
  return :: $a \rightarrow m\ a$
  $(\ggg)$ :: $m\ a \rightarrow (a \rightarrow m\ b) \rightarrow m\ b$

Intuitively, m is a type constructor of computations, return introduces a trivial computation, and $(\ggg)$ (pronounced *bind*) sequences computations by taking a computation returning a value of type a and a function from a into a new computation. Instances of the Monad class are required to satisfy certain coherence equations that ensure that return and $(\ggg)$ are well-behaved.

As an example, in Figure 1 we have defined two monads: Either x is a monad for exceptions of type x, and the identity monad Id is a monad of pure computations.

Combinator libraries for monads come equipped with some standard monads corresponding to different computational effects that provide readily available building blocks for constructing effectful computations. For example, libraries usually provide a State s monad for modelling global state of type s, a Cont r monad for modelling continuations with result type r, a Writer w monad for modelling output of a monoid w, a Reader e monad for modelling environments of

---

[1] http://hackage.haskell.org/cgi-bin/hackage-scripts/package/mmtl

```
data Either x a = Left x | Right a          newtype Id a = Id a
instance Monad (Either x) where            instance Monad Id where
   return a      = Right a                     return a     = Id a
   Left x  >>= f = Left x                       (Id a) >>= f = f a
   Right a >>= f = f a
```

Fig. 1. Either and Identity Monad

type e, and an Exception x monad for modelling exceptions of type x. To see the details of their implementation we refer the reader to an introductory article [1]. These monads provide some of the most common computational effects but, by all means, they are not the only ones. The fact that monad libraries (mostly) only support this limited set of effects and have not been extended to other effects can be seen as evidence of the universality of these effects. Less optimistically, it can be seen as symptomatic of a lack of extensibility (Section 3.2).

In addition to the aforementioned monads, libraries provide the corresponding monad transformer [14] for each effect. A *monad transformer* is a monad parameterised by an arbitrary monad. It can be thought of as a monad with a hole which can be filled by any monad. More formally, a monad transformer is a type constructor with kind $(* \to *) \to (* \to *)$ which is an instance of the type class MonadT.

```
class MonadT t where
   lift :: Monad m ⇒ m a → t m a
```

Each instance T of MonadT is required to map monads to monads (via an instance Monad m ⇒ Monad (T m)), and lift is required to behave well with respect to return and ($\gg\!\!=$).

Using monad transformers, one can easily construct complex monads. For example, the state monad transformer StateT s applied to some monad m will yield a monad StateT s m, which combines the effect of state and the effect(s) modelled by m. One can then stack effects, adding more and more monad transformer layers, in order to construct complex monads. For example, **type** StExc s x = StateT s (Exception x) is a monad for state of type s and exceptions of type x. We can further extend this monad and add continuations simply by applying the continuation monad transformer to obtain **type** ContStExc r s x = ContT r (StExc s x).

Since a monad transformer adds an effect to another monad, monads such as State can be constructed by adding state to the identity monad Id.

$$\text{State } s \equiv \text{StateT } s \text{ Id}$$

Therefore, in principle, only the transformer version of the monad is needed. Also, note that for the combined monads there is no need to verify any monad laws, or define new monad instances. The monad transformers will guarantee that the obtained type is a monad by construction, realising the idea that correct constructions are obtained by combining correct components.

Consider now the monad **type** ExcSt x s = ExcT x (State s), obtained by applying the exception monad transformer to the state monad. Is this monad equivalent to StExc s x? After all, both monads model state together with exceptions. The answer is no, and in general, the order in which the monad transformers are applied is important. To see why, it is necessary to *run* the effectful computations.

Monad transformers and their associated monads come equipped with a run function that allows us to evaluate an effectful computation. For example, the state monad can be run with runState :: s → State s a → (a, s) that given an initial state and a stateful computation, returns the value of the computation together with the final state. The state monad transformer can be run with runStateT :: Monad m ⇒ s → StateT s m a → m (a, s), which given an initial state and a computation, returns an m-computation with a value and final state. The exception monad[2] is run with a function runException :: Exception x a → Either x a, and the exception monad transformer is run with a function runExcT :: Monad m ⇒ ExcT x m a → m (Either x a), that returns an m-computation over either an exception or a value.

In order to obtain a run function for a combined monad we compose the run functions of the components:

$$\begin{aligned}
&\text{runStExc} \quad :: s \to \text{StExc } s\ x\ a \to \text{Either } x\ (a, s) \\
&\text{runStExc } s = \text{runException} \cdot \text{runStateT } s \\[4pt]
&\text{runExcSt} \quad :: s \to \text{ExcSt } x\ s\ a \to (\text{Either } x\ a, s) \\
&\text{runExcSt } s = \text{runState } s \cdot \text{runExcT}
\end{aligned}$$

Analysing the type of the resulting run functions, we can see that in StExc when an exception is raised the computation forgets about the state, while in ExcSt when an exception is raised the computation preserves the state. One can then choose how exceptions should interact with state by choosing the order in which the monad transformers are applied. In general, applying monad transformers in different orders gives rise to different interactions among effects [14].

So far, we have discussed the construction of types with monadic structure for modelling computational effects. In order to write programs that will produce and manipulate these effects, monads and monad transformers come equipped with effectful operations. For example, State comes equipped with operations get :: State s s and put :: s → State s () for getting access to the current state and for setting the current state, and Exception comes equipped with operations throw :: x → Exception x a and handle :: Exception x a → (x → Exception x a) → Exception x a for throwing an exception and handling an exception.

Consider the exception monad Exception x which supports the operation throw. If we extend it with a monad transformer such as StateT s and obtain the monad StateT s (Exception x), we expect this extended monad to not only support get and put as provided by StateT, but also to support throw as provided

---

[2] We distinguish between the Either monad and the exception monad as they might have different implementations. Also, it is precisely when they differ that runException is interesting.

by Exception x. How to make the extended monad to support the operations of its underlying monad is known as the problem of *operation lifting*.

3   Some Problems with the Traditional Design

The current design of monad transformers libraries performs the liftings of operations of an underlying monad to the transformed monad in an ad-hoc fashion, relying crucially on a type-class trick in order to perform the liftings. The basic idea is the following: define a class of monads supporting a certain operation. For example, we define the class of monads supporting the operation callCC, and show that the continuation monad transformer ContT applied to any monad m is an instance of this class:

```
class Monad m ⇒ ContM m where
    callCC :: ((a → m b) → m a) → m a
instance Monad m ⇒ ContM (ContT m) where
    callCC = ...
```

The final step is to show that, for each monad transformer in the library, if the underlying monad supports callCC, then the transformed monad also supports callCC. For example, for the exception monad transformer ExcT:

```
instance ContM m ⇒ ContM (ExcT x m) where
    callCC = ...
```

This type-class trick has some advantages, such as an overloading of the operations that is usually convenient, but libraries that rely on it have some shortcomings which affect the predictability, extensibility, expressive power and portability of the library. In the following, we explain why this is so.

3.1   Non-uniform Liftings

One can replace a computation on the Writer monad by a computation on the more general State monad, and replace the output operation tell by an output operation on State. Similarly, one can do the same replacements on their transformer versions, for example, replacing the operation tell :: Monad m ⇒ String → WriterT String m () that outputs a string, with the following definition:

```
tellˢ    :: Monad m ⇒ String → StateT String m ()
tellˢ w = do s ← get
             put (s ++ w)
```

One would expect that replacing WriterT by StateT, replacing tell by tell^S, and replacing runWriterT by runStateT "", the semantics of a program would be preserved. However, in the mtl [4], the following two programs, which perform computations over WriterT String Cont and StateT String Cont respectively, have different behaviours:

p1 :: (String, String)
p1 = (runCont id · runWriterT)
    (callCC ($\lambda exit \to$ tell "1" $\ggg \lambda\_ \to exit$ "Exit"))

p2 :: (String, String)
p2 = (runCont id · runStateT "")
    (callCC ($\lambda exit \to$ tell^S "1" $\ggg \lambda\_ \to exit$ "Exit"))

While p1 = ("Exit", ""), we have that p2 = ("Exit", "1"). The difference in behaviour is caused by non-uniform liftings in the mtl. In particular, callCC is lifted through the StateT monad transformer in a way which is not coherent with the lifting of callCC through WriterT. Although we can regard this as a bug and change the implementation of the library, since each operation is lifted on a case-by-case basis, there is no intrinsic guarantee that the liftings are coherent. Hence, with no guarantee that the liftings are coherent, the predictability of the semantics of the library is seriously affected.

3.2   Quadratic Number of Instances

Suppose a programmer wants to extend the library with a new monad transformer which comes equipped with some operations. The programmer must write a new class corresponding to the added operations and an instance of this new class for *each* existing monad transformer, so that the added operations can be lifted through other monad transformers. Furthermore, the programmer is required to write instances of *each* class of existing operations for the new monad transformer. In other words, assuming one class of operations per monad transformer, the number of instances increases quadratically with the number of monad transformers.

Not only the extensibility of the library is affected because of the quadratic growth of required lines of code, but also because of the lack of separation of concerns. Extending the library requires understanding the semantics of all the existing monad transformers.

The quadratic number of instances and lack of separation of concerns is a major hurdle. It discourages anyone willing to extend the library and it shows that the traditional design can only work for a library with a very limited number of monads.

3.3   Shadowing of Operations

We have seen in Section 2 how StExc and ExcST give rise to different interactions between exceptions and state. With the former, state changes are lost when an exception is raised, while with the latter state changes are preserved. Suppose that we need both types of exception. We can easily construct such a monad as follows:

type ExcStExc $x1$ s $x2$ = ExcT $x1$ (StExc s $x2$)

runExcStExc :: $s \to$ ExcStExc $x1$ s $x2$ $a \to$ Either $x2$ (Either $x1$ a, s)
runExcStExc s = runStExc s · runExcT

We now have two different types of exceptions with two different exception objects ($x1$ and $x2$). Let us assume that both objects are of the same type, say Int. Since there is no type that will distinguish instances, the function handle will refer to the instance of the outermost monad. We have no way of handling the other type of exceptions, as there is no way of saying "What I mean is the handle operation corresponding to the monad under two monad transformers". The inner handle operation is shadowed by the outer one.

One way to deal with this problem is to define different types of exceptions, but this usually means inserting unnecessary constructors and destructors which clutter the program and make it more difficult to understand. We see shadowing as revealing a limitation in the expressive power of the library.

3.4   Portability

The implementation of the type-class trick requires several extensions to the Haskell 98 standard [12], such as functional dependencies and multi-parameter classes. Although many of these extensions have been around for a while and their semantics are quite stable, they certainly affect the portability of the library. This is particularly so because the whole implementation of the library revolves around this type-class trick. We would like to have the *choice* of paying the price and using the operation overloading provided by the type-class implementation when it is convenient without being *forced* to do so.

4   A New Approach

We now present the new ideas behind our monad transformer library. Specifically, we present an improved lifting mechanism with explicit lifting of functions which addresses the significant shortcomings discussed in the previous section.

The main idea of this approach is to pair each operation to a type of its implementations. For example, implementations of handle for exceptions of type x and a monad m are given by elements of the type Handle x m. Once a type of implementations is given, we define functions parameterised by an implementation. In the exceptions handling example, this means that we will define a function handleX that given an implementation Handle x m performs the handling of an exception.

```
handleX :: Monad m ⇒ Handle x m → m a → (x → m a) → m a
handleX = ...
```

Additionally, we define a function liftHandle that, given an implementation of the operations for a monad m, produces an implementation of the operation for the monad t m, where t is an arbitrary monad transformer (as indicated by the class constraint MonadT t).

```
liftHandle :: (Monad m, MonadT t) ⇒ Handle x m → Handle x (t m)
liftHandle = ...
```

We expect every operation to have a type for its implementations, and a function parameterised by this type which allows programmers to use the operation and a lifting function.

Concrete monads and monad transformers provide their own implementation of the operations:

```
handleExcT :: Monad m ⇒ Handle x (ExcT x m)
handleExcT = ...
```

It is now possible, when using an operation, to state explicitly and precisely which implementation is meant and through how many monad transformers this implementation should be lifted. For example, handleX handleExcT is the operation handle as implemented by handleExcT. Its lifting through two monad transformers is given by handleX (liftHandle (liftHandle handleExcT)).

The approach has several advantages:

Uniform-liftings: operations are lifted uniformly through monad transformers by construction. This means that the semantics of the lifted operations is predictable.

Modularity: operations need to be defined only once for each monad/monad transformer that supports them, effectively taking the quadratic order of instances to linear.

Expressivity: One has the ability to exactly state which operation one is referring to, as it is done in the example above. In fact, if desired, one can have more that one implementation of an operation for a given monad.

The main difference between the traditional approach and ours is that instead of defining a type class for each class of operations, we define a type. This removes the dependency from type classes, but opens the question of what is an appropriate type for the implementation of operations. We answer this question in Section 5.

The implementation that follows the ideas above constitutes the *core* of our library Monatron. This core only needs Haskell 98 extended with rank-2 types [10] and is fully-functional. However, the overloading of operations provided by typeclasses is often convenient. When there is no possible confusion, and using additional language extensions is not a problem, one can let the compiler infer which implementation one is referring to.

4.1   Overloading of Operations

It is simple to add overloading on top of the core functionality. We define the class of monads m with implementations Handle x m, and define the operation handle for this class of monads:

```
class Monad m ⇒ HandleM x m | m → x where
    handleM :: Handle x m
```

```
handle :: HandleM x m ⇒ m a → (x → m a) → m a
handle = handleX handleM
```

Note that in the definition of handle, we are replacing the explicit parameter Handle z m in handleX by an implicit parameter given by the type class.

Finally, we provide instances for the concrete monads that implement the operations: the monad ExcT x m, and any monad transformer applied to a monad of class HandleM.

```
instance Monad m ⇒ HandleM x (ExcT x m) where
    handleM = handleExcT
instance (HandleM x m, MonadT t) ⇒ HandleM x (t m) where
    handleM = liftHandle handleM
```

Of course, implementing this overloading of operations will require the use of many extensions to Haskell 98, as it was the case with the traditional design of monad transformer libraries. However, in this case, the core functionality does not rely on the extensions and one has the choice of using the extensions when they are available and overloading is convenient, as opposed to being forced to always do so.

5   Implementation of Monatron

The key idea of the design is to obtain a suitable representation of the implementations of the operations. Such a representation should allow programmers to both perform the operations and lift them through monad transformers.

5.1   Types for Operation Implementation

Let us consider first the simple case of the operations get and put. A monad m implements these operations for a parameter s with a pair of a computation m s and a function $s → m$ (). Hence, our representation for the operations is a pair as shown in the type GetPut below. The projections give rise to the parameterised operations getX and putX, and lifting an implementation is just post-composing lift.

```
type GetPut s m = (m s, s → m ())
getX           :: GetPut s m → m s
getX (g, _)    = g
putX           :: GetPut s m → s → m ()
putX (_, p) s  = p s
liftGetPut     :: (Monad m, MonadT t) ⇒ GetPut s m → GetPut s (t m)
liftGetPut (g, p) = (lift g, lift · p)
```

The function liftGetPut is simple because in the type of the operations of GetPut the monad only occurs in the result. In general, operations of the form $\forall a.\ S\ a → M\ a$, where S is an instance of Functor, can be lifted simply by applying lift after the operation. Operations of the form above are in one-to-one

```
newtype Cod f a = Cod {unCod :: ∀b. (a → f b) → f b}
runCod :: Monad m ⇒ Cod m a → m a
runCod c = unCod c return
instance MonadT Cod where
    lift m    = Cod (m≫=)
    tmap f m = Cod (λk → f (unCod m (f · k)))
instance Monad m ⇒ Monad (Cod m) where
    return   = lift · return
    c ≫= f   = Cod (λk → unCod c (λa → unCod (f a) k))
```

Fig. 2. Codensity monad transformer

correspondence with operations $\forall x.\ \mathsf{S}\ (\mathsf{M}\ a) \to \mathsf{M}\ a$ that respect the bind of the monad (i.e. operations such that it is the same to bind any function $a \to \mathsf{M}\ b$ before performing the operation or after performing the operation). Because of this correspondence we will say that such operations are S-algebraic.

What happens when the operation in question is not S-algebraic? For example, the operation for handling exceptions of type x has type $\forall a.\mathsf{M}\ a \to (x \to \mathsf{M}\ a) \to \mathsf{M}\ a$, for a monad M which supports exceptions. Although it is equivalent to an operation $\forall a.\ \mathsf{S}\ (\mathsf{M}\ a) \to \mathsf{M}\ a$ for $\mathsf{S}\ a = (a, x \to a)$, it is not S-algebraic, since it doesn't respect the bind of the monad (handling an exception before binding and after binding an arbitrary function $a \to \mathsf{M}\ b$ does not yield the same result).

However, it can be shown that every operation $\mathsf{op} :: \forall a.\ \mathsf{S}\ (\mathsf{M}\ a) \to \mathsf{M}\ a$ is in one-to-one correspondence with an operation $\overline{\mathsf{op}} :: \forall a.\ \mathsf{S}\ a \to \mathsf{Cod}\ \mathsf{M}\ a$. Here, $\mathsf{Cod}\ \mathsf{M}\ a$ is the codensity monad transformer [13,9] defined in Fig. 2. Categorically, the codensity monad transformer takes a functor to the right Kan extension of the functor along itself. The correspondence between op and $\overline{\mathsf{op}}$ shows how an operation which is not S-algebraic for a given monad can be S-algebraic for a different (more powerful) monad.

As with any monad transformer, we can lift a computation $(m\ a)$ into $(\mathsf{Cod}\ m\ a)$ with lift, but also we can use runCod to run a computation $(\mathsf{Cod}\ m\ a)$ and obtain a computation $(m\ a)$ in the original monad. A routine calculation shows that runCod · lift = id.

The obtained operation $\overline{\mathsf{op}}$ can be easily lifted to a monad transformer T by post-composition with lift. However, this does not yield a lifting of op yet. In order to obtain a proper lifting, we need to 'correct' the result of the operation (lift · $\overline{\mathsf{op}}$), by applying (lift · runCod) to every occurrence of the monad inside the transformer T. Hence, we extend the class for monad transformers with an extra member:

```
class MonadT t where
    lift :: Monad m ⇒ m a → t m a
    tmap :: (Monad m, MonadT t) ⇒ (∀x. m x → m x) → t m a → t m a
```

The addition of tmap is essential for lifting the correction function, not only for the case of handle, but also for any other operation which is not S-algebraic.

type Handle $x\ m\ =\ (\forall a.\ a \rightarrow (x \rightarrow a) \rightarrow m\ a, \forall a.\ m\ a \rightarrow m\ a)$

handleX   :: Monad $m \Rightarrow$ Handle $x\ m \rightarrow m\ a \rightarrow (x \rightarrow m\ a) \rightarrow m\ a$
handleX $(h, n)\ m = n \cdot$ join $\cdot\ h\ m$

liftHandle   :: (Monad m, MonadT t) $\Rightarrow$ Handle $x\ m \rightarrow$ Handle $x\ (t\ m)$
liftHandle $(h, n)\ = (\lambda m \rightarrow$ lift $\cdot\ h\ m,$ tmap $n)$

Fig. 3. Type and functions for implementations of handle

type Throw $x\ m\ =\ (\forall a.\ x \rightarrow m\ a)$

throwX   :: Throw $x\ m \rightarrow x \rightarrow m\ a$
throwX $t\ x$ $= t\ x$

liftThrow   :: (Monad m, MonadT t) $\Rightarrow$ Throw $x\ m \rightarrow$ Throw $x\ (t\ m)$
liftThrow t $=$ lift $\cdot\ t$

Fig. 4. Type and functions for implementations of throw

If we lift an operation through two transformers the correction function is no longer (lift $\cdot$ runCod) :: M $a \rightarrow$ M a, but tmap (lift $\cdot$ runCod) :: T M $a \rightarrow$ T M a. Consequently, the correction function will change according to the depth of the lifting. This motivates the following definition of the implementation of handle.

Implementations of handle consist of pairs of an S-algebraic operation and a correction function (see Figure 3). The parameterised operation handleX constructs from these components the usual operation exception handling. The function liftHandle lifts the components with lift and tmap respectively.

As a final example, in Figure 4 we provide the type and functions for implementations of throw. Since throw is an S-algebraic operation, its implementations are simply functions of type $\forall a.\ x \rightarrow m\ a$.

5.2   Implementing Transformers and Operations

So far, we have defined functions that deal with generic implementations of certain operations. For example, handleX and liftHandle deal with implementations Handle $x\ m$. We now define concrete monad transformers and show that they provide an implementation of operations. In particular, we will define the state monad transformer and its implementation of get and put, and the exception monad transformer and its implementation of throw and handle.

State Monad Transformer. We start with the state monad transformer (see Figure 5). Our implementation of the state monad transformer is essentially the traditional one [14].

Note that we give a different name for the constructor and destructor. This is because we only want to export an interface consisting of a type and some operations, leaving room for potential optimizations.

The monad transformer StateT provides an implementation of GetPut, which is simply a pair of functions.

```
newtype StateT s m a = S {unS :: s → m (a, s)}
stateT :: (s → m (a, s)) → StateT s m a
stateT = S
runStateT :: s → StateT s m a → m (a, s)
runStateT s m = unS m s
instance MonadT (StateT s) where
    lift m = S (λs → m ≫ λa → return (a, s))
    tmap f (S m) = S (f · m)
instance Monad m ⇒ Monad (StateT s m) where
    return   = lift · return
    m ≫ k = S (λs → unS m s ≫ λ(a, s') → unS (k a) s')
```

Fig. 5. State monad transformer

```
getPutStateT :: Monad m ⇒ GetPut s (StateT s m)
getPutStateT = (get, put)
    where get _ = S (λs → return (s, s))
          put s = S (λ_ → return ((), s))
```

Once we have defined the implementation of GetPut, we can use it via getX and putX, and lift it with liftGetPut. Importantly, there is a separation of the notion of *implementation* of operations (as provided by getPutStateT) and the *use* of that type of operation (as provided by the functions getX, putX, and liftGetPut).

Exception Monad Transformer. Let us review the traditional definition of the exception monad transformer, which can be found in Figure 6, together with the functions throw^i and handle^i. A computation of type X^i x m a is an m-computation whose value is either an exception of type x or a pure value of type a. The operation throw^i throws an exception, and handle^i takes a computation and a handler, and if the computation throws an exception then it applies the handler.

This monad transformer can provide an implementation Throw x (X^i x m), but it is not powerful enough to provide an implementation Handle x (X^i x m), as we would have no way of providing a lifting function for it.

Consider now a context $[\bullet] \gg k$ that binds a function $k :: a → X^i$ x m b. Given such a context, it is possible to define an exception handling operation which instead of checking if its first argument throws an exception, it checks whether an exception is thrown after binding k:

$$h = \text{handle}^i \ (k \ a) \ (k \cdot h) :: a → (x → a) → X^i \ x \ m \ a$$

Analyzing computations in the context of a bind operation is possible if we transform X^i x m with the codensity monad transformer. Intuitively, the codensity monad transformer adds to a monad the possibility of analysing a computation in the context of a bind.

newtype $X^i \; x \; m \; a = X^i \; \{ unX^i :: m \; (\text{Either } x \; a) \}$

instance MonadT $(X^i \; x)$ **where** lift $m \quad = X^i \; (\text{fmap Right } m)$
$\qquad\qquad\qquad\qquad\qquad$ tmap $f = X^i \cdot f \cdot unX^i$

instance Monad $m \Rightarrow$ Monad $(X^i \; x \; m)$ **where**
$\quad$ return $\qquad = \text{lift} \cdot \text{return}$
$\quad (X^i \; m) \ggeq f = X^i \; (\textbf{do } a \leftarrow m; \textbf{case } a \textbf{ of } \text{Left } x \rightarrow \text{return (Left } x)$
$\qquad\qquad\qquad\qquad\qquad\qquad\qquad\qquad\qquad$ Right $b \rightarrow unX^i \; (f \; b))$

$\quad$ throw$^i \qquad\quad :: \text{Monad } m \Rightarrow x \rightarrow X^i \; x \; m \; a$
$\quad$ throw$^i \; x \quad = X^i \; (\text{return (Left } x))$

$\quad$ handle$^i \qquad\quad :: \text{Monad } m \Rightarrow X^i \; x \; m \; a \rightarrow (x \rightarrow X^i \; x \; m \; a) \rightarrow X^i \; x \; m \; a$
$\quad$ handle$^i \; m \; h = X^i \; (unX^i \; m \ggeq \lambda exa \rightarrow \textbf{case } exa \textbf{ of}$
$\qquad\qquad\qquad\qquad\qquad\qquad\qquad\qquad$ Left $x \rightarrow unX^i \; (h \; x)$
$\qquad\qquad\qquad\qquad\qquad\qquad\qquad\qquad$ Right $a \rightarrow \text{return (Right } a))$

Fig. 6. Traditional exception monad transformer

newtype ExcT $x \; m \; a = X \; \{ unX :: \text{Cod } (X^i \; x \; m) \; a \}$

instance MonadT (ExcT x) **where**
$\quad$ lift $\qquad = X \cdot \text{lift} \cdot \text{lift}$
$\quad$ tmap $f = X \cdot \text{tmap (tmap } f) \cdot unX$

instance Monad $m \Rightarrow$ Monad (ExcT $x \; m$) **where**
$\quad$ return $\; = \text{lift} \cdot \text{return}$
$\quad m \ggeq f = X \; (unX \; m \ggeq unX \cdot f)$

Fig. 7. Exception monad transformer

The proposed correction function (lift · runCod) has the effect of closing the context. In order to illustrate this idea, consider the computation handle $m \; h \ggeq \lambda\_ \rightarrow$ throw (). We do not expect the throw after the bind to affect the result of the handle operation. This means that, even though we are considering computations in a context, at some point we want to "close" the context, perform a computation, and only then consider the result in a resulting context. This is exactly what (lift · runCod) does.

We can define the exception monad transformer as the transformation of the traditional exception monad with the codensity monad transformer. The complete implementation of the obtained monad transformer for exceptions is shown in Figure 7.

We remark that, despite the relative complexity of the obtained monad, the interface for it does not need to be changed. It is still possible to construct elements of the exception monad transformer ExcT $x \; m \; a$ from an element of m (Either $x \; a$), and running the exception monad still yields the type m (Either $x \; a$), as shown below:

$\quad$ excT :: Monad $m \Rightarrow m$ (Either $x \; a) \rightarrow$ ExcT $x \; m \; a$
$\quad$ excT $= X \cdot \text{lift} \cdot X^i$

runExcT :: Monad m ⇒ ExcT x m a → m (Either x a)
runExcT = unX^i · runCod · unX

This means that the complexity of the implementation is actually hidden from the programmer, who can use the library without needing to understand the details of the implementation.

Going to the trouble of defining the exception monad transformer in this manner now pays off. We can now define the implementation of the operations throw and handle as provided by ExcT. Note that the correction function in the implementation of handle is essentially (lift · runCod).

throwExcT :: Monad m ⇒ Throw x (ExcT x m)
throwExcT x = X (lift (throw^i x))
handleExcT :: Monad m ⇒ Handle x (ExcT x m)
handleExcT = $(k, \text{excT} · \text{runExcT})$
  where k a h = X (Cod (λc → handle^i $(c\ a)$ $(c · h)$))

The given semantics for handleExcT is the expected one, as a routine calculation shows that, in essence, it is equivalent to handle^i:

$$\text{handleX handleExcT} \equiv \text{handleE}^i$$

where handleE^i is given by:

handleE^i :: (Monad m) ⇒ ExcT x m a → $(x$ → ExcT x m $a)$ → ExcT x m a
handleE^i m h = xe (handle^i (ex m) (ex · h))
  where xe :: Monad m ⇒ X^i x m a → ExcT x m a
    xe = X · lift
    ex :: Monad m ⇒ ExcT x m a → X^i x m a
    ex = runCod · unX

Once that the implementation of the operations is defined, we are done. Using and lifting the operations can be done by the functions that act on arbitrary implementations of the operations (such as those in Figure 3).

6   Conclusion

Combinator libraries for monads are essential for facilitating the construction of complex monads that naturally appear in applications that go from basic parser libraries [7] to end-user applications [16]. We have shown that the current design of monad transformer libraries has a number of shortcomings that hinder the extensibility, predictability, portability, and expressive power of the library.

By restructuring the design and incorporating uniform liftings of operations we have managed to address all of these issues, except for portability for which, at least, some alternative is given. This new design guided the implementation of the Monatron library [8]. The design requires a deeper understanding from the monad transformer writer, as operations need to be defined in such a way that they can be lifted through arbitrary monad transformers. One way to obtain these liftings is formally explained using system $F\omega$ in [9]. The user of the library sees none of this complexity, and benefits from a more expressive interface that works uniformly on all operations.

The complexities of the design lead us to hide the internal implementation in order to maintain a simple interface. This was unnecessary before, as the implementation was very close to the interface. This change may prove to be useful for improving the efficiency of the library, as hidden implementations allow for optimizations that preserve the interface. For example, the list monad is often used for modelling non-determinism, but its *merge* operation (concatenation) is rather inefficient. Using a different internal structure, but preserving the interface, we can provide an efficient *merge* operation. We leave as future work a further departure from the traditional implementation of monads in search for better performance.

6.1 Related Work

The mtl [4] is the most well-known monad transformer library. It is inspired by the paper of Liang et al. [14], and for many years it has been distributed together with the Haskell compiler GHC. More recently, a new library called MonadLib [3] has been introduced. This library is an improvement over the mtl, but it still suffers from the problems described in Section 3. The library presented in this article owes a lot to the excellent work done by the authors of these two libraries.

The codensity monad transformer has appeared in a number of functional programming papers. For example, it has been derived as a monad transformer for backtracking [5], it has been calculated in a search for efficient parsers [2], and it has been used to optimize substitution in the free monad [17]. In our case, however, we were motivated by its mathematical properties [9].

Acknowledgements. I would like to thank Graham Hutton and the anonymous referees for their comments and suggestions and all the people in the Functional Programming Lab for their support.

References

1. Benton, N., Hughes, J., Moggi, E.: Monads and effects. In: Barthe, G., Dybjer, P., Pinto, L., Saraiva, J. (eds.) APPSEM 2000. LNCS, vol. 2395, pp. 42–122. Springer, Heidelberg (2002)
2. Claessen, K.: Parallel Parsing Processes. Journal of Functional Programming 14(6), 741–757 (2004)
3. Diatchki, I.: Monadlib, http://www.galois.com/~diatchki/monadLib/
4. Gill, A.: Monad transformer library, http://hackage.haskell.org/cgi-bin/hackage-scripts/package/mtl-1.1.0.2
5. Hinze, R.: Deriving backtracking monad transformers. In: ICFP, pp. 186–197 (2000)
6. Hughes, J.: The Design of a Pretty-printing Library. In: Jeuring, J., Meijer, E. (eds.) AFP 1995. LNCS, vol. 925, pp. 53–96. Springer, Heidelberg (1995)
7. Hutton, G., Meijer, E.: Monadic Parsing in Haskell. Journal of Functional Programming 8(4), 437–444 (1998)

248   M. Jaskelioff

8. Jaskelioff, M.: Monatron, http://www.cs.nott.ac.uk/~mjj/monatron
9. Jaskelioff, M.: Modular monad transformers. In: Castagna, G. (ed.) ESOP 2009. LNCS, vol. 5502, pp. 64–79. Springer, Heidelberg (2009)
10. Jones, M.P.: First-class polymorphism with type inference. In: POPL, pp. 483–496. ACM Press, New York (1997)
11. Peyton Jones, S.L., Wadler, P.: Imperative functional programming. In: POPL, pp. 71–84 (1993)
12. Peyton Jones, S. (ed.): Haskell 98 Language and Libraries: the Revised Report. Cambridge University Press, Cambridge (2003)
13. Mac Lane, S.: Categories for the Working Mathematician, 2nd edn. Graduate Texts in Mathematics, vol. 5. Springer, Heidelberg (1971)
14. Liang, S., Hudak, P., Jones, M.: Monad transformers and modular interpreters. In: POPL, pp. 333–343 (1995)
15. Moggi, E.: Notions of computation and monads. Information and Computation 93(1), 55–92 (1991)
16. Stewart, D., Sjanssen, S.: Xmonad. In: Haskell Workshop, Freiburg, Germany, pp. 119–119. ACM, New York (2007)
17. Voigtländer, J.: Asymptotic improvement of computations over free monads. In: Audebaud, P., Paulin-Mohring, C. (eds.) MPC 2008. LNCS, vol. 5133, pp. 388–403. Springer, Heidelberg (2008)
18. Wadler, P.: The essence of functional programming. In: POPL, pp. 1–14 (1992)

Catch Me If You Can

Looking for Type-Safe, Hierarchical, Lightweight, Polymorphic and Efficient Error Management in OCaml

David Teller[1], Arnaud Spiwack[2], and Till Varoquaux[3]

[1] LIFO, Université d'Orléans
David.Teller@univ-orleans.fr
[2] LIX, École Polytechnique
Arnaud.Spiwack@lix.polytechnique.fr
[3] till@pps.jussieu.fr

Abstract. This is the year 2008 and ML-style exceptions are everywhere. Most modern languages, whether academic or industrial, feature some variant of this mechanism. Languages such as Java even feature static coverage-checking for such exceptions, something not available for ML languages, at least not without resorting to external tools.

In this document, we demonstrate a design principle and a tiny library for managing errors in a functional manner, with static coverage-checking, automatically-inferred, structurally typed and hierarchical exceptional cases, with a reasonable run-time penalty. Our work is based on OCaml and features monads, polymorphic variants, compile-time code rewriting and trace elements of black magic.

1 Introduction

Despite our best intentions and precautions, even correct programs may fail. The disk may be full, the password provided by the user may be wrong or the expression whose result the user wants plotted may end up in a division by zero. Indeed, management of dynamic errors and other exceptional circumstances inside programs is a problem nearly as old as programming. Error management techniques should be powerful enough to cover all possible situations and flexible enough to let the programmer deal with whichever cases are his responsibility while letting other modules handle other cases, should be sufficiently noninvasive so as to let the programmer concentrate on the main path of execution while providing guarantees that exceptional circumstances will not remain unmanaged, all without compromising performance or violating the paradigm.

Nowadays, most programming languages feature a mechanism based on (or similar to) the notion of *exceptions*, as pioneered by PL/I [10], usually with the semantics later introduced in ML [12]. A few languages, such as Haskell, define this mechanism as libraries [19], while most make it a language primitive, either because the language is not powerful enough, for the sake of performance, to add

S.-B. Scholz and O. Chitil (Eds.): IFL 2008, LNCS 5836, pp. 249–271, 2011.
© Springer-Verlag Berlin Heidelberg 2011

sensible debugging information, or as a manner of sharing a common mechanism for programmer errors and manageable errors.

As a support for our discussion on the management of errors and exceptional circumstances, let us introduce the following type for the representation of arithmetic expressions, written in OCaml:

```
type expr = Value of float
          | Div   of expr * expr
          | Add   of expr * expr
```

The implementation of an evaluator for this type is a trivial task:

```
let rec eval = function
  Value f        → f
| Div   (x, y) → (eval x) /. (eval y)
| Add   (x, y) → (eval x) +. (eval y)
(*val eval: expr → float*)
```

However, as such, the interpreter fails to take into account the possibility of division by zero. In order to manage this *exceptional circumstance* (or *error*), we promptly need to rewrite the code into something more complex:

Listing 1.1. Ad-hoc error management

```
type (α, β) result = Ok of α | Error of β

let rec eval = function
  Value f          → Ok f
| Div   (x, y) → (match eval x with
    Error e → Error e
  | Ok x'     → match eval y with
      Error e              → Error e
    | Ok y' when y' = 0. → Error "Divison by 0"
    | Ok y'                → Ok (x' /. y'))
| Add   (x, y) → (match eval x with
    Error e              → Error e
  | Ok x'                → match eval y with
      Error e              → Error e
    | Ok y'                → Ok (x' +. y'))
(*val eval: expr → (float, string) result*)
```

While this function succeeds in managing exceptional cases, the code is clumsy and possibly slow. An alternative is to use the built-in mechanism of exceptions – which we will refer to as "native exceptions"– as follows:

Listing 1.2. Error management with native exceptions

```
let rec eval = function
   Value f        → f
 | Div   (x, y) → let (x', y') = (eval x, eval y) in
        if y' = 0. then raise (Error "division by 0")
        else            x' /. y'
 | Add   (x, y) → eval x +. eval y
 (*val eval: expr → float *)
```

This definition of eval is easier to write and read, closer to the mathematical definition of arithmetic operations and faster. While native exceptions appear to be a great win over explicitly returning an error value, the implementation of this mechanism is commonly both less flexible and less safe than ad-hoc error management. In particular, in ML languages, the loss of flexibility appears as the impossibility of defining exceptions which would use any polymorphic type parameters[1]. As for the loss of safety, it is a consequence of eval containing no type information could let us determine that the function may fail and what kind of information may accompany the failure. Worse than that: the compiler itself does not have such information and cannot provide guarantees that every exceptional case will eventually be managed. Arguably, the possibility for a native exception to completely escape is comparable to the possibility for a pattern-matching to go wrong, which in turn is comparable to null-pointer exceptions in most modern industrial languages – while technically not a type error, this remains a source of unsafety which we will refer to as "incomplete coverage" in the rest of this document.

While it is possible to complete the type system to guarantee complete coverage, perhaps as a variation on *types and effects* [17], either as part of the mandatory compilation process, as in Java, or as external tools [14], this guarantee does nothing to improve the lack of flexibility. This is quite unfortunate, as numerous situations thus require the manual definition of many superfluous exceptions with identical semantics but different types, or lead to the overuse of magic constants to specify sub-exceptions, or require impure or unsafe hacks to implement simple features. SML provides a way to regain some polymorphism in exceptions defined *locally* using *generative exceptions*. To improve flexibility one needs to change deeply the type system [1]

Another possible approach which may be used to obtain both the readability of exceptions, guarantee of complete coverage and parametric polymorphism, is to implement error management as monads [19], a path followed by Haskell.

---

[1] For comparison, the Java type-checker rejects subtypes of Exception with parametric polymorphism, the C# *parser* rejects catch clauses with parametric polymorphism but allows general catch clauses followed by unsafe downcasts, while Scala accepts defining, throwing and catching exceptions with parametric polymorphism, but the semantics of the language ignores these type parameters both during compilation and during execution.

However, this approach often results in either not-quite-readable and possibly ambiguous type combinations consisting in large hierarchies of algebraic combinators, in the necessity of writing custom error monads or monad transformers, which need to be manually rewritten as often as the list of exceptional cases changes, or in the use of dynamic types. In addition, these monads are perceived as having a large computational cost, due to constant thunking and dethunking of continuations and to the lack of compiler-optimized stack unrolling.

In this document, we attempt to obtain the best of both worlds: polymorphism, type-safety, coverage-check, with the added benefits of automatic inference of error cases and the definition of classes and subclasses of exceptional cases, all of this without the need to modify the programming language. As this is an OCaml-based work, we also take into account the impact of this programming style in terms of both performance, syntactic sugar, possible compile-time optimizations. Despite the number of claims appearing in the previous sentences, our work is actually based on very simple concepts and does not have the ambition of introducing brand new programming methodologies, nor to revolutionize ML programming. Rather, our more limited objective is to present an interesting design principle and a tiny library for error management, in the spirit of Functional Pearls or of a tutorial, and based on ML-style exceptions, monads, phantom types, polymorphic variants and code rewriting. Some of our results are positive, some negative and, somewhere along the way, we revisit techniques results discarded by previous works on hierarchical exceptions [11] and demonstrate that, when redefined with better language support, they may be used to provide safer (and possibly faster) results.

In a first section we demonstrate briefly an error monad, well-known in the world of Haskell but perhaps less common in the ML family. We then proceed to complete this monad with the use of lightweight types to achieve automatic inference of error cases, before pushing farther these lightweight types to permit the representation of classes and subclasses of exceptional cases, while keeping guarantees of coverage. Once this is done, we study the performance of this monad and progressively move the code from the library to the compiler. Finally, we conclude by a discussion on usability, potential improvements, and comparison with other related works.

The source code for the library is available as a downloadable package [18]. Elements of this work will be included in the rehauled OCaml standard libraries, OCaml Batteries Included.

2   The Error Monad

As we discussed already, Listing 1.1 shows a rather clumsy manner of managing manually whichever errors may happen during the evaluation of an arithmetic expression. However, after a cursory examination of this extract, we may notice that much of the clumsiness may be factored away by adding an operation to check whether the result of an expression is Ok x, proceed with x if so and abort the operation otherwise. Indeed in the world of monads [19], this is the *binding* operation. In OCaml, this function is typically hidden behind syntactic sugar [4] `perform` and ⟵, which allows us to rewrite

Listing 1.3. Towards monadic error management

```
let bind m k = match m with
    Ok x      → k x
  | Error _ → m

let rec eval = function
    Value f        → Ok f
  | Div   (x, y) → perform x' ⟵ eval x ; y' ⟵ eval y ;
    if y' = 0. then Error "Division by 0"
    else              Ok (x' /. y')
  | Add   (x, y) → perform x' ⟵ eval x ; y' ⟵ eval y ;
    Ok (x' +. y')
(*val eval: expr → (float, string) result*)
```

For the sake of abstraction (and upcoming changes of implementation), we also hide the implementation of type (α, β) `result` behind two functions `return` (for successes) and `throw` (for failures):

Listing 1.4. Monadic error management

```
let return  x = Ok x
let throw   x = Error x

let rec eval = function
    Value f        → return f
  | Div   (x, y) → perform x' ⟵ eval x ; y' ⟵ eval y ;
    if y' = 0. then throw "Division by 0"
    else              return (x' /. y')
  | Add   (x, y) → perform x' ⟵ eval x ; y' ⟵ eval y ;
    return (x' +. y')
```

This new definition of `eval` is arguably as easy to read as the version of Listing 1.2. As we have decided to abstract away type `result`, we need functions to run a computation and determine it success. We call respectively these functions `catch` (for catching one error case) and `attempt` (for catching all error cases and entering/leaving the error monad):

Listing 1.5. Catching errors

```
let catch ~handle = function Ok x     → Ok x
                           | Error e → handle e

let attempt ~handle = function Ok   x → x
                             | Error e → handle e
```

Here we use a *labeled argument* ~handle (instead of just handle) so that it can be called by explicitly stating its name, and even reordered:

```
attempt normal_case ~handle:error_case
```

We may now group all the functions of the error monad as one module Error_monad with the following signature:

Listing 1.6. A module for the error monad

```
type (+α, +β) result
val return: α → (α, β) result
val throw : β → (α, β) result
val bind  : (α, β) result → (α → (γ, β) result) →
    (γ, β) result
val catch : handle:(β → (α, γ) result) →
    (α, β) result → (α, γ) result
val attempt: handle:(β → α) → (α, β) result → α
```

The + in (+α, +β) result specify that this type is covariant, *i.e.* an expression of type (α, β) result can be generalized even if it is not a value [8].

This adoption of monadic-style error reporting proves sufficient to convey polymorphic type information. As we will see in the next section, we may take advantage of this to improve flexibility of our library even further.

To convince ourselves of the capabilities of the error monad in terms of polymorphism, let us write a toy implementation of (persistent) association lists. The signature contains two functions: find to retrieve the value associated to a key, and add to add an association to the list. Operation find k l fails when nothing is associated to k in l, while add k u l fails when there is already a value v associated to k in l. In both case the key k is used as the error report.

We give the implementation of this module in Listing 1.7, together with its signature in Listing 1.8. As expected, the type of errors thrown by add and find depends on the type of the input.

Listing 1.7. Association list with polymorphic exceptions

```
type (α,β) assoc = (α*β) list

let empty = []

let rec add k u = function
    []                → return [k,u]
  | (x, v as a)::l → if k=x then throw k
                     else        perform l' ⟵ add k u l ;
                                 return (a::l')
let rec find k = function
    []          → throw k
  | (x,v)::l → if k=x then return v
               else        find k l
```

```
type (α,β) assoc
val empty: (α,β) assoc
val add  : α → β → (α,β) assoc → ((α,β) assoc, α) result
val find : α → (α,β) assoc → (β,α) result
```

In the rest of the paper, we shall concentrate on the `eval` example. However, should need arise, this example could be refined similarly.

3   Representing Errors

While Listing 1.4 presents a code much more usable than that of Listing 1.1 and while this listing is type-safe, the awful truth is that this safety hides a fragility, due to the use of "magic" character strings to represent the nature of errors – here, `"Division by 0"`, a constant which the type-checker cannot take into account when attempting to guarantee coverage. Unfortunately, this fragility is shared by elements of both OCaml's, SML's or Haskell's standard libraries.

Now, of course, it may happen that we need to represent several possible errors cases, along with some context data. For instance, during the evaluation of simple arithmetic exceptions, arithmetic overflow errors could also arise. For debugging purposes, we may even decide that each error should be accompanied by the detail of the expression which caused the error and that overflows should be split between overflows during addition and overflows during division.

The error monad of Section 2 handles propagation for any type β of errors. We shall investigate how to choose this type to handle those cases.

3.1   Errors as Heavy-weight Sums

The first and most obvious choice is to represent errors as sum types. For our running example, we could write

Listing 1.9. Simple arithmetic errors

```
type cause_of_overflow = Addition | Division
type eval_error = Division_by_zero of expr
                | Overflow  of expr * cause_of_overflow
```

Now, as our error monad lets us transmit arbitrary error information along with the error itself, we may rewrite `eval` so as to take advantage of `eval_error` instead of `string`, without having to declare a new exception constructor or to rewrite the interface or implementation of the error monad:

Listing 1.10. Monadic error management with sum types

```
let ensure_finite f e cause =
  if is_infinite f then throw (Overflow(e, cause))
  else                      return f

let rec eval = function
  Value f          → return f
| Div (x,y) as e → perform x' ⟵ eval x ; y' ⟵ eval y ;
    if y' = 0. then throw (Division_by_zero e)
    else                 ensure_finite (x' /. y') e Division
| Add (x,y) as e → perform x' ⟵ eval x ; y' ⟵ eval y ;
    ensure_finite (x' +. y') e Addition
(*val eval: expr → (float, eval_error) result*)
```

While this solution improves on the original situation, it is not fully satisfying. Indeed, it is quite common to have several functions share some error cases but not all. For instance, a basic visual 10-digit calculator and a scientific plotter may share on a common arithmetic library. Both evaluators use division and may suffer from divisions by zero. However, only the scientific plotter defines logarithm and may thus suffer from logarithm-related errors. Should the error-reporting mechanism of the library be defined as one heavy-weight sum type, the visual calculator would need to handle all the same error cases as the scientific plotter. OCaml's built-in pattern-matching coverage test will therefore require all error cases to be managed, even though the functions which may trigger these error cases are never invoked by the visual calculator.

The alternative is to use disjoint possible errors for distinct functions. However, this choice quickly leads to composability nightmares. Since a division by zero and a logarithm-error are members of two disjoint types, they need to be injected manually into a type `division_by_zero_or_log_error`, defined as a sum type, for use by the scientific plotter. While possible, this solution is cumbersome to generalize and tends to scale very poorly for large projects, especially during a prototyping phase. These composability troubles also appear as soon as two different libraries use disjoint types to represent errors: arithmetic errors, disk errors or interface toolkit errors, for instance, must then be injected into an awkward common type of errors, and projected back towards smaller types of errors as need arises.

3.2   Errors as Lightweight Composition of Sums

Another approach, commonly seen in the Haskell world, and actually not very different from the second choice just mentioned, is to define a more general type along the lines of

Listing 1.11. Haskell-style **either** type

```
type (α, β) either = Left of α | Right of β
```

With such a data structure, building lightweight compositions of error cases becomes a trivial task. However, these lightweight compositions are also an easy recipe for obtaining unreadable constructions consisting in trees of **either** and tuples. That is, attempting to convert **eval** to use only such lightweight types typically results in the following expression, and its rather convoluted type:

Listing 1.12. Monadic error management with lightweight **either**

```
let ensure_finite f message =
  if is_infinte f then throw message
  else                       return f

let rec eval = function
    Value f          → return f
  | Div (x,y) as e → perform x' ⟵ eval x ; y' ⟵ eval y ;
     if y' = 0. then throw (Right e)
     else ensure_finite (x' /. y') (Left (Left e))
  | Add (x,y) as e → perform x' ⟵ eval x ; y' ⟵ eval y ;
     ensure_finite (x' +. y') (Left (Right e))
(* val eval : expr →
 ( float,( (expr, expr) either,expr) either ) result *)
```

While it is possible to avoid such chains of **either** by combining this approach with the manual definition of new types – perhaps abstracted away behind modules – the result remains unsatisfactory in terms of comprehension and falls far from solving the composability nightmare.

3.3   Errors as Extensible Types

Another alternative would be the use of *extensible types*, as featured in Alice ML [16]. More generally, one such type is available in languages of the ML family: native exceptions. Instead of our current type **eval_error**, and with the same code of **eval**, we could therefore define two native exceptions, whose role is to be raised monadically:

```
exception Division_by_zero of expr
exception Overflow         of expr * cause_of_overflow
```

If, at a later stage, the set of exceptions needs to be extended to take into account, say, logarithm errors, we may implement the new case with the following definition:

```
exception Logarithm_error  of expr
```

Better even, this solution proves compatible with the existing native exception system and permits trivial conversion of native exceptions for use with the error monad:

```
let attempt_legacy ~handle f arg = try   f arg
                                    with  e  →  handle e
(*val attempt_legacy: handle:(exn  →  β)  →  (α  →  β)  →  α  →  β*)
```

At this point, a first weakness appears: while the addition of brand new error cases such as `Logarithm_error` is a trivial task, extending `cause_of_overflow` is impossible unless we find a way to define `cause_of_overflow` as an extensible type. Assuming that we have a way to express several distinct extensible types, perhaps by using an hypothetical encoding with phantom types, we are still faced with a dilemma: should all errors be represented by items of the same type `exn` or should we use several disjoint extensible types? The question may sound familiar, as we have already been faced with the same alternative in the case of heavy-weight sum types. As it turns out, and for the same reasons, neither choice is acceptable: sharing one type gets into the way of coverage guarantees, while splitting into several types leads, again, to composability nightmares.

Or does it? After all, OCaml does contain an additional kind of types, close cousin to extensible sum types, but with much better flexibility: Polymorphic Variants [7].

3.4   Errors as Polymorphic Variant

Polymorphic variants represent a kind of lightweight sum types designed to maximize flexibility. Indeed, the main traits of polymorphic variants are that

1. no declaration is necessary – rather, definition is inferred from usage
2. declaration is possible, for specification and documentation purposes
3. open variants may be composed automatically into a larger variant
4. constructors may be shared between unrelated polymorphic variants.

When used to represent errors, trait 1. lets us concentrate on the task of building the algorithm, without having to write down the exact set of errors before the prototyping phase is over. Trait 2. proves useful at the end of the prototyping phase, to improve error-checking of client code and documentation, while 3. lets OCaml infer the set of errors which may be triggered by an expression – and check completeness of the error coverage, just as it would do for heavy-weight sum types. Finally, trait 4. lets us define functions which may share some – but not necessarily all – error cases.

Before rewriting the full implementation of `eval`, let us build a smaller example. The following extract defines an expression expression `div_by_zero` which `throws` a division by zero with information `Value 0.`:

```
let div_by_zero = throw ('Division_by_zero (Value 0. ))
(* val div_by_zero : (α,
    [> 'Division_by_zero of expr ]) result *)
```

The type of `div_by_zero` mentions that it may have any result α, much like raising ML-exceptions produce results of type α, and that it may throw an error consisting in an *open* variant, marked by constructor 'Division_by_zero, and containing an **expr**.

Similarly, we may define an expression with the ability to cause an overflow during division, much as we could with a heavy-weight sum type:

```
let overflow_div = throw ('Overflow ('Division (Value 0.)))
(* val overflow_div : (_α, _[> 'Overflow of
   _[> 'Division of expr ] ] ) result *)
```

Finally, both expressions may be composed into an expression which might cause either a division by zero or an overflow during division, resulting in:

```
if true then div_by_zero
else            overflow_div
(* (_α, _[> 'Division_by_zero of expr
       |  'Overflow of _[> 'Division of expr ] ]) result*)
```

As we see from the inferred type of this expression, the result of the composition may produce either results (of any type) or errors marked either by 'Division_by_zero (and accompanied by an **expr**) or by 'Overflow (and accompanied by another tag 'Division, itself accompanied by an **expr**). This error signature remains *open*, which allows us to add further error cases.

As expected, converting **eval** to polymorphic variants is straightforward:

Listing 1.13. Monadic error management with polymorphic variants

```
let rec eval = function
    Value f            → return f
  | Div (x,y) as e → perform x' ←— eval x ; y' ←— eval y ;
      if y' = 0. then throw ('Division_by_zero e)
      else ensure_finite (x' /. y') ('Overflow ('Division e))
  | Add (x,y) as e → perform x' ←— eval x ; y' ←— eval y ;
      ensure_finite (x' +. y') ('Overflow ('Addition e))
(*val eval :
expr → ( float, [> 'Division_by_zero of expr
     |  'Overflow of [> 'Addition of expr
            |  'Division of expr ] ] ) result *)
```

As we hoped, with polymorphic variants, we do not have to manually label error cases. Rather, the compiler may infer error cases from the source code. As this inferred information appears in the type of our function, coverage may be proved by the type-checker. Therefore, we may write:

```
let test1 e = attempt (eval e) ~handle:(function
    'Division_by_zero _→print_string "Division by 0"; 0.
  | 'Overflow _        →print_string "Overflow"; 0.)
(*val test1 : expr → float*)
```

On the other hand, the following extract fails to compile:

```
# let test2 e = attempt (eval e) ~handle:(
  function 'Overflow _ → print_string "Overflow"; 0. )

  function 'Overflow _ →
           ^^^^^^^^^^^^^
This pattern matches values of type
  [< 'Overflow of α ]
but is here used to match values of type
  [> 'Division_by_zero of expr
  | 'Overflow of [> 'Addition of expr
                 | 'Division of expr ] ]
```

In addition, the composability of polymorphic variants, which we have demonstrated, means that we do not have to decide whether to put all the error cases defined by a library in one common type or to split them among several disjoint types: barring any conflicting name or any specification which we may decide to add to prevent composition, there is no difference between one large polymorphic variant type and the automatically inferred union of several smaller ones.

Note that this choice of polymorphic variants does not alter the signature of our module, as featured in Listing 1.6. In particular, a consequence is that function catch can be used to eliminate one (or more) variant type exception while propagating others:

```
let ignore_overflow e = catch (eval e) ~handle:(function
  'Overflow _                   → return 0.
| 'Division_by_zero _ as ex → throw ex)
(*val ignore_overflow: expr →
    (float, [> 'Division_by_zero of expr]) result*)
```

Unfortunately, due to limitations on type inference of polymorphic variants, this elimination requires manual annotations and *a priori* knowledge of both the types of error cases which must be handled and the types of error cases which should be propagated:

```
let ignore_overflow e = catch (eval e) ~handle:(function
  'Overflow _                   → return 0.
| _ as ex                       → throw ex)
(*val ignore_overflow: expr →
    ( float, [> 'Division_by_zero of expr
            | 'Overflow of [> 'Addition of expr
                           | 'Division of expr ] ] ) result *)
```

While this limitation is perhaps disappointing, the upside is that, as we will now see, polymorphic variants and a little syntactic sugar may carry us farther than usual ML-style exceptions.

3.5 From Polymorphic Variants to Exception Hierarchies

We have just demonstrated how polymorphic variants solve the problem of composing error cases. Actually, our examples show a little bit more: we have not only defined two kinds of errors (divisions by zero and overflows), but also defined two sub-cases of errors (overflow due to addition and overflow due to division).

Passing the right parameters to function `attempt`, we may choose to consider all overflows at once, as we have done in our latest examples, or we may prefer to differentiate subcases of overflows:

Listing 1.14. Matching cases and subcases

```
let test3 e = attempt (eval e) ~handle:(function
 'Division_by_zero _    → print_string "Division by 0"; 0.
 |'Overflow 'Addition _ → print_string "+ overflows"; 0.
 |'Overflow _           → print_string "Other overflow"; 0.)
```

In other words, while we have chosen to present sub-cases as additional information carried by the error, we could just as well have decided to consider them elements of a small hierarchy:

- division by zero is a class of errors ;
- overflow is a class of errors ;
- overflow through addition is a class of overflows ;
- overflow through division is a class of overflows.

From this observation, we may derive a general notion of classes of errors, without compromising composability and coverage checking.

Before we proceed, we need to decide exactly what an exception class should be. If it is to have any use at all, it should be possible to determine if an exception belongs to a given class by simple pattern-matching. In order to preserve our results and the features used up to this point, an exception class should be a data structure, defined by one or more polymorphic variant constructors and their associated signature, as well as some error content. In addition, for exception classes to be useful, it must be possible to specify a subtyping relation between classes. We also need to ensure consistency between the error content of classes related by subtyping. Finally, we should be able to define new classes and subclasses without having to modify the definition of existing code.

To achieve all this, we encode classes using a method comparable to tail polymorphism [2] with polymorphic variants[2]. Where classical uses of tail polymorphism take advantage of either algebraic data-types or records, though, the use of polymorphic variants preserves extensibility.

---

[2] A similar idea has been suggested in the context of Haskell [11] but discarded as a "very interesting, but academic" and a "failed alternative".

We first introduce a chain-link record, whose sole use is to provide human-readable field names `sub` and `content`. Field `sub` is used to link a class to its super-class, while field `content` serves to record the class-specific additional error information which the programmer wishes to return along with the error:

```
type (α, β) ex =  {
   content: α;
   sub:        β option;
} constraint β = [> ]
```

The `constraint` β = [>] line binds β to being a polymorphic variant row.

From this, assuming for the course of this example that division by zero is a top-level class of exceptions, we may produce the following constructor:

```
let division_by_zero_exc ?sub content =
 'Division_by_zero {
     content = content;
     sub     = sub;  }
(*val ?sub:([>  ] as α)  →  β  →
    [> 'Division_by_zero of (β, α) ex]*)
```

Argument `content` is self-documented, while `sub` will serve for subclasses to register the link. `?sub` means that it is *optional*, it is realised as a labeled argument of an `option` type.

Similarly, we may now define overflow:

```
let overflow_exc ?sub content =
 'Overflow {
     content = content;
     sub     = sub; }
```

Since we decided to describe overflow during addition as a subclass of overflow, we may define its constructor by chaining a call to `overflow_exc`, passing the new chain-link as argument.

```
let overflow_addition ?sub content =
 overflow_exc ˜sub:('Addition {
     content = ();
     sub     = sub;
}) content
```

Or, equivalently, with a small piece of syntactic sugar introduced to increase readability of exception definitions:

```
let exception overflow_division content =
    Overflow content; Division ()
```

The changes to the library are complete. Indeed, one simple record type is sufficient to move from polymorphic variants to polymorphic variants with hierarchies. To confirm our claim that we preserve composability and coverage guarantees, let us revisit `eval` and our test cases.

Adapting `eval` to our hierarchy is just the matter of replacing concrete type constructors with abstract constructors:

Listing 1.15. Eval with hierarchies

```
let rec eval = function
  Value f            → return f
| Div (x,y) as e → perform x' ←— eval x ; y' ←— eval y ;
    if y' = 0. then throw (division_by_zero_exc e)
    else ensure_finite (x' /. y') (overflow_division e)
| Add (x,y) as e → perform x' ←— eval x ; y' ←— eval y ;
    ensure_finite (x' +. y') (overflow_addition e)
(* val eval : expr →
  (float,
   [> 'Division_by_zero of (expr, α) ex
   |  'Overflow of
     (expr,
       [> 'Addition of (unit, β) ex
       |  'Division of (unit, γ) ex ])
     ex ]) result *)
```

While the type information is painful to read – and could benefit from some improved pretty-printing – it accurately reflects the possible result of `eval`, the nature of exceptions and subexceptions and their contents.

Adapting the test of Listing 1.14 to our more general framework, we obtain the following extract, slightly more complex:

```
let test4 e = attempt (eval e) ~handle:(function
  'Division_by_zero _      →
  print_string "Division by 0"; 0.
| 'Overflow {sub = Some ('Addition _)} →
  print_string "+ overflows"; 0.
| 'Overflow _                →
  print_string "Other overflow"; 0. )
```

For convenience, we introduce another layer of syntactic sugar, marked by a new keyword **attempt**, and which provides a simpler notation for exception patterns. With this sugar, we may rewrite the previous listing as

```
let test5 e = attempt eval e with
  Division_by_zero _      → print_string "Division by 0" ; 0.
| Overflow _; Addition _  → print_string "+ overflows"   ; 0.
| Overflow _              → print_string "Other overflow"; 0.
```

While we do not demonstrate this due to space limitations, this syntactic sugar proves also useful to add optional post-treatment for successes, for failures and for any result (à la `finally`).

With this simplified notation, let us demonstrate coverage guarantees by omitting the case of overflow division:

```
let test6 e = attempt eval e with
  Division_by_zero _        → print_string "Division by 0"; 0.
| Overflow _; Addition _  → print_string "+ overflows"  ; 0.
```

The following error message demonstrates that the type-checker has correctly detected the missing case (and integrates well with our syntax extension). The solution is suggested at the end of the message:

Listing 1.16. Missing subcase (error message)

```
    Division_by_zero _     →
    ~~~~~~~~~~~~~~~~~~~~
This pattern matches values of type
  [< `Division_by_zero of α
   |  `Overflow of (expr,
                [< `Addition of β ]) ex ]
but is here used to match values of type
  [> `Division_by_zero of (expr, _) ex
   |  `Overflow of
     (expr,
       [> `Addition of (unit, γ) ex
        |  `Division of (unit, δ) ex ])
     ex ]
The first variant type does not allow tag(s) `Division
```

Similarly, our encoding lets the type-checker spot type or tag errors in exception-matching, as well as provide warnings in case of some useless catch clauses. We do not detail these error/warning messages, which are not any more readable than the one figuring in Listing 1.16, and which could just as well benefit from some customized pretty-printing.

3.6 Bottom Line

In this section, we have examined a number of possible designs for error reports within the error monad. Some were totally unapplicable, some others were impractical. As it turns out, by using polymorphic variants, we may achieve both inference of error cases, composability of error cases and simple definition of hierarchies of error classes, while retaining the ability of the type-checker to guarantee coverage of all possible cases. All of this is implemented in a meager 29 lines of code, including the module signature.

At this point, we have obtained all the features we intended to implement. Our next step is to study the performance cost – and to minimize it, if possible.

4   Measuring Performance

According to our experience, when hearing about monads, typical users of OCaml tend to shrug and mutter something about breaking performance too much to be as useful as built-in exceptions. Is that true?

At this point, we set out to measure the speed of various representations of errors in OCaml and to search for alternative implementations and variants of the error monad which would let us improve performances. In the course of this quest, we tested several dozens of versions, using sometimes purely functional techniques, mostly imperative primitives, type-unsafe optimizations, compile-time rewriting. Due to space constraints, we can only present a short summary of our results in this document. A more complete overview will be made available as a technical report.

The numbers are presented in Figure 1. The six techniques investigated are

ad-hoc management the technique used in Listing 1.1
native exceptions the technique used in Listing 1.2
pure error monad the error monad demonstrated so far
references and exceptions an implementation of the error monad using native exceptions to handle error propagation:

```
exception Raised
type (α, β) result = β option ref → α
let attempt ~handle v =
  let   result = ref None in
  try   v result
  with Raised  →  match !result with
      None     →  assert false (* Unused *)
    | Some e   →  handle e
let bind m k r = k (m r) r
let return x _ = x
let throw  x b = b := Some x; raise Raised
```

Results are implemented as functions which raise a native exception when an error is found. As native exceptions in OCaml cannot be polymorphic, we pass the error message in a reference, that we give as an argument to the result-function. The reference actually contains a β **option** to be able to initialize it.
phantom types and exceptions another implementation of the error monad using exceptions. Instead of using a reference as a "channel" to convey the error message, we make use of the type-unsafe `Obj.obj`. And make use of phantomtypes [6] to make sure that it is only applied in safe situations:

```
exception Raised of Obj.t
type (α, β) result = unit → α constraint β = [> ]
let attempt (v:(_,β) result) ~handle =
 try  v ()
 with Raised r → handle (Obj.obj r : β)
let bind m k () = k ( m () ) ()
let return x () = x
let throw  x () = raise (Raised (Obj.repr x))
```

pure error monad with rewriting a variation on the error monad implemented in Section 2. The monadic `bind` primitive is meant to be used
mostly in the form p ⟵ m; e, a sort of `let ... in` construction which
is interpreted as `bind m (fun p -> e)`. This produces an unnecessary intermediary closure which OCaml compiler does not optimize out. We adress
that issue by extending the monad primitives with a preprocessor function
`rewrite_bind`:

```
val rewrite_bind : m:Ast.expr → p:Ast.patt →
                   e:Ast.expr → Ast.loc   → Ast.expr
```

We shall use this function directly as the interpretation of p ⟵ m; e, instead of building a term out of traditionnal monadic combinators.

```
let rewrite_bind ~m ~p ~e _loc =
  <:expr< match $m$ with
          | Ok $p$ → $e$
          | Error err → Error err >>
```

Notice that using this function forces to expose the implementation of (α, β)
`result`. An alternative solution would be instead to expose another type
(α, β) `_result` which happens to be the implementation of (α, β) `result`.
Then `rewrite_bind` can convert between both using `Obj.magic`. The beauty
of this approach is that even if after preprocessing the code contains unsafe
type-casts, these are inserted by the preprocessor at safe places, with no need
to ever break the monad abstraction[3].

To obtain this benchmark, we implemented using each technique

an arithmetic evaluator errors are rather uncommon, being raised only in
case of division by zero (300 samples)
the n queens problem only one pseudo-error is raised, when a solution has
been found (5 samples)
union of applicative sets of integers pseudo-errors are raised very often to
mark the fact that no change is necessary to a given set (300 samples).

Every test has been performed with OCaml 3.10.2, under Linux, on native
code compiled for the 32bit x86 platform, with maximal inlining, executed 15
times, after a major cycle of garbage-collection, with the best and the worst

---

[3] Using this technique we have also built a variant of the "phantom types and exceptions" approach, which it proved to be less efficient.

result discarded. The results are presented as a percentage of the number of
samples in which the execution time falls within given bounds:

Very good Execution time of the sample is within 5% of the execution time of
the fastest implementation for this test (the "shortest execution time")
Good Within 5-15% of the shortest execution time.
Acceptable Within 15-30% of the shortest execution time.
Slow Within 30-50% of the shortest execution time.
Bad At least 50% longer than the shortest execution time.

For information, we also provide

Average Average of ratio $\dfrac{\text{duration of test}}{\text{shortest execution time}}$.
Deviation Standard deviation of $\dfrac{\text{duration of test}}{\text{shortest execution time}}$.

	Evaluator	Queens	Union		Evaluator	Queens	Union
Ad-hoc error management				Reference and native exceptions			
Very good	56%	40 %	18%	Very good	0%	0 %	0%
Good	26%	60 %	43%	Good	7%	0 %	0%
Acceptable	12%	0 %	35%	Acceptable	33%	0 %	0%
Slow	3%	0 %	4%	Slow	41%	0 %	0%
Bad	3%	0 %	0%	Bad	19%	100%	100%
Average	1.06	1.05	1.13	Average	1.35	1.75	2.26
Deviation	0.12	0.04	0.10	Deviation	0.20	0.06	0.23
Native exceptions				Phantom types and native exceptions			
Very good	70%	100%	100%	Very good	1%	0 %	0%
Good	16%	0 %	0%	Good	8%	0 %	0%
Acceptable	12%	0 %	0%	Acceptable	39%	0 %	0%
Slow	2%	0 %	0%	Slow	35%	0 %	0%
Bad	0%	0 %	0%	Bad	17%	100%	100%
Average	1.06	1.00	1.00	Average	1.35	1.73	2.22
Deviation	0.13	0.00	0.00	Deviation	0.22	0.06	0.22
Pure error monad				Pure error monad with rewriting			
Very good	37%	0 %	0%	Very good	54%	0 %	0%
Good	35%	20 %	0%	Good	28%	100%	0%
Acceptable	18%	60 %	14%	Acceptable	12%	0%	5%
Slow	7%	20 %	71%	Slow	5%	0 %	56%
Bad	3%	0 %	15%	Bad	1%	0 %	38%
Average	1.12	1.24	1.48	Average	1.07	1.07	1.48
Deviation	0.14	0.02	0.14	Deviation	0.15	0.01	0.14

Fig. 1. Testing the performance of the error monad

The first conclusion we draw from our measurements is that the pure error
monad is inappropriate as a mechanism for optimising returns. While this is
unsurprising, we also notice that the speed of the pure monad is actually quite
reasonable when it is used to deal with errors, and can be largely improved by

plugging-in a little compiler support. Further experiments with improvements, which go beyond the scope of this document, hint that slightly more complex rewriting rules can go even further – and not just for error monads. By opposition, our every attempt to domesticate native exceptions into a construction which could be checked for complete coverage incurred an impressive slowdown which made them useless. Our most successful attempts at native exceptions, which also required plugged-in compiler support, remained a little slower than the pure error monad with rewriting.

At this point, the fastest implementation of our library consists in the pure error monad (29 lines), compile-time optimisations (49 lines) and some (larger) syntactic sugar. To handle circumstances in which exceptions are used as optimised returns, we complete this with a 16 lines-long module, which provides a mechanism of local exceptions with polymorphism, while retaining the speed of native exceptions and adding a little safety. This module can also make use of hierarchical exceptions but is neither safe nor generic enough to replace the error monad.

5   Conclusion

We have demonstrated how to design an error-reporting mechanism for OCaml extending the exception semantics of ML, without altering the language. With respect to OCaml's built-in exception mechanisms, our work adds static checks, polymorphic error reports, hierarchies and support for locally-defined exceptions and relaxes the need of declaring error cases, while retaining a readable syntax and acceptable performance.

To obtain this richer mechanism, we make use of monads, polymorphic variants and code rewriting and demonstrate the folk theorem of the OCaml community that polymorphic variants are a more generic kind of exceptions. We have also attempted to optimize code through numerous techniques, and succeeded through the use of compile-time domain-specific code generators.

Related works. Other works have been undertaken with the objective of making exceptions safer or more flexible. Some of these approaches take the form of compile-time checkers such as OCamlExc [14] or similar works for SML [20]. These tools perform program analysis and thus need to evolve whenever the language's semantic does; their maintenance can be quite involved. Similarly, the Catch tool for Haskell [13] uses abstract interpretation to provide guarantees that pattern matches of a program (including pattern-matching upon errors) suffice to cover all possible cases, even when individual pattern-matches are not exhaustive. All these tools retain the exception mechanism of the underlying language and therefore add no new feature, in particular no hierarchies of error classes.

Other efforts are closer to our approach. In addition to the very notion of monads [19], the Haskell community has seen numerous implementations of extensible sets of exceptions, either through monad transformers or dynamic type reflection. Hierarchical exceptions [11] through typeclass hierarchies and dynamic type reflection have also been implemented for Haskell. These choices could have been transposed and sometimes improved into OCaml. We decided to avoid monad transformers in the simple case of error reporting, as these too often require manual definition and manual composition of program-specific or library-specific error cases. Similarly, several variants on run-time type information are possible in OCaml, either with dynamic type reflection comparable to Haskell's `Data.Typeable`, or combinations of view patterns and either dynamically typed objects or lightweight extensible records, all of which have been implemented for OCaml. However, we preferred avoiding these dynamic typing solutions which, as their Haskell counterpart, forbid any automatic coverage-check. Yet another encoding of hierarchies has been demonstrated for ML languages, through the use of phantom types [6]. While this work is very interesting, our experiments seem to show that the use of this encoding for exceptions leads to a much less flexible and composable library, in which new sub-kinds of errors cannot be added post-facto to an existing design.

Another combination of native exceptions and monad-like combinators for fast error reporting has been designed in the context of ML [15]. While benchmarks obtained with this discipline indicate better performance than what we achieve, this work aims only at reducing redundant error messages and does not improve the flexibility or safety of error management. This difference in purpose allows an efficient mix of native exceptions and monadic ones. Perhaps more interestingly, the author demonstrates a set of error-related function types which may not be obtained with pure monads, such as:

$$((\alpha \to \beta) \to \gamma \to \delta) \to (\alpha \to (\beta, \epsilon)\ \mathtt{result}) \to \gamma \to (\delta, \epsilon)\ \mathtt{result}$$

This combinator, which extends traditional function application to handle erroneous arguments, requires native exceptions, and hence cannot be implemented in our pure monad. It may however be implemented trivially with the complementary library we designed for local exceptions.

Numerous other works focus on performance in ML languages and their kin. In particular, the Glasgow Haskell Compiler is usually able to efficiently inline simple functions or rewrite simple compositions – as the OCaml compiler can do neither automatically in our case, this is what we implement manually to optimize away needless abstractions. As for the technique we employ for performing this inlining, it is essentially a specialized form of multi-stage compilation, as available in MetaOCaml [5] or outside the ML community [9]. In particular, our use of specialized code rewriters to avoid the cost of abstraction is an idea also found in MetaOCaml-based works [3].

Future works. While in this document we have investigated only the problem of exception management, our work has yielded ideas which we believe may be applied to the broader domains of effect regions [17]. Indeed, we have started working on an implementation for OCaml through a combination of libraries and syntactic redefinitions. While early experiments seem to indicate that the limitations of type inference on polymorphic variants will limit inference of effect regions, we hope our implementation incurs only a negligible runtime penalty and allows comfortable interactions with existing libraries.

Part of our work on exceptions will be included in OCaml Batteries Included, the community-maintained standard library replacement for OCaml. Most of the modules of this library are being designed to permit monadic error management.

Acknowledgements

We wish to thank Gabriel Scherer for his help with the elaboration and implementation of the syntactic sugar.

References

1. Blume, M., Acar, U.A., Chae, W.: Exception handlers as extensible cases. In: Ramalingam, G. (ed.) APLAS 2008. LNCS, vol. 5356, pp. 273–289. Springer, Heidelberg (2008)
2. Warren Burton, F.: Type extension through polymorphism. ACM Trans. Program. Lang. Syst. 12(1), 135–138 (1990)
3. Carette, J., Kiselyov, O.: Multi-stage programming with functors and monads: Eliminating abstraction overhead from generic code. In: Glück, R., Lowry, M. (eds.) GPCE 2005. LNCS, vol. 3676, pp. 256–274. Springer, Heidelberg (2005)
4. Carette, J., van Dijk, L.E., Kiselyov, O.: Syntax extension for monads in ocaml, http://www.cas.mcmaster.ca/~carette/pa_monad/
5. Czarnecki, K., O'Donnell, J.T., Striegnitz, J., Taha, W.: Dsl implementation in metaocaml, template haskell, and c++. In: Domain-Specific Program Generation, pp. 51–72 (2003)
6. Fluet, M., Pucella, R.: Phantom types and subtyping. In: TCS 2002: Proceedings of the IFIP 17th World Computer Congress - TC1 Stream / 2nd IFIP International Conference on Theoretical Computer Science, Deventer, The Netherlands, pp. 448–460. Kluwer, B.V., Dordrecht (2002)
7. Garrigue, J.: Programming with polymorphic variants. In: ML Workshop (1998)
8. Garrigue, J.: Relaxing the value restriction. In: Kameyama, Y., Stuckey, P.J. (eds.) FLOPS 2004. LNCS, vol. 2998, pp. 196–213. Springer, Heidelberg (2004)
9. Guyer, S.Z., Lin, C.: An annotation language for optimizing software libraries. In: DSL, pp. 39–52 (1999)
10. Holt, R.C., Wortman, D.B.: A sequence of structured subsets of pl/i. SIGCSE Bull. 6(1), 129–132 (1974)
11. Marlow, S.: An extensible dynamically-typed hierarchy of exceptions. In: Haskell 2006: ACM SIGPLAN Workshop on Haskell, Portland, Oregon, ACM Press, New York (2006)
12. Milner, R., Tofte, M., Macqueen, D.: The Definition of Standard ML. MIT Press, Cambridge (1990)
13. Mitchell, N., Runciman, C.: A static checker for safe pattern matching in Haskell. In: Trends in Functional Programming, vol. 6. Intellect (February 2007)
14. Pessaux, F.: Détection statique d'exceptions non rattrapées en Objective Caml. PhD thesis, Université Pierre & Marie Curie - Paris 6 (2000)
15. Ramsey, N.: Eliminating spurious error messages using exceptions, polymorphism, and higher-order functions. The Computer Journal 42(5), 360–372 (1999)

16. Rossberg, A., Le Botlan, D., Tack, G., Brunklaus, T., Smolka, G.: Alice through the looking glass. In: Trends in Functional Programming, vol. 5, pp. 77–96 (2006)
17. Talpin, J.-P., Jouvelot, P.: The type and effect discipline. Inf. Comput. 111(2), 245–296 (1994)
18. Teller, D., Spiwack, A., Varoquaux, T.: Catch me if you can, Software package available at `http://www.univ-orleans.fr/lifo/Members/David.Teller/software/exceptions/catch_0_2.tgz`
19. Wadler, P.: The essence of functional programming. In: POPL 1992: Proceedings of the 19th ACM SIGPLAN-SIGACT Symposium on Principles of Programming Languages, pp. 1–14. ACM, New York (1992)
20. Yi, K., Ryu, S.: A cost-effective estimation of uncaught exceptions in standard ml programs. Theor. Comput. Sci. 277(1-2), 185–217 (2002)

Between Types and Tables

Using Generic Programming for Automated Mapping between Data Types and Relational Databases

Bas Lijnse and Rinus Plasmeijer

Radboud University Nijmegen
{b.lijnse,rinus}@cs.ru.nl

Abstract. In today's digital society, information systems play an important role in many organizations. While their construction is a well understood software engineering process, it still requires much engineering effort. The de facto storage mechanism in information systems is the relational database. Although the representation of data in these databases is optimized for efficient storage, it is less suitable for use in the software components that manipulate the data. Therefore, much of the construction of an information system consists of programming translations between the database and a more convenient representation in the software.

In this paper we present an approach which automates this work for data entry applications, by providing generic versions of the elementary CRUD (Create, Read, Update, Delete) operations. In the spirit of model based development we use Object Role Models, which are normally used to design databases, to derive not only a database, but also a set of data types in Clean to hold data during manipulation. These types represent all information related to a conceptual entity as a single value, and contain enough information about the database to enable automatic mapping. For data entry applications this means that all database operations can be handled by a single generic function.

To illustrate the viability of our approach, a prototype library, which performs this mapping, and an example information system have been implemented.

Keywords: Generic programming, Functional programming, Clean, Relational databases, Object role models, Model based software development.

1 Introduction

In today's digital society, information systems play an important role in many organizations. Many administrative business processes are supported by these systems, while others have even been entirely automated. While the construction of such systems has become a more or less standardized software engineering process, the required amount of effort remains high. Because each organisation has different business processes, information systems need to be tailored or custom made for each individual organisation.

One of the primary functions of information systems is to create, manipulate and view (large) persistent shared collections of data. The de facto storage mechanism for these data structures is the relational database, in which all information is represented in tables with records that reference other records. Although this representation is optimized for redundancy free storage of data, it is less suited for direct manipulation of that data. The reason for this is that conceptually elementary units are often split up into multiple database records. For example, in a small business system, a project consisting of a name and a number of tasks is broken down into one record for the project and a number of records for the tasks which each reference the project.

In data entry applications it is more convenient for developers to do operations on conceptual units instead of single database records. To reuse the example, adding a project instead of adding a project record and a number of task records. Therefore, in the programming language we use to build the data entry components, we need data structures that represent conceptual units rather than database records. While it is easy to construct a type in most modern languages to represent a conceptual unit as a single data structure, using any type more complex than a single database record means that some translation is required whenever data enters or leaves the database. As a result, since each system has a unique database design, a lot of boiler plate code has to be be written to achieve this translation. This translation code is all very similar except for the types and tables they translate between. Even when a DSEL is used to abstract the database interaction from low level SQL, one still has to define the mapping for each new type. This repetitive programming work is not only mind numbing for developers, it is also time consuming and error-prone. Over the years several tools and libraries have been developed to solve this issue with varying degrees of success and practical use. We discuss these approaches in detail in section 6.

In this paper we present a novel approach based on generic programming in Clean that provides generic versions of the elementary CRUD (Create, Read, Update, Delete) operations that abstract over types and tables. These operations map changes in data structures that reflect the conceptual unit structure of entities, to changes in a relational database. The main prerequisite for enabling this, is that all necessary information about the entities' database representations can be inferred from the types of these data structures. In the spirit of model based development, we do this by deriving both the data types and a relational database from the same high level data model. The language we use for these models is Object Role Modeling (ORM). In this graphic modelling language one can specify what information is to be stored in an information system by expressing facts about the modelled domain. Since ORM has a formally defined syntax and semantics, it enables the derivation of a set of database tables, as done in the standard Rmap algorithm [10], or a set of types in our approach.

Our approach consists of four mappings between representations on different levels of abstraction that are depicted in Fig. 1. The first step (1) is a mapping

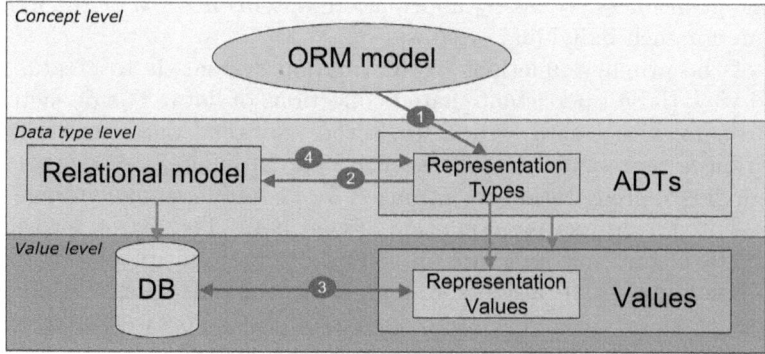

Fig. 1. The four steps in our method

from ORM models on a conceptual level to a set of Clean types on the type level. From these types we derive a matching relational model for storage in a database (2). Our generic library is then used at the value level (3) to do CRUD operations on values of the representations where it automatically maps the values to the database. For many existing databases it is also possible to reverse engineer a set of representation types from a relational model (4).

The key idea behind our approach is that it addresses the representations of data for storage and manipulation as two sides of the same coin. Instead of focusing on either using databases as storage for Clean values, or on Clean values as interface to a storage representation, we consider Clean values and databases as different representations of the same high-level concepts.

Although our approach involves many stages of the software engineering process, we consider the following to be the main contributions of this paper:

- We introduce a structured method to derive Clean data types from ORM models, that allow capturing all information about a conceptual entity in a single data structure. The details of this process can be found in section 3.
- We present a generic library which provides the four CRUD operations as functions on single data structures. These operations also work when the representations in the database span multiple tables. Especially in data entry applications, this library can replace much boiler plate code. The CRUD operations are covered in section 4 and the implementation of the library is discussed in section 5.

2   Motivating Example

To illustrate the various steps in our approach, and to provide some feeling about how it can be applied, we will make use of a running example throughout the remainder of this paper. This example is a simple project management system for a typical small business, which stores information about the following conceptual entities:

- **Projects** are abstract entities which are identified by a unique project number and have a textual description. Projects are containers for tasks and can be worked on by employees. A project can be a sub project of another project and can have sub projects of its own.
- **Tasks** are units of work that have to be done for a certain project. They are identified by a unique task number and have a textual description. The system also keeps track of whether a task is finished or not.
- **Employees** are workers that are identified by a unique name and have a description. They can be assigned to work on projects. An employee can work on several projects at a time and multiple employees may work on the same project.

2.1 ORM Formalization

To enable our generic mapping we need to make the above specification more precise. Using ORM [5], we can make a formal conceptual model of the example as shown in Fig. 2. Using ORM, one models *facts* about *objects*. Facts are expressed as semi-natural language sentences. For example: "**Employee** a *works on* **Project** b". An ORM model abstracts over concrete facts about concrete objects by defining *fact types* (the boxes) and *object types* (the circles). Unlike other data modeling languages like ER [3] or UML[14], ORM does not differentiate between relations and attributes, but considers only facts. ORM also models several basic constraints on the roles that objects have in facts. One can express uniqueness, meaning that a fact about some combination of objects occurs at most once, and mandatory role constraints which enforce that a fact about a certain object must occur at least once. In Fig. 2, these constraint are depicted as arrows spanning unique combinations of roles, and dots on roles that are mandatory.

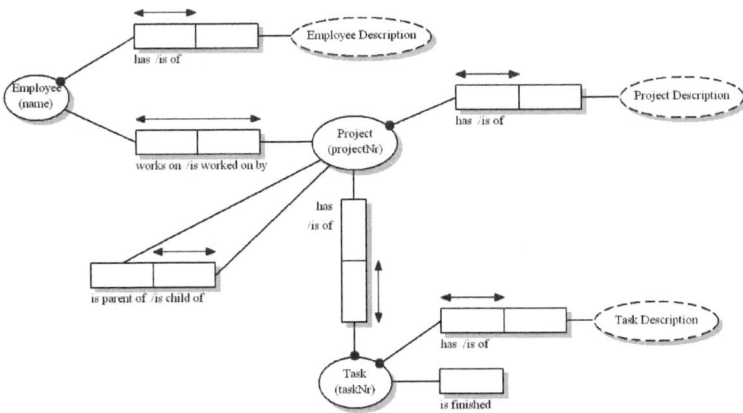

Fig. 2. A simple ORM model for a project management system

3   Types and Tables

The key idea on which our approach is based is that, in data entry applications, we want to manipulate single data structures that represent a conceptual unit. What we do not want, is to manually specify the queries required to build such data structures, or to specify how to update the database after the data structure has been altered. Unfortunately this is often necessary because, since types in data entry applications are often defined ad-hoc for a separately designed database, the relation between types and tables is unclear and inconsistent.

We improve this situation by using a structured process. Since a relational database, and the Clean types used for manipulating it, are simply two different representations of the same abstract entities, the obvious thing to do is define a high level specification of these abstract entities and use it to derive both representations. In the next section we show that when enough information about the storage representation of objects can be inferred from the types of their corresponding Clean representation, we can define an automated mapping once and for all using generic functions. In this section we show how we can obtain a set of types and tables for which this property holds.

3.1   Object Role Models

Instead of defining our own language for defining conceptual entities, we use an existing language from the information modeling field: Object Role Modeling. However, for reasons of simplicity, our approach only considers ORM models that satisfy the following constraints:

- The model only contains entity types, value types and unary and binary fact types.
- Each entity type can be identified by a single value.
- Uniqueness constraints on single facts and mandatory role constraints are the only constraints used.
- Each fact type has at least one uniqueness constraint.
- Uniqueness constraints spanning two roles are only used for facts concerning two entity types.

Although this subset of ORM neglects some advanced ORM constructs, like subtyping or n-ary fact types, it has roughly the same expressive power as the widely used Entity Relationship (ER) [3] modeling language, and is sufficient for most common information systems. Nonetheless, we still use ORM instead of ER because it allows extension of our method to even more expressive conceptual models in the future.

3.2   Representation Types

Although a solid conceptual model is the basis of a well-designed information system, from a programmers perspective however, we are more interested in the concrete representation as types in our (Clean) applications.

Conceptual entities can have different types of relations and constraints. When we want to represent conceptual objects as single Clean data structures we need types that can contain all facts about an entity and also retain information about constraints and relations. This is achieved by defining a subset of Clean's record types with meaningful field names. This set is defined as follows:

- **Entity Records**
  Clean records are used as the primary construct to represent conceptual entities. These records have the same name as the entity type they represent, and have fields for every fact type concerning an entity. The names of these fields have a mandatory structure which can have the following three forms:
  - `<entity name>_<value name>`
    This form is used for values or entities that have a *one-to-one relationship* with this entity. The entity name is a unique name for this entity type, typically the same as the name of the record type. The first field of an entity record must always have this form and is assumed to be a unique identifier for the current entity.
  - `<entity name>_ofwhich_<match name>`
    This form is used for embedding relations between two entities where the relation between the two entities is defined such that the value of the match name of one of the entities is equal to the identity value of another entity. This form is used for *one-to-many relations* between entities. The entity name is the identifier of the "many" part of the relationship. The current entity is the "one" side of the relation.
  - `<relation name>_<select name>_ofwhich_<match name>`
    This form is used for *many-to-many relationships* between entity types. The relation name is a unique name for this relation and is used by both entity records that have a role in the relation. The select and match names are role identifiers for both parts of the relation.

  The types that fields in an entity record are allowed to have, are limited as well. They can be of scalar type, another entity or identification record type, or Maybe or list of scalar or entity or identification record type.
- **Identification Records**
  Because we do not always want to store or load an entire database, we need a representation for references to entities that stay in the database. We represent these references as identification records. These are records that have the same name as the entity record they identify, with an "ID" suffix. These records contain exactly one field which has the same name and type as the corresponding entity record.
- **Scalar Types**
  Value types in ORM are mapped to the basic scalar types in Clean: Int, Bool, Char, String and Real.
- **List and Maybe types**
  When the uniqueness and total role constraints on a fact type define that a fact can be optional, or can have multiple instances, we use Clean's list ([a]) and Maybe (::Maybe a = Nothing | Just a) type to wrap the type of the

object involved in the fact. It is important to note that the order of lists is considered to have no meaning in these types. Storage of an entity record which contains a list does therefore not guarantee that this list has the same order when read again.

Using these types, the ORM model of our project management system (Fig. 2) can be represented by the set of Clean types given below.

```
:: Employee =    { employee_name                            :: String
                 , employee_description                      :: String
                 , projectworkers_project_ofwhich_employee   :: [ProjectID]
                 }
:: EmployeeID = { employee_name                              :: String
                 }
:: Project =     { project_projectNr                         :: Int
                 , project_description                        :: String
                 , project_parent                             :: (Maybe ProjectID)
                 , task_ofwhich_project                       :: [Task]
                 , project_ofwhich_parent                     :: [ProjectID]
                 , projectworkers_employee_ofwhich_project    :: [EmployeeID]
                 }
:: ProjectID =  { project_projectNr                          :: Int
                 }
:: Task =        { task_taskNr                                :: Int
                 , task_project                               :: ProjectID
                 , task_description                           :: String
                 , task_done                                  :: Bool
                 }
:: TaskID =      { task_taskNr                                :: Int
                 }
```

An interesting property of these types is that, unlike database records these Clean records can also contain nested representations of related objects.

3.3   From ORM To Representation Types

To make sure that a set of representation types represent the right concepts, we systematically derive the types from an ORM model (mapping (1) in Fig. 1). The algorithm to perform this mapping groups fact types in a similar fashion as the standard Rmap [10] algorithm and is summarized below. A more elaborate description can be found in [8].

1. For each entity type in the ORM, define an entity and identification record in Clean. They both have one field, which will have the name and type of the primary identification of the entity in ORM.
2. Add fields to the entity records. Each entity record will get a field for all the fact types in which it plays a role. The types and names of the fields are determined based on the object types and constraints in the model.

- When the entity type is related to another entity type, the type of the field is the identification record for that entity. When it is related to a value type, the field will have a scalar value. The name of the field may be freely chosen but has to be prefixed with a globally unique entity identifier. The obvious choice for this is the name of the entity type.
- When the fact type is unary, the field's type will be `Bool`.
- When there is no mandatory role constraint on the role an entity is playing, the field's type will be a `Maybe` type.
- When there is no uniqueness constraint on the role an entity is playing the field's type be a list type.
- Each field name is prefixed with a grouping identifier. If a fact type can be attributed completely to the entity we are defining the type for, we use the name of the entity as prefix. If not, we choose a unique prefix for that fact type, that is to be used in the entity records of both entities playing a role in the fact type.

3. Optionally replace identification record types in record fields to entity record types. This allows the direct embedding of related entities in the data structure of an entity. One has to be careful however to not introduce "inclusion cycles". When an included related entity embeds the original entity again, a cycle exists which will cause endless recursion during execution.

Because step 3. is optional, and the choice between inclusion or reference depends on the intended use of the representation types, this transformation can only be automated by an interactive process or annotation of the ORM model.

3.4   From Representation Types to Tables

The next step in our approach is getting from a set of representation types to a relational model (mapping (2) in Fig. 1). The obvious way would be to map from ORM directly to a relational model as is done in the standard Rmap algorithm [10]. However, since the representation types are already very close to the relational structure, it is easier to derive the tables from these types. A summary of the mapping process is given below. A more detailed version can be found in [8].

1. Define tables for all entities. In these tables all record fields are grouped that have the same entity name as the first (identification) field of the record. The types of the columns are the types of the record fields in the case of scalar types. In the case of entity or identification records the column gets the type of the first field of these record types. When a record field's type is a `Maybe` type, the corresponding column is allowed to have `NULL` values.
2. Define tables for all many-to-many relations. For all many-to-many relationships find the pairs of relation names and define a two-column table by that name. The names of the two columns are the entity names found in the record fields in the representation types.

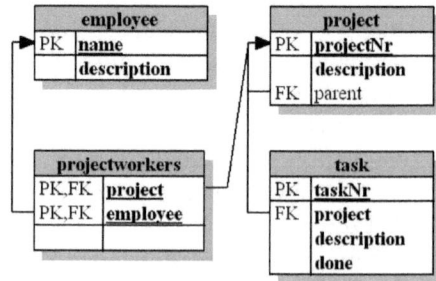

Fig. 3. The derived tables of the ORM model in Fig. 2

3. Add foreign key constraints. Everywhere an entity or identification type in the record field is mapped to a column in a table, a foreign key constraint is defined that references the primary key of the table of the corresponding entity type.

When this algorithm is applied to the set of representation types of section 3.2, we get the set of database tables depicted in Fig. 3. Since this algorithm is completely deterministic it can be easily automated.

With this mapping, we have done all the preparatory work that is required to use our generic library. For new information systems, this is all the initial work one has to do: Define an ORM model, derive a set of representation types and derive a relational model from those types.

3.5   Reverse Engineering: From Tables to Representation Types

In situations where we already have a database, that we want to interface with, we still want to be able to use our generic library. In many situations we are able to reverse engineer a set of representation types from an existing relational model to make this possible.

The process itself (mapping (4) in Fig. 1) is a rather trivial inverse operation of the method to derive a relational model from the representation types. However, this is only possible under certain conditions:

- The relational model must only contain tables indexed on a single column primary key that represent entities and two column tables with a primary key spanning both columns that represent additional facts. When this condition holds, there exists a set of representation types from which we could have derived the existing database.
- We must know which columns are used as references, and what entities they reference. Since the use of foreign keys is not obligatory, it is not always possible to infer the references in a relational model. We can only define a set of representation types if we know which conceptual entities are related and how.

When these conditions hold, which often do for simple information systems, we are able to use our library even in situations where no ORM model of the existing system is available. When these conditions do not hold for the complete database, but do hold for a part of the database, it is still possible to define a set of types for that part. Such partial use of the generic mapping, can still save a lot of work.

4   Generic CRUD Operations

Although having Clean types and database tables that have a clear relation with a formal conceptual model is a merit on its own, the point of that exercise was to enable generic CRUD operations.

What we want to achieve is a set of four generic functions that are available for every possible representation type and enable us to manipulate the entities in the databases of our information systems. Ideally the type definitions of this set would look somewhat like the following code:

```
create :: entity db → (ref,    db)
read   :: ref    db → (entity, db)
update :: entity db →          db
delete :: ref    db →          db
```

Here ref, entity and db are type variables for respectively the identification record type, the entity record type and a database cursor type. Obviously it is not possible to create such a completely polymorphic set of functions, but we can come very close using generics and overloading.

In this section we show how two of these operations, read and update, work by means of an example. The other two are similar and are not covered for the sake of brevity. A full detailed description of all four operations can be found in [8]. In the example we will assume the conceptual model of Fig. 2, the types of section 3.2, and the database tables of Fig. 3.

4.1   Reading Objects

The first operation we will show is the generic read. Suppose we have a database with the following information about some project:

- It has projectNr 84, description "Spring brochure" and the project has no parent project and no sub projects.
- A task is defined for this project with taskNr 481 and description "Draft text" which is not done yet.
- Another task is defined with taskNr 487 and description "Call printer about price" which is also not done yet.
- Employees "john" and "bob" are working on this project.

All of this information can be read into a single Clean value of type Project in just one line of code[1]:

```
(mbError, mbProject, cur) = gsql_read {ProjectID|project_projectNr = 84} cur
```

---

[1] In this code the variable cur is a unique database cursor used to query the database.

If all goes well, this will give us the following data structure:

```
{ Project | project_projectNr = 84
  , project_description = ''Spring brochure''
  , project_parent = Nothing
  , task_ofwhich_project
  = [ { Task | task_taskNr = 481, task_project = 84
      , task_description = ''Draft text'', task_done = False
      }
    , { Task | task_taskNr = 487, task_project = 84
      , task_descrption = ''Call printer about price'', task_done = False
      } ]
  , project_ofwhich_parent = []
  , projectworkers_employee_ofwhich_project
  = [ {EmployeeID | employee_name = ''john''}
    , {EmployeeID | employee_name = ''bob'' } ]
}
```

This single line of code gives us a lot for free. If we had to write a read_product function by hand, it would have required three different SQL queries plus a conversion from flat lists of SQL data values to the nested Project structure.

To achieve this generically, two problems have to be solved: 1. How do we find the information in the database? And 2. how do we construct a value, in this case of type Project? The first problem is solved by interpreting the field names of record types and translating them to SQL queries. The results of these queries are then systematically concatenated to produce a stream of values (tokens) which is a serialized representation of the value we want to construct. This reduces the second problem to deserialization of that representation.

Instead of describing the read operation at an abstract level, it is easier to see what happens by following it step by step when used to read the Project described above.

1. The first step we take is serialization of the ProjecID value to create an initial token stream. Thus in this case, the read operation is started with initial stream [84][2].
2. The next step is to apply the instantiation of the generic read operation for the Project type. When the read operation is applied to read an entity record, the first thing that is done is to expand the token stream by reading additional data for all fields of the record. The head of the token stream is used to match database records and the SQL queries are constructed from the information encoded in the field names. For example, the data for the field project_description is retrieved with the SQL query: SELECT description FROM project WHERE projectNr = 84. When an optional field is empty a NULL token is added to the stream and when a field has multiple values a terminator (TRM) token is added after the last value.

---

[2] To illustrate the intermediate values of the token stream we use an ad-hoc untyped list notation. This is **not** Clean syntax.

So for the example project, the token stream has the value after expansion:
[84, "Spring brochure", NULL, 481, 487, TRM, TRM, "john", "bob", TRM]

3. With the data for all project fields read, the read operation is applied recursively to construct the record fields. When the read operation is instantiated for basic types or identification records no additional data is read. Instead, tokens are consumed to construct values. So after the values of the first three fields (84, ''`Spring brochure`'' and `Nothing`) are constructed the token stream has the value: [481, 487, TRM, TRM, "john", "bob", TRM]

4. The instantiation of the read operation for lists will repeatedly apply the read operation for its element type until the head of the token stream is a terminator. So in this case, the create operation for type `Task` will be called twice. Because `Task`, like `Project`, is an entity record type, we read additional data again. After expansion of the first task the stream has value: [481, 84, "Draft text", false, 487, TRM, TRM, "john", "bob", TRM]
When the list of both tasks is read and constructed the stream is reduced to: [TRM, "john", "bob", TRM]

5. Thus the process continues, and when recursion is completed for all fields we have an empty token stream and can construct the `Project` record.

4.2   Local Changes with Global Meaning

Once all facts about an object are read into a Clean data structure, we can change it in a program. Because this structure is not just some convenient grouping of values for computation, but has a meaningful relationship with both the underlying conceptual model and the relational model in the database, we can interpret changes to this data structure as changes on the conceptual level.

To illustrate this we make some changes to the example `Project` of the previous section and consider their meaning on the conceptual level.

- We change the value of the `project_description` field to ''`Summer brochure`''. The meaning of this change is simple. Since each project has exactly one description, this new description will replace the old value in the database.
- We change the value of the field `task_done` of the first `Task` in the list to `True`. The meaning of this change is simple as well. Since each task is either done or not, this new value will replace the value in the database. So although the task is embedded in the project value, it is still a separate object on the conceptual level which facts can be changed.
- We remove the second `Task` from the list.
  The meaning of this change is less obvious. Since tasks and projects are both conceptual objects that happen to be related, does a removal from the list mean that the conceptual task object and all its facts are removed? Or does it mean that just the relation between the task and project is removed? For the representation types, this choice is dependent on the used type. For entity records, like `Task`, we will interpret removal of the list as complete removal of the object. For identification records, like `TaskID`, we will only remove the relation between objects. Thus in this case task 487 will be deleted completely.

- We add a new `Task` defined as:

```
{ task_taskNr = 0, task_project = {ProjectID | project_projectNr = 0}
, task_description = ''Check online prices'', task_done = False
}
```

This change means that a new task for this project has to be created. The interesting parts however are the `task_taskNr` and `task_project` fields. Each task is related to exactly one project. We have specified in the task record that this is project 0. But this task is created as part of the list of tasks of project 84. When new objects are created in the context of another object we will let the context take precedence and ignore the specified identification. Hence, this change means that a new task is created which is related to project 84, not 0.

The `task_taskNr` field is also interesting. For the identification of new objects we interpret the specified value (0) as a suggestion, but leave it up to the database to determine the actual value. This enables the use of auto incrementing counters which are commonly used in databases.

- We remove ''john'' from the list in `projectworkers_employee_ofwhich_project`. Because the `projectworkers_employee_ofwhich_project` field is a list of identification records, we will interpret the removal of ''john'' from this list as "john no longer works on this project" and not as complete removal of the employee named "john" from the database.

4.3   Updating Objects

In the previous section we have made quite a few changes to our local representation of the project, but all of these changes can be applied to the global representation in the database at once with just the following single line of Clean code:

```
(mbError, mbProjectId, cur) = gsql_update project cur
```

This single line saves us even more programming work than the generic read function. To apply all the changes by hand would in this case require six cusom crafted SQL queries and the necessary conversion code.

As with the read operation, we illustrate the generic update by following its operation step by step.

1. The update operation for entity records is done in three recursive passes. In the first pass we consider only the fields that are single basic values or identity records. In this case the fields that start with `project_`. The update operation or basic values and identification records does no database interaction, but just serializes values to produce the token stream. After this first pass the token stream has the value: [84, "Summer brochure", NULL].

2. After this pass we update the database record for this project. Because new objects can be added (like the new task) we verify that the update query did indeed modify a record in the database. If not, we create a new record.

After this update/create we know the definitive identification of this project (84) and are ready for the next pass.

3. In the second pass we will do a recursive update of the remaining record fields. To make sure that the identification context object takes precedence when updating nested objects we pass along special override tokens (OVR) that specify for which fields in the nested entity records the context must be used instead of its value. In this case the second pass is started with token stream: [OVR task_project ⇒ 84, OVR projectworkers_project ⇒ 84]. The override tokens are used during serialization in the first update pass of a nested entity record. When the second pass finishes the resulting token stream has value: [481, 532, TRM, TRM, "bob", TRM]. The value 532 is an automatically assigned identification for the newly created task.

4. In the third and final pass, the token stream of the second pass is compared with the token stream that a (non-recursive) read operation is for this project produces to determine which list elements have been removed. For these values, the generic delete operation is used to remove them from them from the database.

5. After these three passes, the identification value of the current record is added to the token stream it was started with. In this case returning a token stream of value: [84].

6. The final step is to deserialize the token stream to produce a `ProjectID` value.

4.4 Shared Consequences

An interesting property of the previously illustrated generic operations is that changes in one object have consequences for related objects. Because facts are conceptually shared between objects, the operations maintain that shared structure in the database. If we would have read the `Employee` record of ``john'' before going through the example, the list in the `projectworkers_project_ofwhich_employee` would have contained the value {`ProjectID|project_projectNr=84`}. If we would read it again after updating the project, this value would no longer occur in the list.

5 Implementation in Clean

To validate the generic operations, we have implemented the operations described in the previous section as a prototype library in Clean called "GenSQL".

This library contains about 950 lines of Clean code of which roughly 500 are used for the definition of the main generic function. The rest constitutes about fifty helper functions. Because of its large size, it is not possible to present the generic function in detail. The design of the library as a whole is therefore presented instead[3].

---

[3] Full sources of both the library and the demo application can be found at: http://www.st.cs.ru.nl/papers/2009/gensql-prototype.tgz

5.1   Jack of All Trades

Because the generics mechanism in Clean has some limitations, the implementation of the operations in the GenSQL library has a somewhat unusual design. In Clean it is not possible to call other generic functions of unknown type in the definition of a generic function. The different CRUD operations however, do have some overlap in their functionality. The update operation, for instance, uses the delete operation during a garbage collect step. Because of the limitation we are not able to isolate this overlap in a separate generic function.

To deal with this limitation of the generics mechanism, all operations have been combined into one "Jack of all trades" function. The type signature of this function, gSQL, is as follows:

```
generic gSQL t ::
  GSQLMode GSQLPass (Maybe t) [GSQLFieldInfo] [GSQLToken] *cur   →
  ((Maybe GSQLError), (Maybe t),[GSQLFieldInfo],[GSQLToken],*cur) |SQLCursor cur
```

The first two arguments of this function are the mode and pass of the operation we want gSQL to perform. The mode is one of the four operations GSQLRead, GSQLCreate, GSQLUpdate, GSQLDelete, the type information mode GSQLInfo or GSQLInit. The latter serializes a reference value to the token list in order to start a read or delete operation. The GSQLPass type is simply a synonym for Int.

The next three arguments are the data structures on which the gSQL function operates. All three are both input and output parameters and depending on the mode, are either produced or consumed. The first argument is an optional value of type t. During the read and delete operations, this argument is Nothing in the input and Just in the output because values are constructed from the token list. During the create, update, info and init operations, the argument is Just in the input because values are serialized to the token or info list. The second argument is the token list to which data structures are serialized. The third argument is the info list. In this list, type information about record fields is accumulated. The last argument of the gSQL function is a unique database cursor which has to be in the SQLCursor type class[4]. This is a handle which is used to interact with the database. The return type of the gSQL function is a tuple which contains an optional error an optional value of type t, the token list, the info list and the database cursor.

Although this "Jack of all trades" function is large, it is clearly divided into separate cases for the different types and modes to keep it readable and maintainable.

5.2   Convenient Wrappers

Because of the all-in-one design of the gSQL function, it is not very practical to use. For the read and delete operations, it even has to be called twice. First in the init mode to prepare the token list, and then in the read or delete mode to do the actual work.

---

[4] A | in a type signature is Clean notation for specifying class constraints.

To hide all of this nastiness from the programmer, the GenSQL library provides wrapper functions for each of the four operations. These wrappers have the following type signature.

```
gsql_read   :: a *cur → (Maybe GSQLError, Maybe b, *cur)
    | gSQL{|*|} a & gSQL{|*|} b & SQLCursor cur
gsql_create :: b *cur → (Maybe GSQLError, Maybe a, *cur)
    | gSQL{|*|} a & gSQL{|*|} b & SQLCursor cur
gsql_update :: b *cur → (Maybe GSQLError, Maybe a, *cur)
    | gSQL{|*|} a & gSQL{|*|} b & SQLCursor cur
gsql_delete :: a *cur → (Maybe GSQLError, Maybe b, *cur)
    | gSQL{|*|} a & gSQL{|*|} b & SQLCursor cur
```

Thanks to Clean's overloading mechanism we can use these wrapper functions for any entity for which we have derived gSQL for its identification (a) and entity record (b) type.

5.3 Project Management Example System

In order to test and demonstrate our generic library, we have also implemented the project management system from section 2. This system is a CGI web application written in Clean which runs within an external (Apache) web server and stores its information in a (MySQL) relational database using the GenSQL library. Figure 4 shows the prototype application while updating a project.

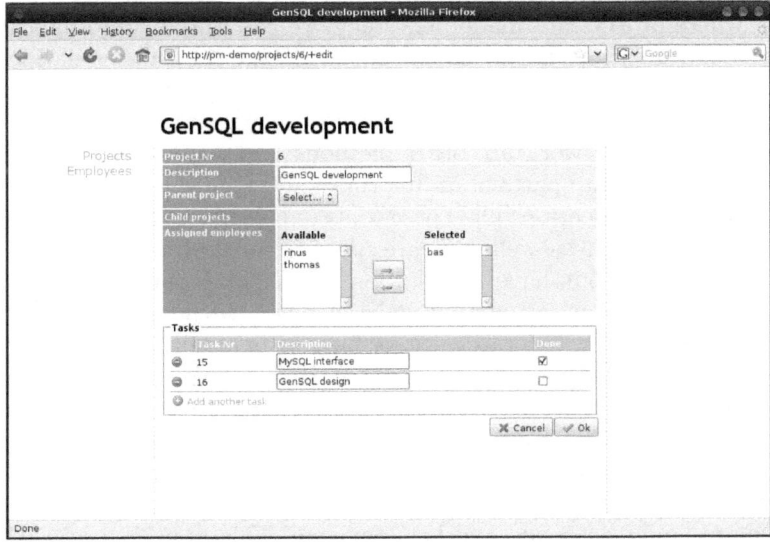

Fig. 4. Screenshot of the project edit page

5.4 Performance

The generic mapping function relieves the programmer of writing much boiler-
plate code and SQL queries. It is however important to realize that there is a
cost associated with this convenience.

First of all there is some overhead cost in space and time consumption of
Clean's generic mechanism. However when optimization techniques [1] are applied by the compiler this can be completely removed.

Secondly there is a cost in the amount of database queries that are performed.
The current implementation of the generic operations is not optimized to minimize the amount of queries. Each retrieval or update of an object does a separate
query. When an object has many facts with embedded related objects this will
result in linearly many queries. Theoretically however, there is no reason why
the generic operations would require more queries than handwritten versions.

6 Related Work

At first glance, our library appears very similar to Object Relational Mapping
[4] libraries in object oriented languages. These libraries achieve persistence of
objects in an OO language by mapping them to a relational database. Although
both approaches relieve programmers of the burden of writing boilerplate data
conversion code, there is an important difference: our approach treats a subset of
all Clean types as a meaningful model of an underlying redundancy free database.
This allows us to easily map binary fact types to the entity records of both
sides without duplicating any information in the database. In object relational
mapping where objects are made persistent, we can only avoid duplication by
mapping binary relations between objects to only one side of the relation. Based
on this property, object relational mapping is more similar to generic persistence
libraries [13] than to the method presented in this paper.

Also related to our work are other methods and tools that use conceptual
data models to generate parts of an information system like user interfaces [6],
or even complete applications [9]. These tools reduce the effort required to build
an information system as well, but are often all-or-nothing solutions that do
a certain trick well, but have no solution when you want something a little
different. Of course you can always make changes to the generated code, but
this means you can only generate once, or have to manually merge your changes
upon regeneration. Because our approach is designed as a generic library, and
generic programming is an integral part of the Clean language, we can combine
a generic solution for common situations together with handwritten code for
exceptional situations in one coherent and type safe solution.

The final related area of research is that of abstraction from SQL by embedding a query language inside another language. This approach is used in the
HaskellDB library in Haskell [7,2], in the LINQ library in C# [11], and more
recently, using dependent types in a database library for Agda [12]. While these
approaches make the programming of data operations easier and type safe, they
do not reduce the amount of work one has to do. When using our library, a

developer no longer needs to define queries at all, thus eliminating the need for easier and safer ways of defining them. These libraries could however, be used complementary to ours to get a generic solution for the common CRUD operations, and type safety for the exceptional custom queries.

7   Conclusions and Future Work

In this paper we have shown that given the right choice of data types and database tables, it is possible to use generic programming to automate the mapping between entities stored in a database and their representation in Clean.

To do so, we have shifted the focus from both the database and the data types, towards the conceptual level of ORM models. By deriving not only a database, but also a set of types from these models, we enable an automatic mapping between them. This means that by just making an ORM model of a perceived system, you get a database design, a set of types for convenient manipulation, and the machinery for doing CRUD operations on values of those types for free. This relieves a Clean programmer of dealing with how changes in a database must be expressed in SQL, and instead enables the manipulation of a database in a more familiar fashion: manipulation of a local data structure.

We have shown the viability of this approach by means of a prototype library and its use in an example information system. While not ready for production systems yet, this library is already useful for rapid prototyping. But, with optimization of the library, and additional generic operations for handling sets of entities, much of the construction effort of information systems can be reduced to just the definition of ORM models.

What remains to be done is extension of our approach to the complete ORM language. While we selected a subset which is useful for many domains, we have ignored some constructs that make ORM more powerful than, for example, ER. We have yet to investigate how these can be integrated in the current approach.

Another area where further work can be done is to explore how the mechanism for locally manipulating parts of a global shared data structure can be used to facilitate sharing in a functional language. Could it for instance be used to implement a heap on top of an in-memory SQL engine?

Acknowledgements

This research is supported by the Dutch Technology Foundation STW, applied science division of NWO and the Technology Program of the Ministry of Economic Affairs. We would like to thank the anonymous reviewers for their constructive comments and suggestions.

References

1. Alimarine, A., Smetsers, S.: Optimizing Generic Functions. In: Kozen, D. (ed.) MPC 2004. LNCS, vol. 3125, pp. 16–31. Springer, Heidelberg (2004)
2. Bingert, B., Höckersten, A.: Student paper: Haskelldb improved. In: Proceedings of 2004 ACM SIGPLAN Workshop on Haskell, pp. 108–115. ACM Press, New York (2004)

3. Chen, P.P.-S.: The entity-relationship model—toward a unified view of data. ACM Trans. Database Syst. 1(1), 9–36 (1976)
4. Fussel, M.: Foundations of object-relational mapping, Whitepaper (1997), http://www.chimu.com/publications/objectRelational/index.html
5. Halpin, T.: Information modeling and relational database: from conceptual analysis to logical design. Morgan Kaufmann Publishers Inc., San Francisco (2001)
6. Janssen, C., Weisbecker, A., Ziegler, J.: Generating user interfaces from data models and dialogue net specifications. In: CHI 1993: Proceedings of the INTERACT 1993 and CHI 1993 Conference on Human Factors in Computing Systems, pp. 418–423. ACM, New York (1993)
7. Leijen, D., Meijer, E.: Domain specific embedded compilers. In: 2nd USENIX Conference on Domain Specific Languages (DSL 1999), Austin, Texas (October 1999); Also appeared in ACM SIGPLAN Notices 35(1), 109–122 (2000)
8. Lijnse, B.: Between types and tables: Generic mapping between relational databases and data structures in clean, Master's thesis, University of Nijmegen, Number 590 (July 2008)
9. Manoku, E., Zwart, J.P., Bakema, G.: A fact approach to automatic application development. Journal of Conceptual Modeling (2006)
10. McCormack, J., Halpin, T., Ritson, P.: Automated mapping of conceptual schemas to relational schemas. In: Rolland, C., Cauvet, C., Bodart, F. (eds.) CAiSE 1993. LNCS, vol. 685, pp. 432–448. Springer, Heidelberg (1993)
11. Meijer, E., Beckman, B., Bierman, G.: LINQ: reconciling object, relations and XML in the .NET framework. In: SIGMOD 2006: Proceedings of the 2006 ACM SIGMOD International Conference on Management of Data, pp. 706–706. ACM, New York (2006)
12. Norell, U.: Dependently typed programming in agda, Tech. Report ICIS-R08008, Radboud University Nijmegen (2008)
13. Smetsers, S., van Weelden, A., Plasmeijer, R.: Efficient and type-safe generic data storage. In: Proceedings of the 1st Workshop on Generative Technologies, WGT 2008, Budapest, Hungary. Electronic Notes in Theoretical Computer Science (April 2008)
14. UML version 2.2 specification (February 2009), http://www.omg.org/spec/UML/2.2/

Author Index

GPSR Compliance

The European Union's (EU) General Product Safety Regulation (GPSR) is a set of rules that requires consumer products to be safe and our obligations to ensure this.

If you have any concerns about our products, you can contact us on ProductSafety@springernature.com

In case Publisher is established outside the EU, the EU authorized representative is:

Springer Nature Customer Service Center GmbH
Europaplatz 3
69115 Heidelberg, Germany

Batch number: 09474011

Printed by Printforce, the Netherlands